European Yearbook of International Economic Law

Special Issue

Series Editors
Marc Bungenberg, Saarbrücken, Germany
Markus Krajewski, Erlangen, Germany
Christian J. Tams, Glasgow, UK
Jörg Philipp Terhechte, Lüneburg, Germany
Andreas R. Ziegler, Lausanne, Switzerland

The European Yearbook of International Economic Law (EYIEL) is an annual publication in International Economic Law, a field increasingly emancipating itself from Public International Law scholarship and evolving into a fully-fledged academic discipline in its own right. With the yearbook, the editors and publisher intend to make a significant contribution to the development of this "new" discipline and provide an international reference source of the highest possible quality. The EYIEL covers all areas of IEL, in particular WTO Law, External Trade Law for major trading countries, important Regional Economic Integration agreements, International Competition Law, International Investment Regulation, International Monetary Law, International Intellectual Property Protection and International Tax Law. In addition to the regular annual volumes, EYIEL Special Issues routinely address specific current topics in International Economic Law.

More information about this subseries at http://www.springer.com/series/8848

Rhea Tamara Hoffmann • Markus Krajewski
Editors

Coherence and Divergence in Services Trade Law

 Springer

Editors
Rhea Tamara Hoffmann
Faculty of Law
University of Erlangen-Nuremberg
Erlangen, Germany

Markus Krajewski
Faculty of Law
University of Erlangen-Nuremberg
Erlangen, Germany

ISSN 2364-8392   ISSN 2364-8406 (electronic)
European Yearbook of International Economic Law
ISSN 2510-6880   ISSN 2510-6899 (electronic)
Special Issue
ISBN 978-3-030-46954-2   ISBN 978-3-030-46955-9 (eBook)
https://doi.org/10.1007/978-3-030-46955-9

This Springer imprint is published by the registered company Springer Nature Switzerland AG.
The registered company address is: Gewerbestrasse 11, 6330 Cham, Switzerland

Preface

The contributions of this EYIEL Special Issue were first presented at an international workshop entitled "Coherence and Divergence in Agreements on Trade in Services" at Friedrich-Alexander-Universität Erlangen-Nürnberg on 14 and 15 March 2019 in Erlangen, Germany. We are extremely grateful to the presenters and participants for stimulating scholarly exchanges and debates. In addition to the presenters, we wish to thank our invited specialists who provided extremely helpful comments on the draft papers: Rudolf Adlung, Martin Roy (WTO), Oliver Prausmüller (Austrian Chamber of Labour), and Christophe Kiener (European Commission). Based on the discussions at the workshop and taking the respective feedback into account, the authors revised and further deepened their contributions and turned them into the chapters of this volume.

The workshop was generously funded by the Dr. German Schweiger-Stiftung and benefited from a research project funded by the Fritz Thyssen Stiftung für Wissenschaftsförderung.

Last but not least, we would like to thank Rachel Höpfner for her invaluable support in handling the manuscripts and proofs.

Erlangen, Germany
March 2020

Rhea Tamara Hoffmann
Markus Krajewski

Contents

List of Contributors

Mira Burri is a Senior Lecturer at the Faculty of Law of the University of Lucerne, Switzerland. She teaches international intellectual property, media, Internet, and trade law. Her current research interests are in the areas of digital trade, culture, copyright, data protection, and Internet governance. She is the principal investigator of the project "The Governance of Big Data in Trade Agreements," sponsored by the Swiss National Science Foundation. She consults the European Parliament, UNESCO, the WEF, and others on issues of digital innovation and cultural diversity. She has co-edited the publications Trade Governance in the Digital Age (Cambridge University Press 2012) and Big Data and Global Trade Law (Cambridge University Press 2020). She is the author of Public Service Broadcasting 3.0 (Routledge 2015). Her personal website is at: www.unilu.ch/mira-burri; her publications are available at: http://ssrn.com/author=483457.

Carlo M. Cantore is a dispute settlement lawyer in the Legal Affairs Division of the WTO. He is also a visiting lecturer in WTO Law at the University of Antwerp. He holds a PhD in law from the European University Institute of Florence and a law degree from the Sant'Anna School of Advanced Studies of Pisa.

Panagiotis Delimatsis is Professor of European and International Trade Law and Director of the Tilburg Law and Economics Center (TILEC), an interdisciplinary Center of Excellence at Tilburg University, the Netherlands. Before joining Tilburg, he was a Senior Research Fellow at the World Trade Institute of the University of Bern. He is a renowned expert and has a keen interest in regulatory policy and regularly publishes on services trade, financial markets, energy, and standardization in Europe and worldwide. He is the author of "International Trade in Services and Domestic Regulations: Necessity, Transparency, and Regulatory Diversity" (International Economic Law Series, Oxford University Press, 2007). He has edited various books, the most recent of which is "the Law, Economics and Politics of International Standardisation" (Cambridge University Press, 2016). His current research relates to the private governance of standard-setting. In this regard, He is the principal investigator of a 5-year project, financed by the European Research Council (ERC Consolidator Grant).

Gabriel Gari is a Reader in International Economic Law at the Centre for Commercial Law Studies, Queen Mary University of London and Academic Director of the LLM in International Economic Law. Prior to joining Queen Mary, he practiced Employment and Commercial Law and worked for the Uruguayan Supreme Court of Justice. He holds degrees in Law and in Sociology from the University of the Republic (Uruguay), an LLM from the London School of Economics and a PhD from Queen Mary University of London. He is a member of the Latin American and Caribbean Research Network on Services, the Latin American Network on International Economic Law, the Society of International Economic Law, and the European Society of International Law.

Rhea Tamara Hoffmann is a post-doc researcher at the University of Erlangen-Nürnberg. Her research focuses on international investment and trade law and fundamental rights, including the principle of nondiscrimination. Previously, she was a researcher at the cluster of excellence "Formation of Normative Orders" at the University of Frankfurt am Main and worked for the United Nations Conference on Trade and Development (UNCTAD) in Geneva.

Markus Krajewski holds the Chair in Public Law and Public International Law at the University of Erlangen-Nürnberg. His research focuses on international economic law, human rights, European external relations, and the law of public services. He is co-editor of the European Yearbook of International Economic Law and serves as Secretary-General of the German Branch of the International Law Association (ILA).

Johanna Jacobsson is Assistant Professor at IE University (Madrid, Spain). She holds a PhD from the European University Institute (Florence, Italy, 2016) and LL. B., LL.M., and BA degrees from the University of Helsinki (Finland). She has previously been a law clerk at the Court of Justice of the European Union, a visiting researcher at the Finnish Institute of International Affairs, and a practitioner in a law firm. Since 2018, she is a member of the Executive Council of the Society of International Economic Law (SIEL).

Marion Panizzon Dr. iur., LL.M. (Duke) is a privatdocent of the University of Bern, fellow of the World Trade Institute, and an associated researcher with the nccr-on the move, University of Neuchatel. Currently on an internship with the Salvation Army's Immigrant and Refugee Services, she is also a Member of the Board of the Center for Migration, University of Göttingen. Her research discusses the shifts of EU external migration law and policy in the wake of the refugee crisis 2015/2016 from a multilevel governance perspective. She has proposed reforming the EU's export-based refugee labor scheme in the Jordan/Lebanon compacts towards including a humanitarian services dimension.

Harjodh Singh is an Independent Legal Consultant from India specializing in international trade law and intellectual property law.

Ines Willemyns obtained her PhD in international economic law in 2019 after having worked as a doctoral researcher at the Leuven Centre for Global Governance Studies at KU Leuven. Her dissertation discussed the international legal framework applicable to digital services trade. Before working as a doctoral researcher, she obtained an LL.M from the University of Barcelona (IELPO) and a bachelor's and master's degree in law from KU Leuven. She researches various aspects of international economic law with a particular focus on digital trade issues.

Svetlana Yakovleva is a PhD candidate at the Institute for Information Law (IViR) of the University of Amsterdam. She also works part-time as a Senior Legal Adviser in Privacy and Cybersecurity practice group at De Brauw Blackstone Westbroek in Amsterdam. Her primary research interests lie at the intersection of data privacy and cybersecurity law, human rights, and international trade law. She received a degree in law (cum laude) from the National Research University Higher School of Economics (Moscow) in 2005. She also holds an LL.M degree in Law and Economics (EMLE) from the Erasmus University, Rotterdam and the University of Hamburg (2007), and a research master degree in Information law from the IViR (2016). Between 2007 and 2014, she worked as a trainee lawyer at the Moscow office of Debevoise & Plimpton LLP, independent legal counsel and Legal and Compliance Officer at Allianz Global Assistance Russia. She also provided legal and methodological advice for the e-Government project of the Russian Government.

Weiwei Zhang is International Trade Advisor at Sidley Austin LLP's Geneva office. Dr. Weiwei Zhang is also Adjunct Professor of International Economic Law at the University of International Business and Economics in Beijing and Visiting Fellow at the Centre for Trade and Economic Integration in the Graduate Institute of International and Development Studies in Geneva.

Lijun Zhao is Senior Lecturer in Law at Middlesex University and Co-founding Director for the China-Europe Commercial Collaboration Association (cecca. org.uk). Before joining academia, she worked as a Judge in P.R. China and later a consultant for several governmental law reform projects. She has expertise in International Business Law and International Law, and her research has been published widely in these areas of law, including International Trade, Commercial Law, Maritime and Transport Law, Comparative and Chinese Law. Many articles of hers have been published in international peer-reviewed journals. Some articles are archived by the UN Library and indexed in the UNCITRAL Bibliography on international trade and maritime law. She has held visiting posts at various institutions including Harvard Law School, the Max Planck Institute for Comparative and Private Law, Swansea University, and Shanghai Maritime University. Currently, she is conducting a research project in the support of Comité Maritime International (CMI).

Introduction

Rhea Tamara Hoffmann and Markus Krajewski

A quarter of a century after the conclusion of the General Agreement on Trade and Services (GATS), the international law on trade in services remains in a state of flux: On the one side, countries increasingly conclude regional trade agreements with chapters on trade in services which aim at a further liberalisation of services trade. On the other side, the GATS structure still remains the dominant model and serves as a basis of many preferential trade agreements (PTAs). Yet, new aspects such as electronic commerce, data protection and taxation emerge while issues, which already existed in the mid-1990s such as financial services regulation, labour mobility, and telecommunications continue to be of current concern.

The present EYIEL Special Issue investigates structures and basic principles of international trade in services law almost 25 years after the GATS entered into force on January 1, 1995. While the founding members of the WTO expected the GATS to become the basis of a coherent and unified legal framework, more than 20 years later the legal regime of trade in services is regulated in numerous bilateral and regional free trade agreements (FTAs) signed since 1995, which complement and override the liberalization of GATS-based trade in services. Therefore, one of the striking features of the development of the international law regarding trade in services is the ever-growing number of regional trade agreements (RTAs[1]) and PTAs since the late 1980. According to the Regional Trade Agreements Information System of the WTO, there are 161 economic integration agreements which cover trade in services.[2]

---

[1]In accordance with WTO terminology, regional trade agreements (RTAs) are defined as reciprocal trade agreements between two or more partners.

[2]See http://rtais.wto.org/UI/PublicSearchByCrResult.aspx.

R. T. Hoffmann (✉) · M. Krajewski
University of Erlangen-Nuremberg, Faculty of Law, Erlangen, Germany
e-mail: rhea.hoffmann@fau.de; markus.krajewski@fau.de

© The Editor(s) (if applicable) and The Author(s), under exclusive licence to Springer Nature Switzerland AG 2020
R. T. Hoffmann, M. Krajewski (eds.), *Coherence and Divergence in Services Trade Law*, European Yearbook of International Economic Law,
https://doi.org/10.1007/978-3-030-46955-9_1

RTAs typically establish for the contracting parties liberalisation commitments going beyond the GATS. Moreover, regional agreements partly develop the basic concepts of the GATS further.

Usually, the debates focus on the question if PTAs serve as a stepping-stone or stumbling block for trade liberalisation at the multilateral level. However, it can be assumed that rules on trade in services in PTAs will coexist with the global GATS regime for the foreseeable future. This raises the question if we are currently witnessing a drive towards greater coherence or more divergence in agreements on trade in services. The book is based on the premise that both trends of divergence and coherence can be found in the current law of international trade in services. Coherence is evident when bilateral and regional FTAs build on and further develop the foundations of GATS. Divergence becomes apparent when the increasing regionalisation and fragmentation of legal rules leads to different approaches to liberalisation and regulation. Therefore, the book investigates which GATS structural principles have been incorporated into regional and bilateral agreements and which have been further developed or replaced. The reasons for the adaptation or transformation of the principles and the consequences for future agreements are also examined by various authors.

This Special Issue contains original contributions on trade in services from various perspectives with a focus on topical questions concerning the legal framework of trade in services and assess how these issues are dealt with in the GATS and in selected preferential trade agreements. The authors address topical questions concerning the legal framework of trade in services and assess how these issues are dealt with in the GATS and in selected preferential trade agreements. The chapters discuss if the differences and similarities (if any) are evidence of greater coherence or greater divergence. The chapters in the volume are arranged around two broad themes: cross-cutting issues and sector specific issues.

Cross-cutting issues cover a historical bird's view on coherence and divergence in agreements on trade in services, services liberalization by sub-central entities as well as recent developments on disciplines on domestic regulations.

The sector specific chapters of this book cover privacy and data protection, digital services, movement of natural persons, telecommunication and media services, financial services, maritime transport and taxation.

The GATS already has sector-specific rules for two service sectors where liberalisation and regulation are particularly closely linked: Financial and telecommunications services. Special provisions to this effect can also be found in NAFTA, for example. The background to these special regulations is the recognition that in certain cases the liberalisation of a sector must be accompanied by its (re)regulation in order to take account of specific market situations or the sector's own laws. In the telecommunications sector, for example, the question arises of how to ensure that dominant market players do not distort competition and how to enable universal services. In the context of the liberalisation of financial services, it should be noted that regulations aimed at the protection of deposits are necessary. The principles already laid down in the GATS have been extended to both sectors in bilateral and regional trade agreements and to other similar sectors such as postal and courier services or tourism services. Other sectors or sub-sectors such as e-commerce[3] (or digital trade[4]) or the provision of services by natural persons is increasingly being made the subject of special legal regimes in FTAs. Given the wide-ranging nature and complexity of the many sectors included within the services area, various sectors have often received special attention. These sectors have been the subject either of separate chapters in various sub-regional integration agreements or of annexes to a chapter or protocol. Such individual chapters or annexes spell out with greater precision the rules and disciplines governing the sector in question, the form of acceptable regulatory intervention, or the definition of the scope of liberalization.

Certain services sectors have been excluded both from GATS and RTAs. One example is the air transport sector, where traffic rights or routing agreements are excluded from many RTAs as they have been from the GATS. Likewise, GATS excludes government services when they are provided on a non-commercial basis and are not in competition with one or more service suppliers. These would include such services as education or health care provided exclusively by the government on a not-for-profit basis (non-commercial basis).

With respect to the services sectors covered by newer trade agreements such as the United States Mexico Canada Agreement (USMCA) and the Comprehensive Economic and Trade Agreement between the European Union and its Member States and Canada (CETA) there are slight variances between these agreements and the GATS. Some sectors are subject to special regulations and some sectors are exempted. GATS covers sectoral regulations on telecommunications, financial services, air transport and maritime transport. The last two sectors are not covered by USMCA.[5] The USMCA, however, covers digital trade. CETA appears to be most comprehensive in terms of sectoral coverage. It covers: financial services (Chapter 13), international maritime transport services (Chapter 14), telecommunication (Chapter 15) and electronic commerce (Chapter 16).

On the basis of the GATS approaches for sector-specific regulations on financial services and telecommunications, the question arises as to how these have been further developed in regional and bilateral trade agreements and, if necessary, transferred to other sectors. This also raises the question of whether further developments are based on technical changes in the sectors concerned (e.g. in the area of electronic communications or e-commerce/digital trade) or on past crisis experiences (e.g. in the area of financial services) or whether they can be explained by internal liberalisation in the countries concerned (e.g. with regard to postal and courier services in EU free trade agreements). This raises the question whether the

---

[3]See e.g. Chapter 16 of the Comprehensive Economic and Trade Agreement between the European Union and its Member States and Canada (CETA).

[4]See e.g. Chapter 19 of United States Mexico Canada Agreement (USMCA).

[5]Financial services are covered by Chapter 17 USMCA. Telecommunications are covered by Chapter 18 USMCA.

development of sector-specific rules is based on the fact that sector-specific rules are more appropriate for the liberalisation and regulation of services than a general regime covering all services in the same way.

This Special Issue commences with reflections and forward-looking perspectives by *Panagiotis Delimatsis* who sets the stage for further analysis of instances of coherence and divergence in trade in services agreements. He offers a chronological view on the services regulation with a focus on coherence and divergence in this specific area of trade policy. He conceptualises 'a drama in three acts' identifying three time periods with respect to the evolution of the law of trade in services. The first act plays before the advent of GATS and the WTO. At this time views on trade in services as a stand-alone topic in the agenda of multilateral trade negotiations were diverging. These regulatory divergences needed to be overcome to achieve the inclusion of services in a multilateral treaty. The second act concerns the creation of the GATS and its characteristics. *Delimatsis* assesses the outcome of the GATS from a viewpoint of coherence. He observes that services liberalisation commitments enshrined in the GATS schedules become increasingly outdated with the effluxion of time. As a consequence, countries came up with their own strategies to open services industries including reforms at the domestic level. The third time act is the time of PTAs which aim at services liberalization. PTAs increasingly diverge from the GATS and may therefore undermine the achievement of minimal coherence in the regulation of services. *Delimatsis* concludes that today services liberalisation at the global level is confronted by diverging views—American isolationism on the one hand and an introspective approach of the biggest developing countries with respect to WTO matters. Even though trade in services is expected to increase in the near future, countries are reluctant to open domestic services markets.

In the next chapter, *Johanna Jacobsson* moves to the impact of services liberalisation in trade agreements on subcentral entities. She senses significant implications because regional and local measures are numerous and often have commercial implications. *Jacobsson* analyses the different ways in which federations and other federal-type structures engage in international services liberalization by reviewing the GATS commitments as well as the services commitments that the EU, the US and Canada have made in some of their recent PTAs. The chapter analyses the many differences in scheduling treaty commitments. *Jacobsson* stresses crucial differences in the way that these federal entities engage in international services liberalisation. For example, in NAFTA, all existing sub-central measures are exempted and are not listed. In other treaties sub-central measures are exempted and provide for an illustrative list of existing measures or a legally binding list. She concludes that deeper service liberalization calls for a more extensive inclusion of sub-central entities in international services negotiations through legally binding commitments instead of services liberalization only on the level of the central government.

Addressing one of the most controversial horizontal topics which remains contested *Gabriel Gari* compares the disciplines on domestic regulations affecting trade in services at regional, plurilateral and multilateral level. He provides an overview of the recent developments on disciplines on domestic regulation both at multilateral and regional level. The chapter examines disciplines on transparency of domestic regulations and disciplines on the development of domestic regulations, the disciplines on the administration of domestic regulation and provisions on special and differential treatment for developing countries. *Gari* analyses thirty PTAs from Australia, Canada, China, EU, Japan and the U.S. and compares them with GATS disciplines. In addition, he assesses three draft texts on disciplines on domestic regulations pursuant to Article VI:4 GATS that have been circulated among WTO Members since 2009. *Gari* identifies a significant degree of convergence between the disciplines adopted at regional level with those that are about to be adopted at plurilateral level. At the same time, discrepancies over the extent and eligibility for special and differential treatment for developing countries are the main obstacle to reach a multilateral agreement. Finally, the chapter argues that the risk of trade diversion that could be generated by the disciplines on domestic regulation adopted at regional or plurilateral level is extremely low due to a soft phrasing of disciplines and an application on a MFN basis via Article XVIII or de facto.

Moving from horizontal to more specific aspects, *Svetlana Yakovleva* addresses privacy and data protection in FTAs. She takes stock of the evolution of provisions on privacy and data protection in the post-WTO FTAs and FTAs currently under negotiation relying on EU- and US-led FTAs as an empirical basis. The chapter evaluates the trends and patterns of the development of these provisions and provides an outlook for the upcoming negotiations on electronic commerce at the WTO. *Yakovleva* highlights the evolution of provisions on privacy and personal data protection in general exceptions, financial and telecommunications chapters, chapters on electronic commerce and digital trade. After identifying trends in the design and wording of these provisions in the EU- and US-led FTAs the author concludes that both trading partners tend to prefer their own template for regional FTAs. Her comparison of these templates demonstrates that they are rooted in domestic regulatory models of information governance. These two different approaches show a divergence in FTAs with respect to privacy and data protection. *Yakovleva* argues that a mutual inconsistency of the EU and US approaches to cross border data flows and the protection of privacy and personal data may prove counterproductive in the multilateral negotiations on electronic commerce at the WTO.

In the next chapter *Ines Willemyns* focuses on digital services in preferential trade agreements. Her chapter maps how digital services trade is addressed under the GATS as well as in the e-commerce chapters in preferential trade agreements. Due to the applicability of the GATS to all measures affecting the supply of digital services WTO Members are be subject to the GATS obligations when they are enacting measures to regulate these services, or the Internet more generally. *Willemyns* identifies three gaps in addressing barriers to digital services trade that adversely affect the liberalisation of digital services trade. Firstly, until today there is a disagreement between WTO Members with regard to the question whether 'digital products' classify as goods or services. Secondly, there is a lack of commitments in the relevant services sectors. Thirdly, there are three barriers/obstacles to digital trade (data localisation requirements, a mandated transfer of source codes and a lack of access to the Internet). The chapter then assesses whether e-commerce chapters in PTAs go further than what can be found at the multilateral level. Moreover, the chapter studies whether existing gaps are being filled in the e-commerce chapters of PTAs. The e-commerce-related content of almost 100 PTAs is identified through a term-frequency analysis, which allows for a mapping of the presence of different barriers to digital services trade in PTAs. *Willemyns* shows that there is a considerably divergence between how e-commerce PTAs address the three issues that have been studied in this chapter.

Addressing the proverbial 'elephant in the room', i.e. the relevance of labour migration in a trade in services context *Marion Panizzon and Harjodh Singh* analyse the regulatory or market-driven coherence of the movement of natural persons across EU and Asian Preferential Trade Agreements. They focus on the movement of natural persons according to mode 4 (M4) of the GATS as well as non-serviced migration in the EU and Asian PTAs. With respect to mode 4, the treatment in regional trade agreements and the GATS varies considerably. In GATS, the ability of service suppliers to move within the region on a temporary basis is dependent upon scheduled commitments. The authors present that liberalisation commitments in PTAs have advanced in GATS-plus and GATS-extra. The way migration and M4-type mobility are regulated however differs between EU and Asian PTAs. With regard to the access of natural persons as service providers to markets in other countries a political controversy has existed since the GATS and has continued into the present day. This type of cross-border trade in services is closely linked to issues of temporary labour migration. Both in the GATS and in most other agreements, the participating states are more restrictive in this respect. In this respect, an element of coherence rather than divergence in international service trade law is also apparent here.

The next two chapters have a specific sectoral focus: *Mira Burri* analyses telecommunications and media services in PTAs while *Carlo M. Cantore* addresses financial services. Burri maps differences in the commitments and treaty language of PTAs (US and EU trade deals in particular) in comparison with corresponding commitments entailed in the GATS. PTAs barely differ from GATS obligations. Rather they follow the path of the GATS and are dependent on previous solutions, negotiated modalities and classifications, and even rely on the same language. Therefore, *Burri* critically concludes that recent PTA developments do not adequately take into account the technological and political developments in the telecommunications and the media services sector after the end of the Uruguay Round.

Cantore compares key provisions of the five recent select FTAs and assesses their convergence (or divergence) with the GATS as well as among themselves. He concludes that despite the different approach to liberalisation followed (negative list versus positive list), the FTAs examined in this study largely import the majority of the discipline from the GATS templates. Moreover, the chapter shows how certain provisions from the GATS Understanding were implemented into FTAs as binding obligations. This development highlights the relevance of the GATS for future reforms and a trend towards convergence with respect to financial services trade.

Maritime transport services are then discussed by *Lijun Zhao*. She analyses whether and how RTAs (and PTAs) may facilitate international trade and enhance liberalisation of maritime transport service along with the GATS under the WTO framework. *Zhao* analysis builds on a historical, legal and economic perspective of maritime transport services. In her chapter *Zhao* concludes that maritime transport services should be governed by WTO rules as well as RTAs. One reason for this is rooted in the economy of maritime transport services itself since regional transport services only need to be liberalised among the involved countries of that specific region. The WTO, on the other hand, plays a crucial role with respect to matters which have a global impact, such as open registry and cabotage.

The final chapter on sectoral issues in the book deals with taxation. *Weiwei Zhang* explores the intersections between the global tax reform launched by the Organization for Economic Co-operation and Development (OECD) and the Group of 20 (G20) to tackle base erosion and profit shifting (BEPS) on the one hand, and international rules on trade in services, mostly—the GATS under the WTO on the other hand. With respect to the intersection of the BEPS Package and the GATS *Zhang* concludes that some recommendations of the BEPS Package may stand in contrast to GATS obligations.

To conclude, all chapters have shown either aspects of convergence or aspects of divergence between GATS rules and trade in services rules of FTAs. Combining the different analyses has led to a more comprehensive and holistic picture of the current law on services trade liberalisation. Despite the above-mentioned differences between GATS and regional and bilateral FTAs, these have not led to a comprehensive fragmentation of the legal framework, as the agreements essentially contain the same or at least similar obligations. In particular, all agreements contain the basic principles of non-discrimination (most-favoured-nation treatment and national treatment) and the obligation to open markets. What the agreements also have in common is that the states can shape the scope of the liberalisation obligations themselves by shaping their own specific commitments, even if this tends to be easier in the case of agreements with a positive list approach. The modalities and techniques of the concrete obligations to liberalise services were extended, supplemented and modified in FTAs. For example, the positive list approach known from the GATS was combined with the NAFTA negative list approach, without a new model having already emerged. The actual economic effects of the modifications of the new approaches are not yet clear.

Regional and bilateral FTAs also adopt the central concepts and structural principles of the GATS. This can be seen, for example, in the conception and definition of the concept of trade in services. The concept of 'trade in services' can either be defined according to the GATS model with a focus on the four modes of supply or as an autonomous concept with a focus on each individual agreement. Today, the GATS still represents the undisputed reference framework concerning trade in services. The definition of trade in services (Art. I GATS) and the basic principles of non-discrimination (most favoured nation treatment and national treatment), market access and general exceptions have been integrated into other FTAs.

Despite certain variances, these principles can be regarded as common law of trade in services. However, compared to the GATS model, the structure of some regional agreements varies.

The chapters of the book showed tendencies and developments towards consolidation of trade in services issues which contribute towards coherence in the law of trade in services. At the same time some developments lead to more divergence between GATS rules and bilateral and regional trade agreements due to differentiations which relativize and complement the GATS structure and basic principles. Against this backdrop, the importance of the GATS becomes less relevant at least for some areas of the law. In other areas, however, the GATS will continue to be the important reference framework and those legal structures and principles will depend on future developments at the WTO.

Rhea Tamara Hoffmann is a post-doc researcher at the University of Erlangen-Nürnberg. Her research focuses on international investment and trade law and fundamental rights, including the principle of nondiscrimination. Previously, she was a researcher at the cluster of excellence "Formation of Normative Orders" at the University of Frankfurt am Main and worked for the United Nations Conference on Trade and Development (UNCTAD) in Geneva.

Markus Krajewski holds the Chair in Public Law and Public International Law at the University of Erlangen-Nürnberg. His research focuses on international economic law, human rights, European external relations, and the law of public services. He is co-editor of the European Yearbook of International Economic Law and serves as Secretary-General of the German Branch of the International Law Association (ILA).

Coherence and Divergence in Agreements on Trade in Services: A Drama in Three Acts

Panagiotis Delimatsis

Contents

1 Introduction

Services liberalization at the global level is currently held hostage of transatlantic divergences of views, American isolationism and the increasingly introspective approach that the biggest developing countries take with respect to international

For insightful comments and suggestions, the author is grateful to Rolf Adlung, Martin Roy and Christophe Kiener. Remaining errors are of the author's alone.

P. Delimatsis (✉)
Tilburg Law and Economics Center, Tilburg, The Netherlands
e-mail: p.delimatsis@uvt.nl

© The Editor(s) (if applicable) and The Author(s), under exclusive licence to
Springer Nature Switzerland AG 2020
R. T. Hoffmann, M. Krajewski (eds.), *Coherence and Divergence in Services Trade
Law*, European Yearbook of International Economic Law,
https://doi.org/10.1007/978-3-030-46955-9_2

trade matters. At the level of rule-making relating to services, a learning-by-doing approach can be observed both unilaterally and at the preferential trade agreement (PTA) level. As the services liberalization commitments enshrined in the Schedules of the General Agreement on Trade in Services (GATS) become increasingly outdated, countries are in the pursuit of the most adequate strategies to reap the positive spillovers from the expansion of their services industries.

Reluctance to open domestic services markets is often associated with fears relating to the interpretation of liberalization commitments that existing GATS case-law has instigated; well-established perceptions about the maintenance of State control over public services; or the impact of services liberalization in under-served areas or vulnerable groups at the domestic level. Additional reasons may relate to the preservation of the natural landscape and fears that the presence of foreign investors will have negative spillovers on the environment. Another cause for a liberalization-averse stance is the recurring fluidity and complexity as to the definition of trade in services and the distinction among modes of supply.

Despite this unfavourable policy climate, services currently dominate economic activity in most countries around the world irrespective of their level of development. Services are a growth engine, not only in terms of economic but also social growth. While financial, telecommunications or transport services come to mind, other services such as health or education can also be key inputs and determinants of the stock and growth of human capital.[1] New technological means 'democratize' the supply of services globally, opening new pathways for interaction. The new collaborative consumption opportunities that are given through the internet expand the pool of potential service suppliers and are capable of ensuring a more equal distribution of trade gains.

Global trade in services has grown in the last 20 years in a steadier manner than merchandise trade. Importantly, services have been more resilient than goods to the macroeconomic upheaval of recent times. Studies suggest that if exports of trade in goods were equally resilient (that is, shared the same elasticity to GDP growth as services exports), then their decrease during the 2008–2009 collapse would have been only half compared to what was observed (i.e. about 15% instead of 30%). Services are crisis-proof and are surprisingly immune to short-term negative shocks when compared to goods exports. They continued to be consumed despite the negative economic situation. Such resilience is particularly apparent in business services. Only transport services saw a decline similar to goods exports, but this is an inevitable consequence of the collapse of such exports.[2]

Trade in services suffered significantly only in 2009, decreasing almost 10%. However, in 2010, it resumed its pre-crisis levels, whereas global services exports grew by 5% in 2014. On average, trade in services has still increased by 8% annually in the last two decades and services exports more than doubled between 2007 and 2017, amidst the Great Recession. Reaching their peak in recent times, world services exports grew by 8% in 2017, accounting for over US$5 trillion.

---

[1]See Hoekman and Mattoo (2008), p. 23.
[2]See Ariu (2016), pp. 138–149.

The EU and the US are the leading traders of services in the world. Nonetheless, the growth of the services industries in the developing world is also quite important. Exports of developing economies in services trade grew by 8% in 2017.[3] The share of developing countries in services trade accounts for almost one third of global trade in services. Again, the distribution of the gains from trade in services is not balanced, as China, India and Singapore account for a disproportionately high share of trade in services. Tourism and travel but also transport and business process outsourcing (BPO) constitute areas whereby low-income economies have a comparative advantage and currently lead the services revolution in the developing world. Furthermore, trade among developing countries has increased from 8% to 13% between 2000 and 2012.[4]

Against this backdrop, the present chapter takes the trade policy drama that is services liberalization and uses it to structure the following analysis. Act I considers the types of divergence that had to be overcome to get to the achievement of including services negotiations in the single undertaking approach of the negotiations that occurred during the Uruguay Round. This is followed in Act II by an assessment of the GATS outcome from a viewpoint of coherence. Finally, Act III picks up the story of services liberalization through the conclusion of PTAs and attempts to identify the thorniest points that may undermine the achievement of minimal coherence regarding the regulation of services industries at the global level.

2 Act I: Trade in Services Before the WTO and the Origins of the GATS—Diverging Views on Trade in Services as a Stand-Alone Topic

2.1 Scene I: Minding the Conceptual Gap

The public perception about the role of services has not always been so rosy—on the contrary. For a very long time, services were regarded as ancillary activities that are not per se productive and have no independent value. Adam Smith had famously suggested that services is a waste of resources, which perish at the moment of their production, 'unproductive of any value'.[5] Drake and Nicolaidis identify a 'conceptual gap' that lasted for centuries and eloquently summarize the rationale for the near contempt vis-à-vis services: first, services did not make any visible contributions to wealth, contrary to goods; second, services could not exist without goods, as they are derivative of goods; lack of demand for goods would also mean no demand for services; third, services were more often than not inputs to the real economy, performed in house by manufacturers rather than external suppliers. Thus, there

---

[3] WTO, World Trade Statistical Review 2018, p. 20.
[4] See Maurer, Magdeleine and Lanz (2016), p. 42.
[5] Smith (1937), p. 315; See, for the quote, Drake and Nicolaidis (1992), p. 43.

was no reason to assess their market value separately; and, fourth, compared with tangible goods, services were invisible and existed only temporarily (i.e. they vanished at the moment of supply) and therefore were insignificant.[6] Physical proximity was necessary for a service to be provided.

This should not be taken to mean that services were totally neglected in any public discussion at the global level. In 1947, the abortive Havana Charter—which was, to a certain extent, a source of inspiration during the Uruguay Round negotiations—recognized services as part of international commerce, but only obliquely: While the Charter recognized that services are important trade enablers, it identified them as a potential source of restrictive business practices, i.e. as a *private* matter.[7] Thus, by providing so, it outrightly left outside its scope State measures that may affect the supply and consumption of services.

On the EU side, the Treaty of Rome establishing the European Economic Community in 1957 enshrined a provision on the freedom to provide services. However, for a long time, services were considered as a subordinate category of economic activity; the freedom relating to services was regarded as ancillary to the other three fundamental freedoms relating to free movement of goods, persons or capital. The wording of the Treaty was also quite unequivocal. Indeed, Article 60 ECT would define services in a tautological but, also crucially, negative manner: 'Services shall be considered to be "services" within the meaning of the Treaty where they are normally provided for remuneration, in so far as they are not governed by the provisions relating to freedom of movement for goods, capital and persons.'[8] Thus, services were defined negatively and in the alternative by reference to the other three fundamental freedoms.[9]

Interestingly, this wording has survived through the various amendments of the EEC/EC/EU Treaties over the years and is currently set out intact in Article 57 of the Treaty on the Functioning of the European Union (TFEU). This description of free movement of services by reference to the other freedoms was also given full colour in early case law by the European Court of Justice: In *Gebhard*, the court found that, based on the Treaty text, it had to prioritize the examination of the compatibility of the measure at issue with the rules on establishment before it can turn to the relevance of the freedom to provide services, thereby alluding to a relationship of subordination between the two freedoms.[10] As a corollary of this line of thinking, the

---

[6]Drake and Nicolaidis (1992), p. 43.

[7]Art. 53:1 of the Final Act; also Krommenacker (1984), p. 141.

[8]See also Delimatsis (2018), p. 195.

[9]See Ehlermann and Campogrande (1988), p. 484; also Snell (2002).

[10]Case C-55/94, *Reinhard Gebhard v Consiglio dell'Ordine degli Avvocati e Procuratori di Milano,* ECLI:EU:C:1995:411, para. 22; See also earlier, Case 60/84, *Cinéthèque,* ECLI:EU: C:1985:329, para. 10; and C-275/92, *Schindler,* ECLI:EU:C:1994:119, para. 30.

CJEU found in *Gebhard* that two freedoms cannot simultaneously apply to a given national measure.[11]

The US, on the other hand, concluded various treaties of friendship, commerce and navigation which included rules with regard to specific services such as aviation, shipping or communications but the conclusion of such agreements was discontinued in the 1950s.[12] In fact, bilateral agreements explicitly covering trade in services were concluded much later (for instance, the US-Canada Agreement in 1987).

The conceptual gap mentioned earlier inevitably led to a policy gap. Regarded as non-tradable,[13] with various public monopolies dominating the supply of backbone services such as financial, telecommunication or transport, services were for a long time virtually absent from any trade-related discussion. Policymakers failed to realize that there were common characteristics and concerns that connect all services sectors which would require an international trade agreement that would supersede the piecemeal, sector-specific approach that dominated at the time.

2.2   Act 2: Services Rising

In the meantime, technological advances and the information revolution started changing the nature of service supply, allowing the performance of a wide variety of services from a distance. In addition, the progressive dismantling of barriers to trade in goods also had a beneficial impact on services which were inputs to goods. Furthermore, studies of that period started adducing evidence proving the importance of services for employment and productivity gains. In addition, the first signs of extensive outsourcing were becoming apparent, enabled by increasing unbundling of services activities and the possibility for delivering a service from a distance in a more cost-efficient manner, without any movement of the service supplier or the service recipient being required.

The role of the OECD in increasing awareness with regard to trade in services and gradually constructing a new trade reality is by now well-documented.[14] An early attempt to address barriers to trade in services was the OECD Decision to adopt a Code of Liberalization of Current Invisible Operations in 1961. Whereas the Code had a quite broad substantive scope covering banking, insurance, transport or business services (and thus, in a way, constitutes the predecessor of subsequent attempts to address barriers to trade in services like the GATS), the OECD, a newly

---

[11]Case C-55/94, *Gebhard*, para. 20. Note that this case law is now abandoned. See C-452/04, *Fidium Finanz AG v Bundesanstalt für Finanzdienstleistungsaufsicht*, ECLI:EU:C:2006:631, para. 32.

[12]See Marchetti and Mavroidis (2011), p. 690.

[13]Feketekuty (1998), p. 80.

[14]See, among many others, Feketekuty (1988).

established subject of international law, at the time had only 20 Members so a broad geographical momentum was still missing. In addition, there was no real follow-up; subsequent discussions rather focused on foreign direct investment and capital movements.

The recognition of the importance of trade in services can be traced in the 1970s. Indeed, it was about a decade after the Invisibles Code, and only shortly before the Tokyo Round negotiations, when an OECD high-level group prepared a report explicitly referring to trade in services at the conceptual level; the increased internationalization of the phenomenon; the fact that from an international trade viewpoint, trade in services raised questions similar to goods; and thus, the need to address protectionist forces that may impede further liberalization of services.[15] However, subsequently, the OECD, once again, put the issue aside.

Yet, the necessary momentum was thereby created, notably in the US. While trade diplomats and economists were reflecting on how to improve the conditions under which trade in goods would take place (in other words, how to tackle non-tariff barriers), companies and interest groups in developed economies started acknowledging the increasing importance of services as a stand-alone area that necessitated its own rules and disciplines.[16] The US and the UK in particular led the relevant discussions and structured their internal trade-related authorities accordingly. The US Trade Act of 1974 mandated the US Trade Representative (USTR) to raise services already during the Tokyo Round but such an attempt was largely unsuccessful except for some references to services in certain Tokyo Codes (for instance, the government procurement code). However, the issue was not abandoned. On the contrary, the US extracted an informal agreement among advanced economies that services would be put back in the OECD agenda.

Once the issue was delegated back to Paris, the OECD Trade Committee—and a newly established working group on trade in services—became the forum that would eventually create a coalition of advanced economies promoting the inclusion of services in the forthcoming multilateral trade agenda at the GATT level and the ensuing liberalization of trade in services across sectors. That was everything but a walkover, as various developed nations, including the EU, believed that a more careful tactic that focused on data gathering, followed by a tailor-made, sector-specific approach was warranted. Recall that services liberalization within the EU was at its infancy, whereas the discussion for the recognition of professional qualifications in major professions like lawyers or architects had barely started. Other countries like Japan supported the US vision.

Nonetheless, the US managed to steer and maintain the discussions in the abstract, issue-framing level, thereby achieving its twofold objective: avoiding the intervention of other international organizations dealing with specific sectors such as the International Telecommunications Union (ITU) but also responding favourably to various US constituents and lobbies representing various services sectors.

---

[15] OECD, 'Report by the High-Level Group on Trade and Related Problems' (OECD, 1973), at 63.
[16] See Kelsey (2008), p. 61.

Absent relatively robust work from other OECD economies, a wave of technical work 'made in the US' demonstrating the potential benefits of services liberalization for the overall sluggish growth that the global economy was experiencing, hit by the oil crises and high inflation of the 1970s, also helped establishing the case for action as far as international services regulation liberalization was concerned. This has culminated to an adopted position by the OECD ministers in 1981 that GATT could be the appropriate forum for multilateral action in services.

3 Act II: Addressing Regulatory Divergence and Bringing Coherence Through Multilateral Action

3.1 Scene 1: Making the Case for Global Services Regulation

Despite opposition by the developing world at the GATT level, which saw services as the 'Trojan horse' used by the US to maintain its comparative advantage and distract from persistent protectionism in manufacturing and agriculture, the US, with reinvigorated force after the election of Ronald Reagan, worked meticulously to build a case for GATT action in services. The first important victory towards this direction was the inclusion—as a last item—of services in the GATT Ministerial declaration in November 1982.[17]

This addition was everything but an easy task: the developing countries were unanimously against any such action. Led by Brazil and India, the developing world insisted that there was no competence and thus no mandate could exist for the GATT regarding the regulation of services. According to various countries with development-related concerns, services were primarily a matter of domestic regulatory conduct and therefore did not belong to the purview of the multilateral trading system. Other than the sovereignty concerns that were raised, the fears of developing countries were also associated with the desire to protect 'infant industries'; the difficulties they faced with regard to balance-of-payments; and the crucial role of infrastructure services.[18]

In addition, several developed countries have not had done convincingly their homework already at the domestic level: many of them were simply in the dark as to the stakes at issue relating to services transactions. The ministerial declaration achieved a significant step in the direction of addressing this issue, as it called for national examinations of the service sector for those that were interested in undertaking such studies.

The declaration left open the question as to the availability, necessity and desirability of the multilateral track. Despite the soft language used in the

---

[17]See GATT, Thirty-Eight Session, Ministerial Declaration adopted on 29 November 1982, L/5424, 29 November 1982, p. 14.

[18]See Sapir (1985), p. 40.

declaration, the issue was on the table for the first time and thus a convergence towards a multilateral consensus was in the making. Opponents would from now on have to justify their foot-dragging. One thing was certain for all GATT parties: they would have to start collecting substantive input relating to services transactions but also strategic input in anticipation of a potential agreement liberalizing services at the global level. Know-how as to the adequacy of the GATT framework for this new area of international relations was also in the making for the most part.

Several empirical studies[19] in that period demonstrated the quantitative and qualitative significance of services in international trade and, thus, confirmed that this trade issue was mooted as mature for inclusion on the trade negotiating agenda. The USTR, W. Brock, also published an influential study coinciding with the GATT ministerial decision and calling for multilateral action before protectionist trends negatively affect the supply of services.[20] The bilateral or regional arrangements and mechanisms that preceded the GATS were considered as insufficient to address concerns relating to market access and discriminatory treatment based on the origin of services and service suppliers beyond their territorial scope.

Thus, the US government became the primary advocate for including services in the agenda with a view to making domestic laws, regulations and administrative practices subject to international rules.[21] Lobbies from the financial and the communications sector did not want the momentum to be lost and were closely following the discussion, also through the Coalition of Service Industries (CSI) whose contributions maintained the growing impetus for strengthening the case for a new regulatory framework on trade in services.[22]

The US strategy for the inclusion of services in the multilateral agenda was enunciated in the US national study on trade in services in 1984.[23] This was the American response to the request for national studies that was included in the GATT ministerial decision of 1982. At the outset, the US proposal entailed an expansion of the GATT in order to include services with the contemplation that the new round of multilateral trade negotiations encompasses the negotiation of the services compact. Essentially, the American proposal tended to focus the negotiations on the sectors that where of export interest to the United States and other developed countries (namely FDI), while excluding liberalization of labour movements, where developing countries might often have a comparative advantage.[24]

By 1985, the diplomatic battle was no longer between the US and the world. Rather, it had already become a North versus South issue.[25] The Group of Ten (G10), led by Brazil and India, preferred such negotiations to be outside the GATT

---

[19]Hill (1977), p. 315; also Krommenacker (1979), p. 510.

[20]Brock (1982), p. 229; also Malmgren (1985), p. 18.

[21]Also Bhagwati (1987), p. 26.

[22]Bhagwati (1984), p. 140; also Reyna (1993), p. 2343.

[23]USTR, *US national study on trade in services*, 25 January 1984.

[24]USTR, *US national study on trade in services*, 25 January 1984, p. 77; also Berg (1987), p. 10.

[25]Drake and Nicolaidis (1992), p. 58.

conceptual and institutional structure, undertaken by governments rather than the GATT contracting parties.[26] At the end of the day, the Punta del Este declaration portrayed a compromise,[27] i.e. two distinct tracks for negotiations on goods and services, but the Uruguay Round as a whole was considered a 'single undertaking' to be conducted within the same time and under the aegis of the Trade Negotiating Committee. This was a key factor for the eventually successful inclusion of services in the new multilateral regime that was in the making in the early 1990s.

3.2   Scene 2: Came, Saw and. . . Conquered Coherence?

After prolonged negotiations culminating in the Punta del Este Ministerial Meeting in September 1986, services became part of the agenda in a convoluted series of trade-offs that shaped the Uruguay Round.[28] Hence, the final constellation had something for everybody to claim victory: developing countries did not succeed in dissociating the GATT from a potential services agreement. They did, however, successfully advocate in favour of a flexible framework agreement with few firm obligations.[29] In any event, from an international political economy perspective, the final inclusion of services in the agenda was an extraordinary event defying all odds, as an influential group of developing countries in the GATT adamantly argued against it.[30]

Under these circumstances, the GATS was a milestone and an unequivocal expression of a cooperative equilibrium moment in global trade history. It constituted a major step in an unchartered territory and an innovative endeavour to establish a pragmatic yet coherent framework to allow for the expansion of trade in services. However, the GATS is also the expression of a compromise that occurred among centrifugal forces that sought to influence the approach taken with regard to services trade. It further was a concerted effort to consolidate at the international level previous efforts of privatization that the service sector underwent in the 1980s within various jurisdictions notably in the developed world. For the EU, for instance, the period of GATS negotiations coincided with the implementation of the single market program in the aftermath of the Single European Act, which changed dramatically the making of the EU economic rulebook.

Furthermore, the GATS was the culmination of the erosion of the public service tradition which had already happened in most of the 1980s and transformations in

---

[26]GATT, 'Communication from Brazil', MTN.GNS/W/3, 11 March 1987.

[27]Reyna (1993), p. 2361.

[28]Marconini (1990), p. 19; Woodrow (1991), p. 222; also Hindley (1990), p. 136; Smeets et al. (1991), p. 197.

[29]See Hoekman B (1993) Developing Countries and the Uruguay Round: Negotiations on Services, PRWP No 1220, The World Bank, p. 14.

[30]See also Croome (1999), pp. 102, 207, 310.

previously non-marketable services that created new business opportunities for companies and private parties. The GATS can be seen as an attempt of a core group consisting of trading powers but also smaller, developing economies with market dynamism to multilateralize these transformations and induce other WTO Members to join them in the deregulatory verve, as liberalism reigned in the most advanced economies and started spreading rapidly in the wake of the collapse of communism. In theory, such a consolidation would be a necessary prerequisite if the objective of the new framework was to bring about a more coherent landscape globally.

However, this was not necessarily the objective in practice—if it was, then the final outcome surely fell short of it. Indeed, in a turning point which has witnessed significant learning-by-doing moments, high levels of flexibility undermined the overall coherence of the agreement from the outset: a soft set of general obligations which should most of the times be read in combination with a given Member's Schedule; legal provisions that called for negotiations (for instance, with respect to government procurement or subsidies); Members' Schedules that did not lock-in existing liberalization, that is, they did not reflect the actual level of openness; a future promise for progressive liberalization, starting 5 years after the end of the Uruguay Round at the latest; and, finally, an abstract sunset clause relating to exemptions from the MFN obligation.

And yet, the potential for a coherent framework which would have satisfactory elements and concepts for everybody was present. Importantly, the substantive, personal and institutional scope of the agreement seemingly was limitless:

- First, the definition of what constitutes a 'measure' affecting trade in services was all-encompassing and revolutionary.
- Second, the GATS would break new ground in the multilateral trading system by covering not only measures taken by governments and public authorities at all levels of governments[31] but also non-governmental bodies with delegated regulatory powers. The latter brought under the GATS coverage, for instance, all self-regulated professions that set conditions for access to and practice of a profession. This was an important extension that was deemed necessary, as delegation of power to private associations had become an important phenomenon globally, covering various services sectors, from business to financial to transport services.
- Third, the GATS, included an all-encompassing definition of what a service is. Inspired by intellectual work during most of the 1980s, which suggested that services can increasingly be supplied independently of physical proximity and also that trade in services does not necessarily happen only via foreign direct investment,[32] the agreement defined services by means of four modes of

---

[31] See the chapter by Jacobsson in this volume.
[32] *Inter alia*, Bhagwati (1984), p. 139; Sampson and Snape (1985), p. 172; See also Chang et al. (1999), p. 94; Arup (2000), p. 121.

supply:[33] the first one, 'cross-border supply', which entailed the movement of service that crosses a physical border,[34] was by now possible due to technological advances and improved means of communication. The second, 'consumption abroad', covering the moment of *receiving* a service abroad recognized the increasing importance of travel due to improved means of transport but also the opportunities arising from developed country citizens travelling to developing countries to consume services.[35] The other two modes would be the most controversial ones. 'Commercial presence', or Mode 3, would cover establishment of an investor in another WTO Member to deliver services. Mode 4 would cover the 'presence of natural persons' which would need to be temporary so that migration-related questions and issues remain outside the scope of the GATS. This Mode would cover low-skilled, independent professionals and contract service suppliers but also intra-corporate transferees.

3.3   Scene 3: The GATS Flexibilities

Despite the good intentions, the potential for greater coherence vanished rapidly. Members were allowed to impose limitations even to the most basic obligations like national treatment, market access or transparency. Even the utmost principle of MFN is not uniformly applicable; rather, each Member was given the opportunity to inscribe exemptions to the MFN. These exemptions, limitations and conditions are inscribed in each Member's Schedule of Commitments (hereinafter 'the Schedule'). Such conditions, however, would have an impact on the applicability of the GATS to the WTO Members, thereby creating a playing field which was unlevelled from the start. According to the logic of the GATS, though, this would be in line with the principle of progressive liberalization. Proposals to ensure a minimum level of liberalization across sectors and Members faced substantial opposition and thus were not taken up any further.

Thus, without reading the Schedule and the MFN exemptions list of a given Member, it would be impossible to assess fully the committed level of openness of

---

[33] Arts I:2 GATS and XXVIII(b) GATS. During the GATS negotiations the original word 'delivery' was replaced by the word 'supply' because the latter was understood as covering those measures directly governing as well as those indirectly affecting the supply of services. See also Panel Report, *EC – Bananas III (US)*, para. 7.281 and fn 455. In *US – Gambling*, however, 'supply' and 'delivery' were used interchangeably. See, for example, Panel Report, *US – Gambling*, paras 6.280ff.

[34] The *1993 Scheduling Guidelines* clarify that in the case of a service supply through mode 1 '. . .*the service supplier is not present within the territory of the Member where the service is delivered*'. GATT, 'Scheduling of Initial Commitments in Trade in Services: Explanatory Note', MTN.GNS/W/164, 3 September 1993, para. 19(a).

[35] To date, transport and travel are the leading sector for the developing world in terms of growth. Tourism accounts for over 40% of Africa's commercial services exports, whereas in the LDC group only this percentage is more than 10% higher.

that Member. The list of MFN exemptions typically is short, identifying those sectors in which Members would want to maintain their right to discriminate among WTO Members (that is, a negative list of 'grandfathering' provisions).[36] These exemptions could, for instance, include derogations in audiovisual services or transport services. These exemptions are still in place although Members had agreed in the end of the Uruguay Round to review them after 10 years with a view to eliminating them. As a general rule, with the exception of financial services, there is an inverse relationship between the number of MFN exemptions and the frequency with which specific commitments were undertaken.[37]

In terms of scheduling limitations and conditions to the obligation on market access and national treatment, variety abounds. The scheduling approach has induced such a variable geometry regarding services liberalization globally. While discussions have included the NAFTA approach of 'negative' listing (that is, explicitly list reservations from market access and national treatment), WTO Members opted for a hybrid approach of scheduling. Members would first decide whether they will liberalize market access and/or national treatment in a given services sector (say, professional services, which is a sub-sector of business services) in an explicit (called 'positive') manner, and subsequently list the type of limitations they want to maintain in this sector for each one of the four modes of supply.[38] These limitations are inscribed in a negative manner.[39] For instance, a given Member may decide, out of the entire business service sector, to fully liberalize only the supply of architectural services in a cross-border manner, but still maintain limitations against (or, by inscribing 'Unbound', not liberalize any aspect of) the temporary presence of foreign architects in the domestic market.

In other words, the applicability of the GATS largely depends on the liberalizing decisions of each WTO Member, most notably the commitments, limitations and conditions made under market access (Article XVI GATS) or national treatment (Article XVII GATS). WTO Members can tailor their obligations based on their country-specific needs and capacities. WTO Members have a wide margin of maneuver as to the substantive features (that is, the sectoral choice) of their

---

[36]The so-called 'negative list' approach means in the GATS jargon that, other than the sectors and sub-sectors that are explicitly listed in a Member's list of MFN exemptions, the MFN principle applies to all sectors. See also Adlung and Carzaniga (2009), p. 357.

[37]Mattoo (2000), p. 67.

[38]Cross-border supply; consumption abroad; commercial presence; and temporary movement of natural persons. There is no doubt that the GATS is an investment agreement, as over 50% of services trade is conducted through Mode 3. See Magdeleine J and Maurer A, Measuring GATS Mode 4 Trade Flows, WTO Staff Working Paper, ERSD-2008-05, October 2008, https://www.wto.org/english/res_e/reser_e/ersd200805_e.pdf (last accessed 3 December 2019).

[39]The so-called 'negative list' approach means in the GATS jargon that, other than the limitations listed in the sectors and sub-sectors that are explicitly listed in a Member's Schedule, Members are bound to fully apply the market access and national treatment obligations in those sectors and subsectors.

liberalizing commitments. The same flexibility would apply as to the timing of such liberalizing commitments (that is, the starting date of the pledge made).

If a service sector does not form part of the Schedule of a given Member, then the GATS has a quite limited influence on the regulation of this sector domestically. For instance, if a Member decides not to include health services in its Schedule, then only the MFN principle applies and some other minor (so-called 'unconditional') obligations. The latter would include an obligation to publish all relevant measures of general application affecting trade in services (Article III:1 GATS) or to allow for independent review of and appropriate remedies for administrative decisions affecting trade in services (Article VI:2).

As another indication of the flexibility enshrined in the agreement, the former obligation depends on a subjective element: it is for each Member to assess whether a given measure affects trade in services. Furthermore, this type of publication is a transparency-related feature that exists in most democracies in the world. Independent review is an important obligation that can create additional costs for domestic authorities and self-regulatory bodies. However, it was not really brought up in a dispute over the years.[40] The EU experience in this respect has shown that the issue of independence can indeed become controversial in the case of decisions by self-regulatory bodies such as professional associations or independent authorities which decide on the granting of licences (for instance, in the telecommunications sector).[41]

In combination with the complex dynamics that were developed during the Uruguay Round and shortly before the conclusion of the negotiations due to the single undertaking approach, this flexibility embedded in the GATS was the essential precondition for the GATS to be broadly accepted. This led to a certain core of countries negotiating with each other deep liberalization commitments that would greatly improve market access in sectors like financial, telecommunication or business services, whereas other countries would decide to leave liberalization for the future.

As noted earlier, WTO Members failed to reach an agreement to lock-in actual liberalization in their respective Schedules. In other words, contrary to the GATT Schedules, the GATS Schedules were outdated from the moment the agreement was concluded. This meant that the much sought-after coherence that a multilateral instrument could bring in identifying the current level of protectionism on trade in services failed to emerge. However, this lack of coherence is associated with high levels of uncertainty that service suppliers face, notably in case the difference between actual and bound level of liberalization is significant. Addressing this gap, also known in the goods realm as 'tariff water', could have important positive effects on trade. Recent studies have attempted to quantify the impact of legal bindings on trade in services that result from a decrease of uncertainty of this type

---

[40]Except for certain GATT-related cases.
[41]See Delimatsis (2007), p. 13.

and found that the average increase of bilateral trade could be between 8% and 12% depending on the sector.[42]

3.4   Scene 4: The Evolving Nature of Services and the Static Classification System

In addition, the entries in the Members' Schedules were based on the Central Product Classification (CPC) List of the United Nations, which found its place in the GATS in a simplified form document, the Services Sectoral Classification List (the so-called 'W/120').[43] Being a relatively short list of sectors and subsectors, the W/120 and the ensuing Schedules of commitments prepared by the WTO Members have left room for ambiguity and varying interpretations, which would not always converge with the intentions and regulatory purposes of the drafters of those Schedules.

At this juncture, a problematic feature of the Classification List has been the lack of a mechanism which would ensure its adaptation to future developments. The Classification List is everything but a living instrument: First and foremost, it failed to keep up with the developments in classification-related matters that were taken up in the CPC List. Indeed, the CPC 1991 that was used for the W/120 has been subsequently revised several times: Version 1.0 was finally published in 1998, Version 1.1. in 2002, Version 2.0 in 2008, and more recently, in 2015, Version 2.1 was adopted.[44] However, the W/120 remained unchanged. Subsequent revisions of the latter have never been taken up at the GATS level.

Yet, technological advances are transforming the way services are supplied. The global economy nowadays is fairly different than 25 years ago, but the GATS has no internal mechanism that would allow updating regularly its sectoral list. More crucially, there is no mechanism that would allow a coordinated effort to update the Schedules but also ensure coherence when an issue of interpretation arises either at the technical level of the dispute settlement level.

In the present state of affairs, modification of Schedules is a burdensome, time-consuming process that takes place in an *ad hoc* manner, and at the initiative of a given WTO Member.[45] The existing mechanism of Article XXI GATS is fairly formalistic and time-consuming. Arguably, financial compensation and expedited arbitration setting the level of damages would be more reliable and sustainable

---

[42]See Lamprecht and Miroudot (2018).

[43]GATT, 'Services Sectoral Classification List' MTN.GNS/W/120, 10 July 1991.

[44]See   https://unstats.un.org/unsd/classifications/unsdclassifications/cpcv21.pdf   (last   accessed 3 December 2019).

[45]For instance, in the aftermath of the *US – Gambling* saga, the US sought to change the entry of its schedule with respect to the cross-border supply of gambling and betting services. However, this has been impossible for more than 2 years now.

options in a Member-driven organization. Also, with the current structure of the GATS, one is left to wonder why Members are not allowed to experiment with liberalizing commitments (for instance, in the highly contentious mode 4) for a pre-agreed number of years. Such a possibility could lead to higher levels of liberalization and also better, more responsive regulation. The idea of rolling-back liberalization in services has been a taboo for several years; however, the lack of such a possibility may partly explain the current lack of ambition in the GATS.

Other than the issue of outdated sectoral classifications, one should also note that services related to a given activity may be dispersed among various sectors or subsectors. Divided into several sectors and subsectors which are regarded as mutually exclusive,[46] the Classification List fails to cater for, simplify and thus facilitate liberalization in certain sectors, as services related to a given activity are dispersed among various sectors and subsectors. While there have been proposals for taking a cluster approach in scheduling commitments, ensuring coherence in one's Schedule was left to governments alone during the Uruguay Round. Even so, in view of the fragmentation of the Classification List, ensuring such a coherence became a Herculean task.

For instance, the entry in the Classification List relating to energy services fails to fully capture contemporary realities and trends in the sector. In the 1980s, gas and electricity were provided for the most part by state-run vertically integrated monopolies. These suppliers were responsible for all energy-related activities, from exploration to production to marketing.[47] The relative insignificance of the sector at that time is also reflected in the Classification List: transport, construction, engineering, distribution and energy-related financial services are dispersed across various services sectors included in the Classification List.[48] In view of the sector's peculiarities at the time, it became clear that substantial trade in energy services could not yet occur. For this reason, preference was given to other, more trade-friendly sectors.

This should not be taken to mean that the existing classification with the three energy-specific sectors in the Classification List may not lead to quite significant results in terms of market access. For instance, services incidental to energy distribution and to mining (both classified under business services) include both downstream and upstream energy-related activities. In addition, pipeline transportation of fuels (classified under transport services) covers all services that relate to the actual operation of a pipeline.

However, this helps us make a crucial point here: careless scheduling may lead to unanticipated results and requests to liberalize sub-sectors that were not intended to be liberalized. Thus, a more detailed and accurate classification would also lead to much more precise liberalization offers, a type of managed liberalization that most WTO Members would feel comfortable with. While, arguably, the existing

---

[46] Also Appellate Body Report, *US – Gambling*, para. 180.

[47] See WTO, Council for Trade in Services, 'Energy Services', S/C/W/311, 12 January 2010, p. 2.

[48] See also WTO, Council for Trade in Services (Special Session), 'Energy Services', Communication from the United States, S/CSS/W/24, 18 December 2000, Annex A.

classification in broad brush strokes may lead to more liberalization, even if unintentional, the long-term effect of such a constellation would most likely be that Members would be reluctant to schedule more commitments next time they are given the opportunity, leading to an overall sub-optimal result that ultimately undermines any trust-building effort towards the multilateral trade regime and defies the rationale of the principle of progressive liberalization.

The current state of affairs does not deviate much of the above-anticipated result: Services Schedules have been at the epicenter of most criticism against the GATS. All disputes relating to services before the WTO judiciary tackled the interpretation of GATS schedules and the scope of the commitments made therein. Recall that pursuant to Article XX:3 GATS, the GATS Schedules, once verified, became treaty text, that is, multilateral obligations that determine the scope of the GATS. As Schedules represent a treaty and a common agreement among all Members, their interpretation inevitably triggers the application of the rules of interpretation of the Vienna Convention on the Law of Treaties (Articles 31–33 VCLT).

Thus, commitments made are treaty terms that must be interpreted in good faith, consistently with the ordinary meaning of the undertaken commitments of a given Member as viewed in their context and understood in the light of the object and purpose of the GATS and the WTO, more generally.[49] Although Schedules are the results of 'a process of reciprocal demands and concessions, of "give and take"',[50] the intent and perceptions of a given Member alone regarding certain concepts will not matter.[51] This seems to come quite close to imposing top-down coherence via judicial interpretation in an inherently incoherent landscape as described above.

On the other hand, the manner Members draft their Schedules and other members perceive similar concepts was regarded as context within the meaning of the VCLT.[52] The latter is of particular importance in the GATS whereby the reference point is the Classification List *in combination with* the CPC.[53] Thus, panels and the Appellate Body, when interpreting a GATS Schedule, will routinely have recourse to GATS Schedules of other Members to extract, if possible, the common understanding of Members regarding—and a reliable, objective meaning of—a particular concept or term. This may not always be possible, though, as certain terms used may be country-specific and unique to a particular Member. In those cases, the ordinary

---

[49]Cf. Leroux (2007), p. 757. The Appellate Body confirmed that treaty interpretation 'is ultimately a holistic exercise that should not be mechanically subdivided into rigid components'. See Appellate Body Report, *China – Publications and Audiovisual Products*, para. 348.

[50]Appellate Body Report, *EC – Computer Equipment*, para. 109.

[51]As the Appellate Body noted in *EC – Computer Equipment* [para. 82] when interpreting GATT Schedules, "the security and predictability of tariff concessions would be seriously undermined if the concessions in Members' Schedules were to be interpreted on the basis of the subjective views of certain exporting Members alone".

[52]See, for instance, Appellate Body Report, *US – Gambling*, para. 182.

[53]This can be contrasted to the GATT where only the Harmonized System of the World Customs Organization (WCO) is the relevant benchmark.

meaning of the term will play the most important role, and thus taking into account the unilateral origin of the commitment will be inevitable.[54]

Revisiting scheduling in services in the GATS in a future negotiating round may be less burdensome than one would consider at first blush. As observed by meticulous research, WTO Members have committed on average about one third of the 160 subsectors of the Classification List. This percentage rises to two thirds for developed countries and countries that went through the WTO accession process.[55] Thus, an overhauling of Schedules and the classification list, as suggested before, may not be a mission impossible, in particular if one considers the long-term benefits (including the positive trust-building spillovers) of such an endeavor.

More complex, however, may be the identification of a future-proof classification list in the light of the growing importance of services inputs that make up a part of manufactured goods (and thus are subject to tariffs) (coined 'Mode 5'). Typical mode 5 services would entail design, engineering and software, as they are very often incorporated and traded as part of manufactured goods. More fundamentally for our purposes, though, such a development calls for a revisiting of the goods/services dichotomy with a view to creating a more coherent approach to scheduling liberalization commitments. Such coherence could be worked out through a long-term partnership with the Expert Group on International Statistical Classifications and the World Customs Organization.

Economically, it appears quite sensible to address this issue: Empirical evidence shows that the share of these embedded services as a percentage of total exports in goods has recorded double digit growth. For a considerable group of countries, these mode 5 services account for about one third of the total value of their manufactured exports. Statistics suggest that, for most WTO Members, the importance of mode 5 ranges from 20% to almost 50%.[56] Estimates also suggest that global GDP gains from liberalizing this type of embedded services at the WTO level could reach some €300 billion by 2025. Such liberalization could also have a beneficial impact on total trade, increasing it by an additional €500 billion.

---

[54]See also Ortino (2006), p. 124. The Appellate Body implicitly agreed with this limitation in *US – Gambling*, para. 182.

[55]See Marchetti and Roy (2008), p. 66.

[56]See Antimiani and Cernat (2018).

4 Act III: ....and Back Again: Increasing Divergence, Deepening Fragmentation?

4.1 Scene 1: The Disconnect Between Political Will and Economic Reality

The multilateral trading system is at the crossroads and the GATS is doubtless affected by the current impasse. Indeed, the initial high hopes of many with respect to prolonged prosperity at the global level thanks to a concerted effort to liberalize the emerging services markets and reap the benefits of technological progress did not materialize in full. Worse, some blame the GATS for unleashing all those forces preaching for unharnessed liberalization in important sectors such as financial services, which proved to be a disastrous recipe for global welfare.[57] Clearly, the occurrence of the recent Great Recession did not help increase the popularity of the agreement. Coupled with a turn to populism globally that focuses on those manufacturing jobs mostly hurt by globalization and considers services as a 'posh' field of economic activity where incomes are higher and thus not of immediate urgency for political fiat, the compromise of any new liberalization effort such as TiSA appears to be a self-fulfilling prophecy. Ironically, TiSA has been the most important effort yet to create a coherence point in the global regulation of services *post*-Uruguay Round.

However, the world does not necessarily brim with pessimistic news when it comes to the regulation of trade in services. In fact, much of trade in services liberalization in recent years happens autonomously. Services are by now too important to be ignored by any regulator. They are crucial components of the information society networks on which relations between producers and consumers depend. Instantaneous interactive communication permits transactions in an increasing number of services to occur at the same time but in different places. This allows overcoming the need for proximity between consumer and service supplier and thus increases the tradability of services across borders and jurisdictions, calling for a more efficient reaction in regulatory-making terms from the side of the regulators at a cross-national level. Furthermore, the growing interpenetration of services and goods in the supply and demand cycles means that any policy seeking the optimal allocation of productive resources must now take into consideration regulatory issues in both goods and services and their intermingling.[58]

This element also renders necessary a closer look into the nature of trade costs in services. In this respect, recent studies demonstrate that trade costs for services

---

[57]See Kelsey (2016), p. 119.

[58]For this intermingling, compare C-390/99, *Canal Satélite Digital*, ECLI:EU:C:2002:34, paras 31–33. In the WTO context, see Appellate Body Report, *China – Publications and Audiovisual Products*. See also Antimiani and Cernat (2018).

continue to be relatively higher than trade costs for goods. In addition, and quite crucially, within the service sector, there is a worrisome discrepancy between trade costs of final services when compared to intermediate services. In sectors like business or construction services, the difference may be as high as 40%. However, trade costs in both intermediary and final services have taken a downward path overtime. Again, this encouraging trend is more observable in the case of intermediate trade costs. This means that trade costs for final services are higher and also that they are falling more slowly.[59] The finding that trade costs in intermediate services decrease more rapidly should be linked to the fact that they play a crucial role in the production and trade of both services and goods in global value chains but also that they are more sensitive to applied trade policies in trade in services than are final services—the latter being more resilient to such changes.

Intermediate services trade costs are lower in trade-enabling sectors such as transport and business services, followed by post and telecommunication services. On the other end of the spectrum, construction services are consistently exposed to the highest level of trade costs, be it as intermediary of final services. Whereas trade costs in transport services but also in other sectors are quite static over time (except for finance, but this is most likely due to the Global Financial Crisis of 2007–2009).

High trade costs in services reveal a rather disappointing picture about the state of trade liberalization in services and the fact that certain trade barriers persist despite various waves of liberalization. It is quite telling that no significant changes in key services sectors are to be observed since the entry into force of the GATS. This would apply to both discriminatory measures but also non-discriminatory regulatory measures that aim to allegedly ensure the quality of the service supplied. This comes to corroborate the claim of some that the GATS commitments may not have had a breakthrough impact on addressing trade costs in services trade.[60]

Some of the most significant barriers to trade in services are embedded in non-discriminatory domestic regulations. Recent studies found, for instance, that domestic regulations affecting trade in professional services can represent as high as an average ad valorem tariff equivalent that ranges between 26% and 88%. Quite astonishingly, it seems that the productivity of firms does not affect the results and the impact remains significant even in the case of the most integrated regional market today, the EU. Such regulations negatively affect export decisions but also the values exported by each firm active in this sector.[61] Unfortunately, the GATS has failed to date to address such measures although negotiations at the WTO level to conclude

---

[59]See Miroudot and Shepherd (2016), p. 66.

[60]Arguably, however, this explains recent initiatives by certain WTO Members such as India for the creation of an agreement on trade facilitation in services as a means of redistributing gains from trade in services.

[61]Crozet et al. (2016), pp. 585–607.

the mandate set out in Article VI:4 GATS advanced reasonably well when compared to other trade areas.[62]

However, these observations also come to substantiate any new argument for the potential gains of further liberalization in trade in services. There is indeed growing evidence of robust nature suggesting that a positive correlation exists between liberalization of trade in services and trade and investment flows in services sectors.[63] This positive relationship requires careful consideration of not only how to facilitate trade at the border, but also a renewed focus on complementary policies that strive for actual liberalization. The sectors with the most immediate benefits from renewed liberalization efforts could be transport logistics and policies relating to distribution services, as both are key trade enablers.[64]

Indeed, increased trade costs have a negative impact not only on services exports but also on trade in goods. Since multiple services are by now important inputs for goods, rising trade costs have a negative impact on trade in goods as well. Thus, this means that lower barriers to trade in services and investment could increase the productivity performance of domestic industries active in manufacturing.[65] Economic studies suggest that the positive downstream productivity effect of full services trade liberalization could be above 20%, and perhaps higher if high-quality domestic institutions are in place to support such liberalization.[66]

These positive results are not developed-country-specific: there is empirical evidence suggesting, for instance, that if the East African Community (EAC) countries as a group decided to decrease the average level of restrictions to trade in services to that of Ghana (which is the African country with the lowest services trade barriers), then trade in goods in Rwanda, Kenya, Tanzania and Uganda could record double-digit increases, between 13% and 20%.[67] Similar findings were found to hold also for liberalization of trade in services in Sub-Saharan Africa.[68] Empirical findings in India also support this positive link between services liberalization in sectors like transport, banking or telecommunications and performance of the manufacturing sector: the productivity of Indian firms improved by 11% due to services liberalization.[69]

Thus, theoretical and empirical analyses quite unequivocally corroborate the case for further liberalization of services trade and also, crucially, point to supportive and corrective action that must be taken by governments, including, for instance, the

---

[62]See Delimatsis (2010), pp. 443–473.

[63]Nordås and Rouzet (2015).

[64]See Hoekman (2016), p. 149.

[65]See Hoekman and Shepherd (2017).

[66]See Beverelli et al. (2017), pp. 166–182.

[67]See Balchin N et al., Trade in services and economic transformation, ODI Report, November 2016, https://set.odi.org/wp-content/uploads/2016/11/SET-Trade-in-Services-and-Economic-Transformation_Final-Nov2016.pdf, p. 47.

[68]See Arnold et al. (2008), pp. 578–599.

[69]See Arnold et al. (2016), pp. 1–39.

strengthening of the relevant institutions or putting mechanisms in place to make sure that domestic service suppliers also benefit from State action in this field.

4.2   Scene 2: The Great Divergence?

Whereas multilateral liberalization would seem to ensure that there is sufficient number of trade-offs to attain results with which every WTO Member would be better off, in practice, recent liberalization has been registered exclusively at the PTA level. Such liberalization efforts have not always led to actual liberalization. In fact, some of them led to less liberalization than the GATS itself, as they include GATS-minus commitments. Quite interestingly, it was demonstrated that NAFTA-type PTA agreements (that is, agreements that follow a negative, or 'top-down', listing) concluded between developed and developing countries (North-South) are more prone to include GATS-minus commitments than PTAs concluded among developed economies (North-North) or among developing economies (South-South).[70]

In terms of architecture, liberalization approach and issue-areas, PTAs vary considerably. Many times, such variations are recorded within a given PTA. For instance, recent PTAs combine a negative listing of investment-related reservations (Mode 3) with a positive listing for commitments relating to cross-border supply (Mode 1) or temporary stay of service suppliers (Mode 4). There is also significant variation of approaches by a single WTO Member. For instance, the EU undertook a hybrid approach in its recent PTA with Japan or the Deep and Comprehensive Free Trade Agreements (DCFTAs) it concluded within the Eastern Partnership (Georgia, Moldova, Ukraine), combining negative and positive listing, but agreed on a negative list approach only with Canada under CETA. The US, but also several Asian countries by now, opt for negative listing in their PTAs. South-South PTAs, on the other hand, follow for the most part the GATS approach, which is evidence of continuous reluctance and even suspicion against negative listing although it is still doubtful whether the approach chosen itself is responsible for more liberalization.

More generally, there are several sources of friction and ensuing divergence between the status quo at the multilateral level and the phenomena we observe at the PTA level. These include:

1. *Negative/positive listing*: This deviation from the GATS approach creates confusion with respect to listing commitments and limitations, which, arguably, is artificial, as it unnecessarily complicates the understanding of the scope of a market opening and blurs the level of liberalization opted for by the parties to the PTA.[71]

---

[70]See Adlung and Miroudot (2012), p. 1045.
[71]Cf. Delimatsis (2017), p. 583.

2. *The splintering of Mode 4*: Labour mobility continues to be one of the most contentious and least tractable issues. Most North-South and North-North PTAs draw a dividing line between temporary stay of high-skilled human capital (e.g., intra-corporate transferees and business visitors) and low-skilled or self-employed labour (e.g. independent professionals). In addition, PTA partners include chapters on business visitors or independent professionals within the agreement which appears to allow these partners to avoid the obligation enshrined in Article VII GATS to offer an adequate opportunity to non-PTA parties. Approaches of this sort appear to broaden the divergence of views between the developed and developing world. At the same time, it is worth noting that even South-South PTAs only narrowly liberalize mode 4 movements, which may be indicative of a general, widespread lack of interest for liberalization in this mode of supply.

3. *Dispersal of Content*: Another source of divergence and thus fragmentation is the choice by some PTA partners to scatter different content for each of the services areas covered. For instance, the rules for e-commerce, professional services and other types of services are incorporated in different chapters, which means that they are not necessarily subject to the same set of obligations. Complicated cross-referencing leads to general obligations be applied to certain services or modes but not to others, depending on the chapter of the agreement at issue.[72] While the consolidation of services and investment in one chapter of a given PTA was to bring more coherence in the regulation of services, this has not always been the ultimate outcome.

4. *Regulatory convergence 1.0*: Regulatory cooperation in certain PTAs, coined under various terms including 'convergence', 'compatibility', 'improvement' or 'coherence' has gone quite far even when compared to the most progressive proposals in the WTO negotiations within the Working Party on Domestic Regulation in the framework of Article VI:4 negotiations.[73] In certain PTAs, upstream regulatory cooperation of authorities, mutual recognition agreements among professional bodies, regulatory impact assessments and creation of new bipartisan committees are foreseen. There is doubtless positive spillovers for non-parties to those PTAs from these regulatory initiatives. Once in the path of good governance, it becomes difficult to exclude beneficiaries from reaping the benefits of better regulatory mechanics at the domestic level.

   However, this is no longer the case once the parties, in PTA practice developed countries, decide to move towards shared institutional settings and solutions. Such phenomena, once again, widen regulatory fragmentation and create

---

[72]The EU-Japan FTA takes a wiser approach by introducing a single chapter with various sub-sections, which means that the general framework is applicable to all sub-sections unless otherwise indicated.

[73]See Polanco and Sauvé (2018), p. 575; and Gari (2020). See also the chapter by Gari in this volume.

unnecessary friction to trade flows in services. By the same token, regulatory fragmentation of this type does not necessarily lead to more legitimate outcomes.

Take the case of the concept of 'regulatory approximation', as preached by the EU in its DCFTAs. The rationale behind it is that the EU does not converge with its DCFTA partner in a commonly agreed regulatory solution; rather, the idea of approximation is essentially synonymous to the integration of the European regulatory regime in the legal order of the DCFTA partner in certain areas such as financial, telecommunications or postal services. This amounts to the exportation of regulatory approaches to the—typically weaker, in terms of negotiating leverage—DCFTA partner, which would be less likely to happen in a multilateral setting where a multi-stakeholder approach and compromise are bound to occur.[74] However, other than this instance of regulatory approximation dominated by the EU, no WTO Member, regardless of its trading power, can claim that it has managed to impose the exact same PTA template to all of its PTA partners.

5. *Regulatory convergence 2.0*: negotiations on domestic regulation under Article VI:4 GATS have progressed substantially, but no consolidated text has been adopted to date. More recently, a group of some sixty WTO Members agreed during the Buenos Aires Ministerial conference to finalize the negotiations in this area with a view to adopting an agreement in this regard, which would be open for everybody to sign up.[75] Absent any tangible outcome at the multilateral level, WTO Members have inserted various proposed domestic regulation disciplines in their PTAs. An example at issue is the inclusion of rules relating to technical standards in services in the Japan-Switzerland PTA. Such divergence does not necessarily undermine any future effort for achieving coherence, as such disciplines can be subsumed within a framework of 'regulatory convergence 2.0' at the multilateral level. Thus, despite the significant work undertaken at the PTA level, the best way to achieve coherence at the regulatory front remains the conclusion of the negotiations on domestic regulation.[76]

Are we then talking about an irreversible divergence-centered drama? Not really (at least for now). While instances of divergence abound, market openness in services continues apace, many times in an autonomous manner via market forces or through accession to the WTO. The overall level of new liberalization has been staggering in certain cases, particularly when it comes to new liberalization by

---

[74]It is worth mentioning that, even in this case, no coherence between the EU and its DCFTA partners as a group is ensured. For instance, based on the Association Agreements that underlie such PTAs, the EU is committed to concluding mobility partnerships with those partners. However, not all EU Member States participate in these partnerships (in fact, participation varies from DCFTA to DCFTA), typically due to Mode 4-related disagreements relating to the timing and breadth of labour market openness but also due to anachronistic views about competences. Such divergence, arguably, undermines the effectiveness of the EU development policy.

[75]See WTO, 'Joint Ministerial Statement on Services Domestic Regulation', WT/MIN(17)/61, 13 December 2017.

[76]See, for an early claim along these lines, Delimatsis et al. (2011), p. 245.

developing countries.[77] Even better news: not much of this new liberalization is necessarily preferential, as most PTAs adopt a quite liberal rule of origin for service suppliers. In addition, there is a substantial number of regulatory concessions (i.e. due process-related improvements and regulatory convergence pledges embedded in PTAs) that de facto apply on an MFN basis, as it may prove impossible to exclude certain foreign suppliers from the regulatory changes and good governance reforms undertaken.[78] Even if unintended, such liberalization is important in the case of services, as they are particularly sensitive to the lack of regulatory transparency.

5 Conclusion

Services liberalization at the global level is currently held hostage of transatlantic divergences of views, American isolationism and the increasingly introspective approach that the biggest developing countries take with respect to WTO matters. US-driven at the outset, the appetite for services liberalization at the global level became a topic that multiple players, albeit with diverging priorities and preferences, were interested. This change of the political economy landscape clearly calls for a renewed and genuine commitment to multilateralism, which is one of the main *desiderata* in international economic regulation nowadays.

At the rule-making front on services, a learning-by-doing approach can be observed both unilaterally and at the PTA level. As the services liberalization commitments enshrined in the GATS schedules become increasingly outdated with the effluxion of time, countries are in the pursuit of the most adequate strategies to open services industries. In many cases, such efforts are coupled with domestic reforms and reshuffling of competences to ensure a coherent regulation of services already at the domestic level.

Reluctance to open domestic services markets is often associated with fears relating to the interpretation of liberalization commitments that existing GATS case-law has instigated; deeply-rooted perceptions about the maintenance of State control over public services; or the impact of services liberalization in underserved areas or vulnerable groups at the domestic level. Additional reasons may relate to the preservation of the natural landscape and fears that the presence of foreign investors will have negative spillovers on the environment. Another cause for insecurity is the recurring fluidity and complexity as to the definition of trade in services and the distinction among modes of supply.[79]

The most recent discussion about the existence of a mode 5 of supplying services does not help alleviate this complexity but creates headaches to regulatory authorities. However, and arguably, the early realization of the importance of looking into

---

[77]See Roy (2014), p. 15.

[78]See Sauve and Shingal (2014), p. 401.

[79]See Rueda-Cantuche et al. (2018).

rules for services and goods as a whole that calls for (more) coherence may generate renewed bottom-up forces which will call for action and coherent convergence at the multilateral level, driven by the rising profile and importance of services.

In the near future, trade in services is expected to increase further to account for one fourth of total trade by 2030, boosted by the intensive use of digital technologies.[80] However, already now a careful look at global trade on a value-added basis would suggest that almost half of world trade is due to services activities.[81] This suggests that the case for multilateral action and coherent State action in this field will not faint any time soon. In the meantime, WTO Members may start thinking about potential mechanisms that would create momentum and allow for a modular approach. This would include the development of a prevailing template which could be used to identify common denominators in any given instance. Based on this chapter, services may not have had a rosy past, but it seems that they will have a rosy, less dramatic future.

References

Adlung R, Carzaniga A (2009) MFN exemptions under the general agreement on trade in services: grandfathers striving for immortality? J Int Econ Law 12(2):357–392

Adlung R, Miroudot S (2012) Poison in the wine? Tracing GATS-minus commitments in regional trade agreements. J World Trade 46(5):1045–1082

Antimiani A, Cernat L (2018) Liberalizing global trade in mode 5 services: how much is it worth? J World Trade 52(1):65–48

Ariu A (2016) Crisis-proof services: why trade in services did not suffer during the 2008–2009 collapse. J Int Econ 98:138–149

Arnold JM, Mattoo A, Narciso G (2008) Services inputs and firm productivity in sub-Saharan Africa: evidence from firm-level data. J Afr Econ 17(4):578–599

Arnold JM, Javorcik B, Lipscomb M, Mattoo A (2016) Services reform and manufacturing performance: evidence from India. Econ J 126(590):1–39

Arup C (2000) The new World Trade Organization agreements: globalizing law through services and intellectual property. Cambridge University Press, Cambridge

Berg TG (1987) Trade in services: toward a "Development Round" of the GATT negotiations benefiting both developing and industrialized states. Harv Int Law J 28(1):1–30

Beverelli C, Fiorini M, Hoekman B (2017) Services trade policy and manufacturing productivity: the role of institutions. J Int Econ 104(C):166–182

Bhagwati J (1984) Splintering and disembodiment of services and developing nations. World Econ 7(2):133–144

Bhagwati J (1987) International trade in services and its relevance for economic development. In: Garini O (ed) The emerging service economy. Pergamon Press, Oxford, pp 3–34

Brock WE (1982) A simple plan for negotiating on trade in services. World Econ 5(3):229–240

Chang P, Karsenty G, Mattoo A, Richtering J (1999) GATS, the modes of supply and statistics on trade in services. J World Trade 33(3):93–115

Croome J (1999) Reshaping the world trading system: a history of the Uruguay Round. Springer, The Hague

---

[80]WTO, World Trade Report 2018, at 114.

[81]See Miroudot and Shepherd (2016).

Crozet M, Milet E, Mirza D (2016) The impact of domestic regulations on international trade in services: evidence from firm-level data. J Comp Econ 44(3):585–607

Delimatsis P (2007) Due process and "Good" regulation embedded in the GATS – disciplining regulatory behaviour in services through Article VI of the GATS. J Int Econ Law 10(1):15–17

Delimatsis P (2010) Concluding the WTO services negotiations on domestic regulation – hopes and fears. World Trade Rev 9(4):643–673

Delimatsis P (2017) The evolution of the EU external trade policy in services – CETA, TTIP, and TiSA after Brexit. J Int Econ Law 20(3):583–625

Delimatsis P (2018) From Sacchi to Uber: 60 years of services liberalization, ten years of the services directive in the EU. Yearb Eur Law 37:188–250

Delimatsis P et al (2011) Developing trade rules for services: a case of fragmented coherence? In: Cottier T, Delimatsis P (eds) The prospects of International Trade Regulation – from fragmentation to coherence. Cambridge University Press, Cambridge, pp 245–228

Drake WJ, Nicolaidis K (1992) Ideas, interests, and institutionalization: "Trade in Services" and the Uruguay Round. Int Organ 46(1):37–100

Ehlermann D, Campogrande G (1988) Rules on services in the EEC: a model for negotiating world-wide rule. In: Petersmann EU, Hilf M (eds) The new GATT round of multilateral trade negotiations: legal and economic problems. Kluwer Law International, Alphen aan den Rijn, pp 481–500

Feketekuty G (1988) International trade in services: an overview and blueprint for negotiations. Ballinger Pub. Co, Cambridge

Feketekuty G (1998) Trade in services – bringing services into the multilateral trading system. In: Bhagwati J, Hirsch M (eds) The Uruguay Round and beyond – essays in honor of Arthur Dunkel. Springer, Heidelberg, pp 481–498

Gari G (2020) Recent preferential trade agreements' disciplines for tackling regulatory divergence in services: how far beyond GATS? World Trade Rev 19(1):1–29

Hill TP (1977) On goods and services. Rev Income Wealth 23(4):315–338

Hindley B (1990) Services. In: Schott JJ (ed) Completing the Uruguay Round: a results-oriented approach to the GATT Trade negotiations. Institute for International Economics, Washington DC, pp 130–146

Hoekman B (2016) The Bali Trade Facilitation Agreement and rulemaking in the WTO: milestone, mistake or mirage? In: Bhagwati J, Krishna R, Panagariya A (eds) The world trade system – trends and challenges. MIT Press, Cambridge, pp 149–192

Hoekman B, Mattoo A (2008) Services trade and growth. In: Marchetti J, Roy M (eds) Opening markets for trade in services – countries and sectors in bilateral and WTO negotiations. Cambridge University Press, Cambridge, pp 21–58

Hoekman B, Shepherd B (2017) Services productivity, trade policy and manufacturing exports. World Econ 40(3):499–516

Kelsey J (2008) Serving whose interests? The political economy of trade in services agreements. Routledge-Cavendish, London

Kelsey J (2016) From GATS to TiSA: pushing the trade in services regime beyond the limits. In: Bungenberg M et al (eds) European yearbook of international economic law, vol 7. Springer, Heidelberg, pp 119–151

Krommenacker RJ (1979) Trade related services and GATT. J World Trade 13(6):510–522

Krommenacker RJ (1984) World-traded services: the challenge for the eighties. Artech House Publishers, London

Lamprecht P, Miroudot S (2018) The value of market access and national treatment commitments in services trade agreements. OECD trade policy papers, no. 231. OECD Publishing, Paris

Leroux E (2007) Eleven years of GATS case-law: what have we learned? J Int Econ Law 10(4):749–793

Malmgren HB (1985) Negotiating international rules for trade in services. World Econ 8(1):11–26

Marchetti J, Mavroidis P (2011) The genesis of the GATS (General Agreement on Trade in Services). Eur J Int Law 22(3):689–721

Marchetti J, Roy M (2008) Services liberalization in the WTO and in PTAs. In: Marchetti J, Roy M (eds) Opening markets for trade in services – countries and sectors in bilateral and WTO negotiations. Cambridge University Press, Cambridge, pp 61–112

Marconini M (1990) The Uruguay Round negotiations on services: an overview. In: Messerlin PA, Sauvant KP (eds) The Uruguay Round: services in the world economy. The World Bank, Washington, pp 19–26

Mattoo A (2000) MFN and the GATT. In: Cottier T, Mavroidis P (eds) Regulatory barriers and the principle of non-discrimination in world trade law. University of Michigan Press, Ann Arbor, pp 51–100

Maurer A, Magdeleine J, Lanz R (2016) Measuring trade in services in a world of global value chains. In: Roy M, Sauvé P (eds) Research handbook on trade in services. Edward Elgar, Cheltenham, pp 42–65

Miroudot S, Shepherd B (2016) Trade costs and global value chains in services. In: Roy M, Sauvé P (eds) Research handbook on trade in services. Edward Elgar, Cheltenham, pp 66–84

Nordås H, Rouzet D (2015) The impact of services trade restrictiveness on trade flows: first estimates. OECD trade policy papers, no. 178. OECD Publishing, Paris

Ortino F (2006) Treaty interpretation and the WTO Appellate Body Report in US – Gambling: a critique. J Int Econ Law 9(1):117–148

Polanco R, Sauvé P (2018) The treatment of regulatory convergence in preferential trade agreements. World Trade Rev 17(4):575–607

Reyna JV (1993) Services. In: Stewart TP (ed) The GATT Uruguay Round: a negotiating history (1986–1992), Commentary, vol II. Kluwer Law International, Zuidpoolsingel, pp 775–828

Roy M (2014) Services commitments in preferential trade agreements: surveying the empirical landscape. In: Sauvé P, Shingal A (eds) The preferential liberalization of trade in services – comparative regionalism. Edward Elgar, Cheltenham, pp 15–36

Rueda-Cantuche J, Cernat L, Sousa N (2018) Trade and jobs in Europe: the role of mode 5 services export. Int Labour Rev 158(1):115–136

Sampson G, Snape R (1985) Identifying the issues on trade in services. World Econ 8(2):171–182

Sapir A (1985) North-South issues in trade in services. World Econ 8(1):27–42

Sauve P, Shingal A (2014) Reflections on the nature of preferences in services. In: Sauvé P, Shingal A (eds) The preferential liberalization of trade in services – comparative regionalism. Edward Elgar, Cheltenham, pp 401–412

Smeets HD, Hofner G, Knorr A (1991) A multilateral framework of principles and rules for trade in services. In: Oppermann T, Molsberger J (eds) A new GATT for the nineties and Europe '92. Nomos, Baden-Baden, pp 191–212

Smith A (1937) The wealth of nations. Random House, Inc., New York

Snell J (2002) Goods and services in EC law – a study of the relationship between the freedoms. Oxford University Press, Oxford

Woodrow RB (1991) Sectoral coverage and implementation within a Uruguay Round services trade agreement: paradox and prognosis. In: Oppermann T, Molsberger J (eds) A new GATT for the nineties and Europe '92. Nomos, Baden-Baden, pp 221–244

Panagiotis Delimatsis is Professor of European and International Trade Law and Director of the Tilburg Law and Economics Center (TILEC), an interdisciplinary Center of Excellence at Tilburg University, the Netherlands. Before joining Tilburg, he was a Senior Research Fellow at the World Trade Institute of the University of Bern. Panagiotis is a renowned expert and has a keen interest in regulatory policy and regularly publishes on services trade, financial markets, energy and standardization in Europe and worldwide. He is the author of 'International Trade in Services and Domestic Regulations—Necessity, Transparency, and Regulatory Diversity' (International Economic Law Series, Oxford University Press, 2007). Panagiotis has edited various books, the most recent of which is 'the Law, Economics and Politics of International Standardisation' (Cambridge University Press, 2016). His current research relates to the private governance of standard-setting. In this regard, Panagiotis is the Principal Investigator of a 5-year project, financed by the European Research Council (ERC Consolidator Grant).

Services Liberalization by Sub-Central Entities: Towards Deeper Commitments?

Johanna Jacobsson

Contents

1   Introduction

The present chapter explores the issue of federalism in the international liberalization of services. It asks how to address a regional subdivision of a WTO Member and the consequences that it possibly has on that Members' services commitments. The issue has so far been largely neglected by research. It is, however, noteworthy considering that several WTO Members have constitutional structures that give powers to states,

Thank you to Ruslan Saleev for his research assistance regarding the services commitments of the Russian Federation.

J. Jacobsson (✉)
IE Law School, IE University, Madrid, Spain
e-mail: johanna.jacobsson@ie.edu

© The Editor(s) (if applicable) and The Author(s), under exclusive licence to
Springer Nature Switzerland AG 2020
R. T. Hoffmann, M. Krajewski (eds.), *Coherence and Divergence in Services Trade Law*, European Yearbook of International Economic Law,
https://doi.org/10.1007/978-3-030-46955-9_3

regions or other local entities in the regulation of economic activities. In the area of services such local measures are particularly abundant and many rules concerning the quality of a specific service or the professional qualifications of service suppliers depend on sub-central regulation. Such lower level regulation is likely to have important commercial implications in cases where it includes directly discriminatory elements or otherwise aims to protect domestic services and service suppliers.

It is therefore not surprising that trade negotiators are increasingly starting to press for the inclusion of regulatory measures imposed on services not only on the level of the central government but also on regional levels. The issue has entered into spotlight especially in the context of the EU-Canada Comprehensive Economic and Trade Agreement (CETA). In that agreement, Canada has for the first time included in a preferential trade agreement (PTA) a binding list of provincial and territorial non-conforming measures in the field of services and investment. In the currently stalled Transatlantic Trade and Investment Partnership (TTIP) negotiations between the EU and the US, on the other hand, addressing the sub-central government both in the area of services and public procurement was one of the negotiating objectives of the EU.[1] Both the CETA and the TTIP are part of an important development, considering that Canada and the US have previously addressed the regional and local levels of government only to a very limited extent in their trade agreements.

Several powerful WTO Members have constitutional structures that give powers to states, regions or other local entities in the regulation of services.[2] The issue is particularly relevant in the case of federal, or quasi-federal, states, such as Australia, Argentina, Brazil, Ethiopia, India, Mexico, Nigeria, Russia and Switzerland among others. The division of powers in federal states that are part of the EU (Austria, Belgium and Germany) is similarly relevant. Moreover, the EU itself can be contrasted to or compared with a federation.[3] In the area of trade such a comparison can be made, at least for practical purposes. The EU has an exclusive competence in trade and negotiates its trade, and nowadays also investment, agreements as a block.

---

[1]See Press Release "European Union and United States to launch negotiations for a Transatlantic Trade and Investment Partnership", available http://trade.ec.europa.eu/doclib/press/index.cfm?id=869, 13 February 2013.

[2]Three-level government (federal, state/provincial and local government) is common to all federal systems; however, there are varieties in the place and role of local government. The impact of regional and local government to international services trade is particularly relevant in the case of federal states but may arise also in the case of unitary states where certain regulatory powers are given to local levels of government. For an overview of the role of local government in federal states, see Steytler (2005).

[3]There is plenty of literature on the question of the extent to which the EU can be compared with federations. The fragmented polity of the EU has often been viewed as exceptional in terms of political development. That distinction, however, is increasingly challenged by scholars who choose to focus on systematic comparison between the EU and federal states. An increasing amount of research spanning across comparative politics, public and constitutional law and international relations no longer treats the EU as *sui generis*. See references in Egan (2015), p. 3. On the EU as a federal-type polity, see Schütze (2009) and Cloots et al. (2012). Much of the research compares the EU and the US. See e.g. Menon and Schain (2006).

The EU institutions make laws on trade matters, negotiate and conclude international trade agreements. In the area of goods, third country products are in free circulation inside the EU once they have crossed an external border of the Union. In services the situation is, however, more complex. Prior to establishment in one of the Member States, third country service suppliers cannot enjoy the free movement of services with the EU. Moreover, rules for service activities remain poorly harmonized. As a result, external liberalization levels largely vary between different Member States. However, EU's trade agreements are always negotiated and concluded on the level of the Union and the Member States do not have the possibility to enter into services agreements individually with third countries.

The chapter analyses services liberalization by federal entities by reviewing selected services agreements of three powerful federal actors: the EU, the US and Canada. It starts by looking into their services commitments in the GATS and shows to what extent sub-central levels of government appear across their GATS commitments. It then reviews the same actors' commitments in their services PTAs concluded with South Korea. In addition, the chapter reviews the CETA (EU-Canada) as well as the North-American Free Trade Agreement (NAFTA) that interestingly involves three federations (Canada, the US and Mexico). The chapter shows that there are crucial differences in the way that the EU, the US and Canada engage in international services liberalization.

Federations and federal-type structures will generally be referred to as "federal entities" across the chapter. This includes the EU, which is here considered to represent a "federal-type structure". Measures taken on different national (domestic) levels of these WTO Members' will be referred to as "sub-central measures". The measures covered by the term "sub-central measures" are understood to cover all measures taken by other than central authorities, mainly be any regional or local governments and authorities. This is in line with the definition given in GATS Article I:3(a)(i) to "measures by Members". When discussing services PTAs, the chapter refers to economic integration agreements (EIAs). The language reflects GATS Article V, which sets the rules for PTAs in services.

2 The Impact of Federalism on Services Trade Liberalization

One of the most often mentioned goals of modern trade agreements is to go deeper in services liberalization. In the area of services, liberalization necessarily means tackling regulation. That regulation is often not limited to central levels of government but reaches regional levels which may be states, territories, provinces or even more local levels such as municipalities. As the supply of services is often dependent on such lower-level regulation, liberalization commitments made only by central authorities may fall short of creating the big gains that relate to truly open markets in services. The economic impact of restrictive sub-central regulation can be significant. Moreover, the role of regions and even cities is likely to only grow in the future and more focus should therefore be directed beyond the central government.[4]

Sub-central measures are typically not completely excluded from EIAs; they are often bound at existing levels (that is, grandfathered), but they are not listed. The US and Canada have traditionally followed this approach. Their EIAs include a reservation for all existing non-conforming measures (NCMs) of sub-central entities (states in the case of the US, provinces and territories in the case of Canada, as well as local level of government). As the sub-central measures are in most cases not listed, it is impossible to understand the scope and restrictiveness of such measures.

The inclusion of services commitments beyond the Canadian central government in the CETA is therefore a significant achievement. In that agreement, Canada has for the first time in its PTA history included detailed lists of provincial and territorial NCMs in the field of services and investment. The lists cover both existing and future NCMs. The Canadian provinces and territories are bound to regulatory *status quo* and have also committed to providing to the EU the benefits of autonomous liberalization in a number of important service sectors (architectural, engineering, foreign legal consultancy, urban planning, tourism, business services).[5]

The US, on the other hand, has recently begun including an illustrative list of existing NCMs in the field of services for state level restrictions. However, the NCMs illustrated at the state and local level are provided for transparency purposes only and do not bind the US nor the US states.[6] And no real liberalization of state level measures seems to be involved as all negatively listed US EIAs exempt *all* existing NCMs of all US states, as well as the District of Columbia and Puerto Rico from the national treatment, market access and MFN disciplines.[7] There is no

---

[4]From climate change and renewable energy to international trade, subnational governments are increasingly active in tackling matters of international concern. Meyer notes that 41% of the claims brought under the investor-state dispute settlement ("ISDS") provisions of NAFTA have challenged subnational government action. Canada, the most frequent respondent under NAFTA Chapter 11, also has the highest percentage of claims involving local action. 22 of its 38 claims involve local action, a remarkable 58% of claims. The WTO has also seen its share of claims challenging local action. Out of 502 cases filed to date, at least 41 have challenged subnational action (including claims against EU Member States)—a bit more than 8% of cases. See Meyer (2017), pp. 276–277.

[5]"Technical Summary of Final Negotiated Outcomes, Agreement-in-principle, documents summarizing the important negotiated outcomes of the Canada-European Union Comprehensive Economic and Trade Agreement as of October 18, 2013", The Government of Canada, available at http://www.international.gc.ca/trade-agreements-accords-commerciaux/assets/pdfs/ceta-aecg/ceta-technicalsummary.pdf, p. 13.

[6]See p. 12 of KORUS, Annex I, the schedule of the United States and Appendix I-A to the same schedule. Page 12 includes the following statement: "For purposes of transparency, Appendix I-A sets out an illustrative, non-binding list of non-conforming measures maintained at the regional level of government".

[7]P. 12 of KORUS, Annex I, the schedule of the United States. The exempted measures are "All existing non-conforming measures of all states of the United States, the District of Columbia, and Puerto Rico". In addition to the KORUS, a similar exclusion is present in all US EIAs that have been concluded in accordance with negative listing (all agreements have been concluded after the entry into force of the GATS). The service schedule of the US-Jordan FTA of 2010 is the only US

indication of any market access opening having been done to state level measures in the course of the negotiations for the US EIAs.

In the course of the TTIP negotiations, it was reported that the EU was pushing for the inclusion of sub-central measures in the US services schedule. According to one news report, the US was offering to follow the same approach as in its recent agreement with South-Korea (KORUS), thus merely providing an illustrative list of state-level NCMs instead of specifying them individually. At the same time, US was pushing to formulate the services schedules in accordance with the negative list approach. The EU, which until the CETA followed a "positive-list" approach, reportedly communicated that it was willing to consider a negative list, but only if the US provided a detailed list of all restrictions on services trade maintained by states and local entities. The EU argued that this was necessary in order to fully assess the value of the US services offer because it would show the exact extent of the market access that EU service suppliers would gain. This was unlikely to happen as the US had thus far refused to engage in such an endeavor arguing that the mapping of state-level services barriers would be a Herculean task and could take "two years to complete".[8]

The blanket inclusion of all non-conforming sub-central measures among one's reservations in practice equals to a complete exclusion from the key service disciplines, and most importantly from national treatment. That is why the listing of sub-central measures in CETA is a big step forward. It should also be noted that with countries that do not list their sub-central measures, it is sometimes possible to find out what these existing measures are from other EIAs where they have been listed. For example, Australia has in some of its EIAs, similarly to the US, included all existing NCMs at the regional level of government in its Annex I, thus exempting all existing NCMs of the Australian states and territories from the key services disciplines.[9] In its later agreements with Korea (2014) and China (2015), Australia has, however, listed NCMs applied at the regional level as well.

From a practical and methodological point of view, it may, however, be difficult, or practically impossible, to map all existing non-conforming measures by regional entities in different countries and thus understand to what extent they do away with the amount of non-discriminatory treatment granted on the central level. That is the

---

EIA that follows a positive listing model and appears to reflect the US GATS commitments to a large extent.

[8]Hennig J, "Under Pressure To Show TTIP Progress, U.S., EU Focus On Market Access", Inside U.S. Trade—04/18/2014, Vol. 32, No. 16 (posted 17 April 2014). According to the news piece, an EU source signaled that the list demanded by the EU also served a tactical reason: once the US had admitted not being able to provide the list, it would give Brussels a free pass to push back on US demands. At that point, the negotiations could begin on services, the source had said.

[9]See e.g. Australia-United States FTA (2005), Schedule of Australia, Annex I, p. 1. In its Annex II, Australia reserves the right to adopt or maintain any measure at the regional level of government that is not inconsistent with Australia's obligations under Article XVI of the GATS. This is similar to the US and the earlier Canadian practice, even though the Canadian reservation applies to the regional level only. With regard to Mode 4 commitments, the reservation applies also to the central government (Australia's Annex II, p. 2).

case especially when sub-central restrictions are not listed in a specific EIA (as in the US EIAs). Sometimes it may be possible. This is the situation in CETA. As a certain baseline, the federal countries' GATS commitments can be used.

3 Sub-Central Entities in the GATS Commitments of the US, Canada and the EU

In contrast to the majority of their EIAs, the GATS schedules of both US and Canada include sub-central measures. This may have to do with the fact that all WTO Members had to engage in a similar scheduling practice under the GATS, whereas in EIAs the partner countries agree among themselves if and how to include any sub-national limitations to the liberalization commitments. The GATS deliberately mentions measures taken by sub-central entities in Article I:3.[10] The exclusion of a Member's regional or local limitations from its schedule would thus go against the GATS.

Both countries have included sub-central measures extensively. In its GATS schedule, the US has specified measures across all levels of government—on federal, state and local levels. For legal services alone, the US schedule is 20 pages long because of differences in state-level regulation. Canada's GATS schedule also includes numerous mentions of the Canadian provinces and territories. They are usually named individually but on a couple of occasions they are referred to together as "Federal and sub-central governments".[11]

In comparison, the EU's GATS schedules also include commitments both for the entire EU as well as individual Member States. The second sub-central level of the EU consists of the regulations applied on the sub-national level of individual Member States. There are, however, only a few examples of limitations described on sub-national levels of the Member States in the reviewed schedules of the EU's GATS, as well as EIA, commitments.[12]

---

[10]"Measures" by Members means measures taken by "central, regional or local governments and authorities" (Article I:3(a)(i)).

[11]See e.g. the horizontal commitments in Canada's GATS schedule. For "commercial presence", Canada has inserted the following limitation on national treatment: "Federal and sub-central tax measures (generally pertaining to small business) may result in a difference in treatment in respect of all or some "Canadian controlled private corporations" as defined by the Income Tax Act". Canada, Schedule of Specific Commitments, GATS/SC/16, 15 April 1994.

[12]One example are the Åland Islands that form an autonomous region in Finland. In contrast to other Finnish regions, Åland enjoys a high degree of home rule. Limitations to the possibility to supply services in Åland are included in the horizontal commitments of Finland. See Draft consolidated GATS Schedule, Communication from the European Communities and its Member States, S/C/W/273, 9 October 2006. The commitments of Finland were upon its accession to the EU in 1995 included in the consolidated EU schedule but are based on the national GATS Schedule of Finland, GATS/SC/33, 15 April 1994.

As there are many limitations and sectors that remain 'unbound' in the Members' GATS commitments, differences in the levels of openness inside a federal country may easily remain unnoticed when looking at the country's GATS schedule alone. If the country's general (central level) liberalization is low, that may hide internal differences between more and less liberal sub-central levels of government. Some WTO Members may also have chosen to liberalize according to the lowest common denominator in cases where there are differences in the openness levels between different regions or local levels of government. A look into different federal countries' GATS commitments shows that in some of their schedules sub-central entities appear widely across both the horizontal and sector-specific schedules (among such WTO Members are the EU, the US, Canada, Australia). In some other federal countries' GATS schedules sub-central entities make only occasional appearances (examples include Switzerland and Mexico with some mentions of regional/local measures) or zero appearances (an example is Russia with no mention of regional/ local measures).

The difference is likely to be based on the way that services are regulated in the WTO Member in question (services regulated either centrally or across different levels of government) or, alternatively, it may be based on the degree of liberalization taken by the country in general (poor central level of liberalization can "hide" differences between different lower levels of government). Finding out what exactly is at stake in each case requires qualitative analysis of the competences of the sub-central authorities in each particular WTO Member. A comparison of the US and Canada to the Russian Federation is an enlightening example in this regard. Russia, unlike the US and Canada, is a very centralized state. According to the Russian Constitution, there is a joint jurisdiction of the Russian Federation and the subjects of the Russian Federation (the regions) over a number of policy areas such as environment, education, science and healthcare. However, in many of the areas, the texts of the regional laws closely follow the wording of the federal laws.[13] It appears that in the case of Russia, regional competences affect Russia's services commitments to a very limited extent.

The GATS schedules of the US and Canada, on the other hand, show a much more extensive division of competencies between the central and regional levels of government. The GATS commitments, however, date to early 1990s and are generally considered shallow.[14] The main avenue for services liberalization today are EIAs. Another way to shed more light on the issue is therefore to look into federal countries' EIAs. As services commitments in such agreements are supposed to go deeper than the same countries' GATS commitments, the agreements can reveal

---

[13]For example, in the area of education the regional laws are almost identical to the federal laws. In the area of culture, some more differences exist, reflecting the cultural diversity of the country.

[14]About the poor level of liberalization in the WTO Members' GATS commitments, see e.g. Adlung and Roy (2005).

internal divisions that are hidden in the same countries' original GATS schedules.[15]
As the following section shows, the mapping and binding of sub-central commitments has, however, proved difficult for the US and Canada. In the case of the EU,
its EIAs continue to show the diversity in the services regulations between different
EU Member States.

4 Sub-Central Measures in Selected EIAs

There are crucial differences in the way that the US and Canada engage in international services liberalization, as compared to the EU. First of all, almost all of their
EIAs follow negative listing[16] and secondly, they include a reservation regarding all
limitations applied on the sub-central levels of government (CETA notwithstanding). All existing sub-central measures are simply exempted, in trade language—
"grandfathered".[17]

In contrast to their commitments under the GATS, measures applied at the level
of regional and local government are not listed in any EIAs of the US and Canada
(in the case of Canada, up until CETA).[18] Both the US and Canada have in their
EIAs exempted all existing non-conforming measures (the so-called Annex I limitations) of all sub-central entities (again, CETA notwithstanding).[19] These two
powerful federal states have thus managed to negotiate preferential agreements

---

[15]Research has shown that the market access commitments in EIAs tend to go significantly beyond
the level of liberalization in the same countries GATS commitments. See Roy (2014). However,
sub-central levels of government have not been addressed in most studies.

[16]The US-Jordan FTA (signed in 2000) follows a positive listing in its services schedules. However,
the commitments appear to be copied from both states' GATS commitments of 1994. In the case of
Jordan, its schedule includes some improvements to its GATS commitments.

[17]In general sense, a "grandfather clause" is an exemption that allows an entity to continue with
activities or operations that were approved before the implementation of new rules, regulations or
laws. See Investopedia: https://www.investopedia.com/terms/g/grandfatherclause.asp. On the use
of the grandfathering clause, see e.g. Adlung and Carzaniga (2009).

[18]In the case of the US, the only exception is the US-Jordan EIA. However, the US commitments
are copied from its GATS commitments and include the same sub-central measures as its GATS
schedule.

[19]We checked this by going through all EIAs signed by the US and Canada. The US EIAs are
available on the website of the USTR: https://ustr.gov/trade-agreements/free-trade-agreement. The
US has PTAs in force with 14 countries. 13 of them include a services agreement. Sub-central
non-conforming measures are exempted through a blanket reservation included in Annex I of the
agreements. The Canadian EIAs are available on the website of the Government of Canada: https://
www.international.gc.ca/trade-commerce/trade-agreements-accords-commerciaux/agr-acc. Canada
has 14 PTAs in force. Nine of them include an EIA. In some of the Canadian EIAs, existing
non-conforming measures applied by Canadian sub-central governments are exempted already in
the text of the agreement (see e.g. Art. 10.07 "Reservations" of the Canada-Panama FTA). In others,
they are exempted through a separate clause in Annex I (e.g. Canada-Chile FTA, Canada's
Annex I).

that allow them to forego any existing limitations to trade in services appearing on the regional and local levels of government.

This is noteworthy considering that EIAs should eliminate substantially all discrimination, as required by GATS Article V. Moreover, the services chapters of the reviewed PTAs include a similar wording as GATS Article I regarding the definition of covered measures. They include those taken by regional and local governments and authorities alike. Based on Article V GATS and the coverage of the reviewed EIAs, one could thus expect the inclusion of sub-central measures, and maybe even expect them to go deeper than the respective GATS commitments. However, this is not the reality. Out of the reviewed agreements by the US and Canada, only the CETA by Canada engages in significant liberalization on the sub-central level. The US has not included the sub-central level in any of its EIAs. In its EIA with Korea, the US has, for the first time, included an illustrative list of sub-central measures. However, the list is not legally binding.[20]

Below we explain to what extent the reviewed EIAs include commitments taken by sub-central levels of government. We go through each agreement, starting from CETA and NAFTA and moving then to the EIAs concluded by the US, Canada and the EU with South Korea. An overview of the presence of sub-central entities in these EIAs as well as in the same countries' GATS commitments is included in a separate summarizing table at the end of the chapter.

4.1 CETA

CETA, provisionally in force since 21 September 2017, follows the negative scheduling method in its description of reservations.[21] This was new for the EU, which has earlier been using GATS-type positive scheduling practice in its EIAs. It was reported that the EU agreed to negative scheduling at least partially due to its motivation to effectively bind the Canadian provinces.[22]

With regard to both existing and future measures applicable in Canada, Canada has included two different annexes. The first applies on the national level (federal level as well as provincial and territorial levels) and the second one applies on the provincial and territorial level. Canada's list of Provincial and Territorial measures

---

[20]The chapter reviews only a couple PTAs but the author has reviewed also earlier PTAs of US and Canada and found that they very limited references to sub-central entities.

[21]However, the commitments for the temporary entry and stay of natural persons for business purposes (the Mode 4 category of CETA) are described in positive manner, sector by sector. See Annexes from 10-B to 10-E of CETA. The negatively schedules reservations apply to Cross-Border Trade in Services (modes 1 and 2) and Investment (covering mode 3 but also non-services sector investment).

[22]Walker J, Negotiation of Trade Agreements in Federal Countries, SPICe Briefing, the Scottish Parliament, 17 November 2007, available at https://sp-bpr-en-prod-cdnep.azureedge.net/published/2017/11/17/Negotiation-of-Trade-Agreements-in-Federal-Countries/SB17-79.pdf.

under Annex I is 271 pages long and under Annex II 88 pages long. This is a radical departure from Canada's earlier EIAs were sub-central NCMs have been excluded. It shows that Canada has engaged in deeper services liberalization with the EU by binding the restrictions applied also in provinces and territories. Through Annex I, the Canadian provinces and territories are bound to regulatory *status quo* and have committed to providing to the EU the benefits of autonomous liberalization in accordance with the ratchet clause of Article 9.7 of CETA. In addition, Canada has bound the sub-central levels of government also with regard to future measures (Annex II).

Unlike GATS Article I:3, in CETA there is no general definition for the authorities whose measures are covered by the agreement's service disciplines. Article 9.1 ("Definitions") and Article 9.2 ("Scope") of Chapter 9 on Cross-Border Trade in Services do not mention anything about the sub-central levels of government. Neither do the respective provisions for Investment (Chapter 8) and for the Temporary Entry and Stay of Natural Persons for Business Purposes (Chapter 10). Instead, the issue is taken up in the substantial obligations. For example, Article 9.3 on national treatment (NT) in cross-border trade in services (Chapter 9) specifies the following:

1. Each Party shall accord to service suppliers and services of the other Party treatment no less favourable than that it accords, in like situations, to its own service suppliers and services.

2. For greater certainty, the treatment accorded by a Party pursuant to paragraph 1 means, with respect to a government in Canada other than at the federal level, or, with respect to a government of or in a Member State of the European Union, treatment no less favourable than the most favourable treatment accorded, in like situations, by that government to its own service suppliers and services.

The formulation thus clarifies that the obligation of NT applies beyond the central level of government and that the point of comparison should be the like service suppliers and services of that particular sub-central entity whose treatment is under scrutiny. In the case of the EU, reference is made both to the central governments of the Member States as well as to the lower levels of government within the Member States (government *of or in* a Member State), thus covering the two levels of sub-central authorities in the EU (national and sub-national).

Another reference to different levels of government is included in Article 9.5 regarding MFN. Article 9.6 includes the MA principle and specifies that the prohibited limitations shall not be adopted or maintained by a Party "on the basis of its entire territory or on the basis of the territory of a national, provincial, territorial, regional or local level of government".

Article 9.7 ("Reservations") specifies in paragraph 1 that NT, MFN and MA disciplines do not apply to any NCM that is maintained by a Party at the level of the EU, a national government or a provincial, territorial, or regional government, as set out in the Parties' schedules to Annex I. The said obligations do not apply to existing NCMs of local governments either. In contrast to provincial, territorial, or regional measures, such local measures are not required to be listed. This means that local measures, such as municipal measures, remain unlisted in CETA. This can, however, be considered a minor shortcoming considering that Canada has in CETA for the first time listed the NCMs of its provinces and territories.

Reservations to future measures (the Annex II measures) are specified in the second paragraph. According to Article 9.7, para. 2, NT, MFN and MA disciplines do not apply to a measure that "a Party" adopts or maintains with respect to a sector, subsector or activity as set out in its Schedule to Annex II. The level of government is not specified. According to Article 1.1 ("General definitions"), "Parties" means, on the one hand, "the European Union or its Member States" or "the European Union and its Member States" within their respective areas of competence as derived from the EU Treaties, and on the other hand, "Canada". It is therefore not entirely clear what levels of sub-central government are covered by the reservations to future measures under Article 9.7, para. 2. However, as Canada has included provincial and territorial NCMs in its schedule to Annex II, it appears that any future NCMs by sub-central entities are meant to be covered as well.

In addition, Article 1.10 (Persons exercising delegated governmental authority) states that unless otherwise specified in the agreement, each Party must ensure that persons with delegated regulatory, administrative or other governmental authority must act in accordance with the Party's obligations. It further specifies that the obligation applies "at any level of government". Furthermore, Article 1.8 specifies that "Each Party shall ensure that all necessary measures are taken in order to give effect to the provisions of this Agreement, including their observance at all levels of government".[23]

Central government is defined in the Party-specific definitions of Article 1.2. For Canada, it means the Government of Canada, and for the EU Party, it means "the European Union or the national governments of its Member States". The definition is interesting as it labels the EU as "central government". CETA thus appears to have the same approach as has been adopted in this chapter as it contrasts the relations of the EU and its Member States to federal states.

4.2 NAFTA

NAFTA, an agreement predating the GATS, lacks a general definition of the authorities whose measures are covered by the agreement. Similarly to CETA, the extent to which regional measures are covered is specified in the substantial obligations of the agreement.

---

[23]The provision can be contrasted with the obligation for WTO Members to take "such reasonable measures as may be available to it" to ensure the observance of the GATS disciplines by regional and local governments and authorities and non-governmental bodies within their territory (Art. I:3 (ii)). The language in CETA appears stronger as it requires each Party to "ensure" compliance by taking any "necessary measures" without any mention of them being "reasonable" or "available" to the Party.

Article 1202 of Chapter Twelve (Cross-Border Trade in Services) includes the discipline on NT. It notes that NT means "with respect to a state or province, treatment no less favorable than the most favorable treatment accorded, in like circumstances, by that state or province to service providers of the Party of which it forms a part".

Article 1206 on "Reservations" states that the NT, MFN and prohibition of local presence disciplines do not apply to existing NCMs listed in Annex I and maintained either at the federal level, by a state or province, or a local government. The explanatory note to Annex I mentions that each reservation sets out the level of government maintaining the measure for which a reservation is taken. In accordance with Article 1206:1(a), only measures taken by local governments do not need to be listed. This appears to mean measures that are adopted on lower levels than state or province. The exclusion of local measures is again similar to CETA.

The categories of measures covered by NAFTA Articles 1206, 1207 and 1108 roughly correspond to Modes 1, 2 and 3.[24] The wording of the said articles confirms that NAFTA was meant to cover sub-central measures. Unlike CETA, NAFTA, however, stops short from listing any NCMs that are applied by sub-central levels of government (state and provincial level). This is because under the second paragraph of Article 1206, "Each Party may set out in its Schedule to Annex I, within 2 years of the date of entry into force of this Agreement, any existing non-conforming measure maintained by a state or province, not including a local government." The Parties thus gave each other a period of 2 years to come up with a list of NCMs that were applied on the level of states and provinces with regard to the NT, MFN and local presence requirements.

The same timeline of 2 years is given for the listing of any NCMs at the state and provincial level for measures in breach of the rules on Investment (Article 1108, "Reservations and Exceptions" of Chapter Eleven).

NAFTA does not have a MA discipline similar to the GATS and later EIAs, but Article 1207 on Quantitative Restrictions specifies that any quantitative restrictions are set out in Annex V. Again, a specific timeline is given to set out restrictions maintained by a state or province (and not including a local government). However, under Article 1207 the timeline for the listing of such sub-central measures is only 1 year (Article 1207:1).

The Parties returned to the issue 2 years later. They did that through an exchange of separate side letters in March 1996 (NAFTA entered into force on 1 January 1994). In those side letters the three states set out a reservation for all existing state and provincial measures in their entirety.[25]

---

[24]NAFTA does not include a list of NCMs for the Temporary Entry of Business Persons but the commitments for them are included in annexes and appendixes directly under the relevant Chapter Sixteen. The commitments appear to apply across all levels of government of all three Parties. There do not seem to be differences in the relevant immigration categories across the different levels of government of the three states.

[25]The side letters of the US, Canada and Mexico are available on the webpage of the NAFTA Secretariat: https://www.nafta-sec-alena.org/Home/Texts-of-the-Agreement/North-American-Free-

The detailed and legally binding listing of the sub-central measures had apparently proved impossible, or overly burdensome.[26] Therefore, each Party ended up exempting (reserving) all NCMs in force on sub-central levels of government. The US has thereafter included a reservation for sub-central NCMs in all of its EIAs. It has put the blanket reservation forward at the signing of the agreement, without any attempt to come up with any such lists at a later stage (excluding a limited, non-binding list in the US-Korea EIA). A similar practice (reservation of all sub-central measures) was followed by Canada, all the way up until the conclusion of CETA with the EU in 2016.

4.3 US-Korea

The US-Korea Free Trade Agreement (KORUS) entered into force on 15 March 2012. Similarly to NAFTA and most US EIAs, its service commitments follow a negative scheduling method. Article 12.1, paragraph 2, of Chapter Twelve on Cross-Border Trade in Services includes the same definition for "measures" as GATS Article 1:3. KORUS thus covers measures adopted or maintained by central, regional, or local governments and authorities. Article 12.3 of KORUS also includes a reference to "a regional subdivision", similarly to GATS Article XVI.

Even if the definition of "measures" follows the GATS, with regard to the actual commitments of the sub-central levels of government KORUS follows the established practice of the US since NAFTA. It exempts all existing NCMs of "all states of the United States, the District of Columbia, and Puerto Rico".[27] The exemption applies to NT (Articles 11.3 and 12.2), MNF (Articles 11.4 and 12.3), Local Presence (Article 12.5), Performance Requirements (Article 11.8) and Senior

---

Trade-Agreement. See all three letters in Annex I, under "Non-Conforming Measures" placed at the top of the page below "Schedule of Canada". Each state's side letter says that, "for transparency", attached are documents that list NCMs maintained at the provincial and territorial level. However, such documents were not attached to the publicly available copies of the original side letters (which are scanned fax documents) and we were not able to locate them elsewhere either. The lists are unlikely to have been very detailed considering that later lists included by the US and Canada for "transparency" purposes in their FTAs with Korea are very vague and non-binding illustrations of the types of measures applied.

[26]The situation has not got any easier over the years. The recently negotiated United States-Mexico-Canada Agreement (USMCA), meant to replace NAFTA, also sets out a reservation for all existing sub-central NCMs. No lists of such measures are available in the version that is currently available on the webpage of the USTR. The lack of legally binding and exhaustive lists of sub-central measures is probably due to a variety of reasons—economic and political, but probably also technical. Going through all such measures may be a Herculean endeavour indeed, as noted by the Obama administration during the TTIP negotiations. See Hennig J, "Under Pressure To Show TTIP Progress, U.S., EU Focus On Market Access", Inside U.S. Trade—04/18/2014, Vol. 32, No. 16 (posted 17 April 2014).

[27]P. 12 of KORUS, Annex I, the schedule of the United States and Appendix I-A to the same schedule.

Management and Boards of Directors (Article 11.9). The formulation is similar to all earlier US EIAs since NAFTA and was followed by the US also in the draft TPP agreement (from which the US later withdrew).

What is new is the illustrative list of state-level NCMs that is provided on the following page of Annex I, as Appendix I-A.[28] However, the NCMs illustrated at the state and local level are provided for transparency purposes only and are not bound by the services provisions of these EIAs.[29] Annex I states "For purposes of transparency, Appendix I-A sets out an illustrative, non-binding list of non-conforming measures maintained at the regional level of government." Footnote 1 specifies that the "document is provided for transparency purposes only, and is neither exhaustive nor binding. The information contained in this document is drawn from U.S. commitments under the General Agreement on Trade in Services, the May 2005 Revised U.S. Services Offer under the Doha Development Agenda negotiations, and related documents". This would seem to indicate that the US is informing its treaty partner of potential sub-central measures (to the extent that they were committed to under the GATS and the Doha Round Offer and revealed by those and related documents) but has not undertaken an updated review to find out what the currently applied measures are. The list is "not exhaustive", which would seem to indicate that also other sub-central measures may be applied, especially if introduced after the GATS. Furthermore, KORUS does not provide for any liberalization of sub-central measures— the list is provided for transparency purposes only. The list of existing sub-central measures is neither binding and thus cannot be relied upon based on the FTA. However, it should be considered a slight improvement to the US scheduling practice as it gives some information on restrictive measures that are applied on the level of the states.

Korea managed to negotiate also another concession related to the sub-central levels of government. Annex 12-C of KORUS integrates a possibility for a party to request "consultations regarding non-conforming measures maintained by a regional level of government". The annex includes only one paragraph which reads:

> If a Party considers that an Annex I non-conforming measure applied by a regional level of government of the other Party creates a material impediment to a service supplier of the Party, an investor of the Party, or a covered investment, it may request consultations with regard to that measure. The Parties shall enter into consultations with a view to exchanging information on the operation of the measure and to considering whether further steps are necessary and appropriate.

The concession may be modest and does not guarantee that any changes to problematic sub-central measures would be agreed upon, but it shows that there is

---

[28]The same list was put forward along the US services commitments in the TPP. The original text and schedules of commitments is provided on the website of the USTR "for reference purposes": https://ustr.gov/trade-agreements/free-trade-agreements/trans-pacific-partnership/tpp-full-text.

[29]In the original TPP agreement, the information can be similarly found in Annex I, the schedule of the United States and Appendix I-A to the same schedule, at page 16. The US has withdrawn from the TPP but the originally negotiated commitments are available at https://ustr.gov/trade-agreements/free-trade-agreements/trans-pacific-partnership/tpp-full-text.

an increasing pressure to open up services markets also on the level of sub-central levels of government.[30] In KORUS, the pressure may have been exerted both ways. Korea has a system of local autonomies where the number of high-level local governments was in 2012 increased to seventeen. The local levels of government, and especially the high-level local governments, may exercise regulatory powers that affect Korea's services commitments.[31]

Interestingly, the US has not excluded sub-central measures with regard to MA commitments under Article 12:4. As was mentioned above, the exclusion of sub-central measures in Annex I applies to the articles on NT, MFN, local presence and a few other disciplines. This omission seems to relate to another Appendix that the US has included as part of its Annex II. That Appendix II-A specifies that "[T]he United States reserves the right to adopt or maintain any measure that is not inconsistent with the United States' obligations under Article XVI of the General Agreement on Trade in Services as set out in the U.S. Schedule of Specific Commitments under the GATS".[32] Considering the blanket reservation included therein, this appears to confirm that the US has not given any new MA commitments under KORUS but limits itself to those given under the GATS. For this purpose, sub-central measures do not need to be specifically exempted as they are tied to the level provided already under the GATS in any case.[33] However, it is also specified that "For purposes of this entry only, the U.S. Schedule of Specific Commitments is modified as indicated in Appendix II-A". Appendix II-A includes limited improvements to the US GATS schedule on MA. The improvements are mostly given at the federal level (at least no regional specification is mentioned), but a few are improvements to state-level measures.[34] However, the list of improvements is short and

---

[30]In the context of the TiSA negotiations the same pressure is visible in the bilateral market access request by the EU to the US. The EU wanted the US to update its TiSA offer by providing full transparency for sub-central measures. As an alternative option, the EU requested the US to provide transparency related to local content in all sectors where the US has MA commitments and to take a commitment to provide the remaining information on transparency with respect to other sectors after TiSA enters into force. See "TiSA – bilateral market access request by the European Union" (June 2016), Copy for the Council and the European Parliament. Available at: https://www.bilaterals.org/?tisa-bilateral-market-access&lang=en (source: Wikileaks).

[31]These high-level local governments are Seoul Special City, six metropolises, eight provinces, and Jeju Special Self-Governing Province. See the webpage of the Korean Culture and Information Service: http://www.korea.net/Government/Constitution-and-Government/Local-Governments. Korea's Annex I in KORUS reveals some sub-central measures applied on local levels of Korean government.

[32]P. 8 of Appendix II-A of Annex II-US.

[33]It is worth noting that the US has included a similar reservation to MA in all of its EIAs since the conclusion of the GATS. The reservations are typically included at the end or towards the end of the US Annex II. The formulations differ to some extent, but all set the US GATS commitments as the baseline of its MA commitments under the EIA.

[34]Appendix II-A starts by the following statement: For the following Sectors, U.S. obligations under Article XVI of the General Agreement on Trade in Services as set out in the U.S. Schedule of Specific Commitments under the GATS (GATS/SC/90, GATS/SC/90/Suppl.1, GATS/SC/90/Suppl.2, and GATS/SC/90/Suppl.3) are improved as described.

limited to a couple sectors only.[35] It indicates little progress in the US market access commitments as compared to its GATS commitments, both on the federal as well as the sub-central level.

4.4 Canada-Korea

The Canada-Korea Free Trade Agreement (CKFTA) has been in force since 1 January 2015. "Measures" are defined similarly to the GATS (Article 9.1:2, "Scope and Coverage", Chapter Nine: Cross-Border Trade in Services). In addition, the second paragraph of Article 9.2 on NT specifies that "the treatment accorded by a Party under paragraph 1 means, with respect to a sub-national government, treatment no less favourable than the most favourable treatment accorded, in like circumstances, by that sub-national government to service suppliers of the Party of which it forms a part".[36] Article 9.4 on MA applies to measures imposed "either on the basis of its [Party's] entire territory or on the basis of a sub-national government". It can thus be interpreted that Canada has agreed to NT and MA disciplines on all levels of the government.

The agreement includes a list of national reservations for existing (Annex I) and future (Annex II) NCMs. The NCMs are set on the federal level but a couple horizontal limitations include a mention of the Canadian provinces. However, the appearances of sub-central measures in Canada's national schedule are only occasional. Otherwise, Canada has included a similar carve-out for sub-central measures as is included in NAFTA. Canada's schedule to Annex I of the agreement includes a statement similar to NAFTA: all existing NCMs of all provinces and territories are included in reservations. In addition, and very interestingly, Canada's Appendix I-A sets out "an illustrative, non-binding list of non-conforming measures maintained at the sub-national level of government". The list is provided "[f]or purposes of transparency only".[37]

The logic of the listing is the same as in the non-binding and illustrative list of state measures included by the US in KORUS (also called Appendix I-A). The wording regarding the nature of the list as "illustrative" and "non-binding" is almost

---

[35]P. 11 of Appendix II-A of Annex II-US.

[36]It is noteworthy that the NT obligation sets as a point of comparison the service suppliers of the Party of which the sub-central entity forms a part, not to the service suppliers of the sub-central entity itself. As noted by Carlo Cantore regarding a similar NT clause in the Comprehensive and Progressive Agreement for Trans-Pacific Partnership (CPTPP), this formulation transforms the NT obligation into a type of "most-favoured region" obligation. See the chapter by Cantore in this volume.

[37]Footnote 2 to the Appendix notes that the document is provided for "transparency purposes only", and is "neither exhaustive nor binding". Furthermore, it states that the information contained in the document is drawn from Canada's May 2005 Revised Conditional Offer on Services (TN/S/O/CAN/Rev.1, 23 May 2005).

identical between the two agreements. The list of sub-central measures in the Canada-Korea agreement is also very general and does not explain in detail what the sub-central measures consist of. Instead, it simply lists which states have existing measures affecting citizenship, residency, local presence, economic needs tests, taxation, and corporate form or training requirements. Both Canada and the US have included the illustrative list of sub-central NCMs only in their EIAs with Korea. It may thus be that the lists exist thanks to the Korean negotiators' efforts to shed some light on the various service-related measures applied by the American and Canadian states and provinces. Canada and the US provided the same lists as part of their Annex I schedules to the original TPP agreement as well. The Canadian list is still part of the re-negotiated Comprehensive and Progressive Agreement for Trans-Pacific Partnership (CPTPP), which was concluded by the remaining 11 TPP states after the withdrawal of the US.[38]

Canada's approach to MA commitments is also the same as in the post-GATS EIAs concluded by the US. Canada has in its EIAs tied its commitments to its MA commitments under the GATS. The binding of the Canadian MA commitments to the level of the GATS is included in all Canadian EIAs, except for CETA. In addition, and again similarly to the KORUS, Appendix II-A to Canada's schedule of NCMs in the Canada-Korea EIA includes a list of commitments that somewhat improve Canada's obligations under Article XVI of the GATS. The list also includes some improvements to Canada's GATS commitments on the level of provinces, across various service sectors.[39]

Similarly to the US-Korea EIA, also the Canada-Korea EIA includes the possibility of consultations with regard to sub-central measures.[40] Consultations are available in case such a measure "creates a material impediment to a service supplier of the Party, an investor of the Party, or a covered investment". The consultation request is also available when a sub-national NCM "prevents the development of a mutual recognition agreement or arrangement or prevents a service supplier of a Party from receiving the benefits of such an agreement or arrangement".

The EIAs concluded by Canada and the US are surprisingly similar with regard to this issue, all the way up until the conclusion of CETA. In NAFTA, the US and Canada[41] have set out a reservation with regard to all existing NCMs (Annex I

---

[38]See Annex I of Canada to the CPTPP, available at https://international.gc.ca/trade-commerce/trade-agreements-accords-commerciaux/agr-acc/cptpp-ptpgp/. At the time of writing, the agreement had entered into force for seven of the 11 states that signed it (including Canada). The original US commitments under the draft TPP are available on the webpage of the USTR.

[39]Many of the new commitments consist of the removal of discriminatory MA requirements, such as commercial presence requirements or foreign ownership restrictions. Several removed restrictions seem to apply to NT, rather than MA, e.g. those that remove citizenship or residence requirements. Therefore, even if the list is provided as an improvement to Canada's MA commitments as compared to the GATS, it does also provide for a limited number of new NT commitments for Canadian provinces.

[40]Article 9.6 and Annex 9-A.

[41]Also Mexico has done the same.

limitations) of all sub-central entities. However, with regard to future measures (Annex II)[42] the agreements have a liberalizing effect also on state and provincial levels. The reviewed EIAs of the US and Canada do not include Annex II measures for sub-national levels of government and it would thus seem that they do not allow for the introduction of new sub-central limitations, beyond the existing ones. However, as the existing NCMs are not explained in detail, it may be hard to keep track of which sub-central measures have been excluded from the commitments in the first place. If a service supplier from a partner country wants to challenge a restrictive measure applied by a US state or a Canadian province, it needs to check the measure's legislative background and try to understand if the measure existed already at the time of the conclusion of the EIA. Annex I measures are subject to a "ratchet" clause. Therefore, any unilateral liberalization should not be subsequently withdrawn. But again, it may be hard for foreign service suppliers to keep track of such developments. Therefore, the detailed inclusion of the measures applied by the Canadian provinces and territories in the CETA agreement is an important step forward. It renders the sub-central level accountable in a way that is radically different to the earlier treaty practice of Canada and the US.

4.5   The EU in EU-Korea and CETA

The EU-South Korea free trade agreement (FTA) has been provisionally applied since July 2011 and was formally ratified in December 2015. The agreement is the first of the EU's new generation PTAs, the so called Deep and Comprehensive Free Trade Areas (DCFTAs) and represented a stepping-stone for future liberalization. According to the EU, at the time of its conclusion the agreement with Korea went further than any of its previous agreements in lifting trade barriers in services.[43]

Similarly to other EU's EIAs, the definitions regarding sub-central levels of government largely match those of the GATS. In the EU-Korea EIA, a definition of "measure" is included in Article 7.2 ("Definitions") of Chapter Seven on Trade in Services, Establishment and Electronic Commerce. The wording is not completely identical to the GATS, but extremely similar and the provision clearly covers all levels of government (central, regional and local governments). The provision

---

[42]The difference between Annex I and Annex II measures is that existing measures that do not comply with the disciplines of the services agreement must be listed in Annex I and cannot be made more restrictive. Annex II includes a list of measures for which the state wants to maintain the freedom to introduce them at a later stage. Either way, a measure must be listed under one of the annexes to be upheld. Typically, an Annex I measure needs to be amended, continued or renewed in order to be validly upheld. If it is discontinued, the trading partner gets to benefit from autonomous liberalization and the measure cannot be re-introduced at a later stage, unless it has been included also in Annex II.

[43]See the European Commission's information page on the EU-South Korea Free Trade Agreement, available at http://ec.europa.eu/trade/policy/countries-and-regions/countries/south-korea/.

regarding MA (Article 7.5.2) also includes a reference to "a regional subdivision" similarly to GATS Article XVI. It specifies that neither party may adopt or maintain either on the basis of a regional subdivision or on the basis of its entire territory MA limitations similar to those included in GATS Article XVI.

The EU's services schedule in the agreement includes a large number Member State-specific reservations. This is due to the fact that the EU still, to a large extent, lacks harmonized legislation with regard to how services and services-related areas of law are regulated in the Member States.[44] For example, the EU has no uniform rules regulating service professions. Each Member State can apply its own qualification and license requirements across the sectors. Moreover, in the absence of an EU-wide immigration policy, service suppliers from third countries face a different immigration scheme in each Member State. Even if the Member States aim at formulating unified conditions relating to issues such as period of stay and prior employment, there is still a separate work and residence permit procedure in each Member State. The complex and Member State-specific sectoral commitments that the EU has offered under the GATS and its EIAs, including the EU-Korea FTA as well as CETA, illustrate how the incompleteness of the EU's internal services market appears in its external trade relations.

The variety of Member State-specific limitations depends on the service sector in question. Interestingly, the commitments of the EU and its Member States are not significantly more uniform in the EU-Korea EIA as compared to the EU's consolidated GATS commitments. The internal diversity in the measures applied by the EU Member States is particularly visible in CETA as the negative listing of reservations requires the detailed explanation of all limitations. The EU's schedule is organized in several parts. The first part includes the reservations applied in the entire EU (13 pages in length). After that, the Member State-specific reservations follow. They are organized separately for each Member State, starting from 14 pages of Austrian reservations and finishing with four pages of UK reservations. The reservations reveal several domestic sub-central measures. They are most frequent in the German reservations and go further than the reservations of the German Länder that are visible as part of the GATS and the EU-Korea EIA. In the case of the federal EU states, CETA has therefore revealed some sub-central limitations that were hiding under the positive scheduling method of the GATS and the EU-Korea EIA. However, such situations are limited and most of the Member State-specific reservations are made of measures that apply on the level of the central (national) government. This may relate to the intra-EU integration through which many divergent sub-national measures of EU Member States have already been brought in line with EU law. Further research should be carried out to confirm this hypothesis.

---

[44]See Langhammer (2005), p. 311, who notes that given the significant amount of national sovereignties that remain in the services trade amongst EU Member States, the EU is not yet even a free trade area.

5 Conclusion

The chapter has given a short analysis of the services commitments of a few key federal entities. In NAFTA, all existing sub-central measures are exempted and are not listed. In KORUS and the Canada-Korea FTA, the US and Canada have similarly exempted existing sub-central measures but as a small improvement they have provided an illustrative list of existing measures. The list, however, is only exemplary and not legally binding. Based on this practice it is clear to see why the legally binding listing of sub-central measures in CETA by Canada is such a big step forward.

In CETA Canada has included in its schedule separate federal, and provincial and territorial annexes, which together form the entirety of its commitments. Canada's two annexes with federal measures take approximately 50 pages of the agreement, whereas the two annexes with provincial and territorial restrictions occupy over 200 pages. This success with the binding inclusion of sub-central commitments is arguably related to the unprecedented participation of the Canadian sub-central entities in the CETA negotiations.[45]

The EU follows a scheduling practice of its own. It is still far from putting forward a common EU offer but instead describes Member State-specific limitations in cases where they exist. This goes further than what can be observed in the case of the US that has not yet engaged in extensive state-specific liberalization. However, each EU Member State is a WTO Member also in its own right and this can affect the conclusions to be drawn from the EU's commitments. However, meaningful services liberalization in any federal entity, whether a state or a special structure such as the EU, should encompass sub-central measures. In the case of the EU, the same issue arises with regard to the Member States' own sub-national measures. There are some but in general very few appearances of sub-national entities, such as the German or Austrian Länder. This may mean that such sub-central limitations do not exist, or that such sub-central limitations have not been listed to a sufficient degree. In any case, truly deeper service liberalization calls for a more extensive inclusion of sub-central entities in international services negotiations through legally binding commitments.

Services liberalization is likely to be weak in such federal states that liberalize services only on the level of the central government. The same applies to some other areas of trade liberalization, especially to commitments taken with regard to public procurement. Investment liberalization can be similarly affected. The general scarcity of sub-central commitments in trade agreements is noteworthy considering that many of the purported gains of modern trade agreements relate to the liberalization of behind-the-border barriers, such as discrimination against foreign service suppliers. Therefore, true and deep liberalization of services should not neglect sub-central actors but demand their greater engagement with international services trade negotiations.

---

[45]For an overview of the sub-central participation of the Canadian provinces and a comparison between sub-national perspectives in Canada and the EU in the context of the CETA negotiations, see Omiunu (2017).

Annex: Summarizing Table

GATS Commitments

Country/ entity	Sub-central measures covered in the treaty text	Inclusion of sub-central commitments in the sector-specific commitments	Comments
United States	Yes	Yes	Sub-central measures appear widely
Canada	Yes	Yes	Sub-central measures appear widely
European Union	Yes	Yes (on the level of EU Member States)	A very limited appearance of EU MSs' internal (national) sub-central measures

Table reproduced with permission of Cambridge University Press through PLSclear; first published in Johanna Jacobsson, Preferential Services Liberalization—The Case of the European Union and Federal States, CUP 2019

EIA Commitments

Agreement	Sub-central measures covered in the treaty text	Inclusion of sub-central commitments in sector-specific commitments by US, Canada and EU	Comments
KORUS	Yes	No	Reservation for all existing sub-central non-conforming measures (a non-binding list is provided)
Canada-Korea	Yes	No	The same as in KORUS
EU-Korea	Yes	Yes (on the level of EU Member States)	A very limited appearance of EU MSs' internal (national) sub-central measures
CETA	Yes	Yes	Sub-central non-conforming measures described in detail
NAFTA	Yes	No	Reservation for all existing sub-central non-conforming measures

Table reproduced with permission of Cambridge University Press through PLSclear; first published in Johanna Jacobsson, Preferential Services Liberalization—The Case of the European Union and Federal States, CUP 2019

References

Adlung R, Carzaniga A (2009) MFN exemptions under the general agreements on trade in services: grandfathers striving for immortality. J Int Econ Law 12(2):357–392

Adlung R, Roy M (2005) Turning hills into mountains? Current commitments under the GATS. J World Trade 39(6):1161–1194

Cloots E, De Baere G, Sottiaux S (2012) Federalism in the European Union. Hart, Oxford

Egan M (2015) Single markets: economic integration in Europe and the United States. Oxford University Press, New York

Langhammer R (2005) The EU offer of service trade liberalization in the DOHA Round: evidence of a not-yet-perfect customs union. J Common Mark Stud 43(2):311–325

Menon A, Schain M (2006) Comparative federalism: The European Union and the United States in comparative perspective. Oxford University Press, Oxford

Meyer T (2017) Local liability in international economic law. N C Law Rev 95(2):261–338

Omiunu O (2017) The evolving role of sub-national actors in international economic relations: a case study of the Canada-European Union CETA. In: Amtenbrink F, Prévost D, Wessel R (eds) Shifting forms and levels of cooperation in international economic law: structural developments in trade, investment and financial regulation, Netherlands Yearbook of International Law, vol 48. T.M.C. Asser Press, Den Haag, pp 173–205

Roy M (2014) Services commitments in preferential trade agreements: surveying the empirical landscape. In: Sauvé P, Shingal A (eds) The preferential liberalization of trade in services: comparative regionalism. Edward Elgar, Cheltenham, pp 13–36

Schütze R (2009) From dual to cooperative federalism: the changing structure of European law. Oxford University Press, Oxford

Steytler N (2005) The place and role of local government in federal systems, Konrad-Adenauer Stiftung. Occasional Chapters, Johannesburg

Johanna Jacobsson is Assistant Professor at IE University (Madrid, Spain). She holds a PhD from the European University Institute (Florence, Italy, 2016) and LL.B., LL.M. and BA degrees from the University of Helsinki (Finland). She has previously been a law clerk at the Court of Justice of the European Union, a visiting researcher at the Finnish Institute of International Affairs and a practitioner in a law firm. Since 2018, Johanna is a member of the Executive Council of the Society of International Economic Law (SIEL).

Disciplines on Domestic Regulations Affecting Trade in Services: Convergence or Divergence?

Gabriel Gari

Contents

The article has benefited from useful feedback provided by Martin Roy. Usual caveats apply.

G. Gari (✉)
Queen Mary University of London, Centre for Commercial Law Studies, London, UK
e-mail: g.gari@qmul.ac.uk

59

R. T. Hoffmann, M. Krajewski (eds.), *Coherence and Divergence in Services Trade
Law*, European Yearbook of International Economic Law,
https://doi.org/10.1007/978-3-030-46955-9_4

1 Introduction

A quarter of a century has gone since the GATS entered into force in January 1995. A quick review of multilateral negotiations on trade in services over this period point at two main findings. First, reciprocal negotiations of specific market access and national treatment commitments have played a limited role. At best, they have contributed to consolidate applied regulatory policies.[1] Second, even assuming success in removing overt quantitative restrictions and discriminatory measures, effective market access conditions for foreign service suppliers cannot be achieved unless the trade restrictive effect stemming from disparities of non-discriminatory domestic regulations is addressed in one way or another.

The scale of this problem is best appreciated when looked at from the perspective of a service exporter that needs to get authorisation to supply a service abroad.[2] The first hurdle is to find out the regulatory requirements to get such permit. It is not an easy task for a foreign supplier to navigate through the interstices of a foreign regulatory system to identify the licensing criteria and other administrative provisions applicable to specific service sectors, let alone when the transparency standards of this type of regulations are sub-optimal.[3] The second hurdle is to meet different licensing or qualification requirements and technical standards, which, inevitably, will vary across jurisdictions, and may well depart from international practice or impose excessive burdens which have no strong public policy justifications.[4] Finally, the foreign service supplier has to follow a procedure to demonstrate compliance with such licensing requirements, qualification requirements or technical standards. Service exporters claim that such procedures often take too long or seem open-ended, without any clarity or certainty for business on how long they should reasonably expect to wait for approvals.[5] Clearly, these regulatory hurdles can easily dilute the value of specific commitments on market access and national treatment, no matter how ambitious the commitments may be. This problem is not new.[6] It is compounded by the regulatory intensity of service sectors, and there is mounting empirical evidence of its trade restrictive effects.[7]

---

[1]See, e.g. Hoekman and Mattoo (2013).

[2]See Statement from New Zealand, Report of the Meeting of the Working Party on Domestic Regulations held on 16 June 2016 (S/WPDR/M/67, 28/06/16).

[3]Ibid.

[4]Ibid.

[5]Ibid.

[6]Back in 1988, a Price Waterhouse's survey to service exporters identified that discriminatory treatment is not written into the published laws and regulations but is a matter of official practice, "the way things have always been done", "general bureaucratic tendency not to approve new activities", etc. Cited by Feketekuty (1988).

[7]See, for example, Kox and Lejour (2005); Schwellnus (2007); Kox and Nordås (2007, 2009); Van der Marel and Shepherd (2013). The recently created OECD database on regulatory barriers to trade in services has the potential to make a valuable contribution on this matter. See Nordås (2016); for professional services, see Mattoo and Mishra (2009); Crozet et al. (2016).

GATS negotiators were not oblivious to this problem, but facing the daunting task of adopting the first ever multilateral rules for trade in services, they focused on disciplines aimed at addressing overt quantitative restrictions and discriminatory measures, paying less attention to disciplines on domestic regulations. They were assigned an ancillary role in the liberalization of trade in services compared with the negotiation of specific commitments on market access and national treatment. Such disciplines are prescribed by Article VI.[8] Paragraphs 4 and 5 contain disciplines relating to the content of the measures and thus of a substantive nature, whereas paragraphs 1–3 and 6 contain disciplines of a procedural nature, i.e. relating to the application, administration and review of measures.[9] At the time of its drafting, GATT Contracting Parties could not agree on a final text for the substantive disciplines, so they just pledged to develop them in the future.

Treaty drafters continue facing a difficult choice that lies at the heart of the controversy surrounding this particular area of the international law of trade in services, i.e. how to balance trade liberalisation goals *vis a vis* the need to protect the right to regulate the supply of services in order to meet national policy objectives. The right to regulate is one of the key means by which a State formulates and implements its policy objectives, whatever those objectives may be according to its own sovereign preferences. In this sense, the right to regulate is a political right *par excellence*. On the other hand, it is the result of the exercise of such right in the form of licensing and qualification requirements and procedures and technical standards that could make the difference between the ability to enter a market or not. The choice, therefore, is how far should treaty drafters go in bringing domestic policy-making processes under international oversight subject to trade sanctions.

Recent developments both at multilateral and regional level merit a review of the international law on trade in services relating to disciplines on domestic regulation. At multilateral level, since September 2016, the negotiations to develop substantive disciplines for domestic regulations mandated by Article VI.4 have picked up.[10] So much so that a sub-group of WTO members consisting mainly of developed and high or middle income developing countries are close to adopting a reference paper on services. At regional level, recent Preferential Trade Agreements (PTAs) adopted by the world largest players in trade in services, include very detailed disciplines on domestic regulation with great potential to address the trade costs stemming from regulatory diversity. However, these innovations are far from being representative of the whole universe of PTAs currently in force.[11]

---

[8]For a detailed analysis of this provision see Krajewski (2008).

[9]Krajewski (2008).

[10]See below, Sect. 2.1.

[11]See below Sect. 2.2.

Against this background, the aim of this paper is to analyse the recent developments on disciplines on domestic regulations affecting trade in services both at multilateral and regional level, shed light on the extent to which such developments are converging or diverging, and identify the factors driving or preventing convergence. More specifically, how do PTAs' disciplines on domestic regulation compare with multilateral ones (vertical convergence)? How do they compare among themselves (horizontal convergence)? Does the evidence suggest a trend towards convergence or divergence? If so, which are the factors driving or preventing convergence?

To answer these questions, the paper builds on and further expands the findings of a recent study of twenty three PTAs entered into by China, the EU, Japan, and the U. S.[12] First, as it stems from Table 1, the sample of PTAs reviewed by this paper has been expanded from twenty three to thirty.

In addition, to better assess the degree of vertical convergence, PTAs' disciplines are compared not only with GATS disciplines, but also with the three draft texts on disciplines on domestic regulations pursuant to Article VI:4 that have been circulated among WTO Members, i.e. the Working Party on Domestic Regulations' Chairman draft text of 20 March 2009 (hereinafter CMT2009);[13] the Chairman's Progress Report of 14 April 2011 (hereinafter CPR2011)[14] and the Draft Reference Paper on Services Domestic Regulation (hereinafter DRP2019).[15]

The analysis will focus on disciplines on domestic regulations found in PTAs' chapters on trade in services and stand-alone chapters on transparency where they exist. It will not cover disciplines on domestic regulations included on chapters on specific service sectors, movement of natural persons and e-commerce.

The disciplines reviewed are classified according to the following categories: (a) disciplines on transparency of domestic regulations, i.e. provisions prescribing duties aimed at disseminating information about measures affecting trade in services; (b) disciplines on the development of domestic regulations, i.e. substantive standards to be met by the regulator when adopting requirements and procedures for licenses and qualifications and technical standards; and (c) disciplines on the administration of domestic regulations, i.e. procedural standards to be observed by the regulator when processing applications to obtain the authorisation necessary to supply a service. Further specifications for each category of disciplines are provided below in the corresponding sections. In order to assess the likely impact of these provisions

---

[12]Gari (2020).

[13]Second Revision, Draft Disciplines on Domestic Regulation Pursuant to GATS Article VI.4, Informal Note by the Chairman, Room Document, 20 March 2009.

[14]Disciplines on Domestic Regulation Pursuant to GATS Article VI4, Chairman's Progress Report (S/WPDR/W/45, 14 April 2011).

[15]Draft Reference Paper on Services Domestic Regulation, Note by the Chairperson, INF/SDR/W/1/Rev.1, 12 December 2019. Copy on hold.

Table 1 Recent preferential trade agreements from Australia, Canada, China, EU, Japan and U.S.

Name	Code	Year of signature
Free Trade Agreement between the Government of Georgia and the Government of the People's Republic of China	CHN-GEO	2017
Free Trade Agreement between the Government of Australia and the Government of the People's Republic of China	CHN-AUS	2015
Free Trade Agreement between the Government of the People's Republic of China and the Government of the Republic of Korea	CHN-KOR	2015
Free Trade Agreement between the Swiss Confederation and the People's Republic of China	CHN-CHE	2013
Free Trade Agreement between the Government of Iceland and the Government of the People's Republic of China	CHN-ISL	2013
Free Trade Agreement between the Government of the People's Republic of China and the Government of the Republic of Costa Rica	CHN-CRC	2010
Free Trade Agreement between the European Union and the Socialist Republic of Vietnam	EU-VNM	2019
Agreement between the European Union and Japan for an Economic Partnership	EU-JPN	2018
EU Mexico Trade Agreement	EU-MEX	2018[a]
Free Trade Agreement between the European Union and the Republic of Singapore	EU-SGP	2018
Comprehensive and Enhanced Partnership Agreement between the EU and its Member States and the Republic of Armenia	EU-ARM	2017
Comprehensive Economic and Trade Agreement between Canada and the EU and its Member States	CETA	2016
Trade Agreement between the European Union and its Member States and Colombia and Peru	EU-COL	2012
Agreement establishing an Association between the European Union and its Member States and Central America	EU-CEN	2012
Free Trade Agreement between the European Union and its Member States and the Republic of Korea	EU-KOR	2010
Economic Partnership Agreement between the CARIFORUM States and the EC and its Member States	EU-CARIFORUM	2008
Agreement between Japan and Mongolia for an Economic Partnership	JPN-MNG	2015
Agreement between Japan and Australia for an Economic Partnership	JPN-AUS	2014
Agreement between Japan and the Republic of Peru for an Economic Partnership	JPN-PER	2011
Comprehensive Economic Partnership between the Republic of India and Japan	JPN-IND	2011
Agreement on Free Trade and Economic Partnership between Japan and the Swiss Confederation	JPN-CHE	2009
Agreement between the United States of America, The United Mexican States and Canada	USMCA	2018

(continued)

Table 1 (continued)

Name	Code	Year of signature
Free Trade Agreement between the United States and the Republic of Korea	USA-KOR	2007
United States Panama Trade Promotion Agreement	USA-PAN	2007
United States Colombia Trade Promotion Agreement	USA-COL	2006
United States Peru Trade Promotion Agreement	USA-PER	2006
Agreement between the Govt. of the USA and the Govt. of the Sultanate of Oman on the Establishment of a FTA	USA-OMN	2006
Comprehensive and Progressive Agreement for Trans-Pacific Partnership	CPTPP	2018
Indonesia-Australia Comprehensive Economic Partnership	AUS-IDN	2019
Canada Korea Free Trade Agreement	CAN-KOR	2014

^aAgreement in principle

in tackling regulatory divergence, the paper also evaluates their legal enforceability.[16]

The remaining of the paper is organized as follow: Sect. 2 provides an overview of the recent developments on disciplines on domestic regulation both at multilateral and regional level; Sect. 3 examines disciplines on transparency of domestic regulations; Sect. 4 examines disciplines on the development of domestic regulations; Sect. 5 examines the disciplines on the administration of domestic regulation; Sect. 6 examines provisions on special and differential treatment for developing countries and Sect. 7 concludes.

2 Recent Developments on Disciplines on Domestic Regulation

2.1 Developments at Multilateral Level

Article VI.4 of GATS calls upon WTO members to develop any necessary disciplines to ensure that measures relating to qualification requirements (QRs) and procedures (QPs), technical standards (TSs) and licensing requirements (LRs) and procedures (LPs) do not constitute unnecessary barriers to trade in services and with a view to ensure that such requirements are, *inter alia*: "based on objective and

---

[16]Trade disciplines are classified as 'hard' or 'soft' according to the extent to which they are legally enforceable. This is a text-based classification. When the text of the provision includes an unqualified expression such as "shall", it is regarded as 'hard'. By contrast, when the text qualifies the verb "shall" by terms such as 'to the extent possible', or where there is an explicit textual exclusion of the said provision from the jurisdiction of the PTA's enforcement mechanisms, then it is regarded as 'soft'. This criteria is inspired by the methodology developed by Horn et al. (2010), pp. 1572–1573.

transparent criteria", "not more burdensome than necessary to ensure the quality of the service", and "in the case of licensing procedures, not in themselves a restriction on the supply of the service". The provision does not specify a timeframe for the completion of such task, but Article VI:5 prescribes a temporary obligation not to apply such measures in a way that nullifies or impairs Members' specific commitments.

WTO Members addressed Article VI:4's mandate early on with eagerness. Only 2 months after the agreement entered into force, the Council of Trade in Services (CTS) established a Working Party on Professional Services (WPPS) to make recommendations for the elaboration on multilateral disciplines in the Accountancy Sector.[17] By December 1998, the WPPS had concluded its task and the CTS adopted the Disciplines on Domestic Regulation in the Accountancy Sector.[18] The CTS stipulated that the disciplines should be integrated into the GATS "No later than the conclusion of the forthcoming round of services negotiations...", but it did not specify the process to do this.[19] In the end, the round of services negotiations were never concluded and the disciplines were not incorporated into the GATS. Nevertheless, the final product is a comprehensive document whose scope, structure and level of ambition—including the adoption of a necessity test,[20] set a strong precedent for the negotiations on horizontal disciplines on domestic regulation that followed.

Prompted by this early success, by July 1999 the CTS replaced the WPSS with a Working Party on Domestic Regulation (WPDR) entrusted with the much more ambitious task of developing "generally applicable disciplines..." on domestic regulation.[21] It soon became clear that WTO Members had miscalculated the difficulty to complete such task. For over a decade, deep differences came to the fore and prevented Members from making any progress. It was only by March 2009 that the Chairman of the WPDR circulated an informal note including a draft prepared under his responsibility (CMT2009). The document reflects proposals which the Chairman felt had enjoyed wide support by delegations during their discussions. It keeps the same structure as the disciplines for the Accountancy Sector, including separate sections on Transparency, LRs, LPs, QRs, QPs and TSs, but extends their scope of application to all sectors where specific commitments are undertaken. It uses hard language for all operational provisions and adds a development chapter to address the special needs of individual developing countries in implementing the measures.

In early 2011, Members undertook a paragraph by paragraph review of the CMT2009. Based on the results of this "sweeping exercise", the chairman of the WPDR circulated a progress report identifying parts of the draft that were stabilized, and those on which further work was required (CPR2011). Since the circulation of

---

[17]Decision on Professional Services, 1 March 1995 (S/L/3).

[18]See Decision of the CTS adopted on 14 December 1998 (S/L/63, 15/12/98 and S/L/64, 17/12/98).

[19]Para 2, S/L/63.

[20]See paragraph 2, Decision of the CTS adopted on 14 December 1998 (S/L/64, 17/12/98).

[21]CTS Decision on Domestic Regulation adopted on 26 April 1999 (S/L/70, 28/04/99).

the CPR2011, text-based negotiations remained dormant, until a meaningful exchange of views took place prior and immediately after the tenth Ministerial Conference held in Nairobi in December 2015. Building on those meaningful exchanges, a number of Members called for a resumption of the negotiations.[22] Concrete text proposals were subsequently tabled on specific matters previously covered by the CMT2009, but structured in a different way, including proposals on "transparency",[23] "development of measures"[24] and "administration of measures".[25]

By December 2017, during the eleventh Ministerial Conference in Buenos Aires, a consolidated text proposal was circulated (hereinafter CTP2017).[26] Its sponsors, including all developed countries (but the U.S.), China and a number of high and middle income developing countries, issued a statement reaffirming their commitment to advancing negotiations on the basis of such text, and calling Members to conclude the negotiations in advance of the twelfth Ministerial Conference.[27] Others, however, voiced their strong opposition to the consolidated text proposal, both on strategic and substantive grounds.

Bolivia, Cuba, India, the African Group and the LDC group argued that progress on the negotiation on disciplines on domestic regulation should be balanced with progress on the market access side of the services negotiations in sectors and modes of supply of interest to developing countries and, more broadly, with progress in

---

[22]Communication from Australia; Chile; China; Colombia; Hong Kong, China; the Republic of Korea; Mexico; New Zealand; Norway; the Russian Federation; Singapore; Switzerland; the Separate Customs Territory of Taiwan, Penghu, Kinmen And Matsu; and Turkey—Elements for Discussion (JOB/SERV/231/Rev.1, 13/06/16).

[23]Communication on "Transparency" from Australia, Colombia, the European Union, Japan, Republic of Korea, Mexico, New Zealand and the Separate Customs Territory of Taiwan, Penghu, Kinmen and Matsu (JOB/SERV/251/Rev.1).

[24]Communications on "Development of Measures" from Australia, Canada, Colombia, the European Union, Israel, Japan and Mexico (JOB/SERV/250) and Hong Kong, China, New Zealand, Switzerland and Chile (JOB/SERV/252/Rev.2).

[25]Communication on "Administration of Measures" from Australia, Chile, Colombia, the European Union, Japan, Mexico, Norway, Peru, Republic of Korea, and the Separate Customs Territory of Taiwan, Penghu, Kinmen and Matsu (JOB/SERV/239/Rev.1).

[26]Communication from Albania; Argentina; Australia; Canada; Chile; China; Colombia; Costa Rica; The European Union; Hong Kong, China; Iceland; Israel; Japan; The Republic Of Kazakhstan; The Republic of Korea; Liechtenstein; The Former Yugoslav Republic of Macedonia; Mexico; The Republic of Moldova; Montenegro; New Zealand; Norway; Peru; The Russian Federation; Switzerland; The Separate Customs Territory Of Taiwan, Penghu, Kinmen And Matsu; Turkey; Ukraine; and Uruguay, Disciplines on Domestic Regulation, 13 December 2017 (WT/MIN(17)/7/Rev.2).

[27]Communication from Albania; Argentina; Australia; Canada; Chile; China; Colombia; Costa Rica; The European Union; Hong Kong, China; Iceland; Israel; Japan; The Republic Of Kazakhstan; The Republic of Korea; Liechtenstein; The Former Yugoslav Republic of Macedonia; Mexico; The Republic of Moldova; Montenegro; New Zealand; Norway; Peru; The Russian Federation; Switzerland; The Separate Customs Territory Of Taiwan, Penghu, Kinmen And Matsu; Turkey; Ukraine; and Uruguay, Disciplines on Domestic Regulation, 13 December 2017 (WT/MIN(17)/7/Rev.2).

other areas of the Doha Development Agenda.[28] In addition, both India and the African Group made detailed technical objections to the text circulated during the Buenos Aires Ministerial Conference.

India's position claims that many of the provisions included in the draft fall outside the terms of the negotiation mandate prescribed by Article VI:4.[29] It also argues that the disciplines fail to tackle those domestic regulations affecting exports in those sectors and modes of supply of particular interest to India such as professional services supplied by Mode 4.[30] In its turn, the African Group position paper raises strong concerns about the impact of the proposed disciplines on the right to regulate the supply of services and the risk of imposing a single regulatory model to very diverse situations as well as the lack of clear evidence about the costs and benefits of these disciplines, particularly for developing countries suffering from institutional weaknesses and resource' constraints.[31]

Given the opposition of a number of developing countries, negotiations continued after the Buenos Aires Ministerial Conference within the WTO, but on a plurilateral basis, outside the WPDR. In its turn, the WPDR limited its agenda to the discussion of a number of proposals submitted by India for disciplines concerned with barriers affecting the supply of services through Mode 4.[32]

In November 2018, the sponsors of the plurilateral negotiations replaced the CTP2017 with a new draft text (hereinafter DR8-A).[33,34] In May 2019, they issued a joint statement welcoming the progress made in the negotiations, committing to continue working on outstanding issues and encouraging all WTO Members to participate in the negotiations in order to improve the regulatory environment for

---

[28]See, inter alia, statements by South Africa, Bolivia, Cuba and Uganda, in the meeting of the WPDR held on 15, 16, 22 June and 5 July 2017 (S/WPDR/M/71, 29/09/17).

[29]Comments by India on Co-Sponsors' Text on Disciplines on Domestic Regulation (WT/MIN(17)/ 7; WT/GC/190), WT/MIN(17)/19, 5/12/17.

[30]Ibid.

[31]Disciplines on Domestic Regulation African Group Elements for Ministerial Decision, WT/MIN (17)/8, 4 December 2017.

[32]See Communication from India GATS Article VI:4—Disciplines for Supply of a Service through the Presence of a Natural Person of a Member in the Territory of Another Member (S/WPDR/W/61/ Rev.1, 8/08/19).

[33]DR8-A, GATS Article VI:4 Disciplines, Non-Attributed Working Text, 9 November 2018. Copy on hold.

[34]It is interesting to note that at the same time, outside the WTO, the APEC Members adopted the APEC Non-binding Principles for Domestic Regulation of the Services Sector, which closely resemble the DR8-A text. See https://www.google.com/url?sa=t&rct=j&q=&esrc=s& source=web&cd=1&ved=2ahUKEwi_2KLI6o_kAhUwIrkGHQA1DqoQFjAAegQIBhAC& url=https%3A%2F%2Fapec.org%2F-%2Fmedia%2FAPEC%2FPublications%2F2018%2F11% 2F2018-CTI-Report-to-Ministers%2FTOC%2FAppendix-13%2D%2D-APEC-Nonbinding-Princi ples-for-DR-Drafting-Group.pdf&usg=AOvVaw2zUHeK96YcZx1XUto-z1v4.

trade in services globally.[35] In addition, the statement included a commitment to incorporate the outcome of the negotiations in the sponsors' schedules of specific commitments by the twelfth WTO Ministerial Conference. The statement was signed by fifty nine WTO Members which accounted for 57% of world exports of commercial services in 2018.[36] The U.S., which accounted for almost 19% of such exports,[37] is actively participating in the negotiations although it is not formally endorsing the statements of the plurilateral group.

At the open-ended meeting of the plurilateral group of 19 July 2019, participants welcomed a draft Reference Paper on Services Domestic Regulations produced by the Chairperson of the plurilateral negotiations, which was last updated on 4 December 2019 (DRP2019).[38] Section II contains the substantive disciplines which are to be inscribed into Members' Schedules of Specific Commitments. By February 2020, a total of 26 indicative draft schedules were submitted by 53 WTO Members.[39]

The participants' pledge to conduct the plurilateral negotiations within the WTO and in accordance with open, transparent and inclusive principles, as well as their pledge to incorporate the results of the negotiations into their GATS schedules as additional commitments under Article XVIII of the Agreement (and thus extending the benefits of the disciplines on a Most Favoured Nation basis to WTO Members that have not participated in the negotiations) are of critical importance to facilitate the convergence of multilateral disciplines on domestic regulation.

---

[35]Joint Statement on Services Domestic Regulation, 23 May 2019 WT/L/1059, circulated at the request of the delegations of Albania; Argentina; Australia; Brazil; Canada; Chile; China; Colombia; Costa Rica; El Salvador; European Union; Hong Kong, China; Iceland; Israel; Japan; Kazakhstan; Republic of Korea; Liechtenstein; Mexico; Republic of Moldova; Montenegro; New Zealand; Nigeria; North Macedonia; Norway; Paraguay; Peru; Russian Federation; Switzerland; the Separate Customs Territory of Taiwan, Penghu, Kinmen and Matsu; Turkey; and Uruguay. While not formally subscribing to the Joint Statements, the U.S. is participating on the negotiations.

[36]World Trade Statistical Review (WTO, 2019), available at https://www.wto.org/english/res_e/statis_e/wts2019_e/wts19_toc_e.htm.

[37]World Trade Statistical Review (WTO, 2019), available at https://www.wto.org/english/res_e/statis_e/wts2019_e/wts19_toc_e.htm.

[38]Draft Reference Paper on Services Domestic Regulation, Note by the Chairperson, INF/SDR/W/1/Rev.1, 12 December 2019. Copy on hold.

[39]Indicative draft schedules have been submitted by the following participants: Albania; Australia; Brazil; Canada; Chile; China, Colombia; Costa Rica; the European Union; Hong Kong, China; Iceland; Israel; Japan; Liechtenstein; North Macedonia; Mexico; Rep. of Moldova; Montenegro; Norway; Paraguay; Rep. of Korea; New Zealand; Switzerland; Chinese Taipei; Turkey; and Uruguay. Minutes of Meeting held on 4 February 2020, INF/SDR/R/9.

2.2 Developments at Regional Level

The inclusion of disciplines on trade in services in PTAs is relatively recent. During the GATT years, almost all PTAs but for the European Economic Community (1957) and the Free Trade Agreement between Canada and the United States (1989), dealt exclusively with trade in goods. The number of PTAs with disciplines on trade in services began to gain traction by 2000.[40] It was the U.S. that started including provisions aimed at the liberalisation of trade in service in its PTAs in accordance with its 'competitive liberalisation' strategy prevailing in the early 2000s. As of 7 August 2019, of the 301 PTAs notified to the WTO and in force, 149 have provisions liberalizing trade in goods only, 151 liberalize goods and services and one just services.[41]

Currently, each of the largest trading players of the world (China, EU, Japan, U. S.) has its own extensive network of PTAs covering trade in services. At the same time, there are many developing countries that remain outside these networks, which have only entered into a few PTAs, the majority of which just cover trade in goods. From a geographical perspective, the distribution of PTAs is also uneven. A recent report notes that today's PTAs, and especially the negotiation of future agreements, is concentrated in the East Asian region and Europe.[42]

There are few studies that look at the extent of innovation of these PTAs on services rules compared with the GATS.[43] Lim, Marchetti and Roy note that PTAs appear to offer limited value added over GATS rules on domestic regulation, with the exception of rules found in separate chapters on Telecom and Financial Services, additional transparency provisions, as well as some sector-specific provisions relating to recognition in certain agreements.[44] Ortino and Lydgate highlight CETA's, CTPP's and USMCA's novel approaches to tackle regulatory diversity affecting trade in services, but warn that it is too early to tell whether they will have any ground-breaking impact in terms of trade liberalisation.[45]

Our previous review of twenty three PTAs entered into by China, the EU, Japan, and U.S. identified a remarkable expansion in the number and extent of PTAs' disciplines on domestic regulations compared with GATS.[46] But it also found that such innovations were not evenly spread across the PTAs examined. While a few of them include significant developments on their disciplines on transparency, development and administration of domestic regulations compared with GATS,[47] others are much less innovative, with either no specific provisions on the development of

---

[40]For instance, Shingal et al. (2018).

[41]WTO RTAs database, available http://rtais.wto.org/UI/publicsummarytable.aspx.

[42]Acharya (2016).

[43]See, inter alia, Latrille and Juneyoung (2012) and Araujo (2014).

[44]Roy et al. (2007).

[45]Ortino and Lydgate (2019).

[46]Gari (2020).

[47]For example, CPTPP, CETA, EU-Japan FTA.

domestic regulations[48] or just a commitment to review the results of multilateral negotiations pursuant to Article VI.4 of GATS, with a view to incorporating them into their services Chapter.[49] The remaining of this paper will provide further evidence of the extent of PTAs innovations' on disciplines on domestic regulation compared not just with GATS but also with those disciplines included in multilateral (CMT2009, CPR2011) and plurilateral (DRP2019) draft texts.

3 Disciplines on Transparency of Domestic Regulations

3.1 Overview

Disciplines on transparency of domestic regulations encompass duties aimed at disseminating information about measures affecting trade in services. For analytical purposes, and without prejudice of minor variations found in the Article VI:4 draft texts and the PTAs examined by this paper, such disciplines are classified in three categories: duty to publish, duty to consult and duty to inform. In its turn, as indicated below, each of them are further classified in sub-categories.

Table 2 illustrates which of these disciplines are found in the Article VI:4 draft texts and in those PTAs with the most ambitious provisions on this matter for China, the EU, Japan and the U.S. It also specifies whether the disciplines are phrased in hard (i.e. 'shall') or soft (e.g. 'to the extent possible') terms. With respect to the PTAs, the review covers transparency provisions irrespective of whether they are included in the horizontal chapter on transparency or in the services chapter. Transparency provisions on sector specific chapters are not considered.

3.2 Duty to Publish

The duty to publish includes: (a) the duty to publish or otherwise make publicly available measures of general application affecting trade in services (PUB I); (b) when a member requires authorisation for the supply of a service, the duty to publish or otherwise make publicly available the information necessary for service suppliers or persons seeking to supply a service to comply with the requirements and procedures for obtaining, maintaining, amending and renewing such authorisation (PUB II); and (c) the duty to allow a reasonable interval between publication and entry into force of measures of general application affecting trade in services (REP).

---

[48]For example, the agreement between the EU and Central America.

[49]For example, the agreements between China and Australia, EU and Colombia, Peru and Ecuador and Japan and India.

Table 2 Disciplines on transparency of domestic regulations

	PUB I	PUB II	REP	ADP	OTC	NOT	POI	ENP
GATS	H	–	–	–	–	H	H	H
CMT2009	–	H	–	S	S	–	–	H
CPR2011	–	H	–			–	–	H
DRP2019	–	H	S	S	S	–	–	H
CHN-AUS	H	H	–	S	S	S	H	–
EU-ARM	H	–	H	S	H	–	H	H
JPN-PER	H	–	S	–	S	–	H	S
USA-PAN	H	–	S	S	S	S	H	H
CPTPP	H	–	S	S	S	S	H	H

"H": Hard, "S": Soft

Same as CMT2009

Minor changes in wording without altering the content, scope or enforceability of the discipline

Changes altering the content, scope or enforceability of the disciplines

Applicable to the services chapter only

As it stems from Table 2, the GATS already includes a hard obligation to publish measures of general application affecting trade in services (PUB I),[50] so none of the Article VI:4 draft texts include it. At regional level, all five PTAs examined include stand-alone chapters on transparency that include a provision that at least matches the one prescribed by GATS.

On the duty to publish the information necessary for obtaining, maintaining, amending and renewing an authorisation to supply a service (PUB II), there is divergence between the multilateral and regional level. The CMT2009 covered this duty, spelling out an open-ended list of items to be published, including applicable LRs and LPs, QRs and QPs and TSs, applicable procedures relating to appeals or reviews of decisions concerning application and the established timeframe for processing of an application.[51] The CMPR2011 reflects the fact that WTO Members reached an agreement to keep this provision on an *ad referendum* basis,[52] and the DRP2019 also includes a provision that keeps this duty under slightly modified terms.[53] At PTA level, however, none of the agreements reviewed

---

[50]Article III.1 and 2.

[51]Paragraph 13.

[52]Paragraph 13.

[53]Paragraph 13, Section II.

contain a similar provision in their services chapter but for the CHN-AUS PTA. Even in this case, the duty to publish refers only to licences, with no reference to qualifications or technical standards.[54] This is without prejudice from the fact that such duty is sometimes included in chapters for specific service sectors.[55]

By contrast, neither the GATS nor the CMT2009 include a duty to allow a reasonable interval between publication and entry into force of measures of general application affecting trade in services (REP). However, the DRP2019 does include such duty.[56] It is also included in the horizontal chapter on transparency of all the PTAs reviewed but for CHN-AUS.

3.3   Duty to Consult

The duty to consult includes: (a) the duty to publish in advance proposed measures of general application affecting trade in services (ADP), and (b) the duty to provide interested persons and other parties a reasonable opportunity to comment on such proposed measures before their adoption (OTC). A number of WTO Agreements include a duty to consult for product regulations, although in almost all cases the opportunity to comment is extended only to other Members and not to interested persons.[57] The GATS does not include a duty to consult. Extending the duty to consult to service regulations remains controversial, both because of the high implementation costs to be faced by those countries whose domestic legal systems do not include such duty, and the risk of capture of the regulatory process by foreign corporations to the detriment of the public interest.[58]

The CMT2009 draft text included a soft duty to provide reasonable opportunities for service suppliers to comment and to address collectively in writing substantive issues raised by the comments received.[59] But it was removed during the early 2011 scooping review exercise (CPR2011), revealing the lack of consensus among WTO Members on this matter.[60] The DRP2019 text reintroduced a soft duty to provide interested persons and other Members a reasonable opportunity to comment and to

---

[54]Article 8.18.2.

[55]See, e.g., Article 13.22, Telecommunications Chapter, CPTPP.

[56]Paragraph 20.

[57]See Article 2.9 WTO Agreement on Technical Barriers to Trade; paragraph 5, Annex B Agreement on Sanitary and Phytosanitary Measures; Article 1.4(b) Agreement on Import Licensing Procedures; and Article 2 of the Agreement on Trade Facilitation. The latter is the only case where the opportunity to make comments is extended to "traders and other interested parties".

[58]See Abugattas Majluf L (2006) Policy Paper on Trade in Services and Sustainable Development: Domestic Regulation. Domestic Regulation and the GATS: Challenges for Developing Countries, www.ictsd.org/downloads/2008/06/dom_reg.pdf.

[59]Paragraph 15.

[60]S/WPDR/W/45, at 23.

consider comments received,[61] triggering specific objections both from India[62] and the African Group of WTO Members.[63]

At PTA level, by contrast, the four largest players in trade in services are part to at least one PTA that includes a transparency chapter with a duty to provide reasonable opportunities for interested persons to comment on any proposal to adopt or amend any measure of general application. However, only the EU-ARM PTA includes a soft duty to take into consideration the comments received from interested persons with respect to any such proposal.[64] This is without prejudice of duties to consult included in chapters for specific service sectors such as financial services[65] and telecommunications.[66]

3.4 Duty to Inform

Finally, the duty to inform includes: (a) the duty to notify the other Party of any measure that the Party considers that affects the operation of the Agreement (NOT); (b) on request of the other Party, the duty to provide information and respond to questions pertaining to any actual or proposed measure that the other Party considers might materially affect the operation of this Agreement, whether or not the other Party has been previously notified of that measure (POI), and (c) the duty to establish or maintain appropriate mechanisms for responding to enquiries from service suppliers or persons seeking to supply a service regarding the information necessary to comply with the requirements and procedures for obtaining, maintaining, amending and renewing such authorisation (ENP).

With respect to this particular transparency duty, the risk of divergence is minimal because the GATS already includes all three sub-categories mentioned above[67] and there are only minor differences between them and those included in the PTAs reviewed. The only element of divergence relates to the duty to establish enquiry points. The GATS imposes a hard obligation on developed countries and, to the extent possible, on other Members, to supply information to service suppliers from developing countries.[68] The CMT2009 maintains the duty to establish enquiry

---

[61]Paragraphs 17 and 18, Section II.

[62]India's Comments on Communication JOB/SERV/268—Disciplines on Domestic Regulation (RD/SERV/145, 29/09/17) at 7.

[63]African Group Elements for Ministerial Decision, WT/MIN(17)/8, 4/12/17, para. 2.1.

[64]Article 309.2(c).

[65]For example, Annex 11-B, Section E of the CPTPP.

[66]For example, Article 13.22 of the CPTPP and 21.1 of USA-KOR includes a duty to consult that requires to make publicly available all relevant comments filed by interested persons and to respond to all significant and relevant issues raised in comments filed.

[67]Articles III.3, III.4 and IV.2.

[68]Article IIV.2.

points but extending its scope of application to all Members, irrespective of their development status.[69] In 2011, this was agreed by all Members on an *ad referendum* basis (CPR2011).[70] The DRP2019 includes a similar duty, but watered down by a footnote that acknowledges that resource constraints may be a factor in determining whether a mechanism for responding to enquiries is appropriate.[71] India objected this specific footnote arguing that it diluted the GATS obligation of developed countries to establish 'contact points' for service suppliers from developing countries.[72]

4   Disciplines on the Development of Domestic Regulations

4.1   Overview

Disciplines on the development of domestic regulations deal with standards of a substantive nature, i.e. relating to the content of regulations. As mentioned, the GATS simply includes a mandate for the development of minimum substantive standards for LPs, LPs, QRs, QPs and TSs. At multilateral level, the differences between the three draft texts produced in fulfilment of Article VI:4 mandate clearly suggests the lack of convergence among WTO Members on this matter.

At regional level, there are also major differences. As it stems from Table 3, out of the thirty PTAs reviewed, only twenty one include substantive standards for selected measures (ISS). Of the remaining nine that do not include such standards, six include a temporary obligation not to apply the relevant measures in a manner that would nullify or impair their specific commitments, equivalent to that prescribed by Article VI:5 of GATS (TNI). All U.S. PTAs include such standards, whereas only two of the six Chinese PTAs reviewed include them. The other PTAs without substantive standards include developing country parties.[73]

One provision that is particularly relevant is the duty to review the results of multilateral negotiations on disciplines on LRs and Ps, QRs and Ps and TSs pursuant to Article VI.4 of GATS, with a view to incorporating them into the PTA (DTR). Twenty out the thirty PTAs reviewed include such provision which, in theory, should pave the way for vertical convergence. However, because WTO negotiations are now conducted on a plurilateral rather than a multilateral basis, it remains unclear whether the conclusion of these negotiations would trigger this duty, particularly in those cases such as JPN-IND PTA, where only one of the parties participates in the plurilateral negotiations.

---

[69]Paragraph 14.

[70]S/WPDR/W/45, at 22.

[71]Paragraph 14, Section II.

[72]Comments by India on Co-Sponsors' Text on Disciplines on Domestic Regulation (WT/MIN(17)/ 7; WT/GC/190) (WT/MIN(17)/19, 5/12/17).

[73]EU-CARIFORUM, EU-COL-PER, EU-CENTRAM, JPN-IND and CAN-KOR.

Table 3 PTAs' disciplines on development of domestic regulations

	ISS	TNI	DTR		ISS	TNI	DTR
CHN-CRC	Y	–	Y	**JPN-CHE**	Y	–	Y
CHN-ISL	N	Y	Y	**JPN-IND**	N	Y	Y
CHN-CHE	Y	–	N	**JPN-PER**	Y	–	Y
CHN-KOR	N	Y	Y	**JPN-AUS**	Y	–	Y
CHN-AUS	N	Y	Y	**JPN-MNG**	Y	–	N
CHN-GEO	N	Y	Y	**USA-OMN**	Y	–	Y
EU-CARIFORUM	N	N	N	**USA-PER**	Y	–	Y
EU-KOR	Y	–	Y	**USA-COL**	Y	–	Y
EU-COL-PER	N	Y	Y	**USA-PAN**	Y	–	Y
EU-CEN	N	N	N	**USA-KOR**	Y	–	Y
CETA	Y	–	N	**USMCA**	Y	–	N
EU-ARM	Y	–	N	**CPTPP**	Y	–	Y
EU-JPN	Y	–	N	**AUS-IDN**	Y	–	Y
EU-SGP	Y	–	N	**CAN-KOR**	N	N	Y
EU-VNM	Y	–	N				
EU-MEX	Y	–	Y				

4.2 Substantive Standards

Table 4 compares the substantive standards for LRs, LPs, QRs, QPs and TSs included in the Article VI:4 draft texts and in the China, EU, Japan and U.S. PTAs with the most ambitious provisions on this matter.

The first aspect to consider is the scope of application of the substantive disciplines on domestic regulation. With respect to the measures covered, the mandate of Article VI:4 refers to measures relating to LRs, LPs, QRs, QPs and TSs but does not

Table 4 Substantive standards

	SCO	OTC	NEC	PRO	RIS	ENF
GATS	–	–	–	–	–	–
CMT2009	SC	Y	–	Y	Y	H
CPR2011	SC	Y	Y	Y	Y	H
DRP2019	SC	Y	–	Y	–	H
CHN-CHE	HR	Y	Y	Y	Y	S
EU-JPN	HR	Y	N	Y	N	H
JPN-MNG	HR	Y	Y	Y	N	H
USMCA	HR	Y	N	N	N	H
CPTPP	HR	Y	N	Y	Y	S

"SC": Specific Commitments; "HR": Horizontal, "Y": Yes, "N": No, "H": Hard, "S": Soft

Same as CMT2009

Minor changes in wording without altering the content, scope or enforceability of the discipline

Changes altering the content, scope or enforceability of the disciplines

define them. The CMT2009 provides definitions for each of them which in 2011 where agreed to on an *ad referendum* basis but for the case of technical standards.[74] The DRP2019 also refers to measures by Members relating to LRs, LPs, QRs, QPs and TSs affecting trade in services,[75] but does not provide a definition for of any of these measures. It also specifies that the disciplines do not apply to any terms, limitations, conditions, or qualifications set out in a Member's schedule pursuant to Articles XVI or XVII of the Agreement.[76] At regional level, only a few of the agreements reviewed include definitions for LRs, LPs, QRs and QPs but none of them defines the meaning of technical standards.[77]

The lack of a definition for technical standards leaves unresolved whether voluntary standards fall within the scope of the disciplines and if so, how Members can effectively discipline action by private actors outside the scope of the GATS.[78] This is a serious handicap for the liberalisation of trade in services considering that voluntary standards on services are growing fast and that they can act as market

---

[74]See CMT2009, paragraphs 5–9 and CPR2011, pp. 10–14.

[75]Paragraph 1 Section II.

[76]Paragraph 2 Section II.

[77]See EU-VNM, EU-SGP, EU-ARM and CETA.

[78]See CPR2011, p. 4.

entry barriers, particularly those imposed by leading firms concentrating large market power within Global Value Chains (GVCs).[79]

Notwithstanding the lack of a definition that expressly includes voluntary standards, some of the texts reviewed include provisions aimed at disciplining non-governmental organizations' standard setting processes. The CMT2009 encourages Members "... to ensure maximum transparency of relevant processes relating to the development and application of domestic and international standards by *non-governmental bodies* (emphasis added)".[80] However, during the early 2011 scooping review exercise, Members remained divided on the exact terms to use for such provision.[81] The DRP2019 also imposes an obligation on Members to encourage "... any body, including relevant international organizations, designated to develop technical standards to use open and transparent processes."[82] The reference to "...any body..", seems wide enough to include both domestic and international non-governmental organizations, particularly when the term is used in addition to "competent authorities". At regional level, similar provisions are included in USMCA[83] and EU-JPN.[84]

With respect to the sectors covered (SCO), as shown in Table 4, the multilateral and regional approaches differ. At multilateral level, the CMT2009 stipulates that the disciplines apply to measures by Members relating to LRs, LPs, QRs, QPs and TSs affecting trade in services where specific commitments are undertaken (SC).[85] In 2011, WTO Members agreed on an *ad referendum* basis to limit the disciplines' scope of application to sectors were specific commitments are undertaken.[86] The DRP2019 also limits the application of the disciplines to sectors were specific commitments are undertaken.[87] It also includes two additional provisions that remain bracketed. One of them allows Members to negotiate adjustments to the sectoral application of the disciplines provided[88] and the other one clarifies that the disciplines shall also apply to sectoral preferences that have been notified pursuant to the Ministerial Decision on Preferential Treatment to Services and Service Suppliers of Least-Developed Countries (WT/L/847).[89]

By contrast, at regional level the substantive standards apply horizontally. As Table 4 shows, this is true both for PTAs that follow a positive list approach for specific commitments (CHN-CHE and JPN-MNG), and for those that follow a

---

[79]See Gari (2016).

[80]Paragraph 40.

[81]CPR2011, p. 41.

[82]Paragraph 21, Section II.

[83]Article 15.8.5.

[84]Article 8.32.

[85]Paragraph 10.

[86]CPR2011, at 16.

[87]Paragraph 7, Section I.

[88]Paragraph 8, Section I.

[89]Paragraph 9, Section I.

negative list approach (EU-JPN, USMCA, CPTPP). For the latter, it is specified that the disciplines do not apply to non-conforming measures included in the Annexes. The fact that PTAs de-link the scope of application of the substantive disciplines on domestic regulation from their specific market access and national treatment commitments, lends support to the argument that disciplines on domestic regulation are moving away from the narrower objective of protecting the value of specific commitments to a broader 'good governance' goal.

With respect to the substantive standards themselves, there are also major discrepancies both vertically and horizontally. As Table 4 indicates, the requirement to base the relevant measures on "objective and transparent criteria" (OTC) is the only one that is included in all the texts considered, with only minor variations in its phrasing. For example, the DRP2019 and USMCA clarify that "objective criteria" include criteria that may not be quantifiable, such as competence, ability to supply the service and environmental, social and health effects.[90] The only difference to note is that in the case of USMCA and EU-JPN, this particular substantive standard applies only to LRs, LPs, QRs and QPs but not to technical standards.[91]

The requirement that the relevant measures are "not more burdensome than necessary to ensure the quality of the service" (NEC) is, by far, the most controversial one. The CMT2009 did not include it, but during the scooping exercise carried out in early 2011, proposals were tabled to add a necessity test and the matter remained unresolved.[92] Some WTO Members are ardent supporters of a necessity test for domestic regulations,[93] whereas others are strongly opposed to it.[94] The DRP2019 does not include such test, which seems to suggest that its demandeurs flexibilized their position in order to reach a plurilateral consensus. At regional level, while CHN-CHE and JPN-MNG include a necessity test, EU-JPN, USMCA and CPTPP do not.

Substantive requirements applicable to licensing and qualification procedures (PRO) vary both vertically and horizontally. The mandate of Article VI:4 refers only to licensing procedures stipulating that they must "not in themselves be a restriction on the supply of the service". At regional level, CHN-CHE, JPN-MNG and the CPTPP replicate this standard in these exact terms.[95] The CMT2009 extends the application of this standard to both LPs and QPs and adds that they must be "as simple as possible".[96] The extension of this standard to QPs is particularly relevant

---

[90] See footnote 16, DRP2019 and Article 15.8.2(a), USMCA.

[91] Article 8.30 EU-JPN and Article 15.8.2 USMCA.

[92] See the multiple alternatives suggested for the necessity test in CPR2011, pp. 7 and 18.

[93] See proposal from Chile; Hong Kong, China; The Republic Of Moldova; Peru; New Zealand And Switzerland in WT/MIN(17)/7/Rev.2, 13/12/17, para 6.3.

[94] Most developing countries, but also Canada and the U.S.

[95] Article 8.7.3 CHN-CHE, Article JPN-MNG and Article CPTPP.

[96] Paras 17 and 31.

for developing countries with a strong competitive advantage on professional services. However, during the early 2011 review, some WTO Members tabled proposals to dilute these provisions and others to enhance them.[97] The DRP2019 also applies this standard to both LPs and QPs but slightly changing the wording by stipulating that "the procedures do not in themselves unjustifiably prevent fulfilment of requirements".[98] USMCA follows this wording as well.[99] The EU-JPN also adds that both LPs and QPs "shall be clear, made public in advance and be such as to ensure that the applications are dealt with objectively and impartially".[100]

A few WTO Members tabled a proposal to add a substantive standard to prevent gender discrimination on the supply of services.[101] Such proposal did not gain multilateral consensus. India, for example, questions that gender is a trade related issue which can be meaningfully addressed through DR disciplines.[102] The DRP2019 includes the proposal, but as of December 2019 the text remains bracketed.[103] At regional level, none of the PTAs examined include such criteria.

Only a few of the texts reviewed assign a minor role to international standards for the development of domestic regulations (RIS). The CMT2009 includes a soft provision on this matter applicable only for technical standards: "Where technical standards are required and relevant international standards exist or their completion is imminent, Members should take them or the relevant parts of them into account in formulating their technical standards, except when such international standards or relevant parts would be an ineffective or inappropriate means for the fulfilment of national policy objectives."[104] During the early 2011 review, Members failed to endorse this provision. Some Members were of the opinion that rather than "take into account", Members should "base" technical standards on relevant international standards where available.[105] The DRP2019 does not include any obligation on

---

[97]CPR2011, p. 25.

[98]Para 22(c), Section II.

[99]Article 15.8.2(c).

[100]Article 8.31.1.

[101]See proposal from Albania; Argentina; Australia; Canada; Chile; Colombia; The European Union; Iceland; The Republic of Kazakhstan; Liechtenstein; The Former Yugoslav Republic of Macedonia; Mexico; The Republic of Moldova; Montenegro; New Zealand; Norway; Pakistan; Panama; Paraguay; Peru; The Russian Federation; Switzerland; Ukraine and Uruguay in WT/MIN (17)/7/Rev.2, 13/12/17, para 6.2. The wording of the proposal reads as follows: "With a view to promoting women's economic empowerment, where a Member adopts or maintains measures relating to authorisation for the supply of a service, the Member shall ensure that such measures do not discriminate against women".

[102]Comments by India on Co-Sponsors' Text on Disciplines on Domestic Regulation (WT/MIN (17)/7; WT/GC/190), para 8.

[103]See para 22(d), Section II.

[104]Paragraph 41.

[105]CPR2011, p. 43.

this matter. At regional level, only CHN-CHE[106] and CPTPP[107] offer a weak incentive to apply international standards of relevant international organizations. Both agreements provide that when a Party applies such standards, "account shall be taken" of them in determining whether such Party is in conformity with the obligations on domestic regulation. This restrained use of international standards for disciplining domestic measures contrasts with that prescribed by WTO disciplines applicable to product regulations.[108]

Finally, in terms of their enforceability (ENF), the evidence suggests that save for two PTAs, there is both vertical and horizontal convergence. As it stems from Table 4, in all three Article VI:4 texts, disciplines on substantive standards are drafted in hard terms ('... shall ensure...'). At regional level, JPN-MNG,[109] EU-JPN[110] and USMCA draft them in hard terms ("... shall ensure...), whereas the CPTPP ("... shall endeavour to ensure...")[111] and CHN-CHE ("... shall aim to ensure...")[112] draft them in soft terms.

4.3 Good Regulatory Practices

The most recent EU PTAs, CPTPP and USMCA have taken a further step with respect to disciplines on the development of domestic regulations. In addition to substantive standards, they also include a set of requirements applicable to the rule-making process known as "Good Regulatory Practices". Notwithstanding some variations among these PTAs, the extent of such requirements tends to cover the whole regulatory cycle, including transparency and public consultation requirements, regulatory impact analysis, interagency coordination and compatibility, and ex-post scrutiny of judicial or administrative review. Their aim is to avoid unnecessary, duplicative or inefficient regulations through evidence-based and coherent decision-making.

Tracing the origins of these good regulatory practices, Han-Wei Liu & Ching-Fu Lin identified the U.S. as the primary driving force behind them.[113] They note that such practices mirror key elements of the U.S. Administrative Procedure Act enacted

---

[106] Article 8.7.4.

[107] Article 10.8.3.

[108] See, for example, Article 2.4 and 2.5 of the TBT Agreement, and 3.1 and 3.2 of the SPS Agreement.

[109] Article 7.8.3 JPN-MNG.

[110] Articles 8.30 and 8.31 EU-JPN.

[111] Article 10.8.3 CPTPP.

[112] Article 8.7.3 CHN-CHE.

[113] Han-Wei and Ching-Fu (2017).

in 1946 and subsequent Presidential Executive Orders.[114] They also show how the U.S. pushed for their inclusion in trade agreements at both multilateral and regional levels,[115] and how western-led international organisations such as APEC, the OECD and the World Bank actively contributed to their diffusion.[116]

At multilateral level, the use of Good Regulatory Practices has gained some traction but only with reference to product regulations.[117] Neither the GATS nor the Article VI:4 texts refer to them in any shape or form. At regional level, only four of the thirty PTAs examined—CPTPP, EU-JPN, EU-MEX and USMCA—have included stand-alone chapters on Good Regulatory Practices that apply to measures of general application adopted at central government level related to *any* matter covered by the agreements with which compliance is mandatory.[118] In the case of the CPTPP, the disciplines apply only to "covered regulatory measures" determined by each Party.[119]

Table 5 illustrates the extent of Good Regulatory Practices per agreement. The data shows that provisions on such practices are quite detailed and demanding across all PTAs. In addition to duties relating to transparency, public consultation, regulatory impact assessment and retrospective evaluations, they all include an obligation to establish internal processes to facilitate an effective interagency coordination among domestic authorities in the development of regulations to identify potential overlaps between proposed and existing regulations, and prevent the creation of inconsistent requirements across domestic authorities. Most of them also include an obligation to establish and maintain a national or central coordinating body for this purpose.

---

[114]Han-Wei and Ching-Fu (2017) cite, inter alia, the following examples: Reagan's Presidential Executive Order 12291 of 17 February 1981 implementing a mandatory Regulatory Impact Analysis (RIA); replaced by Clinton's Executive Order 12866 of 30 September 1993. The latter strengthened the RIA process and introduced a centralized planning mechanism providing for early interagency coordination to avoid inconsistency, incompatibility, or duplication among various regulations adopted by federal agencies. The interagency coordination was to a entrusted to a central coordinating body, the Office of Management and Budget (OMB), with the advisory assistance of its Office of Information and Regulatory Affairs (OIRA).

[115]Han-Wei and Ching-Fu (2017), pp. 15–23.

[116]See, e.g., the APEC-OECD Integrated Checklist on Regulatory Reform (2005), a voluntary tool to evaluate regulatory reforms checklist aimed at promoting efficiency, transparency and accountability of regulations; the OECD—Recommendation of the Council on Regulatory Policy and Governance (2012), available at https://www.oecd.org/gov/regulatory-policy/2012-recommendation.htm.

[117]For example, the most recent TBT triennial reviews include thematic sessions that illustrate about Members' practice on this matter. See in particular sixth, seventh and eighth TBT triennial reviews. See also G/TBT/26, 13 November 2009, paras. 8–9.

[118]Four other EU PTAs reviewed include a single provision on good regulatory practice and administrative behaviour which expresses the consent of the Parties to cooperate in promoting regulatory quality and performance, including through exchange of information and best practices on their respective regulatory reform processes and regulatory impact assessments. See Article 14.7 EU-VNM, Article 13.7 EU-SGP, Article 12.7 EU-KOR and Article 313 EU-ARM.

[119]Article 25.1, CPTPP.

Table 5 Good regulatory practices

	Interagency coordination	Central coordinating body	Transparency	Early planning	Public consultation	Impact assessment	Use of plain language	Retrospective evaluation	Regulatory register	Subject to dispute settlement
CPTPP	✓	✓	✓	✓	–	✓	✓	✓	✓	NO
EU-JAP	✓	–	✓	✓	✓	✓	–	✓	–	NO
EU-MEX	✓	✓	✓	✓	✓	✓	–	✓	✓	NO
USMCA	✓	✓	✓	✓	✓	✓	✓	✓	✓	YES

The USMCA is the PTA that includes the more extensive provisions on this matter.[120] It is also the only one which allows the parties to have recourse to dispute settlement for the breach of provisions on Good Regulatory Practices, although claims for this purpose are limited only to address "a sustained or recurring course of action or inaction that is inconsistent with a provision of this Chapter".[121] Other than this, there tends to be a high degree of convergence on the extent of disciplines on this area. But it is important to highlight that such convergence is limited only to four agreements. None of the Chinese PTAs, nor the Japanese PTAs (other than EU-JPN) and certainly not the Article VI:4 texts include provisions on Good Regulatory Practices, and it is unlikely that convergence on this matter could be achieved any time soon, for at least two reasons.

First, wide differences in regulatory infrastructure across countries are a key obstacle to convergence. While the Good Regulatory Practices examined are already embedded in the domestic administrative legal systems of the U.S. and other OECD countries,[122] that is not the case for the majority of developing and least developed countries.[123] Most of them would need to undertake costly reforms to align their rule-making processes to these requirements, beyond their means or outside their development priorities. With this in mind, it is extremely unlikely that multilateral consensus could be reached for the adoption of this kind of disciplines without generous development provisions suitable to address the special needs of the majority of WTO members. At regional level, due to asymmetries in bargaining power, these disciplines could end up being imposed on developing countries without proper special and differential treatment to compensate for disparate needs.[124]

Second, these disciplines closely resemble the Anglo-American regulatory model. They reflect values and governance patterns which are not necessarily shared in other regions of the world characterized by very different economic, social, political and institutional environments. Detractors argue that there is no one-size-fits-all approach model to regulation and that it would be inconvenient to prescribe a single regulatory model because it would close off important options and space for legitimate policy and regulatory innovation.[125] And although, theoretically, the observance of common rule-making practices should contribute to mitigate regulatory divergence and foster regulatory compatibility, so far there is no empirical evidence available specifically on this matter.

---

[120]See Chapter 28 USMCA.

[121]Article 28.20 USMCA.

[122]See OECD Regulatory Policy Outlook 2018, available at https://read.oecd-ilibrary.org/governance/oecd-regulatory-policy-outlook-2018_9789264303072-en#page5.

[123]See World Bank's Worldwide Governance Indicators, available at http://info.worldbank.org/governance/wgi/index.aspx#home.

[124]The case of Vietnam in the CPTPP could entail a risk of forced regulatory alignment, although such risk is minimized by the fact that the parties to define the scope of application of these disciplines.

[125]Disciplines on Domestic Regulation African Group Elements for Ministerial Decision, WT/MIN (17)/8, 4 December 2017.

5 Disciplines on the Administration of Domestic Regulations

5.1 Overview

Disciplines on the administration of domestic regulations prescribe minimum standards of a procedural nature, i.e. relating to the application, administration and review of domestic regulations. The analysis in this section is limited to procedural standards to be observed by the regulator when processing applications for an authorisation to supply services. Minimum standards for the administration of measures of general application affecting trade in services and for the independent review of administrative decisions affecting trade in services are not considered.[126]

At the outset, it is important to highlight a controversy surrounding the extent of the mandate of Article VI:4 for the development of procedural disciplines on authorisation processes that is obstructing the achievement of multilateral convergence on this matter. On the one hand, Article VI:4 mandates Members to develop disciplines on measures relating, inter alia, to licensing and qualification procedures designed to demonstrate compliance with licensing and qualification requirements. On the other hand, Article VI.3 of GATS prescribes due process obligations for processing applications for authorization to supply services, namely, (a) duty to inform the applicant of the decision within a reasonable period of time after a complete submission of an application; and (b) duty to provide, at the request of the applicant, information concerning the status of the application. The question, therefore, is how far can Members go in developing procedural disciplines in fulfilment of Article VI:4, in light of the final agreement on procedural obligations for authorisation processes prescribed by Article VI:3. The matter is further complicated by the DRP2019 which structures all the procedural disciplines with reference to the authorisation to supply services.[127] India argues that other than the two specific obligations prescribed by Article VI:3, there are neither other disciplines nor mandate for negotiating disciplines on authorization.[128] As a result, India is of the view that the inclusion of procedural disciplines on authorisation processes in the DRP2019, falls outside the remit of the mandate of Article VI.4.[129]

---

[126]In the GATS these standards are prescribed by Articles VI.1 and VI.2. In most PTAs these standards are included in horizontal Transparency or Anti-corruption chapters and their scope of application is extended to laws, regulations, procedures and administrative rulings of general application on any mattered covered by the Agreement.

[127]Paragraph 3, Section II defines authorisation as the "means the permission to supply a service, resulting from a procedure a person must adhere to in order to demonstrate compliance with licensing requirements, qualification requirements or technical standards."

[128]Comments by India on Co-Sponsors' Text on Disciplines on Domestic Regulation (WT/MIN (17)/7; WT/GC/190), WT/MIN(17)/19, 5/12/17, paragraph 2.1.

[129]Ibid.

Table 6 displays the results of the review of the procedural standards to be observed by the regulator when processing applications for an authorisation to supply services included in the GATS, the three Article VI:4 texts and in those PTAs with the most ambitious provisions on this matter for China, the EU, Japan and the U.S. It also specifies whether the disciplines are phrased in hard terms (i.e. 'shall') or soft terms (e.g. 'to the extent possible'). The review does not consider the minimum due process standards for processing applications for authorisation to supply telecommunication services, financial services and applications for visas, permits and other documents necessary for temporary entry included in specific chapters for Telecommunications, Financial Services and Movement of Natural Persons.

Two general observations stand out. First, it is apparent that the extent of the disciplines included in the Article VI:4 texts and in the PTAs go a long way beyond GATS disciplines, including much more comprehensive provisions not just on the processing of application *strictu sensu*, but also on many other procedural and institutional matters, ranging from application timeframes to licensing fees and the independence of the decision maker.

Second, the scope of application of the disciplines on authorisation (SCO) are very similar to those corresponding to the disciplines on the development of domestic regulations observed above, i.e. at multilateral level, GATS disciplines and the three Article VI:4 texts limit their scope of application to sectors where specific commitments have been undertaken (SC), whereas at regional level, all PTAs but CHN-CHE, apply the disciplines horizontally across all sectors. This provides further evidence that the centre of gravity of recent PTAs is moving away from the narrow task of weeding out quantitative restrictions and discriminatory measures from international trade in services, to a more ambitious endeavour to promote good governance of service markets.

For the sake of clarity, the analysis that follows groups the disciplines in three different categories: (a) procedural standards applicable to the submission of applications (Sect. 5.2 below); (b) procedural standards applicable to the processing of applications *strictu sensu* (Sect. 5.3 below), and (c) other procedural requirements (Sect. 5.4 below).

5.2   Submission of Applications

Disciplines relating to the submission of applications include the duty to avoid requiring an applicant to approach more than one competent authority for each application for authorisation, i.e. a Single Window Requirement (SWI); duty to permit the submission of an application at any time (AAT); the duty to allow applicants a reasonable period for the submission of an application when specific time periods for applications exist (RPS); the duty to accept applications in electronic format (AEF) and the duty to accept authenticated copies of documents (AAC).

Table 6 Disciplines on authorisation process

	Submission of applications					Processing of applications							Other pro req			
	SWI	AAT	RPS	AEF	AAC	PIT	IAS	PAR	IAD	IAE	IAR	WUD	FAR	EFI	IFS	SCO
GATS	–	–	–	–	–		H		H				–	–	–	SC
CMT2009	S	S	H	S	S	S	–	H	–	H	S	H	H	H	H	SC
CPR2011	SC		H	S	S		–	H	–	S	S	H	H	H	H	SC
DRP2019	S	S	H	S	H	S	H	H	H	H	S	H	H	H	H	SC
CHN-CHE	–	–	–	–	–	H	H	H	H	H	H	H	H	–	–	SC
EU-MEX	–	S	H	S	H	S	H	H	H	S	S	H	H	H	–	HR
JPN-AUS	–	–	–	–	–	–	H	H	H	S	H	–	–	–	–	HR
USMCA	S	S	H	S	H	S	H	H	H	S	S	H	H	H	H	HR
CPTPP	–	–	H	–	S	S	H	H	H	S	S	S	H	H	–	HR

"H": Hard, "S": Soft "SC" Specific Commitments "HR" Horizontal

Same as CMT2009

Minor changes in wording without altering the content, scope or enforceability of the discipline

Changes altering the content, scope or enforceability of the disciplines

All these disciplines are included in the CMT2009. During the early 2011 scooping review exercise, Members agreed to maintain the duty to allow applicants a reasonable period for the submission of an application (RPS) on an *ad referendum* basis, and proposed alternatives to the duty to establish a single window (SWI), accept documents in electronic format (AEF) and accept authenticated copies of documents (AAC) that introduced only minor changes. The main discrepancy revolved around the use of hard or soft language for phrasing the duty to permit the submission of an application at any time (AAT). Ten years later, the DRP2019 includes all these disciplines in almost identical terms as the CMT2009, with the sole difference that instead of separate duties for licensing procedures and qualification procedures, it includes a single duty for authorisation processes.

At regional level, apart from USMCA, none of the PTAs go as far as the DRP2019. The CHN-CHE and JPN-AUS agreements do not include any of these disciplines. This appears to suggest that some countries have been more forthcoming in their plurilateral negotiations than in their PTA negotiations.

5.3 Processing of Applications

Disciplines on the processing of applications *strictu sensu* include the duty to provide an indicative timeframe for processing an application (PIT); duty to provide, at the request of the applicant, information concerning the status of the application (IAS); duty to process applications within a reasonable timeframe (PAR); duty to inform the applicant of the decision within a reasonable period of time after a complete submission of an application (IAD); duty to inform applicant and provide opportunity to correct minor errors and omissions in the application (IAE); duty to inform, upon request, reasons for rejection of application (IAR) and duty to ensure that authorisation, once granted, enters into effect without undue delay (WUD).

Again, all these disciplines are included in the CMT2009 other than the duty to provide, at the request of the applicant, information concerning the status of the application (IAS) and the duty to inform the applicant of the decision within a reasonable period of time after a complete submission of an application (IAD), which are already prescribed by Article VI:3 of GATS. However, apart from the duty to process applications within a reasonable timeframe (PAR); none of the other disciplines outlived the early 2011 review exercise. Most of the disagreements revolved around the use of hard or soft language to phrase such disciplines. The DRP2019 keeps the same duties included in the CMT2009 but applicable to authorisation processes instead of licensing or qualification procedures. At regional level, apart from JPN-AUS, all PTAs include all these disciplines with only minor differences on their enforceability.

5.4   Other Procedural Requirements

Other procedural requirements include disciplines on fees, i.e. the duty to ensure that fees are reasonable, transparent and not in themselves restrict the supply of the service (FAR); disciplines on the assessment of qualifications; i.e. the duty to schedule examinations at frequent intervals (EFI) and, finally, duties on independence, i.e. the duty to ensure that the competent authority reaches and administers its decisions in a manner independent from any supplier of the services for which authorization is required (IFS).

The CMT2009 included all these duties and phrased them in hard terms. But following the early 2011 scooping review exercise, none of them remain unchanged. Alternative proposals were tabled to reduce the scope of application of the duties on fees, and to carve out fees charged for a variety of public purposes. Alternative proposals were also tabled to the duty referred to the independence of the decision maker from the service suppliers applying for authorisation. At regional level, none of the PTAs reviewed but for USMCA include a duty to ensure the independence of the decision maker, the CHN-CHE PTA only includes the one on fees, and the JPN-AUS agreement does not include any of them.

All in all, and save for the minor discrepancies identified above, the data shows a significant degree of both vertical and horizontal convergence on disciplines on the administration of domestic regulations. The procedural disciplines included in the CMT2009 are almost identical to those included in the DRP2019. In its turn, the procedural disciplines included in the USMCA, which is the most ambitious of all the PTAs reviewed on this matter, are almost identical to those included in the DRP2019. JPN-AUS and CHN-CHE include less duties than those proposed by the DRP2019 but, given that the parties to these PTAs are also sponsoring the DRP2019, this should not be a source of divergence.

However, the case for multilateral convergence for disciplines on the administration of domestic regulations is not there yet. First, the disciplines reviewed appear to assume the existence of an ideal bureaucratic model for the development, administration, application and review of domestic regulations that all countries should aspire to achieve. Yet, in reality, rather than a purely technical and neutral matter, the specific features of any national administrative system are influenced by diverse, and frequently opposing, interests. Also, differences in countries' institutional, social, cultural and developmental circumstances are apparent and, inevitably, they too will have a bearing on the specific features of each country's administrative system. Thus, it remains to be seen whether these minimum due process obligations are also good for developing countries with completely different institutional capacities and regulatory traditions.

Second, it is unquestionable that the path to convergence will have different costs for different countries. Less developed countries will have to undertake profound domestic reforms in order to align their domestic legal systems with these international obligations, compared with developed Parties, whose domestic administrative systems already mirror most, if not all, of the standards required by these obligations.

Finally, the rise and extent of procedural disciplines on domestic regulation on services is part of a broader trend of using international law to prescribe rules and standards that control national administrative conduct.[130] Some scholars have raised concerns about the merits of this trend. Cassesse argues that it paves the way for an intrusion of global rules on national administrations.[131] These international norms, he argues, penetrate domestic legal systems, thus having an effect on national administrative, laws without passing through the filters of national law, which transform them into national rules, before they discipline domestic administrations.[132] Cassesse also argues that subjecting national administrations to both domestic and international rule of law is problematic, because administrative governance should find its source exclusively in national law.[133]

From a strictly functional perspective, it goes without saying that disciplines on the administration of domestic regulations equip trade agreements with a far more sophisticated set of legal tools to address trade restrictions caused by unnecessary red tape, unreasonable and inconsistent administrative practices, delays or arbitrary handling of authorisation process, differences or simply lack of information about authorisation processes across jurisdictions. However, for the reasons just explained, the case for using international trade agreements as drivers of convergence of domestic administrations to this extent remains debatable.

6 Special and Differential Treatment for Developing Countries

The extent and eligibility for special and differential treatment for developing countries is, without a doubt, one of the major obstacles to secure multilateral support for the adoption of the disciplines on domestic regulation examined above. It has always been acknowledged that WTO Members at lowers levels of development should be accorded some flexibility to comply with trade rules in accordance with their particular development, financial and trade needs. However, the sharp economic rise of some developing countries, has sparked an acrimonious debate over differentiated rights and obligations between developed and developing countries, turning it into one of the most contentious issues currently faced by the multilateral trading system.[134] Inevitably, this controversy has affected the negotiations of disciplines on domestic regulation.

---

[130]See Hepburn J, Global Administrative Law and the Role of Domestic Administrative Lawyers. AdminLawBlog, 29 November 2017, https://adminlawblog.org/2017/11/29/global-administrative-law-and-the-role-of-domestic-administrative-lawyers/.

[131]See Cassesse (2005), p. 113.

[132]Ibid, at 112.

[133]Ibid.

[134]See contrasting views between Communication from U.S. An Undifferentiated WTO: Self-Declared Development Status Risks Institutional Irrelevance (WT/GC/W/757, 16/01/19), and Communication from China, India, South Africa and The Bolivarian Republic of Venezuela: The Continued Relevance of Special and Differential Treatment in Favour of Developing Members to Promote Development and Ensure Inclusiveness (WT/GC/W/765, 18/02/19).

The main concerns raised by many developing countries on this particular matter are twofold: the risk of imposing a single regulatory model to very diverse institutional contexts, unduly interfering with the right to regulate the supply of services, and the lack of clear evidence about the costs and benefits of these disciplines, particularly for developing countries suffering from institutional weaknesses and resource' constraints.[135]

Differences on export capacity and institutional development lie at the heart of this controversy. It is net service exporters across sectors and modes of supply who are more likely to reap the benefits of stringent rules on domestic regulations. Understandably, net service importers are less keen to undertake new obligations designed to create new market opportunities they are unlikely to tap on. In addition, variations on the degree of development and sophistication of regulatory infrastructure, government resources and capacities across WTO Members will result in an uneven distribution of implementation costs, with some of them having to face much higher costs in adjusting their domestic legal systems to international benchmarks on domestic regulations than others.

The CMT2009 includes a chapter with five provisions on special and differential treatment for developing countries that remained almost entirely unsettled after the early 2011 scooping review exercise. Paragraph 42 of the CMT2009, stipulates a longer phase-in period for developing countries to implement the disciplines based on their level of development, size of the economy and regulatory and institutional capacity, but it does not define the extent of such period. During the early 2011 review exercise, some countries tabled proposals to tighten this provision (e.g. fix the transitional period to 1 year, with the possibility to apply for an extension but subject to stringent conditions), while others tabled proposals to flexibilize it even further (e.g. a transitional period of 5–7 years, with the possibility of extension if the developing country Member considers that it still faces particular difficulties which impair its ability to implement the disciplines).[136]

Paragraph 43 of the CMT2009 includes a soft obligation to accord reduced administrative fees to service suppliers from developing country Members, while paragraph 44 obliges Members to consider longer phase-in periods for the introduction of new LRs, LPs, QRs, QPs and TSs in service sectors and modes of supply of export interest to developing country Members, if circumstances so allow to do it. Yet again, during the 2011 review exercise, multiple proposals were tabled to water down these obligations.[137]

Paragraph 45 of the CMT2009 imposes a hard obligation on Developed country Members, and to the extent possible, on other Members, to provide technical assistance to developing country Members aimed, *inter alia*, at developing and

---

[135]Disciplines on Domestic Regulation African Group Elements for Ministerial Decision, WT/MIN (17)/8, 4 December 2017.

[136]CPR2011, pp. 45 and 46.

[137]CPR2011, pp. 47 and 48.

strengthening their institutional and regulatory capacities to implement these disciplines, but during the review exercise, Members could not agree on whether the obligation should be phrased on hard or soft terms.[138] Finally, paragraph 46 includes the only provision agreed on an *ad referendum* basis by all WTO Members, namely, a total exemption for Least Developed Countries (LDCs) from the obligation to apply the disciplines.[139]

According to the African Group, the 2009 negotiations ceased because developed countries could not agree to the proposed Special and Differential Treatment provisions, while the 2011 negotiations ceased because such provisions were significantly diminished, and developing countries were opposed to discarding the 2009 text.[140]

The DRP2019 includes a transitional period for Developing Countries that is more restrictive than the one included in the CMT2009. Akin to the technique used in the Agreement on Trade Facilitation,[141] the provision allows developing country Members to designate *ex ante* those specific provisions which would require a transitional period after the entry into force of the agreement for their implementation.[142] It also envisages the possibility of limiting the scope of the designation to individual services sectors or subsectors. However, the exact extension of the transitional period remains bracketed.[143]

Like the CMT2009, the DRP2019 exempts LDCs from the disciplines, further stipulating that upon graduation of their LDC status they would still be entitled to request transitional periods for their implementation.[144] It also includes a provision encouraging developed and developing country Members, in a position to do so, to provide specific technical assistance and capacity building to developing country Members and in particular LDCs, upon their request and on mutually agreed terms and conditions aimed, inter alia, to implement these disciplines.[145]

By contrast, at regional level, the CPTPP is the only one that includes some flexibilities that take into account the different levels of economic development of the Parties, but not specifically related to disciplines on domestic regulation. CPTPP Parties also acknowledge the importance of cooperation and capacity building activities and commit to undertake and strengthen these activities to assist in implementing the Agreement and enhancing its benefits.[146] But when it comes to define the resources to fund such activities, the agreement simply states that "... the

---

[138]CPR2011, p. 49.

[139]See CPR2011, p. 50.

[140]Disciplines on Domestic Regulation African Group Elements for Ministerial Decision, WT/MIN (17)/8, 4 December 2017.

[141]See Agreement on Trade Facilitation, Section II.

[142]Paragraph 12, Section I.

[143]Paragraph 12, Section I.

[144]Paragraph 13, Section I.

[145]Paragraph 14, Section I.

[146]Article 21.1 CPTPP.

Parties shall work to provide the appropriate financial or in-kind resources for cooperation and capacity building activities. . .".[147]

In sum, to redress the asymmetrical distribution of implementation costs among WTO Members, the disciplines on domestic regulation should be complemented with international assistance for domestic regulatory reforms but, multilateral agreement on the eligibility and extent for such assistance remains elusive, and at regional level the matter remains unaddressed.

7 Conclusions

This paper compared the disciplines on domestic regulations affecting trade in services included in a sample of thirty PTAs entered into by China, EU, Japan and the U.S. with the draft texts negotiated pursuant to Article VI:4 GATS mandate at multilateral (CMT2009, CPR2011) and plurilateral level (DRP2019).

Save for some minor differences, the study identified a significant degree of convergence between the disciplines adopted at regional level with those currently negotiated at plurilateral level (DRP2019). With respect to the substantive standards, the main difference lies on the disciplines' scope of application. At regional level, they apply horizontally, whereas at plurilateral level they apply only where specific commitments are undertaken. Another difference relates to the highly controversial necessity test. While two of the PTAs reviewed include a necessity test phrased in hard terms, the DRP2019 does not include such test. With respect to the procedural requirements, the duty to ensure that the competent authority reaches and administers its decisions in a manner independent from any supplier of the services for which authorization is required, is included in the DRP2019, but absent in all the PTAs reviewed other than the USMCA.

At the same time, the study identified key obstacles that are standing against a multilateral agreement on this matter. Such obstacles revolve around the duty to consult, the necessity test, a few procedural requirements and, in particular, the extent and eligibility for special and differential treatment for developing countries. Many developing countries argue forcibly against the duty to grant interested persons, including foreign corporations, the right to comment on regulatory proposals on services for fear of regulatory capture. They are also extremely concerned about the potential impact of the necessity test on the right to regulate the supply of services and the risk of imposing a single regulatory model to very diverse institutional contexts. They condition the adoption of such disciplines to the provision of generous technical assistance to meet the implementation costs they would generate.

Finally, the paper argued that the risk of trade diversion that could be generated by the disciplines on domestic regulation adopted at regional or plurilateral level is extremely low. First, in most cases the disciplines are phrased in soft terms, giving

---

[147] Article 21.5 CPTPP.

countries plenty of flexibility to decide how and when to comply with them. Second, those sponsoring the plurilateral negotiations account for 57% of world exports of commercial services (seventy six cent including the U.S.) and have pledged to incorporate the results of the negotiations into their GATS schedules as additional commitments under Article XVIII of the Agreement (and thus extending the benefits of the disciplines on a Most Favoured Nation basis to WTO Members that have not participated in the negotiations). Finally, even those few PTA disciplines that go beyond those included in the DRP2019 are, for practical reasons, applied *de facto*, on an MFN basis as it may prove impossible to exclude certain foreign suppliers from the benefits of an improved regulatory environment.

The chances for trade divergence may be generated not by the disciplines on domestic regulation examined in this paper but by new commitments on regulatory cooperation and mutual recognition of professional qualifications. As Mattoo argues, regulatory cooperation may lead to patterns of trade based on mutual trust rather than on comparative advantages.[148] This is particularly the case when regulatory cooperation goes beyond the mere exchange of information or best regulatory practices to formal agreements on joint supervision and enforcement of cross border activities. Areas where these "trade based on trust" patterns could arise are those where close cooperation between regulators is critical, e.g. financial services, data protection and movement of natural persons. By the same token, the conditions for the mutual recognition of the professions is something that can be applied on a discriminatory basis. Agreements such as CETA include advanced provisions on this matter. The preferential recognition of professional qualifications is clearly a preference with material implication for trade in professional services.

References

Acharya R (2016) Regional trade agreements and the multilateral trading system. Cambridge University Press, Cambridge

Araujo M (2014) Regulating services trade agreements – a comparative analysis of regulatory disciplines included in EU and US free trade agreements. Trade Law Dev 6(2):393–416

Cassesse S (2005) Global standards for national administrative procedure. Law Contemp Probl 68 (3):109–126

Crozet M, Milet E, Mirza D (2016) The impact of domestic regulations on international trade in services: evidence from firm-level data. J Comp Econ 44(3):585–607

Feketekuty G (1988) International trade in services. An overview and blueprint for negotiations. American Enterprise Institute and Ballinger, Cambridge

Gari G (2016) Is WTO approach to international standards on services outdated? J Int Econ Law 19 (3):589–605

Gari G (2020) Recent preferential trade agreements' disciplines for tackling regulatory divergence in services: how far beyond GATS? World Trade Rev 19(1):1–29

Han-Wei L, Ching-Fu L (2017) China and regulatory coherence: an uneasy relationship? Institute for International Law and Justice, New York

---

[148]Mattoo (2015), p. 11.

Hoekman B, Mattoo A (2013) Liberalizing trade in services: lessons from regional and WTO negotiations. European University Institute Working Papers, RSCAS 2013/34. European University Institute, Italy

Horn H et al (2010) Beyond the WTO? An anatomy of EU and US preferential trade agreements. World Econ 33(11):1565–1588

Kox H, Lejour A (2005) Regulatory heterogeneity as obstacle for international services trade. CPB discussion paper, no. 49. CPB, The Hague

Kox H, Nordås HK (2007) Services trade and domestic regulation. OECD trade policy working papers, no. 49. OECD Publishing, Paris

Kox H, Nordås HK (2009) FREIT trade working paper, no. 040. Regulatory harmonization and trade in services: volumes and choice of mode. https://freit.org//WorkingPapers/Papers/TradePolicyMultilateral/FREIT040.pdf

Krajewski M (2008) Article VI GATS. In: Wolfrum R, Stoll PT, Feinagule C (eds) WTO – trade in services, Max Planck Commentaries on world trade law, vol 6. Martinus Nijhoff, Leiden, pp 165–196

Latrille P, Juneyoung L (2012) Services rules in regional trade agreements. How diverse and how creative as compared to the GATS multilateral rules? WTO staff working paper ERSD-2012-19. WTO Economic Research and Statistic Division, Geneva

Mattoo A (2015) Services Trade and Regulatory Cooperation, E15 Initiative. International Centre for Trade and Sustainable Development (ICTSD) and World Economic Forum, Geneva

Mattoo A, Mishra D (2009) Foreign professionals in the United States: regulatory impediments to trade. J Int Econ Law 12(2):435–456

Nordås H (2016) Services Trade Restrictiveness Index (STRI): the trade effect of regulatory differences. OECD trade policy papers, no. 189. OECD Publishing, Paris

Ortino F, Lydgate E (2019) Addressing domestic regulation affecting trade in services in CETA, CPTPP and USMCA: revolution or timid steps? J World Investment Trade 20(5):680–704

Roy M, Marchetti J, Lim AH (2007) Services liberalization in the new generation of preferential trade agreements: how much further than the GATS? World Trade Rev 6(02):155–192

Schwellnus C (2007) The effects of domestic regulation on services trade revisited. CEPII working paper no. 2007–08. CEPII, Paris

Shingal A, Roy M, Sauve P (2018) Do WTO+ commitments in services trade agreements reflect a quest for optimal regulatory convergence? Evidence from Asia. World Econ 41(5):1223–1250

Van der Marel E, Shepherd B (2013) Services trade, regulation, and regional integration: evidence from sectoral data. World Econ 36(11):1393–1405

Gabriel Gari is a Reader in International Economic Law at the Centre for Commercial Law Studies, Queen Mary University of London and Academic Director of the LLM in International Economic Law. Prior to joining Queen Mary, Gabriel practised Employment and Commercial Law and worked for the Uruguayan Supreme Court of Justice. Gabriel holds degrees in Law and in Sociology from the University of the Republic (Uruguay), an LLM from the London School of Economics and a PhD from Queen Mary University of London. He is a member of the Latin American and Caribbean Research Network on Services, the Latin American Network on International Economic Law, the Society of International Economic Law and the European Society of International Law.

Privacy and Data Protection in the EU- and US-Led Post-WTO Free Trade Agreements

Svetlana Yakovleva

Contents

1 Introduction

Regulating privacy and personal data protection has traditionally been a prerogative of domestic legal regimes. These areas were traditionally outside the scope of international trade law. Until very recently, free trade agreements (FTAs), starting from the Marrakesh Agreement on the Establishment of the World Trade Organization (WTO),[1] referred to privacy and personal data protection as public policy

The author would like to thank Rudolf Adlung, Christoph Kiener, Markus Krajewski, Joanna Pocztowska, Oliver Prausmueller, Martin Roy and Benjamin Zasche.

[1]Marrakesh Agreement on the Establishment of the World Trade Organization (WTO) (WTO Agreement).

S. Yakovleva (✉)
Institute for Information Law (IViR), University of Amsterdam, Amsterdam, The Netherlands

De Brauw Blackstone Westbroek, Amsterdam, The Netherlands
e-mail: Mail@svyakovleva.com

R. T. Hoffmann, M. Krajewski (eds.), *Coherence and Divergence in Services Trade Law*, European Yearbook of International Economic Law,
https://doi.org/10.1007/978-3-030-46955-9_5

objectives that can justify derogation from a party's (or member's) commitments in trade in services, financial or telecommunications sectors. The WTO Agreement mentions the protection of privacy and(or) personal data in the general exception of Article XIV(c)(ii) of the General Agreement on Trade in Services[2] (GATS), exceptions in the GATS Annex on Telecommunications[3] and in the Understanding on Financial Services.[4] The EU- and US-led FTAs concluded after the WTO Agreement (post-WTO FTAs) and before 2018 generally followed the same path with the only difference that privacy and data protection also appeared in some e-commerce chapters.

As (personal) data and its unrestricted flows became an important ingredient of cross-border digital trade, regulating such flows as well as the protection of the rights to privacy and personal data protection, which is often viewed as reason to restrict the flows of personal data, gradually became contentious and politically sensitive issues in domestic and international trade politics.[5]

The European Union (EU) was one of the first to regulate cross-border transfers of personal data in the 1995 Data Protection Directive.[6] The recently adopted General Data Protection Regulation (GDPR)[7] further developed this framework by making it more robust on the one hand, and flexible on the other. Limitations on cross-border transfers under EU law are grounded in the protection of the rights to privacy and personal data as binding fundamental rights under the EU Charter of Fundamental Rights.[8] The EU privacy and data protection framework, arguably one of the strictest in the world, is deeply rooted in a European cultural preference for strong privacy protection and is viewed as integral part and key instantiation of the protection of human dignity.[9]

In short, under the GDPR, personal data can flow as freely as within the European Economic Area (EEA) to third countries that obtained a so-called adequacy decision from the European Commission, stating that they ensure an adequate level of

---

[2]General Agreement on Trade in Services, Annex 1B to the WTO Agreement.

[3]Article 5(d) GATS Annex on Telecommunication.

[4]Article B.8 of the 1994 Understanding on Commitments in Financial Services (Understanding).

[5]Wolfe (2019), p. s64.

[6]Directive 95/46/EC of the European Parliament and of the Council on the protection of individuals with regard to the processing of personal data and on the free movement of such data OJ 1995 L 281, 31.

[7]Regulation (EU) 2016/679 of the European Parliament and of the Council of 27 April 2016 on the protection of natural persons with regard to the processing of personal data and on the free movement of such data, and repealing Directive 95/46/EC, OJ 2016 L 119/1-88.

[8]Charter of Fundamental Rights of the European Union, OJ 2012 C 326.

[9]Article 1 of the EU Charter; Explanation on Article 1—Human dignity in Explanations Relating to the Charter of Fundamental Rights, OJ 2007 C 303/17, https://eur-lex.europa.eu/LexUriServ/LexUriServ.do?uri=OJ:C:2007:303:0017:0035:en:PDF; Opinion of the European Data Protection Supervisor (EDPS) 4/2015 Towards a New Digital Ethics Data, Dignity And Technology, p. 12, 11 September 2015; Rodota (2009), p. 80.

personal data protection (currently 13 countries,[10] including the EU-US Privacy Shield framework,[11] and the mutual adequacy arrangement with Japan[12]). Transfers of personal data to other countries are only allowed if the data exporter has implemented adequate safeguards, such as the standard contractual clauses (SCCs) approved by the European Commission, binding corporate rules for multinational companies or companies conducting joint economic activity, approved industry codes of conduct or certification.[13] If it is not reasonably possible for a data exporter to adopt any of the above-mentioned safeguards, it may rely on specific derogations of Article 49 GDPR, which include explicit consent of an individual, necessity of transfer for the conclusion or performance of a contract, or necessity for the establishment, exercise or defence of legal claims. The EU's "border control" approach to cross-border transfers of personal data has always been in sharp contrast with the US "open skies" policy in this domain.[14] Several scholars warned that it may even run afoul of the EU's WTO trade in services commitments.[15]

Shortly after the conclusion of the WTO agreement, negotiated before the proliferation of Internet, WTO members realised the importance of e-commerce for international trade. As the WTO Work Programme on E-Commerce, launched in 1998,[16] was not yielding any meaningful results, the negotiations on this issue have shifted to bi-lateral and regional fora. Starting from early 2000s, non-binding provisions on electronic commerce appeared in FTAs, which also often mentioned the protection of privacy and personal data.[17] With these provisions trading partners embarked on a learning curve that paved the way for the "next generation" of binding electronic commerce (or digital trade) provisions.[18]

In the spirit of its "digital trade" agenda, the United States has been a pioneer in including provisions on free cross-border data flows in international trade

---

[10]European Commission, Adequacy of the protection of personal data in non-EU countries https://ec.europa.eu/info/law/law-topic/data-protection/data-transfers-outside-eu/adequacy-protection-personal-data-non-eu-countries_en.

[11]Commission Implementing Decision (EU) 2016/1250 of 12 July 2016 pursuant to Directive 95/46/EC of the European Parliament and of the Council on the adequacy of the protection provided by the EU-U.S. Privacy Shield, OJ 2016 L207/1.

[12]European Commission, European Commission adopts adequacy decision on Japan, creating the world's largest area of safe data flows, 23 January 2019 http://europa.eu/rapid/press-release_IP-19-421_en.htm.

[13]Articles 40(2), 42(2), 46 GDPR.

[14]Svantesson (2011), p. 184; LeSieur (2012), pp. 101, 103, 104.

[15]Swire and Litan (1998), pp. 188–196. On the contrary, Shaffer argued that a hypothetical US claim regarding WTO inconsistency of EU's framework for personal data transfers "would likely not prevail." Shaffer (2000), pp. 46–51.

[16]WTO, Work programme on electronic commerce, WT/L/274, 30 September 1998.

[17]Burri (2017b), pp. 18 and 22.

[18]Wolfe (2019), p. s78.

agreements.[19] The United States first proposed a *binding* horizontal provision on free cross-border data flows in the drafts of the currently stalled Trans-Atlantic Trade and Investment Partnership (TTIP) and Trade in Services Agreement (TiSA).[20] This attempt later, as discussed in Sect. 5.2 below, proved successful in the negotiations of the Comprehensive and Progressive Trans-Pacific Partnership (CPTPP),[21] drafted before the US withdrawal from the Agreement,[22] the United States – Mexico – Canada Agreement (USMCA),[23] and the U.S. – Japan Digital Trade Agreement.[24] The e-commerce chapter of the CPTPP, and the digital trade chapter of the USMCA and the U.S. – Japan Digital Trade Agreement not only include a legally binding horizontal obligation on cross-border data flows, but also extensive provisions on the protection of privacy and personal information[25] (I will refer to these provisions jointly as "digital trade provisions"). In 2018, the European Commission reached a political agreement on the EU position on the model provisions for EU-led trade agreements on cross-border data flows. While tackling the same issues, the EU model provisions reserve a wide policy space for the protection of privacy and personal data as fundamental rights. These developments unfolded against the backdrop of an emerging patchwork of domestic rules hampering cross-border data flows, such as those adopted by Russia and China and are underway in India, Indonesia, Malaysia, Singapore and Chile.[26] The new digital trade provisions not only set boundaries on domestic restrictions on cross-border data flows, but also create a basis for regulatory cooperation.[27] On January 25, 2019, 76 members of the World Trade Organization (WTO) launched talks on electronic commerce, which,

---

[19]Burri (2017a), p. 99; Aaronson (2016), p. 59; Geist M (2018) Data rules in modern trade agreements: toward reconciling an open internet with privacy and security safeguards. CIGI International Policy Considerations, https://www.cigionline.org/articles/data-rules-modern-trade-agreements-toward-reconciling-open-internet-privacy-and-security.

[20]Le Roux (2017); Fontanella-Khan J., Data Protection Ruled out of EU-US Trade Talks, Financial Times, 4 November 2013.

[21]Comprehensive and Progressive Agreement for Trans-Pacific Partnership, 8 March, 2018, https://www.mfat.govt.nz/assets/Trans-Pacific-Partnership/Text/14.-Electronic-Commerce-Chapter.pdf.

[22]Letter from the Executive Office of the President, Office of the United States Trade Representative, 30 January 2017, https://ustr.gov/sites/default/files/files/Press/Releases/1-30-17%20USTR%20Letter%20to%20TPP%20Depositary.pdf.

[23]Agreement between the United States of America, the United Mexican States, and Canada (USMCA), signed 30 November 2018, https://ustr.gov/trade-agreements/free-trade-agreements/united-states-mexico-canada-agreement/agreement-between.

[24]United States – Japan Digital Trade Agreement, signed on 7 October 2019, https://ustr.gov/sites/default/files/files/agreements/japan/Agreement_between_the_United_States_and_Japan_concerning_Digital_Trade.pdf.

[25]"Personal information" is a U.S. law term for "personal data."

[26]Geist M (2018) Data rules in modern trade agreements: toward reconciling an open internet with privacy and security safeguards. CIGI International Policy Considerations, https://www.cigionline.org/articles/data-rules-modern-trade-agreements-toward-reconciling-open-internet-privacy-and-security.

[27]Wolfe (2019), pp. s65–s66.

among other things will cover rules on cross-border data flows and the protection of the rights to privacy and personal data.[28]

This chapter takes stock of the evolution of provisions on privacy and data protection in the post-WTO FTAs and FTAs currently under negotiation. It evaluates the trends and patterns of the development of these provisions and provides an outlook for the upcoming negotiations on electronic commerce at the WTO.

The analysis in this chapter relies on the EU-led FTAs concluded after 2000, which include provisions on e-commerce: the 2000 EU–Mexico economic partnership agreement[29] complemented by the 2001 EU–Mexico Joint Council Decision implementing this agreement[30] (collectively referred to as "EU-Mexico EPA"); the 2003 EU–Chile association agreement;[31] the 2012 EU–Central America association agreement;[32] the 2011 EU–Korea FTA;[33] the 2012 trade agreement between the EU, Colombia, and Peru;[34] the 2014 EU–Singapore FTA;[35] the 2016 EU–Canada Comprehensive Economic and Trade Agreement (CETA),[36] EU-Japan Economic

---

[28]European Commission, 76 WTO Partners Launch Talks on E-commerce, 25 January 2019, http://trade.ec.europa.eu/doclib/press/index.cfm?id=1974&title=76-WTO-members-launch-talks-on-e-commerce; Foroohar R., Nations Move to Avoid Global Ecommerce 'Splinternet', Financial Times, 24 January 2019.

[29]Economic Partnership, Political Coordination and Cooperation Agreement between the European Community and its Member States, of the One Part, and the United Mexican States, of the Other Part, 8 December 1997 OJ 2000 L 276/45, https://eeas.europa.eu/sites/eeas/files/28.10.2000_mexico.pdf.

[30]Decision No. 2/2001 of the EU–Mexico Joint Council of 27 February 2001 implementing Articles 6, 9, 12(2)(b), and 50 of the Economic Partnership, Political Coordination and Cooperation Agreement (2001/153/EC) OJ 2001 L70, https://eur-lex.europa.eu/legal-content/EN/TXT/?uri=uriserv%3AOJ.L_.2001.070.01.0007.01.ENG.

[31]Agreement Establishing an Association between the European Community and Its Member States, of the One Part, and the Republic of Chile, of the Other Part, 11 November 2002 OJ 2002 L 352/3, http://eur-lex.europa.eu/resource.html?uri=cellar:f83a503c-fa20-4b3a-9535-f1074175eaf0.0004.02/DOC_2&format=PDF.

[32]Agreement Establishing an Association between Central America, on the one hand, and the European Union and its Member States, on the other, 29 June 2012 OJ 2012 L 346/3, http://eur-lex.europa.eu/legal-content/en/TXT/PDF/?uri=CELEX:22012A1215(01)&rid=1.

[33]Free Trade Agreement Between the European Union and its Member States, of the One Part, and the Republic of Korea, of the Other Part, 6 October 2010 OJ 2011 L. 127/6, http://eur-lex.europa.eu/legal-content/en/TXT/PDF/?uri=CELEX:22011A0514%2801%29&rid=1.

[34]Trade Agreement Between the European Union and its Member States, of the One Part, and Colombia and Peru, of the Other Part, 31 May 2012 OJ 2012 L 354/1, http://publications.europa.eu/resource/cellar/e4c7ab87-4a17-11e2-8762-01aa75ed71a1.0001.04/DOC_30.

[35]EU-Singapore Free Trade Agreement (not yet ratified by the EU). Text available at https://trade.ec.europa.eu/doclib/press/index.cfm?id=961.

[36]Comprehensive Economic and Trade Agreement (CETA) between Canada, of the one part, and the European Union and its Member States, of the other part, 14 September 2014 OJ 2017 L 11/23, http://eur-lex.europa.eu/legal-content/EN/TXT/HTML/?uri=CELEX:22017A0114(01)&from=EN.

Partnership Agreement (JEFTA)[37] and draft EU-Mexico FTA (revision of EU-Mexico EPA).[38] The analysis also considers the EU proposals for the electronic commerce negotiations at the WTO,[39] FTAs with Australia,[40] Chile,[41] Indonesia,[42] New Zealand[43] and Tunisia.[44] Among the US-led FTAs the chapter analyses the FTAs concluded after the so-called US "Digital Agenda,"[45] namely FTAs with Australia,[46] Bahrain,[47] the Central American countries,[48] Chile,[49] Morocco,[50]

---

[37]EU-Japan Economic Partnership Agreement (JEFTA), text after legal revision available at https://trade.ec.europa.eu/doclib/press/index.cfm?id=1684.

[38]European Commission, New EU-Mexico agreement: The Agreement in Principle and its texts, http://trade.ec.europa.eu/doclib/press/index.cfm?id=1833.

[39]European Commission, EU Proposal for WTO Disciplines and Commitments Relating to Electronic Commerce, INF/ECOM/22, 2.7–2.8, 26 April 2019, http://trade.ec.europa.eu/doclib/docs/2019/may/tradoc_157880.pdf.

[40]EU Proposal for the Digital Trade Chapter of EU-Australia *FTA* (Oct. 10, 2018), http://trade.ec.europa.eu/doclib/docs/2018/december/tradoc_157570.pdf.

[41]On file with Author. EU's proposal for Digital Trade chapter of a possible modernised EU-Chile Association Agreement is not yet publicly available.

[42]European Commission, Report of the 5th Round of Negotiations for a Free Trade Agreement Between the European Union and Indonesia, 9–13 July 2018, http://trade.ec.europa.eu/doclib/docs/2018/july/tradoc_157137.pdf.

[43]EU Proposal for the Digital Trade Chapter of EU-New Zealand *FTA*, 25 September 2018, http://trade.ec.europa.eu/doclib/docs/2018/december/tradoc_157581.pdf.

[44]On file with Author. EU's proposal for Digital Trade chapter of a possible modernised EU-Tunisia FTA is not yet publicly available.

[45]Bipartisan Trade Promotion Authority Act of 2002, sections 2102(b)(8) and 2102(b)(9). Wunsch-Vincent (2003), p. 7.

[46]United States-Australia Free Trade Agreement, with Annexes and Related Exchange of Letters, 18 May 2004, 43 I.L.M. 1248, https://ustr.gov/trade-agreements/free-trade-agreements/australian-fta/final-text.

[47]United States-Bahrain Free Trade Agreement, 14 September 2004, 44 I.L.M. 544, https://ustr.gov/trade-agreements/free-trade-agreements/bahrain-fta/final-text.

[48]Dominican Republic-Central America-United States Free Trade Agreement, 28 May 2004, 43 I.L.M. 514, https://ustr.gov/trade-agreements/free-trade-agreements/cafta-dr-dominican-republic-central-america-fta/final-text.

[49]United States-Chile Free Trade Agreement Implementation Act, Pub. L. No. 108-77 (2003) https://ustr.gov/trade-agreements/free-trade-agreements/chile-fta/final-text.

[50]United States-Morocco Free Trade Agreement, 15 June 2004, 44 I.L.M. 544, https://ustr.gov/trade-agreements/free-trade-agreements/morocco-fta/final-text.

South Korea (KORUS),[51] Oman,[52] Panama,[53] Peru,[54] Singapore,[55] Colombia,[56] and the most recent USMCA and U.S. – Japan Digital Trade Agreement. The analysis also includes CPTPP (to which the US is not a party) because the relevant digital trade provisions were not altered after the US withdrawal from the agreement. They also formed the basis for the US model approach implemented in the USMCA and other smaller FTAs.[57]

The chapter proceeds as follows. Sections 2–5 map out, respectively, the evolution of provisions on privacy and personal data protection in general exceptions, financial and telecommunications chapters, chapters on electronic commerce and digital trade. Each section identifies trends in the design and wording of these provisions in the EU- and US-led FTAs and explicates the points of convergence and divergence between the EU and US approaches. Section 6 concludes.

2   General Exception for Privacy and Data Protection

The GATS general exception explicitly mentions privacy and personal data protection as legitimate policy objectives that could justify a violation of a WTO member's commitments under the GATS. Article XIV(c)(ii) reads as follows:

> Subject to the requirement that such measures are not applied in a manner which would constitute a means of arbitrary or unjustifiable discrimination between countries where like conditions prevail, or a disguised restriction on trade in services, nothing in this Agreement shall be construed to prevent the adoption or enforcement by any Member of measures . . .

> (c) *necessary* to secure compliance with laws or regulations which are not inconsistent with the provisions of this Agreement including those relating to . . .

---

[51]United States-Korea Free Trade Agreement, 1 April 2007, 46 I.L.M. 642 https://ustr.gov/trade-agreements/free-trade-agreements/korus-fta/final-text.

[52]United States-Oman Free Trade Agreement, 1 January 2006, https://ustr.gov/trade-agreements/free-trade-agreements/oman-fta/final-text.

[53]United States-Panama Trade Promotion Agreement, 31 October 2012, https://ustr.gov/trade-agreements/free-trade-agreements/panama-tpa/final-text.

[54]United States-Peru-Trade Promotion Agreement, 12 April 2006, https://ustr.gov/trade-agreements/free-trade-agreements/peru-tpa/final-text.

[55]United States-Singapore Free Trade Agreement, 3 September 2003, 117 Stat. 948 https://ustr.gov/trade-agreements/free-trade-agreements/singapore-fta/final-text.

[56]United States-Colombia Trade Promotion Agreement, 15 May 2012, https://ustr.gov/trade-agreements/free-trade-agreements/colombia-fta/final-text.

[57]Geist M (2018) Data rules in modern trade agreements: toward reconciling an open internet with privacy and security safeguards. CIGI International Policy Considerations, https://www.cigionline.org/articles/data-rules-modern-trade-agreements-toward-reconciling-open-internet-privacy-and-security; Burri (2017a), p. 101.

(ii) the *protection of the privacy of individuals in relation to the processing and dissemination of personal data* and the protection of confidentiality of individual records and accounts
<...> (emphasis added)

One of the core elements of the general exception is the "necessity test." Although
the application of this test has been uneven in the past, it could be argued that, in
most cases, "necessity" boils down to an assessment of whether a less trade
restrictive measure is "reasonably available" to a defending party.[58] This test has
been criticized for being insufficiently broad to justify domestic fundamental rights-
based restrictions on cross-border data flows, such as those adopted by the EU,
should they be challenged under the GATS most-favored nation treatment or
national treatment provisions.[59]

In all the EU and US-led post-WTO FTAs considered in this article the wording
of the general exception for domestic privacy and data protection legal frameworks
has been either modelled after the above-mentioned general exception of the GATS
or incorporated this exception *mutatis mutandis*.[60] This, however, does not mean
that the EU and US agree on the breadth of the regulatory space that FTAs should
grant domestic privacy and data protection regulation. On the contrary, in the context
of digital trade negotiations, as Sect. 5 explicates, this has become one of the most
controversial issues on which the EU and US positions are widely divergent.

3   Telecommunications and Financial Services Chapters

Starting from the WTO Agreement, financial and telecommunications services
chapters mention the protection of confidentiality of messages, privacy or personal
data as an exception or a counterbalancing provision to the obligation to provide
access to public telecommunications infrastructure and to allow free cross-border
flows of financial data.

Under article 5(d) of the GATS Annex on Telecommunication, a member may
derogate from an obligation to provide access to public telecommunications infrastructure if this is *"necessary* to ensure the *security and confidentiality of messages*,
subject to the requirement that such measures are *not applied in a manner which
would constitute a means of arbitrary or unjustifiable discrimination or a disguised*

---

[58]Regan (2007), p. 350; Venzke (2011), p. 1138.

[59]Yakovleva (2018), pp. 497–499.

[60]See e.g. Article 28.3(2)(c)(ii) CETA, Article 8.62(e)(ii) EU-Singapore FTA, Article 167(1)(e)
(ii) FTA between EU, Colombia and Peru, Article 27(2) EU-Mexico Joint Council Decision, Article
7.50(e)(ii) EU-Korea FTA, Article 203(1)(e)(ii) EU Association Agreement with Central America,
Article 135(1)(e)(ii) EU-Chile Association Agreement, Article 22.1(2) US-Australia FTA, Article
23.1(2) KORUS FTA, Article 21.1(2) US-Singapore FTA, Article 21.1(2) Dominican Republic-
Central America-United States FTA, Article 21.1(2) US – Panama PTA, Article 32.1(2) USMCA,
Article 29.1(3) CPTPP.

restriction on trade in services." The wording of this exception closely resembles the structure and wording of the general exception discussed in the previous section.

While the GATS Annex on Telecommunications does not specifically mention privacy, CETA and some of the US-led FTAs refer to privacy in addition to the security and confidentiality of the communications.[61] EU-led FTAs before and after CETA follow the GATS Annex on Telecommunications model in this respect.[62] Until very recently, all EU-led FTAs considered in this article no longer formulated this provision as an exception, but as a positive obligation of the parties to take appropriate measures to protect privacy of electronic communications ("a Party shall").[63] Furthermore, these provisions contained a lower threshold, as compared with the GATS Annex on Telecommunications, that the measures to protect privacy and/or confidentiality of electronic communications should meet ("necessity" of such measures was not required).[64] This trend has reversed in the most recent EU-led FTA – JEFTA—and the draft EU-Mexico FTA, which almost verbatim repeat the GATS model.[65] While the EU approach to formulating privacy-related provisions has varied, post-WTO US-led FTAs consistently follow the model of the exception from the GATS Annex on Telecommunications.[66]

In the WTO Agreement, a privacy and data protection-related provision in financial services sector is included in Article B.8 of the 1994 Understanding on commitments in financial services (Understanding) to counterbalance the provision on the free flow of financial information. The provision reads as follows:

> ... Nothing in this paragraph restricts the right of a Member to protect *personal data, personal privacy* and the confidentiality of individual records and accounts so long as such right is *not used to circumvent* the provisions of the Agreement. (emphasis added)

As compared to the general exception for privacy and data protection, this sectoral exception does not provide for a "necessity" requirement.

---

[61] Article 15.3(4) of CETA, article 9.2(4) of US – Singapore FTA, article 13.2(4) of Dominican Republic-Central America-United States FTA, article 13.2(4) of the US – Panama TPA, article 13.2 (4) of US-Chile FTA, article 13.2(4) of US-Morocco FTA, article 14.2(4) of US-Peru FTA, article 14.2(4) of US-Colombia FTA, article 18.3(4) of USMCA, article of 13.4(4) CPTPP.

[62] Article 8.27 of EU-Singapore FTA, article 149 of FTA between EU, Colombia and Peru, article 7.35 of EU-Korea FTA, article 192 of the EU association agreement with Central America, article 8.44(4) of JEFTA, article TS.6(4) of draft Telecommunications chapter of modernised EU-Mexico FTA.

[63] For discussion see Yakovleva (2018), pp. 492–294.

[64] See e.g. article 15.3(4) of CETA.

[65] Article 8.44(4) of JEFTA, article TS.6(4) of draft Telecommunications chapter of modernised EU-Mexico FTA.

[66] Article 9.2(4) of US – Singapore FTA, article 13.2(4) of Dominican Republic-Central America-United States FTA, article 13.2(4) of US – Panama TPA, article 13.2(4) of US-Chile FTA, article 13.2(4) of US-Morocco FTA, article 14.2(4) of US-Peru FTA, article 14.2(4) of US-Colombia FTA, article 12.2(4) of US – Australia FTA, article 14.2(4) of KORUS FTA, article 12.2(4) US-Bahrain FTA, article 13.2(4) of US-Oman FTA, article 18.3(4) USMCA, article 13.4(4) CPTPP.

Provisions on privacy and data protection in financial services chapters of EU-led post-WTO FTAs exhibit a similar dynamic as in that in telecommunications chapters. While the wording of obligations on free flow of financial information remained constant,[67] until very recently all post-WTO EU-led FTAs formulated the provision on the protection of privacy and personal data as a positive obligation ("[e]ach Party shall maintain adequate safeguards to protect privacy").[68] Furthermore, as compared with that of Understanding, these provisions do not contain an anti-circumvention requirement; instead they state that measures protecting privacy and personal data be "appropriate" or "adequate."[69] In JEFTA, however, the EU has returned to the model of the Understanding.[70] The financial services chapter of the draft EU-Mexico FTA does not contain provisions on cross-border data flows of financial data and the protection of privacy and personal data; it merely includes a three years' review clause allowing the parties to reassess whether such provisions are necessary.[71]

Research into the US-led post-WTO FTAs reveals a remarkably different approach to cross-border data flows and privacy and data protection in financial services. Only KORUS and USMCA include provisions on cross-border flows of financial data.[72] In CPTPP financial data flows are regulated by a horizontal provision on data flows discussed in Sect. 5 below. While financial services chapter of KORUS does not contain a specific exception or counterbalancing provision on data protection, this exception in CPTPP and USMCA follow the model of Understanding. The exception for privacy and data protection in these FTAs is broader than the exception from a horizontal provision on cross-border data flows discussed in Sect. 5 below because it does not require that measures to protect privacy and personal data should be "necessary."

To conclude, in the last two decades the US approach to including and formulating provisions on privacy and data protection into telecommunications and financial services chapters has been more internally consistent and more coherent with the WTO Agreement, than that of the EU. Until a recent return to the WTO model in JEFTA and the draft EU-Mexico FTA, the EU tended to afford more policy space to domestic privacy and data protection rules vis-à-vis its international trade

---

[67]Article B.8 of Understanding on commitments in financial services, article 13.15(1) of CETA, article 157(1) of FTA between EU, Colombia and Peru, article 22(1) of the EU association agreement with Mexico, article 7.43(a) of EU-Korea FTA, article 198(1) of FTA between the EU and Central America, article 122(1) of the EU-Chile association agreement, article 8.54(1) of EU-Singapore FTA.

[68]Article 8.54(2) of EU-Singapore FTA, article 157(2) of FTA between EU, Colombia and Peru, article 198(2) of the EU association agreement with Central America, article 7.43(b) of EU-Korea FTA, article 22(2) of EU-Mexico Joint Council Decision, Article 13.15(2) of CETA.

[69]See e.g. article 8.54(2) of EU-Singapore FTA, article 157(2) of FTA between EU, Colombia and Peru, article 198(2) of the EU association agreement with Central America, article 7.43(b) of EU-Korea FTA, article 22(2) of EU-Mexico Joint Council Decision.

[70]Article 8.63(2) of JEFTA.

[71]Article XX.10 Chapter 12 of draft EU-Mexico FTA.

[72]Annex 13-B, section B of KORUS FTA, article 17.17 of USMCA.

obligations to provide access to public telecommunications infrastructure and to allow free cross-border flows of financial data than the WTO Agreement.

4 E-commerce Chapters

Before I delve into the privacy and data protection provisions in the e-commerce and digital trade chapters, an important clarification is in order. I make a distinction between e-commerce and digital trade solely for the purposes of this chapter to underscore a qualitative shift in regulating privacy and data protection in the FTAs concluded in 2018 or later, which make a special emphasis on digital trade. These include the US-led CPTPP, USMCA and the U.S. – Japan Digital Trade Agreement, EU-led JEFTA and the EU's negotiation position on cross-border data flows, which has not yet been included in any concluded FTA. The discussion on the difference between e-commerce and digital trade is beyond the scope of this chapter.

Unlike the WTO agreement, most EU- and US-led post-WTO FTAs contain a chapter on e-commerce.[73] However, while all e-commerce chapters in EU-led FTAs considered in this chapter mention privacy and data protection (some more extensively than others), this is the case in only a few of their US counterparts.

The e-commerce chapters in EU-led FTAs refer to privacy and data protection in three respects: in the chapter on the objectives of electronic commerce, as an alonestanding non-aspirational commitment to protect personal data and in the context of regulatory cooperation. None of these provisions are legally binding.[74] While the wording of each type of provision throughout different FTAs is fairly consistent, the combination of these provision from one FTA to another is heterogeneous.[75]

An example of the first type of provision is Article 8.57(4) "Objectives [of electronic commerce]" of the FTA with Singapore:[76]

> The Parties agree that the development of electronic commerce *must* be fully compatible with *international standards of data protection*, in order to ensure the confidence of users of electronic commerce. (italics added)

---

[73] Chapter 16 of CETA, chapter 8 Section F of EU-Singapore FTA, chapter 6 of FTA between EU, Colombia and Peru, chapter 7 section F of EU-Korea FTA, chapter 6 of the EU association agreement with Central America, chapter 16 of US-Australia FTA, chapter 15 of KORUS FTA, chapter 14 of US-Singapore FTA, chapter 14 of US-Central America FTA, chapter 14 of US-Panama FTA, chapter 13 of US-Bahrain FTA, chapter 15 of US-Chile FTA, chapter 14 of US-Morocco FTA, chapter 14 of US-Oman FTA, chapter 15 of US-Peru FTA, chapter 15 of US-Colombia PTA.

[74] Yakovleva (2018), p. 496.

[75] See also Monteiro and Teh (2017), p. 71.

[76] See also article 162(2) of FTA between EU, Colombia and Peru, article 7.48(2) of EU-Korea FTA, article 201(2) of the EU association agreement with Central America.

The reference to international standards on data protection is of marginal relevance, as these standards are highly fragmented.[77]

An example of the second type of provision is Article 164 of the FTA with Colombia and Peru, which requires that parties "shall endeavour, insofar as possible, and within their respective competences, to develop or maintain, as the case may be, regulations for the protection of personal data".[78]

The third type of provision typically requires that the parties maintain a dialogue on regulatory issues relating to, raised by or relevant for the development of electronic commerce.[79] As a rule, this provision contains an open list of relevant issues, which sometimes explicitly mentions the protection of personal data (or personal information).

Of all e-commerce chapters in US-led FTAs concluded before 2018 and considered in this chapter, only three mention the protection of privacy or personal information.

Article 15.8 of KORUS FTA includes a non-binding provision on cross-border information flows—the first of its kind—which in passing also refers to the protection of personal information:

Recognizing the importance of the free flow of information in facilitating trade, and *acknowledging the importance of protecting personal information*, the Parties *shall endeavor to refrain* from imposing or maintaining unnecessary barriers to electronic information flows across borders.

The US-Panama PTA and the US-Chile FTA mention the protection of privacy in the context of regulatory cooperation on e-commerce.[80]

To conclude, the EU has been more proactive than the US in including privacy and data protection-related provisions in e-commerce chapters. Although all those provisions are purely aspirational, their consistent presence in e-commerce chapters asserts the particular importance of privacy and personal data protection as (at times) competing public policy objectives in regulation of e-commerce by international trade.

5   Regulating Privacy and Data Protection in Digital Trade Chapters

Both the EU and the US are actively negotiating digital trade provisions, which include clauses on the protection of privacy and personal data. These provisions take the form of exceptions from horizontal obligations on cross-border data flows and

---

[77]For a discussion see Yakovleva (2018), pp. 482–487 and 498.

[78]Article 164 of FTA between EU, Colombia and Peru.

[79]Article 202 of the EU Association agreement with Central America, article 7.49(1) of EU-Korea FTA, article 16.6(1) of CETA, article163(1) of FTA between EU, Colombia and Peru.

[80]Article 14.5 of US-Panama TPA, article 15.5 of US-Chile FTA.

extensive clauses on the protection of privacy and personal data (information). Although both the EU and the US aim at achieving the same goal—curtailing "digital protectionism"—their understanding of what it entails and the appetite for domestic regulatory autonomy to protect privacy and personal data are sharply contrasting.[81] While the US often labels onerous data protection rules as "digital protectionism," the EU excludes from "digital protectionism" measures that "can be justified with legitimate privacy considerations."[82] This section explicates the differences in the EU and US approaches.

5.1 The EU Approach to Privacy and Data Protection in Digital Trade Chapters

Most of the discussions on privacy and personal data protection in the context of digital trade revolve around horizontal obligations prohibiting restrictions of cross-border data flows. The source of the controversy is that these provisions could be in direct conflict with the EU's restrictions on cross-border transfers of personal data under the GDPR. Therefore, the EU can undertake this obligation, while ensuring internal consistency of its *aquis*, only under the condition that an exception from such an obligation is sufficiently broad to accommodate the EU's limitations on personal data transfers.[83] Overall, the EU has been cautious in including commitments on cross-border data flows in its FTAs.[84]

The possibility of inclusion of a binding cross-border data flow provision accompanied by a GATS Article XIV(c)(ii)-type exception for data protection in the Trade in Services Agreement (TiSA) and the Transatlantic Trade and Investment Partnership (TTIP)—both now stalled—sparked a strong push back from academics and civil society in 2015–2016.[85] The main point of concern was that the exception was too narrow and the EU's framework for personal data transfers may not be able to

---

[81]For discussion, see Yakovleva (2020).

[82]Compare Aaronson (2017), pp. 8–10 with Communication from the European Commission, *Exchanging and Protecting Personal Data in a Globalised World*, 10 January 2017, p. 6 (Jan. 10, 2017), https://eur-lex.europa.eu/legal-content/EN/TXT/HTML/?uri=CELEX:52017DC0007& from=EN. See also Yakovleva (2020).

[83]Yakovleva and Irion (2020).

[84]Burri (2017b), p. 22.

[85]See Irion et al. (2016), pp. 44–45 and 59–60, Fernández Pérez M., Corporate-sponsored privacy confusion in the EU on trade and data protection, EDRI, 12 October 2016, https://edri.org/ corporate-sponsored-privacy-confusion-eu-trade-data-protection/, European Parliament resolution of 8 July 2015 containing the European Parliament's recommendations to the European Commission on the negotiations for the Transatlantic Trade and Investment Partnership (TTIP) (2014/2228 (INI)), European Parliament resolution of 3 February 2016 containing the European Parliament's recommendations to the Commission on the negotiations for the Trade in Services Agreement (TiSA) (2015/2233(INI)).

pass its threshold. This opposition lead to an interinstitutional dialogue within the European Commission. In the meantime, the EU refrained from including any provision on cross-border data flows in the JEFTA and the draft EU-Mexico FTA. In both cases this provision was replaced by a review clause, allowing the parties to revisit the issue in three years' time.[86] In the case of Japan, the absence of such clause was ameliorated by the adoption of a mutual adequacy decision under the GDPR shortly before JEFTA took effect. In addition, JEFTA's Regulatory Cooperation chapter contains an additional safeguard for the Parties' level of privacy and data protection. Articles 18.1(2)(h) and 18.1(3) allow each Party, notwithstanding regulatory cooperation measures, to "to define or regulate its own levels of protection in pursuit or furtherance of its public policy objectives in areas such as personal data and cybersecurity" and to adopt, maintain and apply regulatory measures "in accordance with its legal framework, principles and deadlines, in order to achieve its public policy objectives at the level of protection it deems appropriate."

In 2018 the European Commission reached a political agreement on the EU position on cross-border data flows. This position was expressed in the model clauses, which consist of a model provision on cross-border data flows (Article A), an exception for the protection of privacy and personal data (Article B), and a provision excluding the parties' rules and safeguards for the protection of personal data and privacy, including cross-border data transfers of personal data, from the scope of regulatory cooperation (Article X).[87] For the purposes of this chapter, I will only consider model Articles A and B.

The EU has already included the model provisions in its negotiating proposals for digital trade chapters in the currently negotiated trade agreements with New Zealand, Australia, Indonesia, Chile and Tunisia.[88] The same model clauses are incorporated into the recent EU proposal for WTO rules on electronic commerce.[89]

---

[86]Article 8.81 of JEFTA, article XX Chapter 16 of draft EU-Mexico Free Trade Agreement, Fortnam (2017).

[87]Horizontal provisions for cross-border data flows and for personal data protection (in EU trade and investment agreements) http://trade.ec.europa.eu/doclib/docs/2018/may/tradoc_156884.pdf.

[88]EU's proposal for the Digital Trade Chapter of EU-New Zealand FTA, 25 September 2018, http://trade.ec.europa.eu/doclib/docs/2018/december/tradoc_157581.pdf, EU's proposal for the Digital Trade chapter of EU-Australia FTA, 10 October 2018, http://trade.ec.europa.eu/doclib/docs/2018/december/tradoc_157570.pdf, European Commission, Report of the 5th round of negotiations for a Free Trade Agreement between the European Union and Indonesia, 9 to 13 July 2018 http://trade.ec.europa.eu/doclib/docs/2018/july/tradoc_157137.pdf, EU's proposal for a Digital Trade chapter for a Deep and Comprehensive Free Trade Area (DCFTA) with Tunisia, 9 November 2018, https://trade.ec.europa.eu/doclib/docs/2019/january/tradoc_157660.%20ALECA%202019%20-%20texte%20commerce%20numerique.pdf, the available EU's proposal for Digital Trade chapter of a possible modernised EU-Chile Association Agreement of 5 February 2018 only contains a placeholder for provisions on data flows, https://trade.ec.europa.eu/doclib/docs/2018/february/tradoc_156582.pdf.

[89]Communication from the European Union, EU proposal for WTO disciplines and commitments relating to electronic commerce, INF/ECOM/22, 26 April 2019, http://trade.ec.europa.eu/doclib/docs/2019/may/tradoc_157880.pdf.

Article A prohibits four types of restrictions of cross-border data flows: (1) a requirement to use local computing facilities or network elements; (2) a requirement to localize data on a Party's territory for storage or processing; (3) the prohibition to store or process data in the territory of the other Party; and (4) the prohibition of making the cross-border transfer of data contingent upon use of computing facilities or network elements in the Parties' territory or upon localisation requirements in the Parties' territory. None of these prohibitions capture the EU's own restrictions on cross-border transfers of personal data.

Article B declares the protection of personal data and privacy as a fundamental right, which reflects the EU's own approach to the protection of these policy interests. In addition, it contains a broad national security-type exception for domestic privacy and data protection regime, which allows each party to adopt and maintain the safeguards it '*deems appropriate* to ensure the protection of personal data and privacy, *including through the adoption and application of rules for the cross-border transfer of personal data*' (emphasis added).

In the existing body of international trade law, a similar formula was used for a national security exception in Article XXI of the General Agreement on Tariffs and Trade of 1947 (GATT 1947), which was later incorporated into GATT 1994, and Article XIVbis(1)(b) of the GATS, which states:

> Nothing in this Agreement shall be construed:
>
> (b) to prevent any Member from taking any action which *it considers necessary for* the protection of its essential security interests <...>.[90] (emphasis added)

The scarce practice of the GATT/WTO Council relating to the national security exception,[91] and the recent WTO Panel decision in *Russia – Traffic in Transit*[92] show that although the exception is not totally "self-judging" and the WTO adjudicating bodies have a power to review that that the objective requirements of the exception are met,[93] the WTO member invoking the exception has a wide margin of appreciation.[94] It is up to this member to decide *whether* an action is required, and *which* action should be taken; this choice cannot be questioned by a trade adjudicating body.[95] In *Russia – Traffic in Transit*, the WTO Panel explicitly stated that the

---

[90]The same provision is also envisaged in Article 73 of the Agreement on Trade Related Aspects of Intellectual Property Rights (TRIPS), and several international trade agreements adopted after the Uruguay Round.

[91]Cottier and Delimatsis (2008), pp. 329–348.

[92]*Russia — Measures Concerning Traffic in Transit* WT/DS512/R 5 April 2019 (*Russia – Traffic in Transit*).

[93]*Russia – Traffic in Transit*, paras. 7.102–7.104.

[94]Westin (1997), pp. 181–182; Jackson (1989), p. 205, Article XXI Security Exceptions, WTO Analytical Index of the GATT, at 600–601, https://www.wto.org/english/res_e/booksp_e/gatt_ai_e/art21_e.pdf.

[95]Westin (1997), pp. 181–182; Jackson (1989), p. 205, Article XXI Security Exceptions, WTO Analytical Index of the GATT, at 600–601, https://www.wto.org/english/res_e/booksp_e/gatt_ai_e/art21_e.pdf.

legal meaning of the adjectival clause "which it considers" allows a WTO member *itself* to determine "the 'necessity' of the measures for the protection of its essential security interests."[96] This "necessity test" is therefore easier to satisfy than the "necessity test" of the general exception. As the WTO Panel in *Russia – Traffic in Transit* clarified, to satisfy the "necessity test" in the national security exception

> there is no need to determine the extent of the deviation of the challenged measure from the prescribed norm in order to evaluate the necessity of the measure, i.e. that there is no reasonably available alternative measure to achieve the protection of the legitimate interests covered by the exception which is not violative, or is less violative, of the prescribed norm.[97]

The recent WTO Panel decision, however, also confirms that the breadth of the margin of appreciation in determining "necessity" in the national security exception is limited by the obligation to interpret and apply the exception in good faith, a general principle of law and a principle of general international law.[98] This means that a WTO member cannot use the security exception "as a means to circumvent their obligations under the GATT 1994."[99] In other words, by means of interpretation the WTO Panel implicitly injected the general exception's chapeau requirements, which are absent in the wording of the national security exception.

This analysis suggest that the model clauses aim to provide for a bullet-proof protection for the EU's regime for transfers of personal data under the GDPR from any possible review by trade adjudicators. At the same time, the clauses are not out of the woods yet as they only represent a starting point in negotiations. It may be difficult for the EU to convince its trading partners to accept the proposal for at least two reasons. First, some of them, such as Indonesia, are in the process of adopting data localization rules.[100] Second, other trading partners, like Australia and New Zealand are already parties to CPTPP which, as the next section demonstrates, implements an entirely different—US—approach. Even if the EU model provisions are included in the actual FTAs, their effectiveness could be diminished due to remaining uncertainty on the relationship between the specific exception for privacy and data protection in these provisions and the general exception for privacy and data protection in the services chapter. Although the model exception is clearly intended as *lex specialis* as opposed to the *lex generalis* of the general exception for privacy and data protection, a trading partner could still argue that the general exception should apply when the EU restrictions on cross-border transfers of

---

[96]*Russia – Traffic in Transit*, para. 146. Before this decision was adopted, scholars were sharply divided on whether the national security is self-judging. Compare Alford (2011), pp. 701–702 with Schloemann and Ohlhoff (1999), pp. 426–427, 438, 443ff, arguing that it is not.

[97]*Russia – Traffic in Transit*, para. 7.108.

[98]*Russia – Traffic in Transit*, para. 7.132. Several scholars made the same argument before this decision was adopted. See e.g. Schloemann and Ohlhoff (1999), pp. 446–447.

[99]*Russia – Traffic in Transit*, para. 7.133.

[100]Herbert Smith Freehills LLP, Indonesia proposes amendments to its data localisation requirement, Lexology, 11 December 2018, https://www.lexology.com/library/detail.aspx?g=a116020b-cee3-433f-b62b-a5e988477d8e.

personal data are challenged as violating a non-discrimination provision in trade in services (and not the digital trade provisions) and by doing so by-pass the national security-type exception.

5.2   The US Approach to Privacy and Data Protection in Digital Trade Chapters

The US approach to digital trade ingrains the country's regulatory model of privacy and data protection. The obligation not to restrict cross-border data flows, an exception from such provision and an article on the protection of personal information included in the CPTPP, USMCA, U.S. – Japan Digital Trade Agreement and the US proposal for WTO negotiations on electronic commerce[101] reflect the US regulatory preference for free cross-border data flows and an economic—as opposed to fundamental rights—approach to the protection of personal information in commercial sphere.[102]

CPTPP and USMCA are the first FTAs, which contain a binding provision requiring each Party to allow (or not to restrict) the cross-border transfer of information by electronic means, including personal information, when this activity is for the conduct of the business of a covered person.[103] Both FTAs also contain an exception which allows the Parties to adopt or maintain measures inconsistent with this obligation to achieve a *legitimate public policy objective*, provided that the measure:

    (a) is not applied in a manner which would constitute a means of arbitrary or unjustifiable discrimination or a disguised restriction on trade; and
    (b) does not impose restrictions on transfers of information *greater than are required* [*necessary*—in the USMCA] to achieve the objective. (emphasis added)[104]

The structure and text of the exception strongly resembles the general exception of Article XIV (c) of the GATS, but are nevertheless different in two respects. First, instead of the "necessity" requirement in the general exception, the CPTPP exception requires that restrictions should not be "greater than are *required* to achieve the objective". This difference seems, however, purely semantic. "Required" is a synonym of "necessary"[105] and, according to the WTO Secretariat is yet another way to

---

[101]Manak I., U.S. WTO E-commerce Proposal Reads Like USMCA, International Economic Law and Policy Blog, 8 May 2019, https://worldtradelaw.typepad.com/ielpblog/2019/05/us-wto-e-commerce-proposal-reads-like-usmca.html.

[102]Wolfe (2019), pp. s75 and s77. For a comparison between EU and US approaches to privacy and data protection see Schwartz and Solove (2014).

[103]Article 14.11(2) of CPTPP, article 19.11(1) of USMCA.

[104]Article 14.11 (3) of CPTPP. Article 19.11(2) of USMCA contains an almost identical provision.

[105]Merriam-Webster online dictionary, https://www.merriam-webster.com/dictionary/necessary.

convey the concept of "necessity."[106] Second, as compared with the general exception, exceptions from the obligation on cross-border data flows do not explicitly name public policy objective that could trigger its application. It could be reasonably argued that privacy and data protection constitute the policy objectives implied in the CPTPP and USMCA exceptions. However, unlike the EU' model exception, these policy objectives are not limited to privacy and data protection. To sum up, while the exception in CPTPP and USMCA embraces an unrestricted scope of public policy objectives, by incorporating the "necessity test" of the general exception it allows for a sufficiently narrower regulatory autonomy to pursue those objectives than the national security-type exception proposed by the EU.

Another novelty introduced in the CPTPP and later in the USMCA is an extensive article on the protection of personal information.[107] Article 14.8 "Personal Information Protection" in the CPTPP includes a mixture of binding and aspirational provisions:

i. An aspirational provision recognising the economic and social benefits of protecting personal information in the context of digital trade (para. 1);
ii. An obligation to ("each Party shall") adopt or maintain a legal framework for protection of personal data of users of electronic commerce and to consider principles and guidelines of relevant international bodies (para. 2);
iii. An aspirational provision to adopt non-discriminatory practices in protecting the users' personal information (para. 3);
iv. An obligation to ("each Party should") publish information on how individuals can pursue a remedy in case of violation of personal information protections and on how business can comply with the local personal information protection requirements (para. 4);
v. An aspirational provision requiring to encourage the development of mechanisms ensuring compatibility between different data protection regimes, such as recognition of regulatory outcomes and to endeavour to exchange information on such mechanisms (para. 5).

Article 19.8 of the USMCA, which incorporates all the provisions mentioned above, is different in two important aspects. First, it endorses the APEC Privacy Framework and the 2013 OECD Guidelines governing the Protection of Privacy and Transborder Flows of Personal data as examples of such framework as an example of a legal framework for the protection of personal information (para. 2). Second, paragraph 3 explicitly lists the key principles of the personal information framework: limitation on collection; choice; data quality; purpose specification; use limitation; security safeguards; transparency; individual participation; and accountability. Furthermore, this paragraph embraces a Parties' recognition of the importance to ensure that "any restrictions on cross-border flows of personal information are necessary and proportionate to the risks presented."

---

[106]WTO, Note by the Secretariat, '"Necessity" in the WTO', S/WPDR/W/27, 2 December 2003, para. I.A.5.
[107]Article 14.8 of CPTPP and article 19.8 of USMCA.

On the one hand, these articles remotely resemble the provisions included in the EU's e-commerce chapters, discussed in Sect. 4 of this chapter (especially provisions (i) and (ii)), which are not present in JEFTA, and the model clauses on cross-border data flows discussed in Sect. 5.1 above. On the other hand, they go a step further by incorporating—for the first time in international trade law—substantive principles of US personal information protection. Another important novelty is an emphasis on developing mechanisms for compatibility between different data protection regimes (provision v) supported by a transparency obligation (provision iv). In addition to its, perhaps, primary function of facilitating cross-border digital trade, the latter obligation can also serve an important starting point for the trading partners to learn about each other's legal regimes for personal data protection in commerce.

6 Conclusion

The analysis of international trade provisions in EU- and US-led post-WTO FTAs referring to privacy and data protection confirms that, apart from the wording of the general exception, both trading partners tend to prefer their own template for regional FTAs.[108] Comparison of these templates demonstrates that they are rooted in domestic regulatory models of information governance, which, in particular, embrace normative underpinnings for privacy and data protection. In addition, each of the trading partners respond differently to particular business demands.[109] This chapter also showed that compared to the EU, the US template for provisions mentioning privacy and data protection in telecommunications and financial services chapters, e-commerce and digital trade chapters has been internally more coherent and aligned with the WTO Agreement.

Returning to digital trade, it could be argued that both the EU and the US attempt to harmonize the standards for cross-border transfers and the protection of privacy and personal data using their own regulatory model as a benchmark.[110] For example, the EU's model provision prohibiting restrictions on cross-border data flows is carefully crafted to outlaw data localization measures adopted by, for example, Russia and China. The US, in its turn, aims to set the level of data protection at a level lower than that in the EU, aligned with its own market-based approach to data protection.

Against this backdrop, convergence of the EU and US models is unlikely. Although some predict[111] and others even consider desirable[112] the diffusion of

---

[108]Wolfe (2019), p. s66.

[109]Wolfe (2019), p. s65.

[110]Bradford (2012), p. 22ff. In contrast, Young disagrees that the EU is exporting its regulatory model. Young (2015), p. 1255.

[111]Burri (2017a), p. 128.

[112]Mattoo and Meltzer (2018), pp. 5–6 and 25.

the CPTPP template for cross-border data flow provisions in international trade agreements, the EU is unlikely to adhere to it as this would require compromising on its constitutional legal regime for privacy and data protection.[113] This may be problematic for other countries, such as Japan or Canada. On the one hand, Japan and Canada are parties to the CPTPP; Canada is party to USMCA and Japan to the U.S. – Japan Digital Trade Agreement modelled after the digital trade provisions in the USMCA. These FTAs provide for a broad prohibition on restrictions on cross-border data flows. On the other hand, both Japan and Canada have an adequacy decision from the EU, which among other things require limitations on onward transfers of personal data obtained from the EU to other countries, which have not been granted adequacy, such as the US (beyond the EU-US Privacy Shield certification mechanism[114]) or Australia. Mutual inconsistency of the EU and US approaches to cross-border data flows and the protection of privacy and personal data may prove counterproductive in the multilateral negotiations on electronic commerce at the WTO.[115] Finding a common ground on data protection could allow the two trading partners to strengthen their negotiating power and offset that of less democratic states, such as China.[116]

References

Aaronson SA (2016) Redefining protectionism. Int Econ 30(4):58–88

Alford RP (2011) The self-judging WTO security exception. Utah Law Rev 2011(3):697–759

Bradford A (2012) The Brussels effect. Northwest Univ Law Rev 107(1):1–68

Burri M (2017a) The governance of data and data flows in trade agreements: the pitfalls of legal adaptation. UC Davis Law Rev 51(65):65–132

Burri M (2017b) Current and emerging trends in disruptive technologies: implications for the present and future of EU's trade policy. Study commissioned by the European Parliament's Committee on International Trade, 1–37 http://www.europarl.europa.eu/RegData/etudes/STUD/2017/603845/EXPO_STU(2017)603845_EN.pdf

Cottier T, Delimatsis P (2008) Article XIVbis security exceptions. In: Wolfrum R, Stoll PT, Feinäugle C (eds) Max Planck commentaries on world trade law, WTO – trade in services, vol 6. Martinus Nijhoff, Leiden, pp 329–348

Irion K, Yakovleva S, Bartl M (2016) Trade and privacy: complicated bedfellows? How to achieve data protection-proof free trade agreements. Study commissioned by BEUC et al. Institute for Information Law (IViR), Amsterdam

Jackson J (1989) The world trading system: law and policy of international economic relations. MIT Press, Cambridge MA

---

[113]Yakovleva and Irion (2020).

[114]European Commission implementing decision pursuant to Directive 95/46/EC of the European Parliament and of the Council on adequacy of the protection provided by the EU-U.S. Privacy Shield of 12.07.2016 C(2016) 4176 final.

[115]Yakovleva and Irion (2020), p. 14.

[116]Yakovleva and Irion (2020), p. 14.

Le Roux G (2017) TTIP negotiations, policy convergence, and the transatlantic digital economy. Bus Polit 19(4):709–737

LeSieur F (2012) Regulating cross-border data flows and privacy in the networked digital environment and global knowledge economy. Int Data Privacy Law 2(2):93–104

Mattoo A, Meltzer JP (2018) International data flows and privacy the conflict and its resolution, policy research working paper 8431. World Bank Group, Washington D.C.

Monteiro JA, Teh R (2017) Provisions on electronic commerce in regional trade agreements. WTO working paper ERSD-2017-11. ERSD, Geneva

Regan DH (2007) The meaning of "necessary" in GATT Article XX and GATS Article XIV: the myth of cost-benefit balancing. World Trade Rev 6(3):347–369

Rodota S (2009) Data protection as fundamental right. In: Gutwirth S et al (eds) Reinventing data protection? Springer, Heidelberg, pp 77–82

Schloemann HL, Ohlhoff S (1999) Constitutionalization and dispute settlement in the WTO: national security as an issue of competence. Am J Int Law 93(2):424–451

Schwartz PM, Solove DJ (2014) Reconciling personal information in the United States and European Union. Calif Law Rev 102(4):877–916

Shaffer G (2000) Globalization and social protection: the impact of EU and international rules in the ratcheting up of U.S. privacy standards. Yale J Int Law 25(1):1–88

Svantesson DJB (2011) The regulation of cross-border data flows. Int Data Privacy Law 1 (3):180–198

Swire P, Litan RE (1998) None of your business: world data flows, electronic commerce, and the European Privacy Directive. Brookings Institution Press, Washington

Venzke I (2011) Making general exceptions: the spell of precedents in developing Article XX GATT into standards for domestic regulatory policy. German Law J 12(05):1111–1140

Westin RA (1997) Environmental tax initiatives and multilateral trade agreements: dangerous collisions. Kluwer Law International, Alphen aan den Rijn

Wolfe R (2019) Learning about digital trade: privacy and e-commerce in CETA and TPP. World Trade Rev 18(S1):s63–s84

Wunsch-Vincent S (2003) The digital trade agenda of the U.S.: parallel tracks of bilateral, regional and multilateral liberalization. Aussenwirtschaft 58(I):7–46

Yakovleva S (2018) Should fundamental rights to privacy and data protection be a part of EU's international trade "deals"? World Trade Rev 17(3):477–508

Yakovleva S (2020) Privacy protection(ism): the latest wave of trade constraints on regulatory autonomy. University of Miami Law Review 416

Yakovleva S, Irion K (2020) Towards compatibility of the EU external trade policy on cross-border data flows with the general data protection regulation. Am J Int Law Unbound 114:10–14. Symposium on the GDPR and International Law

Young AR (2015) Liberalizing trade, not exporting rules: the limits to regulatory co-ordination in the EU "New Generation" preferential trade agreements. J Eur Public Policy 22(9):1253–1275

Svetlana Yakovleva is a PhD candidate at the Institute for Information Law (IViR) of the University of Amsterdam. She also works part-time as a Senior Legal Adviser in Privacy and Cybersecurity practice group at De Brauw Blackstone Westbroek in Amsterdam. Her primary research interests lie at the intersection of data privacy and cybersecurity law, human rights and international trade law. Svetlana received a degree in law (cum laude) from the National Research University Higher School of Economics (Moscow) in 2005. She also holds an LL.M degree in Law and Economics (EMLE) from the Erasmus University, Rotterdam and the University of Hamburg (2007), and a research master degree in Information law from the IViR (2016). Between 2007 and 2014, Svetlana worked as a trainee lawyer at the Moscow office of Debevoise&Plimpton LLP, independent legal counsel and Legal and Compliance Officer at Allianz Global Assistance Russia. Svetlana also provided legal and methodological advice for the e-Government project of the Russian Government.

Addressing Digital Services in PTAs: Only Convergence in the 11th Hour?

Ines Willemyns

Contents

1   Introduction

In the World Trade Organization (WTO), the concept of electronic commerce has been on the radar of the negotiating membership since 1998. With the establishment of the Work Programme on Electronic Commerce (WPEC), Members decided to

I. Willemyns (✉)
Leuven Centre for Global Governance Studies, KU Leuven, Leuven, Belgium

© The Editor(s) (if applicable) and The Author(s), under exclusive licence to   117
Springer Nature Switzerland AG 2020
R. T. Hoffmann, M. Krajewski (eds.), *Coherence and Divergence in Services Trade Law*, European Yearbook of International Economic Law,
https://doi.org/10.1007/978-3-030-46955-9_6

examine "*all trade-related issues relating to global electronic commerce*".[1] The discussions in the context of the WPEC have mainly succeeded at highlighting the diverging views of Members on the issues related to e-commerce. So far, substantive output from the WPEC has been limited to an extended moratorium on customs duties on electronic transmission.[2]

Members are however increasingly aware of the economic impact of barriers to digital services trade and have progressively been addressing such issues at a regional or bilateral level. More and more preferential trade agreements (PTAs) include a chapter dedicated to electronic commerce. This chapter maps how digital services trade is addressed under the General Agreement on Trade in Services (GATS), identifies three issues in the multilateral framework on electronic commerce and studies whether such gaps are being filled in the e-commerce chapters of PTAs. The e-commerce-related content of these PTAs is identified through a term-frequency analysis, which allows for a mapping of the presence of different barriers to digital services trade in PTAs.

2   Digital Services Within the GATS Framework

The first section of this chapter sets out the applicability of the GATS to digital services trade and identifies three elements of the current framework that adversely affect the liberalisation of digital services trade and that can be addressed at the PTA level. It thereby provides the basis for the second section of the chapter, which will analyse the content of existing e-commerce PTAs and assess whether they successfully fill the identified gaps.

2.1   The Broad Scope of the GATS Encompasses Digital Services

Article I:1 GATS clarifies the scope of the agreement as applying to "*measures by Members affecting trade in services*". Services are moreover understood as including any service in any sector.[3] It can therefore be observed that the GATS is supposed to cover all services (except for those supplied in the exercise of governmental

---

[1] WTO, 'Work Programme on Electronic Commerce – Adopted by the General Council on 25 September 1998', WT/L/274, 30 September 1998, p. 1.

[2] The last extension of this moratorium was done in the General Council Decision of 10 December 2019 until the 12th Ministerial Conference, to be held in June 2020. WTO, 'Work Programme on Electronic Commerce – General Council Decision of 10 December 2019', WT/L/1079, 11 December 2019. For a brief history of the work in the context of the WPEC until 2004, see Wunsch-Vincent (2004), pp. 8–24.

[3] Article I:3(b) GATS.

authority), which entails that measures that affect the electronic delivery of services fall within the scope of the agreement. Moreover, the WTO Secretariat opined that it is clear that electronic delivery of digital services can fall within any of the four modes of delivery as defined in paragraph 2 of Article I GATS.[4] In the 1999 Progress Report to the General Council in the framework of the WPEC, it was set out that

> [i]t was the general view that the electronic delivery of services falls within the scope of the GATS, since the Agreement applies to all services regardless of the means by which they are delivered, and that electronic delivery can take place under any of the four modes of supply.[5]

This statement, together with the technologically neutral language used in Article I GATS confirms that digital services fall within the scope of this agreement.[6]

The applicability of the GATS to all measures affecting the supply of digital services entails that Members will be subject to the GATS obligations when they are enacting measures to regulate these services, or the Internet more generally. Members that regulate digital services must therefore ensure the consistency of their measures with the most-favoured-nation (MFN) treatment obligation in Article II GATS and the transparency obligations in Article III GATS. Depending on the commitments Members have taken in services sectors, they also have to provide market access and national treatment to foreign service suppliers and respect the substantive obligations on domestic regulation.[7]

2.2 Three Gaps in Addressing Barriers to Digital Services Trade

However, even if the applicability of the GATS to digital services is accepted, there are several outstanding questions or elements that are not being addressed. First, it is not a straightforward exercise to determine whether digital products qualify as goods or services and there seems to be a persisting disagreement between WTO Members on this. Secondly, many, if not all, services can now be supplied through electronic means. They therefore classify not only as telecommunications and computer services but also as audiovisual services or any other service sector. Some of these

---

[4]WTO Council for Trade in Services, 'The Work Programme on Electronic Commerce', Note by the Secretariat, S/C/W/68, 16 November 1998, para. 37.

[5]WTO Work Programme on Electronic Commerce, 'Progress Report to the General Council adopted by the Council for Trade in Services on 19 July 1999', S/L/74, 27 July 1999, para. 4. The Chairman of the Council for Trade in Services also reported that "*Members agreed that all services delivered electronically were covered by the GATS*". WTO Council for Trade in Services, 'Report of the Meeting Held on 14 and 15 December 1998 – Note by the Secretariat' S/C/M/32, 14 January 1999, para. 16.

[6]The principle of technological neutrality was explicitly recognised by the Panel in *US – Gambling*, stating that technological neutrality encompasses all means of delivery, including the Internet. Panel Report, *US – Gambling*, para. 6.285. See also Farrokhnia and Richards (2016), p. 806.

[7]Respectively, Articles XVI, XVII and VI:5 GATS.

service sectors are however subject to no or limited commitments by WTO Members, leading to an overall low level of obligation under the GATS. Thirdly, even though digital services fall within the scope of the GATS, its text, which dates back to the early 1990s, does not explicitly address several specific barriers to digital services trade.

2.2.1 How to Classify 'Digital Products'

With the process of digitisation, creative content (literature, music, film) can nowadays be traded in electronic form, over the Internet, without ever taking a physical form. This leads to an increased trade in 'digital products', most often content that is transmitted electronically.[8] Content however used to be distributed on a physical carrier and was therefore treated as a good, crossing physical borders and subject to customs duties (examples include books, movies on VCR and DVD, music on LP, cassette and CD and software on CD). Everyone is familiar with the concept of e-books, online access to movies and music as well as purchasing and downloading software online. So far, it is however quite unclear how these 'digital products' fit within the WTO framework.[9] Should they still be classified as goods, even though they have become intangible and no longer physically cross borders? Does their mode of delivery (from physical distribution to electronic distribution) change their nature and should they therefore be considered as services? How does this impact the application of WTO obligations? Do different regimes apply to digital products and their physically stored counterparts?

In the context of the debate on whether digital products qualify as goods or services, two elements have so far been (implicitly) agreed upon.[10] First, goods that are ordered over the Internet but delivered physically still qualify as goods (which entails applicability of the GATT). Second, online services that do not implicate downloaded or stored content are still services (which entails applicability of the GATS). The main interpretative problem is however caused by those products which used to be traded on physical carriers but that can now be traded over the Internet, without ever being transferred to a physical carrier or physically crossing borders.

This issue has been discussed by WTO Members in the WPEC but, so far, they have not managed to agree on a solution. A clear juxtaposition regarding the classification of digital media emerged between the European and U.S.' view. Whereas the EU classifies all electronic deliveries as "*supplies of services which fall within the scope of the GATS*" (arguably allowing it to classify digital media as 'audiovisual services', entailing limited commitments),[11] the U.S. focusses on the

---

[8]Or, put differently, "*products that are digitally encoded and that –before the rise of the Internet– were traditionally traded as part of a physical carrier medium*" in Wunsch-Vincent (2004), p. 10.

[9]As also discussed in Farrokhnia and Richards (2016).

[10]Wu (2006), p. 268.

[11]WTO Work Programme on Electronic Commerce, 'Communication from the European Communities and their Member States', S/C/W/183, 30 November 2000, p. 3.

principle of technological neutrality, stating that the classification should focus on the nature of the products, regardless of whether these services have been delivered electronically or not.[12] The WTO Secretariat in 1998 noted that "*there is no classification which would permit us to say that all intangible products, or even all electronically delivered products, are services by definition*".[13] It additionally clarified that the legal regime applicable to transactions is determined by the *nature* of the product being traded, rather than their means of delivery, thereby arguably aligning with the US' view.[14] So far, however, the disagreement on this issue between the Members continues.

2.2.2 Limited Commitments in Relevant Service Sectors

The GATS has a somewhat peculiar structure, as not all of its obligations apply to all measures affecting trade in services. As indicated above, several of its obligations are subject to Members' sector-specific commitments as contained in their Services Schedule of Commitments. These specific commitments are based on a positive list approach. This approach entails that only those service sectors that are included in the list are committed and whatever is not included in the list is not covered. This possibility of listing commitments allowed Members quite some leeway not to liberalise certain services at the multilateral level. More specifically, Members could focus on what they *did* want to liberalise. This leads to an overall low level of commitment for developing Members which drafted their Services Schedule during the Uruguay Round.[15] Adlung argues that the level of services liberalisation in the context of the Uruguay Round is negligible as Members merely bound their existing level of liberalisation.[16] This is also the case for high income Members, some of which (e.g. the EU) have considerably limited commitments in sensitive service sectors (e.g. audiovisual services).[17]

2.2.3 Specific Barriers to Digital Services Trade Are Not Explicitly Addressed

Digital services trade is confronted with several specific barriers or obstacles which are not explicitly addressed in the GATS framework. Three examples of such

---

[12]WTO Work Programme on Electronic Commerce, Submission by the United States, WT/GC/16, G/C/2, S/C/7, IP/C/16, WT/COMTD/17, 12 February 1999, p. 5.

[13]WTO Council for Trade in Services, 'The Work Programme on Electronic Commerce', Note by the Secretariat, S/C/W/68, 16 November 1998, para. 37.

[14]WTO Council for Trade in Services, 'The Work Programme on Electronic Commerce', Note by the Secretariat, S/C/W/68, 16 November 1998, para. 37.

[15]Adlung (2006), p. 873.

[16]Liberalisation of services has occurred more in accessions and PTAs. Adlung (2007), p. 560.

[17]For the history of the EU-US discussions on audiovisual services, see Pauwels and Loisen (2003).

barriers or obstacles are used in this study: data localisation requirements, mandated source code transfer and lack of ensured access to and use of the Internet for foreign service suppliers. The GATS does not contain any provisions that specifically deal with these barriers. That does however not mean that such barriers cannot be addressed in the context of the GATS or that relevant GATS obligations do not apply to such obstacles to trade.

Data localisation requirements (DLRs) take many different forms, some being more onerous than others, but all of them limit efficiency and raise costs, often to be borne by the consumers.[18] DLRs are measures that require companies to locate data servers within the host country for which they provide services or that require storing or processing original data or a copy in that territory or that generally hinder the flow of data to other countries.[19] They can however amount to a violation of both Members' market access and national treatment obligations. If a Member has committed to data processing services but imposes a requirement on service suppliers to store and process citizens' data locally, this could amount to a zero quota in the sense of Article XVI GATS. Such a DLR effectively prevents foreign data processing service suppliers from supplying their services across borders, in the same sense as how the US prevented online provision of gambling services in its territory in the *US – Gambling* case. The Appellate Body found the de facto prohibition of cross-border supply of gambling services to violate Article XVI:2 (a) and (c) GATS.[20] Depending on the facts of the case, a similar violation could be found for DLRs.

Even if a Member did not commit to the market access obligation in the service sector of data processing, a violation of the national treatment obligation can still be found. It has been argued that DLRs will very likely constitute a violation of the national treatment obligation as the prohibition to process data abroad considerably modifies the conditions of competition to the detriment of foreign services suppliers who supply any kind of digital service across borders (which per definition requires the movement and processing of data).[21] Where a Member made a national treatment commitment in a service sector relevant to digital services,[22] a DLR affecting that service sector will probably violate the national treatment obligation. DLRs have become a much discussed topic in the literature in recent years[23] and Members have started to address them in the ongoing plurilateral negotiation at the WTO on the

---

[18]See also the chapter by Yakovleva in this volume.

[19]Chung (2018), pp. 188–189; Porges and Enders (2016), p. 5.

[20]Appellate Body Report, *US – Gambling*, WT/DS285/AB/R, para. 265.

[21]Several other articles have pointed out the disproportionate burden of DLRs on foreign companies: Chander (2019), p. 15; Meltzer (2019), p. 25; Wolfe (2019), p. 80.

[22]Which can be almost any service sector, considering that many services can now be supplied through electronic transmission.

[23]See *inter alia:* Aaronson and Leblond (2018); Bauer et al. (2014); Chung (2018); Crosby (2016); Ferracane and Lee-Makiyama (2017); Mattoo and Meltzer (2018); Mihaylova (2016); Mitchell and Mishra (2018); Peng and Liu (2017); Tuthill (2016).

trade-related aspects of electronic commerce.[24] So far, however, only a limited number of Members have included prohibitions on data localisation requirements in their proposals.[25]

Mandated transfer of source code[26] creates concerns for companies as it entails the risk of leakage of trade secrets. It discourages or even blocks companies from exporting their products to countries which impose such requirements as a condition to supply goods or services in that market.[27] Neither the GATS nor the Agreement on Trade-Related Aspects of Intellectual Property Rights (TRIPS) contain provisions which expressly address the requirement of transfer of source code as a condition for market access.[28] The mandated transfer of source code has however been discussed multiple times in the context of the WPEC. Countries like the US, the EU, Canada, Chile, Colombia, Côte d'Ivoire, Japan, Korea, Mexico and Singapore have called for multilateral rules prohibiting requirements of source code transfer as a condition for market access.[29] Other Members have however condemned hard rule proposals on non-disclosure of source code.[30] Also in recent proposals in the context of the plurilateral negotiations on trade-related aspects of electronic commerce, Members have suggested such provisions.[31]

---

[24]These plurilateral negotiations were initiated by a group of 73 WTO Members following the WTO Ministerial Conference in Buenos Aires in 2017. WTO Ministerial Conference 11th session, Buenos Aires, 'Joint Statement on Electronic Commerce', WT/MIN(17)/60, 13 December 2017.

[25]WTO Joint Statement on Electronic Commerce Initiative, 'Proposal for the exploratory work by Japan', INF/ECOM/4, 25 March 2019, para. 3.8; WTO Joint Statement on Electronic Commerce Initiative, 'Communication from the United States', INF/ECOM/5, 25 March 2019, para. 2.1; WTO Joint Statement on Electronic Commerce, 'EU Proposal for WTO disciplines and commitments relating to electronic commerce', INF/ECOM/22, 26 April 2019, para. 2.7.1(a); WTO Joint Statement on Electronic Commerce, 'Communication from Singapore', INF/ECOM/25, 30 April 2019, p. 3.

[26]Source code is the basis of any software and mainly written by human programmers.

[27]As explained by Japan in WTO Joint Statement on Electronic Commerce Initiative, 'Proposal for Exploratory Work by Japan', INF/ECOM/4, 25 March 2019, para. 3.13.

[28]However, for an overview of possibly relevant WTO obligations, see Neeraj (2017).

[29]WTO General Council, 'Work Programme on Electronic Commerce – Non-Paper from the United States', JOB/GC/94, 4 July 2016, para 2.7; WTO Work Programme on Electronic Commerce, 'Trade Policy, the WTO, and the Digital Economy', Communication from Canada, Chile, Colombia, Côte d'Ivoire, the European Union, the Republic of Korea, Mexico and Singapore, JOB/GC/97/Rev. 3, 14 July 2016, p. 6; WTO Work Programme On Electronic Commerce, 'Non-Paper for the Discussions on Electronic Commerce / Digital Trade from Japan', JOB/GC/100, 25 July 2016, p. 3.

[30]WTO General Council, 'Statement by the African Group', Work Programme on Electronic Commerce, JOB/GC/144, 20 October 2017, para. 3.5.

[31]WTO Joint Statement on Electronic Commerce Initiative, 'Proposal for the exploratory work by Japan', INF/ECOM/4, 25 March 2019, para. 3.13; WTO Joint Statement on Electronic Commerce Initiative, 'Communication from the United States', INF/ECOM/5, 25 March 2019, para. 4.1; WTO Joint Statement on Electronic Commerce, 'Communication from Ukraine', INF/ECOM/14, 25 March 2019, para. 4.2; WTO Joint Statement on Electronic Commerce, 'Communication from Brazil', INF/ECOM/17, 25 March 2019, p. 8 (interestingly, this provision was omitted in Brazil's later proposal (INF/ECOM/27)); WTO Joint Statement on Electronic Commerce, 'EU Proposal for

Lack of access to the Internet is not a trade barrier in the classical sense of the word as it is mostly not a government imposed limitation to accessing a certain market[32] but it can be qualified as an 'obstacle' to the provision of digital services. As digital service suppliers require access to the Internet as a network to trade internationally, hindered access to mobile networks, broadband or reliable power supply inhibits trade in digital services. Hindered access to telecommunication facilities was already considered undesirable by WTO Members in the 1990s, when Members drafted the Annex on Telecommunications. The Annex has a broad scope and *inter alia* requires Members to ensure access to and use of public telecommunications transport networks and services for the supply of any service.[33] It can be argued that the Internet qualifies as a public telecommunications transport network as it is equivalent to other basic telecommunications services which are a means of conduit for the cross-border supply of services. As the network of networks that, through data transfer, has enabled global cross-border supply of a vast group of services, the Internet is the prototype of a telecommunication transport network. Moreover, the reference to 'public' telecoms transport networks does not relate to the ownership structure (the networks and services can be either public or private) but rather implies an assigned universal service or public service requirement.[34]

The GATS itself does not explicitly address this obstacle to digital services trade but if the Internet constitutes a public telecommunications transport network, then any measure that prevents access to and use of the Internet by foreign service suppliers to supply their services in that market would violate Section 5 of the Telecoms Annex. Members are under a positive obligation to ensure such access. However, WTO Members do not (yet) agree on the applicability of the Annex to the Internet, as is illustrated by the fact that provisions related to open networks and a freely accessible Internet are being proposed only by some Members in the context of the plurilateral negotiations.[35]

WTO disciplines and commitments relating to electronic commerce', INF/ECOM/22, 26 April 2019, para. 2.6; WTO Joint Statement on Electronic Commerce, 'Communication from Singapore', INF/ECOM/25, 30 April 2019, para. 4.1.

[32]See the definition of 'barrier' in Van den Bossche and Zdouc (2017), p. 479: "*all government imposed and sponsored actions or omissions that act as prohibitions or restrictions on trade, other than ordinary customs duties and other duties and charges on imports and exports*".

[33]Section 5 of the Telecoms Annex. On the scope, see also the interpretation by the panel in *Mexico – Telecoms* at para. 7.278.

[34]See para. 3(a) of the GATS Annex on Telecommunications: "*'public telecommunications transport service' means any telecommunications transport service require, explicitly or in effect, by a Member to be offered to the public generally.*" Gao (2008), p. 692.

[35]WTO Joint Statement on Electronic Commerce Initiative, 'Proposal for the exploratory work by Japan', INF/ECOM/4, 25 March 2019, para. 3.9; WTO Joint Statement on Electronic Commerce Initiative, 'Communication from the United States', INF/ECOM/5, 25 March 2019, para. 2.1; WTO Joint Statement on Electronic Commerce, 'EU Proposal for WTO disciplines and commitments relating to electronic commerce', INF/ECOM/22, 26 April 2019, para. 2.9; WTO Joint Statement on Electronic Commerce, 'Communication from Singapore', INF/ECOM/25, 30 April 2019, p. 4; WTO Joint Statement on Electronic Commerce, 'Communication from Brazil', INF/ECOM/27, 30 April 2019, p. 2.

Interestingly but not unexpectedly, neither China nor Russia have included provisions addressing DLRs, source code transfer or limits to access and use of the Internet in their proposals in the plurilateral negotiations at the WTO. Looking at the parties who did propose such provisions (EU, Japan, US and Singapore; Brazil only regarding access and source code), it is expected that they will have taken a similar approach in their PTAs. This will be assessed in the subsequent section of this chapter.

3   Digital Services Within the PTA Framework

This section assesses whether e-commerce chapters in PTAs go further than what can be found at the multilateral level. Confronted with a stand-still at the WTO level, Members have in large numbers turned to preferential trade agreements to further liberalise trade with selected trading partners.[36] This is no different for issues related to digital services trade.

UNCTAD highlights five strengths of PTAs when it comes to regulating international data flows (and hence digital trade). Not only do PTAs increase the potential to engage more countries in the discussion, they generally allow for a higher level of binding and further interoperability between the parties. They additionally have the potential to address the balance between data flows and protection, to address new technologies and to manage cross-border data flows.[37]   UNCTAD however cautiously points out the limitations PTAs are faced with: the secretive negotiations, exclusion of consumer and civil society stakeholders, complex dispute resolution procedures, inability to adequately address gaps in coverage and the difficulty to establish jurisdiction (compared to domestic regulation).[38] The question therefore remains whether the strengths outweigh the perceived weaknesses of regulating trade at a preferential rather than at the multilateral level.

There is additionally a risk of fragmentation and disruption of the global framework when PTAs go further than what can be found at the multilateral level and do so in a diverging way.[39] This is especially the case when both multilateral and bilateral dispute settlement systems are used, with potentially contradictory outcomes.[40] In addition, there are various advantages to dealing with such a broad issue

---

[36]As already observed and aptly termed the 'spaghetti bowl' effect in Bhagwati (1995).

[37]UNCTAD (2016), pp. 37–38.

[38]UNCTAD (2016), p. 38.

[39]Mitchell and Mishra refer to the various new provisions in the CPTPP and warn about risks of fragmentation. Mitchell and Mishra (2018), p. 1097.

[40]This however requires that the provisions on e-commerce in PTAs are subject to the PTA's dispute settlement mechanism, which is sometimes not the case.

at the multilateral level. Burri points out that the law of the WTO is intrinsically flexible but at the same time provides a stable basis of substantive and procedural rules, complemented with an effective dispute settlement system that fosters legal evolution.[41] Moreover, the multilateral level is the more suitable fit for policy in an area that requires fluid interoperability to work.[42] Multilateral negotiations additionally have the largest trade creation effects and (almost) zero trade diversion effects.[43]

Contrastingly, it is pointed out that generally, PTAs are better suited to reconcile diverging interest and are thereby in a better position to address new generation trade barriers.[44] Wu argues that, regardless of this potential, many PTAs continue to skirt around the shortcomings he identified in existing WTO obligations related to electronic commerce.[45] It is worthwhile to test this statement and assess the added value of these PTAs in addressing digital trade issues. Especially considering the ongoing plurilateral negotiations at the multilateral level, PTAs can serve as building blocks, enabling convergence between Members' views on these issues.

For the purpose of this study, 98 PTAs with e-commerce provisions were identified.[46] Through a term-frequency analysis, the presence of certain specific provisions in these PTAs can easily be detected. The following terms were searched for: 'digital products', 'location of computing facilities', 'source code' and 'use of Internet'.[47] They allow for the identification of provisions on digital products and provisions addressing three specific barriers to digital services trade: data localisation requirements, mandated source code transfer and provisions requiring ensured access to and use of the Internet.

---

[41]Burri (2017), pp. 93–95.

[42]Burri (2017), p. 128.

[43]Herman (2010), p. 11.

[44]Burri (2017), p. 127.

[45]The shortcomings he identifies are related to the definition of digital trade/products, classification of digital services, lack of market access liberalisation, lack of provisions on cross-border data flows, consumer-related regulatory measures, security-related regulatory measures and trade facilitation. Wu (2017), p. 5.

[46]This list was compiled on the basis of information from the WTO's Regional Trade Agreements Information System (RTA-IS), WTO documents and literature. Including WTO Work Programme On Electronic Commerce, 'Non-Paper for the Discussions on Electronic Commerce / Digital Trade from Japan', JOB/GC/100, 25 July 2016, 5–8; Burri and Polanco Lazo (2020); Lopez-Gonzalez and Ferencz (2018); Monteiro and Teh (2017); Wu (2017). This list is up to date until 23 August 2019.

[47]First, because parties use (slightly) different terms in their PTAs to address the same kind of provisions, many variations of each of these terms were also included in the search. Secondly, as the text of several PTAs could only be provided in Spanish, the Spanish translation of these terms has also been included in the search. Both of these elements allowed for a complete mapping of these provisions in all e-commerce PTAs.

3.1   General Trends in E-Commerce PTAs

Ever since the early 2000s, countries have started including e-commerce provisions in their PTAs.[48] The New-Zealand – Singapore PTA (2001) was the first to include a provision on paperless trading.[49] This example was swiftly followed in the Japan – Singapore PTA (2002). The US – Jordan PTA (2001) was the very first PTA to include a dedicated e-commerce provision.[50] The Australia – Singapore PTA (2003) was the first to include a dedicated chapter on electronic commerce.[51] The US started including e-commerce chapters and stronger obligations in its PTAs from 2004 onwards.[52] In the US – Australia PTA (2005) provisions on authentication, digital products, online consumer protection and paperless trade were added.[53] The KORUS PTA, concluded in 2012, was the first regional trade agreement to include specific language on the principle of open networks and the free flow of information in its e-commerce chapter.[54]

Figure 1 displays the number of PTAs that have been concluded between 1990 and 2018, coloured in by whether they contain e-commerce provisions or not. The figure indicates that there is a clear increase in the number of e-commerce PTAs, but also that this increase is not linear. The pace of including e-commerce provisions in PTAs has significantly started picking up from 2011 onwards. Notably, more PTAs with e-commerce provisions entered into force than those without in 2014, 2015, 2016 and 2018. This seems to hint at e-commerce provisions in PTAs slowly becoming the rule rather than the exception.

Two-thirds of the WTO Membership is now party to a PTA that includes e-commerce related provisions.[55] Based on the perceived trend in Fig. 1, these parties are more likely to conclude even more e-commerce PTAs in the future. It is therefore worthwhile to look into whether these e-commerce provisions and chapters successfully address the gaps and unclarities that were identified in the first section of this chapter.

---

[48]With perhaps the exception of the EEA Agreement, which entered into force in 1994 and which contained a reference to 'information services', in the context of further cooperation outside of the four freedoms (article 78).

[49]Monteiro and Teh (2017), p. 5.

[50]Huang (2017), p. 316.

[51]Monteiro and Teh (2017), p. 5; Wu (2017), p. 6 The advantage of including e-commerce rules in a separate chapter of a PTA is that it avoids the discussion on the goods v services classification. Wunsch-Vincent and Hold (2012), p. 202.

[52]See the US – Chile PTA and the US – Singapore PTA, both of which entered into force on 1 January 2004.

[53]Huang (2017), p. 316.

[54]Aaronson and Leblond (2018), p. 255; Huang (2017), pp. 316–317. See articles 15.7 and 15.8 KORUS PTA.

[55]111 out of 164 WTO Members are party to a PTA that includes at least one e-commerce related provision. Calculations based on own database.

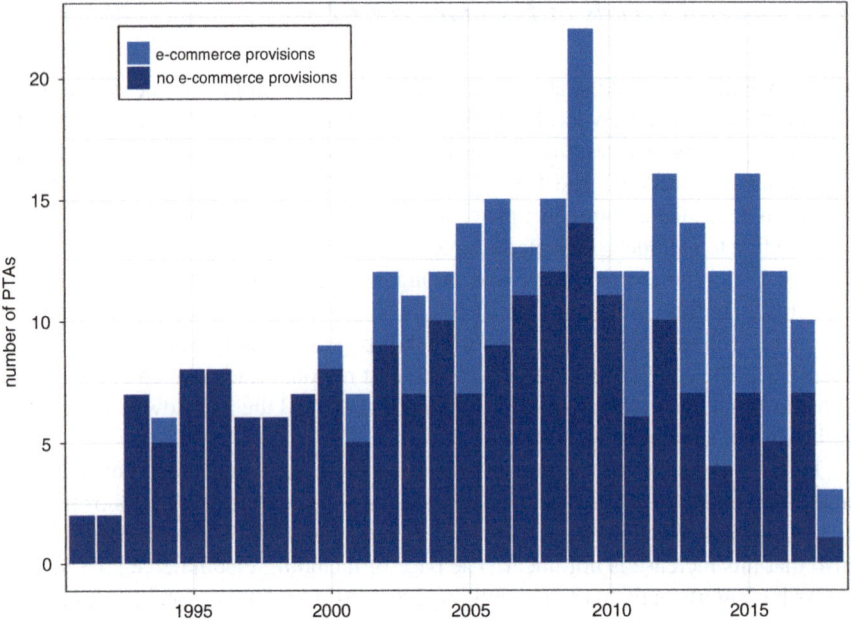

Fig. 1 PTAs concluded between 1990 and 2018

3.2   National Interests Dictate the Classification of 'Digital Products'

WTO Members have taken a disparate approach to the classification of digital products in their PTAs, illustrating the continuing divergent opinions on how to qualify content that is being transmitted electronically. The disagreement between the EU and the US that governs this discussion at the multilateral level is equally present at the bilateral level. This is reflected in the use of the term 'digital product' in PTAs. This term is most often included in US PTAs, which define digital products as (variations on) "*a computer program, text, video, image, sound recording, or other product that is digitally encoded, produced for commercial sale or distribution, and that can be transmitted electronically*". The US additionally consistently includes a non-discrimination obligation, requiring no less favourable treatment of digital products to like (domestic or foreign) digital products.[56]

The EU takes a completely different approach in its PTAs, not ever referring to the term 'digital product'. It prefers the terminology of 'electronic transmissions' and 'by electronic means'. Moreover, the EU often does not include provisions on e-commerce in a separate chapter but rather groups these in a subsection of the

---

[56]It does not require this treatment for digital products and like *offline* products.

chapter on cross-border trade in services.[57] A final element that supports the EU position in this debate is that the EU does not include a prohibition on applying customs duties to electronic transmissions in several of its e-commerce sections/ chapters. Rather it limits itself to clarifying that "*electronic supply constitutes trade in services*" and can therefore not be subject to customs duties.[58] This approach contrasts significantly with the US', who always includes a clear prohibition on the application of customs duties to electronic transmissions. In its more recent PTAs, however, the EU also seems to prefer the clear prohibition over the clarification.

Other countries seem to take a mixed approach in their PTAs when it comes to the use of the term 'digital products'. Out of all 98 e-commerce PTAs, only 42 contain the term 'digital product'. Apart from the US, other 'heavy users' include Singapore, Australia, Canada, Japan and Mexico. All of them include the term 'digital product' in at least half of their e-commerce PTAs. Moreover, all of them define 'digital products' in a very similar way to the US. Australia, Singapore, Japan and Mexico stick closely to the US model, including a non-discrimination obligation on digital products.[59] Canada generally limits itself to a ban on customs duties on digital products that are transmitted electronically.[60] Interestingly, Australia always includes the caveat that the definition of digital products in its PTAs does not prejudge the position of either party in the debate at the WTO as to the qualification of these products as goods or services.[61]

3.3   Use of Negative Lists Results in More Commitments in Relevant Service Sectors

PTAs that cover trade in services are generally characterised by a deeper level of services commitments than what the parties agreed to at the multilateral level. This of course fits within the very *raison d'être* of preferential liberalisation with trading partners: to allow for deeper liberalisation with preferred trading partners. Moreover, any services PTA should be in accordance with Article V GATS, which allows for agreements liberalising trade in services between certain WTO Members provided

---

[57]See EU – Korea PTA, EU – Georgia PTA, EU – Moldova PTA, EU – Ukraine PTA, EU – Armenia PTA, JEEPA, EU – Singapore PTA and EU – Vietnam PTA.

[58]Article 119 EU – CARIFORUM PTA, Article 127 EU – Georgia PTA, Article 254 EU – Moldova PTA, Article 139 EU – Ukraine PTA and Article 193 EU – Armenia PTA. EU PTAs containing the prohibition are: the EU – Korea PTA, EU – Central America PTA, CETA, JEEPA, EU – Mexico PTA, EU – Singapore PTA and EU – Vietnam PTA.

[59]E.g. Article 13.4 Australia – Peru PTA, Article 12.4 Costa Rica – Singapore PTA, Article 9.4 Japan – Mongolia PTA and Article 15.4 Mexico – Central America PTA.

[60]E.g. Article 1503 Canada – Peru PTA.

[61]E.g. fn 3 to Chapter 14 on Electronic Commerce in the Australia – Singapore PTA. Mexico also does so in the Mexico – Panama PTA (fn 1 to Chapter 14) but not in its PTA with Central American countries.

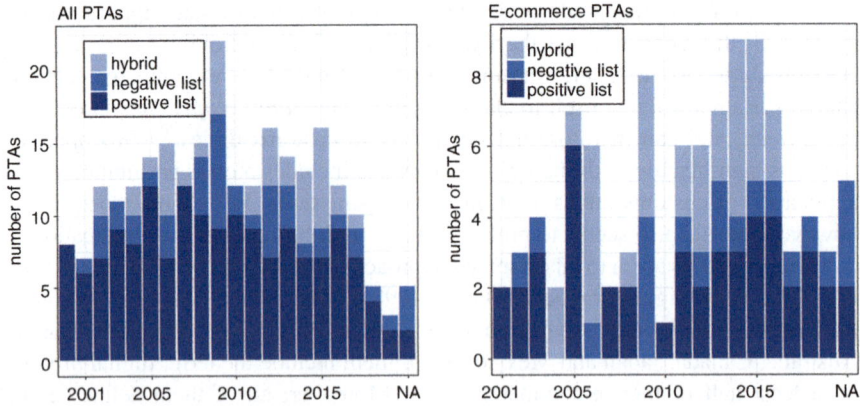

Fig. 2 Negative-list approach in PTAs

that the agreement has substantial sectoral coverage and eliminates substantially all national treatment discrimination.[62]

Several PTAs take the 'negative list' approach to services liberalisation. Different from the positive list approach as used in the GATS (see *supra*), the negative list approach starts from the liberalisation of all service sectors and allows parties to list the service sectors or specific measures for which trade in services is not liberalised, through listed reservations. Very often, reservations take two forms: non-conforming (existing) measures and future measures.[63] Moreover, PTAs taking the negative-list approach regularly include ratchet clauses, whereby any future liberalisation is automatically locked in.[64] The negative-list approach has two significant benefits: transparency and predictability.[65] Overall, this approach leads to a higher level of improved liberalisation commitments, which is in line with the objective to remove all limitations on market access and all discrimination connected to national treatment.[66] It has however been cautioned that negative list PTAs cover substantially more service sectors but that the extent to which they result in actual reduction of barriers to trade is limited.[67] Furthermore, it has been shown that a positive-list approach doesn't necessarily entail less liberalisation than when a negative list is used.[68]

Negative list PTAs are however not yet the rule, as can be inferred from Fig. 2, which indicates the number of positive and negative list PTAs (and hybrid PTAs,

---

[62]Article V:1 GATS.

[63]Roy et al. (2007), p. 158.

[64]Roy et al. (2007), p. 158; Sauvé and Shingal (2011), p. 955.

[65]See Roy et al. (2007), pp. 173 and 179; Stephenson (2002), p. 194.

[66]Hufbauer and Stephenson (2007), p. 619; Jara and Domínguez (2006), p. 114; Roy et al. (2007), p. 173.

[67]Hoekman and Mattoo (2013), p. 14.

[68]Roy et al. (2007), p. 173.

containing elements of both approaches) that entered into force every year since 2000.[69] It can be observed that e-commerce PTAs generally have a slightly higher proportion of negative list PTAs[70] and that quite a number of them takes a hybrid approach.[71] For both graphs it is however noteworthy that even recent PTAs mainly take the positive list-approach.

The overall trend of including more services commitments in PTAs is undisputed and it is this fact which ensures the added value created by PTAs in the liberalisation of digital services trade. Even where PTAs do not contain e-commerce chapters or even provisions, the mere fact that the parties have committed to a higher level of services liberalisation enables the trade in digital services. Because digital services take a wide variety of forms, ranging from social media to online consulting, online banking services and internet telephony, the liberalisation of any mode of supply, but especially cross-border supply (mode 1), of a large group of services sectors ensures applicability of the market access and national treatment obligations to digital services. In this sense, PTAs *per definition* to a certain extent address the GATS issue of limited liberalisation of service sectors relevant to digital services trade.[72]

As a side note, it should be cautioned that the adoption of a negative list approach to services commitments does not solve the discussion on the classification of digital services. Even if only the service (sub)sectors that are not committed are listed, it is key for Members to be able to clearly classify digital services in order to identify both committed and uncommitted services, in order to understand the extent of their obligations.[73]

3.4 Only the Newest and Most Extensive E-Commerce PTAs Address Specific Barriers

Some WTO Members have already discussed the three specific barriers to digital services trade in the context of the WPEC, thereby highlighting the fact that they are not explicitly being addressed within the GATS (see *supra*). As Members are aware of these gaps in the existing legal framework, it makes sense for them to address these lacunae in their preferential agreements. Through the term-frequency analysis, the presence of terms related to these three barriers was mapped for all e-commerce

---

[69]'NA' refers to PTAs whose text has been agreed upon but that have not yet entered into force.

[70]19% of all PTAs entered into force since 2000 take the negative-list approach, compared to 21% of e-commerce PTAs.

[71]16% (all PTAs since 2000) compared to 32% (e-commerce PTAs).

[72]It should however be cautioned that it has been argued that many PTAs contain 'GATS-minus commitments', thereby committing to a lower level of liberalisation than at the multilateral level. See Adlung and Morrison (2010); Adlung and Miroudot (2012).

[73]The classification issue for digital services is discussed and a solution is proposed in Willemyns (2019).

PTAs. Figure 3 shows the amount of mentions of these terms for every single e-commerce PTA, which have been ordered chronologically. The points are slightly scattered, in order to allow for the visibility of overlapping points. All points dancing around the 0 value of the y-axis should therefore be interpreted as that term not being mentioned in that specific PTA.

So far, the presence of these three barriers in PTAs has not exhaustively been mapped. However, other studies have been conducted, addressing some of these barriers or providing an overall estimation of the content of e-commerce chapters.[74] The ICTSD reports that most PTAs include provisions on the elimination of customs duties, consumer protection, authentication methods and signature and paperless trading. Provisions on data localisation, cross-border data flows and mandated transfer of source code are deemed more rare.[75] These findings are confirmed by the term-frequency analysis conducted on the text of 98 e-commerce PTAs. Provisions on customs duties on electronic transmission can be found in 65 PTAs, provisions on online consumer protection in 48 PTAs, provisions on e-authentication in 34 PTAs, provisions on e-signatures and on paperless trade in 50 PTAs each. Provisions on source code, data localisation and access to and use of the Internet are however much less prevalent and have only been included in more recent e-commerce PTAs, as shown in Fig. 3.

The terms related to data localisation provisions were found in six PTAs: Article 9.10 Japan – Mongolia PTA, Article 15 of Chapter 14 Australia – Singapore PTA, Article 14.13 CPTPP, Article 9.10 Singapore – Sri Lanka PTA, Article 19.12 USMCA and Article 13.12 Australia – Peru PTA. Looking closer into the content of these agreements, it becomes clear that all of them include a clear prohibition on DLRs. The language used is very similar, all of them prohibiting the parties to require covered persons to use or locate computing facilities in their territory as a condition for conducting business. These provisions allow for the imposition of DLRs where necessary to achieve legitimate public policy objectives if they are applied in a manner which does not constitute arbitrary or unjustifiable discrimination or a disguised restriction on trade.[76] The only exception to this is Article 19.12 of the USMCA which only sets out the obligation, not the exception. Moreover, the USMCA contains a second prohibition on DLRs in its financial services chapter, stating that the prohibition on DLRs is subject to the condition that financial regulatory authorities have immediate, direct, complete and ongoing access to information processed and stored outside of a party's territory.

The terms related to provisions on source code transfer were found in seven different PTAs: Article 9.11 of the Japan – Mongolia PTA, Article 19 of Chapter 14

---

[74]See *inter alia* Burri (2017); Gao (2018); Herman (2010); Huang (2017); Kim (2019); Monteiro and Teh (2017); Weber (2012); Willemyns (2020); Wunsch-Vincent and Hold (2012).

[75]ICTSD (2018), p. 3.

[76]In the spirit of the chapeau of the general exceptions in Article XIV GATS. It should be noted that the necessity requirement is not included in the Singapore – Sri Lanka PTA and the Australia – Peru PTA.

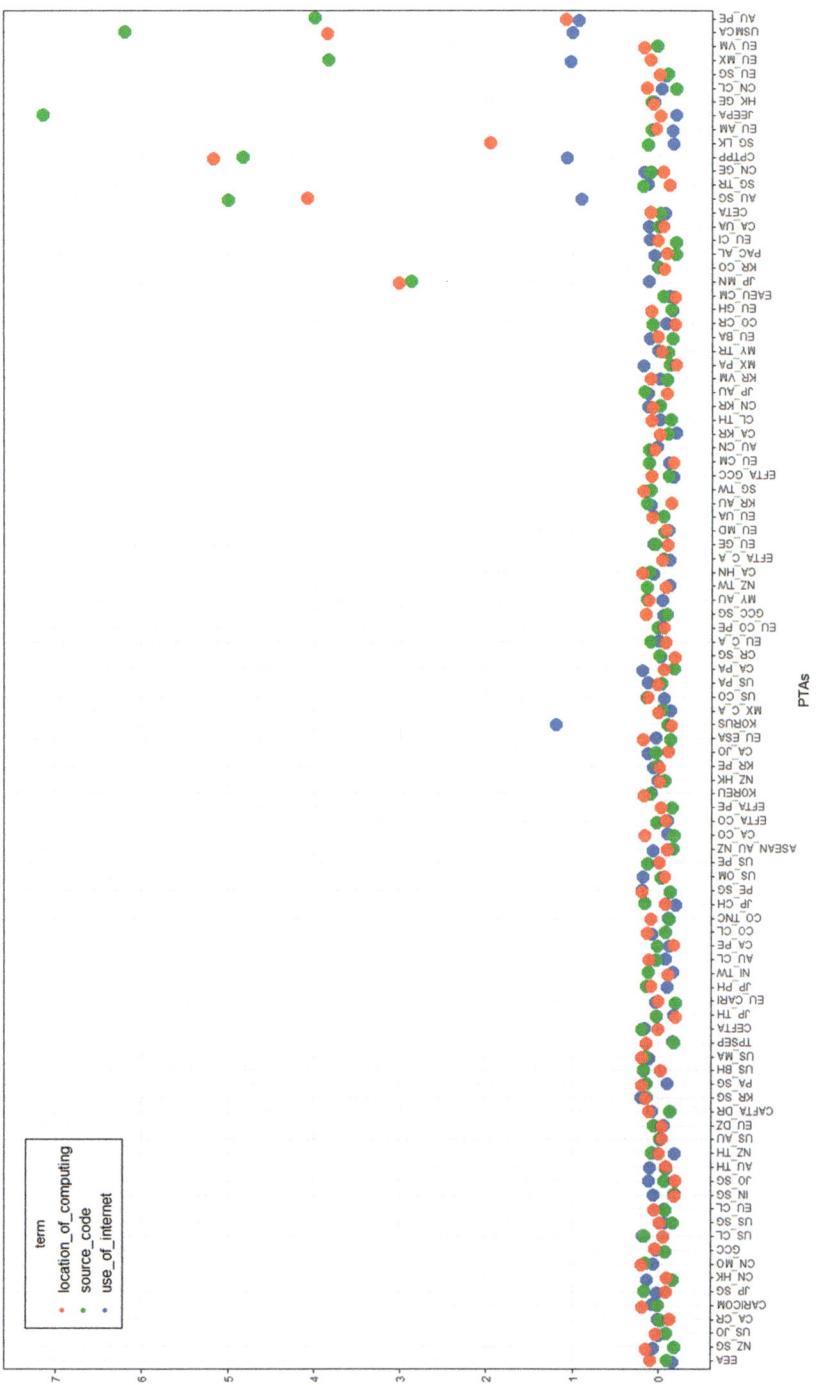

Fig. 3 Specific barriers in e-commerce PTAs

Australia – Singapore PTA, Article 14.17 CPTPP, Article 8.73 JEEPA, Article 9 of the Chapter on Digital Trade EU – Mexico PTA, Article 19.16 USMCA and Article 13.16 Australia – Peru PTA. Even though the language of these provisions is similar, there are small differences. All of these PTAs set out the prohibition for parties to require the transfer of, or access to, source code of software owned by a person of the other party as a condition for import, distribution, sale or use of software in its territory. Most provisions clarify that this obligation only applies to mass-market software and not to software which is used for critical infrastructure.[77] Both of the EU PTAs prohibit requirements of source code transfer without any mention of the condition for market access. Different PTAs contain different exceptions to this obligation: voluntary transfer on commercial basis,[78] transfer required by courts,[79] requirements by regulatory bodies or judicial authorities,[80] general and security exception clauses,[81] requirements related to patents[82] and requirements of modification necessary for compliance with laws and regulations in accordance with the PTA.[83] These differences are quite consistent along country lines, with different approaches taken by Japan, Australia, the US and the EU.

Finally, six PTAs contain provisions that set out the 'principles on access to and use of the Internet for electronic commerce'.[84] Contrary to the provisions on DLRs and source code, parties only *recognise* that consumers should be able to access and use the services and applications of their choice, connect the devices of their choice to the Internet and to access information on the network management practices of Internet access service providers. Only slightly different language is used in the very first provision on this: Article 15.7 KORUS recognises that consumers should be able to *"access and use services and digital products of their choice"* and have the *"benefit of competition between network providers, app and service providers and content providers"*. Especially the language of the first section is interesting. By juxtaposing 'services' and 'digital products', the article implies that services are not digital products, which is in line with the US' position in this debate as discussed above. The EU also takes a slightly different approach, stating that parties *"shall endeavour to ensure"* and choosing a different heading for this provision ('open Internet access').

---

[77]Only USMCA and the EU PTAs do not include this limitation of the scope.

[78]Article 8.73.1 JEEPA and Article 9.2 Chapter Digital Trade EU – Mexico PTA.

[79]Article 8.73.2 JEEPA and Article 9.3 Chapter Digital Trade EU – Mexico PTA.

[80]Article 19.16.2 USMCA.

[81]Article 8.73.3 JEEPA, Article 9.2 Chapter Digital Trade EU – Mexico PTA.

[82]Article 19.4 Chapter 14 Australia – Singapore PTA, Article 14.17.4 CPTPP, Article 13.16.4 Australia – Peru PTA.

[83]Article 19.3 Chapter 14 Australia – Singapore PTA, Article 14.17.3 CPTPP, Article 13.16.3 Australia – Peru PTA.

[84]Article 15.7 KORUS, Article 12 Chapter 14 Australia – Singapore PTA, Article 14.10 CPTPP, Article 10 Chapter on digital trade EU – Mexico, Article 19.10 USMCA and Article 13.10 Australia – Peru PTA.

Overall, it can thus be observed that only a handful of PTAs have addressed these three barriers. Clear frontrunners are Australia, the EU, Japan, Singapore and the US. Most of them have also proposed similar provisions in the ongoing plurilateral negotiations.[85] Brazil's proposals in this context are interesting, considering that it has so far not concluded any e-commerce PTA, let alone included provisions addressing these barriers.[86] With regard to data localisation requirements and mandated transfer of source code, PTAs are considerably more explicit than what is found in the GATS. Even where these provisions do not necessarily fill a legal lacuna –DLRs can be addressed through the market access and national treatment obligations in the GATS– they do however considerably clarify Members' obligations with regard to these specific barriers. This is arguably different for the provisions on access to and use of the Internet which do not utilise sufficiently strong language to add substantially to the existing obligations in the Telecoms Annex. PTA parties would contribute more to the discussions on this point at the multilateral level through an endorsement of the Internet as a 'public telecommunications transport network'.

4 Conclusion

Analysing both the gaps in the application of the GATS framework to digital services trade and the answers to these issues that WTO Members have formulated in their PTAs has uncovered the so-far limited contribution most e-commerce PTAs make to the issues surrounding digital services trade. It has been shown that there is a considerably divergence between how e-commerce PTAs address the three issues that have been studied in this chapter.

Regarding the classification of digital products, it is clear that the juxtaposition between the EU and the US on this issue persists. Only a handful of developed countries seem to be adopting the US approach, including the term 'digital product' in their PTAs. Some however still include the caveat that the inclusion of this term in the e-commerce chapters of their PTAs does not prejudice their position in this debate at the WTO. Therefore, arguably one of the main challenges of the ongoing plurilateral negotiations will be to reconcile Members on the meaning of 'digital products' and the agreements that should be deemed relevant to measures affecting such products.

---

[85]WTO Joint Statement on Electronic Commerce Initiative, 'Proposal for the exploratory work by Japan', INF/ECOM/4, 25 March 2019; WTO Joint Statement on Electronic Commerce Initiative, 'Communication from the United States', INF/ECOM/5, 25 March 2019; WTO Joint Statement on Electronic Commerce, 'EU Proposal for WTO disciplines and commitments relating to electronic commerce', INF/ECOM/22, 26 April 2019; WTO Joint Statement on Electronic Commerce, 'Communication from Singapore', INF/ECOM/25, 30 April 2019.

[86]WTO Joint Statement on Electronic Commerce, 'Communication from Brazil', INF/ECOM/27, 30 April 2019, p. 2.

PTAs already in their very nature address the issue of lack of commitments in relevant services sectors, especially where they take a negative list or hybrid approach. For e-commerce PTAs specifically, there is a slightly higher number of negative lists and a considerably higher number of hybrid list approaches, adding to the overall liberalising nature of e-commerce PTAs. It can therefore be concluded that overall, e-commerce PTAs address the issue of limited commitments, albeit to a more or lesser extent depending on whether a negative list is employed. However, further study into the exact reservations is necessary to provide an in-depth assessment of whether parties considerably go beyond their commitments at the multilateral level, especially concerning sensitive service sectors.

Even though already 98 e-commerce PTAs have been concluded, only half a dozen of them explicitly address the three barriers/obstacles to digital services trade identified in this chapter. These are all PTAs which have been concluded in the last couple of years. To each of them, a strong e-commerce advancing country is a party. Strong obligations on DLR and source code seem feasible to agree to among this small group of countries, but even among them, provisions ensuring access to and use of the Internet seem to remain a sensitive issue, with only some endeavours and recognitions of importance included in their PTAs.

The divergence in approaching these issues is apparent throughout the whole timeline of e-commerce PTAs. However, it should be noted that some convergence can be observed in the newest PTAs concluded by countries like the US, the EU, Japan and Singapore. Considering that similar provisions are now being proposed in the plurilateral negotiations at the WTO, they might become staple provisions in future, far-reaching e-commerce chapters in PTAs or even become part of a plurilateral agreement on the trade-related aspects of electronic commerce. It however remains to be seen whether the handful of e-commerce pioneering developed countries will be able to persuade the other countries at the table of the necessity to develop new provisions on electronic commerce that go beyond what Members have so far agreed to at the multilateral level.

References

Aaronson S, Leblond P (2018) Another digital divide: the rise of data realms and its implications for the WTO. J Int Econ Law 21(2):245–272

Adlung R (2006) Services negotiations in the Doha Round: lost in flexibility. J Int Econ Law 9 (4):865–893

Adlung R (2007) The contribution of services liberalization to poverty reduction: what role for the GATS? J World Investment Trade 8(4):549–570

Adlung R, Miroudot S (2012) Poison in the wine? Tracing GATS-minus commitments in regional trade agreements. J World Trade 46(5):1045–1082

Adlung R, Morrison P (2010) Less than the GATS: "Negative Preferences" in regional services agreements. J Int Econ Law 13(4):1103–1143

Bauer M, Lee-Makiyama H, van der Marel E, Verschelde B (2014) The costs of data localisation: friendly fire on economic recovery, occasional, paper. ECIPE, Brussels

Bhagwati J (1995) US trade policy: the infatuation with FTAs. Colombia University discussion paper series 726, Columbia University, Columbia

Burri M (2017) The governance of data and data flows in trade agreements: the pitfalls of legal adaptation. UC Davis Law Rev 51(1):65–132

Burri M, Polanco Lazo R (2020) E-commerce and data flows provisions in preferential trade agreements: introducing a new dataset. J Int Econ Law 23(1):187–220

Chander A (2019) The Internet of Things: both goods and services. World Trade Rev 18(S1):9–22

Chung C (2018) Data localization: the causes, evolving international regimes and Korean practices. J World Trade 52(2):187–208

Crosby D (2016) Analysis of data localization measures under WTO services trade rules and commitments. International Centre for Trade and Sustainable Development (ICTSD), Geneva

Farrokhnia F, Richards C (2016) E-commerce products under the World Trade Organization agreements: goods, services, both or neither? J World Trade 50(5):793–818

Ferracane M, Lee-Makiyama H (2017) China's technology protectionism and its non-negotiable rationales. Trade working paper. ECIPE, Brussels

Gao H (2008) Annex on telecommunications. In: Wolfrum R, Stoll P, Feinäugle C (eds) WTO – trade in services. Martinus Nijhoff, Leiden, pp 683–711

Gao H (2018) Digital or trade? The contrasting approaches of China and US to digital trade. J Int Econ Law 21(2):297–321

Herman L (2010) Multilateralising regionalism: the case of e-commerce. OECD trade policy papers 99. OECD Publishing, Paris

Hoekman B, Mattoo A (2013) Liberalizing trade in services: lessons from regional and WTO negotiations. Florence, European University Institute – Robert Schuman Centre for Advanced Studies, EUI Working Papers, RSCAS 2013–14. European University Institute, Italy

Huang J (2017) Comparison of e-commerce regulations in Chinese and American FTAs: converging approaches, diverging contents, and polycentric directions? Netherlands Int Law Rev 64 (2):309–337

Hufbauer G, Stephenson S (2007) Services trade: past liberalization and future challenges. J Int Econ Law 10(3):605–630

ICTSD (2018) Updating the multilateral rule book on e-commerce, policy brief. ICTSD, Geneva

Jara A, Domínguez C (2006) Liberalization of trade in services and trade negotiations. J World Trade 40(1):113–127

Kim E (2019) E-commerce in South Korean FTAs: policy priorities and provisional inconsistencies. World Trade Rev 18(S1):85–98

Lopez-Gonzalez J, Ferencz J (2018) Digital trade and market openness, Working Party of the Trade Committee, TAD/TC/WP(2018)3/FINAL. OECD Publishing, Paris

Mattoo A, Meltzer J (2018) International data flows and privacy: the conflict and its resolution. J Int Econ Law 21(4):769–789

Meltzer J (2019) Governing digital trade. World Trade Rev 18(S1):23–48

Mihaylova I (2016) Could the recently enacted data localization requirements in Russia backfire? J World Trade 50(2):313–333

Mitchell A, Mishra N (2018) Data at the docks: modernizing International Trade Law for the digital economy. Vanderbilt J Entertain Technol Law 20(4):1073–1134

Monteiro J, Teh R (2017) Provisions on electronic commerce in regional trade agreements, WTO staff working papers, ERSD-2017-11. World Trade Organization, Economic Research and Statistics Division, Geneva

Neeraj RS (2017) Trade rules on source code – deepening the digital inequities by locking up the software fortress, working paper CWS/WP/200/37. Centre for WTO Studies, Delhi

Pauwels C, Loisen J (2003) The WTO and the audiovisual sector: economic free trade vs cultural horse trading. Eur J Commun 18(3):291–313

Peng S, Liu H (2017) The legality of data residency requirements: how can the trans-Pacific partnership help? J World Trade 51(2):183–204

Porges A, Enders A (2016) Data moving across borders: the future of digital trade policy. E15 initiative. International Centre for Trade and Sustainable Development (ICTSD), Geneva

Roy M, Marchetti J, Lim A (2007) Services liberalization in the new generation of preferential trade agreements (PTAs): how much further than the GATS. World Trade Rev 6(2):155–192

Sauvé P, Shingal A (2011) Reflections on the preferential liberalization of services trade. J World Trade 45(5):953–963

Stephenson S (2002) Regional versus multilateral liberalization of services. World Trade Rev 1 (2):187–209

Tuthill L (2016) Cross-border data flows: what role for trade rules? In: Sauve P, Roy M (eds) Research handbook on trade in services. Edward Elgar, Cheltenham, pp 357–382

UNCTAD (2016) Data protection regulations and international data flows: implications for trade and development. United Nations Publications, New York

Van den Bossche P, Zdouc W (2017) The law and policy of the World Trade Organization. Text, cases and materials. Cambridge University Press, Cambridge

Weber R (2012) Regulatory autonomy and privacy standards under the GATS. Asian J WTO Int Health Law Policy 7(1):25–47

Willemyns I (2019) GATS classification of digital services – does 'The Cloud' have a silver lining? J World Trade 53(1):59–81

Willemyns I (2020) Agreement Forthcoming? A Comparison of EU, US, and Chinese RTAs in Times of Plurilateral E-Commerce Negotiations. J Int Econ Law 23(1):221–244

Wolfe R (2019) Learning about digital trade: privacy and e-commerce in CETA and TPP. World Trade Rev 18(S1):63–84

Wu T (2006) The World Trade Law of censorship and internet filtering. Chic J Int Law 7 (1):263–287

Wu M (2017) Digital trade-related provisions in regional trade agreements: existing models and lessons for the multilateral trade system. ICTSD and IDB, Geneva/Washington

Wunsch-Vincent S (2004) WTO, e-commerce, and information technologies – from the Uruguay Round through the Doha development agenda. Markle Foundation, Germany

Wunsch-Vincent S, Hold A (2012) Towards coherent rules for digital trade: building on efforts in multilateral versus preferential trade negotiations. In: Burri M, Cottier T (eds) Trade governance in the digital age. Cambridge University Press, Cambridge, pp 179–221

Ines Willemyns obtained her PhD in international economic law in 2019 after having worked as a doctoral researcher at the Leuven Centre for Global Governance Studies at KU Leuven. Her dissertation discussed the international legal framework applicable to digital services trade. Before working as a doctoral researcher, she obtained an LL.M from the University of Barcelona (IELPO) and a bachelor's and master's degree in law from KU Leuven. Ines researches various aspects of international economic law with a particular focus on digital trade issues.

Upping the *Ante*: The Movement of Natural Persons (Mode 4) and Non-Services Migration in EU and Asian PTAs

Marion Panizzon and Harjodh Singh

Contents

This work has benefitted from the support of the National Center for Competence in Research, nccr-on the move at the University of Neuchatel, funded by the Swiss National Science Foundation. We have also been supported by a visiting scholarship of the World Trade Institute. We thank Markus Krajewski for his most valuable comments and encouragement.

M. Panizzon (✉)
University of Bern, Bern, Switzerland
e-mail: marion.panizzon@wti.org

H. Singh
Mumbai, India
e-mail: Harjodh.singh@m16.wti.org

© The Editor(s) (if applicable) and The Author(s), under exclusive licence to   139
Springer Nature Switzerland AG 2020
R. T. Hoffmann, M. Krajewski (eds.), *Coherence and Divergence in Services Trade Law*, European Yearbook of International Economic Law,
https://doi.org/10.1007/978-3-030-46955-9_7

Tough issues do not get solved in PTAs (Marchetti and Roy 2011)

Mobility is not just about travelling across borders. Mobility promotes the dissemination of fresh ideas and skills, and the understanding of other cultures and traditions. (Peng et al. 2018, p. 128)

1   Introduction

Up until the creation of the World Trade Organization (WTO) in 1994, the rules governing the cross-border mobility of production factors i.e. capital and persons, were not considered to be a part of trade *stricto sensu*. Hence, national laws regarding the entry, stay and return of natural persons remained outside the purview of the GATT 1947 regulatory framework and its principles of Most Favoured Nation (MFN) and National Treatment. With the adoption of the General Agreement on Trade in Services (GATS) in 1994, WTO Members sent a signal that the cross-border mobility of services and capital included those mobile foreign workers,[1] who were involved in the supply of services, and were subject to the same bilaterally negotiated and multilateralised commitments on market access and national treatment that governed the three other modes of service supply under the WTO/GATS. Article XXVIII of the GATS defines mode 4 as the "supply of a service by a service supplier of one member, through the presence of natural persons of a member in the territory of any other member". Recent 'measurements by the WTO Secretariat have found Mode 4 (M4) to account for 1.4 of world services trade'.[2]

Labour migration and M4 emerge from two distinct paradigms;[3] M4 follows from the trade negotiations perspective and temporary labor migration from the labour market perspective, the latter which correlates to immigration law in the sense that in most migrant host countries, immigration law regulates the entry and admission onto the labor market by drawing up different categories of admission for migrant work (self-employed/independent professional, employee, intra-corporate transferee, contractual service supplier, skills and talents, researcher, stagiaires/trainees, au-pairs which are then approximated or directed to a type of entry visa.[4] The GATS Annex MNP takes care to keep M4 separate from immigration law,[5] so much so that it still

---

[1]Carzaniga (2009), Chetail (2003), and Reyna (1999).

[2]Kemekliene and Watt (2010).

[3]Carzaniga (2009).

[4]Tullao JR and Cortez (2006).

[5]A strict reading of the language of Annex MNP of GATS reveals that WTO Members were not ready to relinquish their sovereign prerogative to decide who is to enter their territory and be admitted. Furthermore, Human demands of the service suppliers on the foreign market, including

remains contested whether the US's increase in the H1-B1 visa fee, contested by India under the GATS Art. VI, the market access, falls within the scope of GATS or not or else remains an issue of immigration outside the reach of WTO dispute settlement.[6]

For migrant sending, labor exporting WTO Members, the fact alone that GATS Art. 1:1(d) defines M4 as an admission category outside the reach of national immigration laws and thus leaves open to national immigration authorities to decide which entry visa and other admission regulation applies is a nuisance. The watertight distinction between the movement of natural persons under the GATS and labor migration more generally which Art. 1:1(d) GATS read in the context of the GATS Annex MNP has been operating waters down the potential for persons to supply their services abroad—in far too many cases, have traditional migrant receiving countries tweaked and tailored their national immigration laws so that there are, outside of the prohibited numerical quotas or ENTs, still obstacles for nationals from other WTO Members to deliver their services abroad, including standards issued by professional regulation bodies, no access to landownership or to subsidies and stipends and, in many instances mismatched market access commitments under GATS and visa/entry rules under national law. Hence, under the categorization of the MMN put forward by nccr-on the move (2019), M4 and labor migration are treated, by authority of norms, the GATS and national immigration law, as two distinct categories, which stand in opposition or conflict to each other, rather than in a relationship of complementarity or overlap. However, this clinical isolation between M4 in trade and labor migration, has over time become opaque. Seen from a continuum, with fragmentation on the one end of the spectrum and labor migration and G4 overlapping at the other, the increased proliferation of PTAs has led to a convergence, such that one can no longer treat M4 as a category outside labor migration. In 2015, Cottier and Sieber-Gasser found that in relation to labor migration and advances in M4, PTAs, which are 'building upon and extending beyond the commitments under WTO law have been labelled 'WTO-*plus*'. PTAs including new areas of regulation have been termed 'WTO-*extra*'' (Horn et al. 2010).

Marchetti and Roy wrote that 'tough issues do not get regulated by PTAs', yet, they might not have thought of M4. In our view, certain PTAs in the EU and Asian PTAs have been pathbreaking, with the EU's going GATS-*plus* by adding the categories installers and maintainers and graduate trainees (GT), while Asian PTAs move GATS-*extra*. PTAs may serve as a laboratory for the future of the multilateral level and may inform amendments to the GATS.[7]

---

access to social welfare, inclusion, citizenship and residence are categorically exempt from the GATS with the exception of national treatment principle.

[6]United States—Measures Concerning Non-Immigrant Visas, WT/DS503, Request for consultations of 3 March 2016. See: Panizzon M (2016) US—India Visa Fee Controversy before the WTO: A Migration-Mobility Nexus for the WTO? Blog post, nccr-on the move, https://blog.nccr-onthemove.ch/us-india-visa-fee-controversy-before-the-wto-a-migration-mobility-nexus-for-the-wto/?lang=de.

[7]Cottier and Sieber-Gasser (2011), p. 14.

Since the DDA of 2001, researchers from the fields as varied as law, political science and economics, have been busy identifying areas of GATS-*plus/extra* in draft Doha Round GATS M4 commitments, but also in PTAs. In so doing, a few have focussed on GATS-*extra,* to identify the policy space which the GATS architecture might offer, to allow policy makers—beyond admitting M4 workers on their markets—to regulate the TMNP through migration measures. The regulation of M4 in GATS and PTAs comes in light of demands by the Global South for more meaningful commitments in the lower-skill range. For industrialized countries to respond appropriately, it is necessary to alleviate anti-immigrant politics, which flare up more easily when low-skilled migration is at stake. Hence, several studies have been discussing how GATS Members can on the one hand offer commitments in the lower-skill range of M4, while regulating this cross-border movement more tightly than they would in the pre-existing, rather highly skilled commitments on M4. Measures thus range from visa requirements, pre-training facilities to return obligations.[8]

In literature, a solid corpus of scholarship on mapping and measuring the M4 GATS-*plus/extra* advances, emerged with the onset of the Doha Development Round in 2001; legal scholars and economists like Chanda 2002; Carzaniga 2003; Jacobsson 2015; Ward 2011 identified loopholes and architectural limitations in GATS scheduling for constructing more low-skilled market access in M4 negotiations. Around that time, scholars in IR started large-scale, H-studies (Lavenex and Jurje 2019) to cross-compare M4 commitments in PTAs as the missing piece of regional migration governance, the latter which included bilateral migration agreements, provisions unifying national immigration laws in regional integration zones (ECOWAS, MERCOSUR; ASEAN). Next, a third wave of research, predominantly legal scholars, compared how the status of certain categories of migrant workers or service suppliers, whose cross-border movement had been liberalized in a multilateral or preferential trade setting was simultaneously liberalized in a bilateral migration management agreement, e.g. graduate trainees/young professionals, installers and maintainers and how the visa/entry conditions at the multilateral, bilateral levels often failed to match an admission category at the level of national immigration law (Tans 2017; Jurje 2019; de Lange 2019).

This chapter introduces a dynamic element to the trade/mobility-migration *nexus,* which traces the direction in which there is greater proximity between M4 and other MNP or not, and amongst which trading partners.

Firstly, we identify when a M4-type provision in a PTA is more likely to be taken up by regional and national immigration law. This has the direct consequence on a service providing natural person, whose so likelihood of obtaining a national immigration status is higher, when the M4 admission category is matched by national immigration law. We want to know under which circumstances PTAs guarantee a certain vertical permeability or have trickling down effect on national or regional (EU labor directive) immigration law formulation. This can be measured,

---

[8]Chanda (2002).

by 'inverse diffusion', in the sense that a PTA puts pressure on national immigration law to simplify procedures and facilitate admission criteria, a finding we have corroborated for the category of installers and maintainers as well as for graduate trainees in EU and Swiss immigration law.

Secondly, we screen the PTAs for any non-M4 services provision by natural persons to be able to correlate M4 to such non-services movement of natural persons within a single PTA in select EU/Asian PTAs. Here, we hypothesize based on findings for cultural-oriented professions in Asian PTAs or, also, GTs in the European context that bilateral or national categories of foreign workers' admission diffuse horizontally into PTAs.

Thirdly, we measure the proximity of liberalizing M4 and regulating the M4 mobility in PTAs. We trace how regulation on visa facilitation, special visa, mutual recognition etc. in PTAs[9] diffuses into national immigration laws and regional integration agreements, including the European Union (EU), the Economic Community of West African States (ECOWAS), the Association of Southeast Asian Nations (ASEAN), which are then reformed for a more liberal solution,[10] in what this chapters labels a process of 'inverse diffusion'.[11]

1.1 Cross-Regional Differences in M4: EU versus Asian PTAs

A cross-regional assessment can be defined as "assess liberalization commitments in recent PTAs and compare them with achievements under GATS and the DDA".[12] The "Hoekman index" is used to identify where there are GATS plus and PTA plus commitments. However, the Hoekman index[13] only includes liberalization commitments. It does not cover the regulatory advances, which certain PTAs make over

---

[9]This chapter uses the term 'PTA' and 'FTA' to refer to any trade agreement or trade arrangement between two or more countries.

[10]Free movement regimes in RTAs or mega-regionals (e.g. AANZFTA 2009, TISA, ASEAN MNP Agreement 2012) and the interconnections between these and PTAs over labour migration is another field of research and is outside the scope of this chapter.

[11]This label has been designed by Panizzon and Lavenex for the nccr-on the move' work package 'migration governance thru trade mobilities', a 4-year research project funded by the Swiss National Science Foundation: https://nccr-onthemove.ch/projects/migration-governance-through-trade-mobilities/.

[12]Roy M (2011) Services Commitments in Preferential Trade Agreements: An Expanded Dataset. WTO Staff Working Paper ERSD-2011-18, https://www.wto.org/english/res_e/reser_e/ersd201118_e.htm.

[13]Hoekman, Assessing the General Agreement on Trade in Services. World Bank, World Bank Discussion Paper No. 307, 1995. see also Hoekman (1996).

GATS and the Doha Development Agenda (DDA), both GATS-plus or GATS-minus.[14] Regulatory advances can be offensive, such as those that facilitate the opening of services markets,[15] or defensive, such as those that respond to a migration-securitization nexus.[16] Regardless of whether they function in a defensive or offensive paradigm, regulatory advances contribute to consolidating a vertical coherence between the PTA, supranational and national immigration law in what is a process, which political scientists label 'diffusion'.[17]

We formulate the hypothesis that Asian PTAs disaggregate the horizontal M4 commitments by adding sector-specific commitment, a phenomenon missing out from EU PTAs. The way that EU PTAs have responded to the call for more medium or low skilled services, is a different one, by adding lower-skilled categories of service suppliers, for example by including installers, maintainers, repairers or graduate trainees.

The Asian approach is 'responsive' in M4, because it directly targets a labour market demand or an export interest, which neither a bilateral agreement nor national immigration law seems to be able to fill in for. M4 in the Asian PTAs stands for 'responsive' coherence.[18] The desire to increase regulatory convergence is, in Asian countries, a main driver for entering into a regional PTA also as a way to reduce 'over dependency' from the US and the EU and to go regional to diversify their economies. One way which demonstrates that M4 is liberalized in Asia to recruit foreign work to fill in for labour market shortage, is that mutual recognition provisions are more detailed, more stringent than in EU PTAs, insofar as in Asian PTAs, government is often required to cooperate with professional bodies to conclude bilateral, plurilateral or multilateral mutual recognition agreements. Often, a fast-track lane is established to complement an underused formal negotiating mandate for an MRA, the latter which has been the typical way trade agreements address the issue of recognition in services (see section below). Besides, Asian PTAs seem to experiment with weaving in migration steering policy elements directly into a trade framework, including visa, spousal employment, and in the case of Japan, even return obligations.

The EU approach is 'constructed coherence' in M4 because it often seems that M4 is artificially constructed to be able to obtain a better negotiating position in another category of trade policy, including intellectual property protection, or investment. In addition the EU uses the template of M4 including its Doha Round advancements of installers and maintainers and graduate trainees, across the board

---

[14]Horn et al. (2010).

[15]Found in Asian FTAs.

[16]Found in Deep and Comprehensive Free Trade Agreements (DCFTAs) which the EU has signed. There are six DCFTAs with the eastern partners (Armenia, Azerbaijan, Belarus, Georgia, Moldova and Ukraine (EaP) and four are being negotiated with Euromed countries, including Jordan, Morocco, Egypt and Tunisia.

[17]See for instance: Tans (2017), Jurje and Lavenex (2018), and Shivakoti (2019).

[18]Cottier and Sieber-Gasser (2015).

towards most trading partners according to a pre-defined, orchestrated scheme. Of course, this has also has to do with the EU Member States retaining competence over labour market access quotas, so that a common position by the EU on M4 is more difficult to come by with than for other WTO Members not facing a supranational system with its complex divisions of power among various levels of territorial jurisdictions.[19]

1.2   How Does the Migration-Mobility Nexus (MMN) Play Out in PTAs?

The 'right to enter another country than one's own', can be negatively defined by international humanitarian law with the *non-refoulement* customary legal principle. Positively, the separate opinion of Judge Trindade in the *Diallo* case held that Art. 14 (2) ICCPR establishes the duty of states to let in non-nationals, if these are long-term residents, which have developed a close and enduring relationship to a country so that it becomes a 'home country'.[20]

Following the incomplete human right to leave any country, including one's own, under Art. 13 Universal Declaration of Human Rights, is the right of nationals and the abovementioned long-term residents to 're-enter', but since this human right fails to include a mirror image, the right to enter any country of one's choice, there is under public international law no 'right to migrate' as such. This general statement has become permeable over time, as various international treaties, regional integration communities and bilateral trade, investment and labor agreements postulate a free movement of persons between two or more countries. At the international level, the only treaty to provide for the temporary movement of natural persons, is the GATS.

The emphasis on service supply reduces the TMNP under GATS to a technicality, the human face of this cross-border movement disappearing behind the service being transnationally supplied. Human demands of the service suppliers on the foreign market, including access to social welfare, inclusion, citizenship and residence are categorically exempt from the GATS with the exception of national treatment principle requiring no less favourable treatment than to a national. Human rights and labour standards of the foreign persons supplying services in another WTO Member are not expressly included within the TMNP, thus fuelling the assumption that for WTO law, they are not relevant.

A third concept next to MNP and temporary (labour) migration, associated with GATS M4, is mobility. Mobility has a different meaning whether it applies to WTO/GATS or the EU. In WTO/GATS it stands for a type of MNP confined to a cross-border movement within an enterprise or business, typically labelled an

---

[19]See generally on regulatory convergence in PTAs.
[20]Chetail (2019), p. 92.

intra-corporate transfer within a mode 3 investment, or an investor or business visitor moving abroad temporarily to set up business is mobile within her business. Mobility is further discussed in Sect. 1.2. For purposes of EU law, mobility conjures the imagery of free movement across the perimeters of Schengenland, i.e. most of geographical Europe with the exception of now, the UK.

Mobility, on the other hand, assumes a completeness which implies the absence of constraints and connotes the freedom of choice of when and where to move for family and personal or work-related motives. Mobility, defined as the cross-border movement determined by choice, rather than by necessity, is not driven by flight due to the threat to life and health. Mobility seems to be a derivate of free movement (EU, ECOWAS, others) or a synonym for the rights exercised by investors, business sellers, ICTs, CSS and those other lucky few service providers, whose cross-border movement is being liberalized by a regional (NAFTA, TISA etc.) or multilateral agreement (GATS). Finally, mobility in EU law denotes the scope of intra-EU geographic mobility of a third country national (TCN).[21] It is a notion deriving from the EU's freedom of movement for EU citizens and for TCN without requiring a residence permit from the Member State concerned. With the exception perhaps of GATS M4, there is no other multilateral treaty or agreement codifying mobility so universally. Mobility captures a fraction of migratory movement, it relates to regulation limited to liberalize people-to-people movement often by granting market access to categories of highly-skilled workers and by facilitating its circularity. Realizing a migration-mobility nexus means that security (migration) and market-driven (mobility) elements are united in a single coherent framework.

In its Annex on the Temporary Movement of Natural Persons (TMNP), the GATS expressly restricts its competence to market access and national treatment,

---

[21]Mobility' has acquired a distinct legal notion under EU law, in particular the concept was developed in the EU labor market directives (ICT, Blue Card, researchers). For example, the EU researcher Directive 2016/801/EU, combining the Study Directive (2004/114/EC) and the Research Directive (2005/71/EG) provides for intra-mobility for third-country students, researchers and their family members, and trainees and volunteers, of up to 180 or 360 days, respectively a year in another EU Member state without the TCN needing to apply for a separate residence permit from the Member State concerned (for TCN researchers requesting a long-term intra-EU mobility (360 days), need to apply for this separate residence permit from the MS concerned. In the, ICT directive 2004/66/EU, similar provisions (Arts. 20ss) provide for long- and short- term intra-EU mobility for TCN ICTs. For posted workers (or CSS) in GATS-speak, the Directive 2018/957/EU replacing 96/71/EC are no mobility rights, in contrast the Council Directive 2009/50/EC of 25 May 2009 on the conditions of entry and residence of third-country nationals for the purposes of highly qualified employment foresees mobility rights for highly qualified TCN as a first step to circular migration coming out of a longer-term residence of a highly qualified TCN in the EU and contributing to "sustain the EU's competitiveness" and "economic growth". Amongst others the intra-EU mobility is being achieved by fast-tracking the admission procedure and offering equal social and economic rights without prejudice to the EU MS reception capacities and labour market demand. EU PTAs have taken this point of fast-tracking admission up, but have not followed-through with guaranteeing economic and social rights parity. The occupational and geographical mobility of third-country highly qualified workers should be recognised as a primary mechanism for improving labour market efficiency, preventing skill shortages and offsetting regional imbalances.

and equally expressly denies any jurisdiction over visa, and other border measures, integration, return and readmission. The GATS thus delineates precisely, what it counts as mobility and what it negates, as migration.

However, in recent years, many regional and trans-regional trade agreements with a services chapter, have begun to mix up the GATS' clear-cut or 'watertight' distinction between what is considered migration and outside its competence and what qualifies as mobility and forms part of GATS, including intra-company transfer and subsidiary to headquarter movement, restrictions (or not) on geographical mobility, spousal employment and transfer.

The challenge of the Migration-Mobility nexus (MMN) is to what extent is such an interconnection between two antagonist versions of movement of persons sufficiently dense and programmatic to qualify as regime and to what extent the coherence it suggests aspires to be governance and if so, what type—global or multilevel.[22]

This chapter discusses the interface of these three concepts i.e. MNP, temporary (labour) migration and mobility, in EU and Asian PTAs, where a research gap seems to exist with regards to combining the cross-regional comparative mapping of mode 4 in PTAs with implementation in regional, bilateral or national laws and regulation, as well as vis-à-vis GATS on MNP. In doing so, we combine a cross-regional analysis of EU and Asian PTAs with a vertical, multi-level analysis of M4 categories and procedural advances cutting across firstly, the GATS/DDA offers, secondly, PTAs and thirdly, bilateral agreements (which are neither an FTA nor a PTA) or unilateral immigration law. We will lay out the differences in three areas: scheduled commitments, domestic regulations and methods of scheduling. Before concluding, we lay out the return and readmission policies found in PTAs.

2 Advances in M4 since the Doha Round of Multilateral Trade Negotiations

From its inception, M4 has been the most restricted mode of supply of a service because it was delivered by natural persons, who moved to stay, even if only temporarily, in a country other than the one of their birth or residence.[23] Restrictiveness was introduced in GATS M4 by three different ways: firstly, by regulating the visa or implementing other border restrictions, which can restrict movement of persons across a border. Secondly, by liberalising the market access and national

---

[22]For more information see: von Bernstorff (2015), p. 988.

[23]In contrast in mode 1 like for trade in goods under GATT 1994 no physical cross-border movement of a natural person is involved. In contrast to mode 2, where the consumer moves to the service provider or mode 3 where the provider is a natural person from another country, in both cases, the natural person brings capital along when crossing the border and thus in many ways 'securitizes' her movement by the way of the collateral of 'capital', which is not the case for mode 4.

treatment in services, meaning that the foreign natural person accesses the market because of a negotiated services or employment contract prior to arrival, and is not free to take on any remunerated occupation, as under the EU's freedom of movement paradigm. Thirdly, most countries offered market access commitments in M4 by employing a horizontal approach only, which identified the categories of service suppliers by their skill levels and functions such as contractual service supplier (CSS), independent professional (IP), installers and maintainers, intra-corporate transferee (ICT), investors and short-term business visitor, managers, executives and specialists. At the insistence of labour sending countries, during the DDA negotiations, it was proposed to lower the high skill bias of M4 as a measure to increase the development-friendliness of GATS.[24]

This section lays out the advances found in PTAs, over the GATS, in three different ways: firstly, by looking at whether they open up specific sectors rather than going for a horizontal commitment with unspecific mentioning in the sectors, i.e. blanket referencing in the sectors, as apparent in the formula 'unbound, except for . . . .' Secondly, by opening up to new categories of persons, or liberalizing new types of M4 commitments such as those which are strengthened by rules, cooperation, and dialogue on tourism, 'infrastructural' services, such as telecommunications and maritime transport, and e-commerce. Thirdly, the inclusion of additional categories of persons, requested by the Least Developed Countries (LDCs) to be included by the industrialized countries in their PTAs, but not necessarily via a GATS commitment in M4, but through a side-letter instead.

For example, the quota for Chinese youth granted by Australia under its work and holiday program associated with the China–Australia Free Trade Agreement (ChAFTA) thru a side-letter.[25] The explicit mentioning of the work and holiday type of entry visa, in a PTA, is a gain in the legal predictability of M4 regime, at least by more closely aligning a well-established immigration legislation traditionally deployed in bilateral labor agreements, to a trade agreement.

The section first discusses the M4 categories found in EU Agreements, and thereafter discusses the categories found in the Asian PTAs. Subsequently, this section discusses the use of side letters in PTAs.

2.1 Upping the Ante: Maintainers and Installers in the EU and Swiss DDA Offer

We discuss the liberalisation of M4 workers in EU under two broad headings: the case of installers and maintainers in the bilateral Swiss-German agreement and of graduate trainees in Franco-African bilateral migration agreements. It appears that the categories of service providers liberalized in both bilateral labour migration

---

[24]Chanda (2002), pp. 631–654; Carzaniga (2003), pp. 21–26.
[25]Shi (2018), p. 115.

agreements influenced the EU and the Swiss Doha offer on M4. Certainly, both France's bilaterals with African countries and the Swiss MoU with Germany were contravening the GATS MFN of Art. II (at least in the case of Switzerland) and could not be justified by an Art. V regional integration agreement exception. Hence, it was necessary to put on offer multilaterally, what was being liberalized bilaterally.

2.1.1 Installers and Maintainers in the 1999 MoU Between Germany and Switzerland

In an exchange of notes on 5 March 1999,[26] Switzerland agreed to liberalize entry to German installers and maintainers of equipment used for fairs by eliminating the requirement to get a work authorization, however they were still required to give notice to the Swiss authorities.[27] At that time, Switzerland was not yet in a free movement of persons regime with the EU, which only came in 2001. The exchange of notes between Germany and Switzerland of 1999 eventually got incorporated into the EU-Switzerland agreement on free movement of persons of 2001. The MFN issue under Article V GATS remained, since Switzerland carved-out the financial/banking sector from its bilateral agreements with the EU. However, the free movement of persons is deemed to be exempt under a 1994 GATS MFN exemption for Switzerland's relations with the EU.[28] Switzerland with its binary system of professions—that are split into university-educated professions and vocational training schools—had an export interest for plumbers and introduced this category into its M4 on offer in the DDA. In response to demands by the Global South to deliver more development-sensitive GATS mode 4 commitments the EU similarly put the category of installers and maintainers into its DDA offer and started deploying it in its PTAs, In this sense, the category of installers and maintainers experienced an upwardly mobile diffusion from bilateral labor migration agreements to the trade setting, whether in a prospective multilateral M4 DDA offer or in PTAs.[29]

Hence, in what seems to be a case of inverse policy diffusion, Switzerland took the occasion of that exchange of notes on installers and maintainers with Germany, to propagate this new category to GATS M4 as its response to the demand for

---

[26]Vereinbarung durch Notenaustausch vom 23. Februar und 5. März 1999 zwischen der Regierung der Schweizerischen Eidgenossenschaft und der Regierung der Bundesrepublik Deutschland über die Erleichterung des grenzüberschreitenden Dienstleistungsverkehrs im Bereiche von Messestandbau- und Montagearbeiten, https://www.admin.ch/opc/de/official-compilation/2000/2664.pdf AS 2000 2664, SR 0.823.291.361.

[27]Weisung ANAG Anhang 4/6 (Ziffern 431 und 433.23).

[28]Council for Trade in Services Special Session, Communication from Switzerland: Temporary Admission of Installers and Maintainers under the GATS: A Case for Mode 4 Commitments. World Trade Organization, TN/S/W/61 2 April 2007.

[29]Nonnenmacher (2012), p. 330.

lower-skilled commitments in the DDA.[30] The category of installers and maintainers (IM) has been included by Switzerland in some FTAs,[31] while excluded in others and it remains to be studied what factors make or unmake the decision for exporting this category into a M4 trade context[32] It seems that with China, Switzerland had been granting market access in M4 to Chinese professionals and hence wanted to secure a M4 commitment in return, while the same was not the case for Korea. In both cases though, the services category becomes M4 and does not stand apart, as a non-services category.

2.1.2 Graduate Trainees (GT): A Hybrid Category of M4 and Non-services Mobility

Graduate trainees (GTs), are a category of services supply and non-services move-ment of natural persons, which are being currently included in the EU DDA offer and in various EU PTAs, including the EU Singapore FTA (EUSFTA) of 2014,[33] the EU C&P FTA and the EU-Georgia DCFTA. GT are a sub-category, which the EU includes either in the ICT category of M4 service suppliers or else, which are considered to a "temporary presence of natural persons for business persons", without any link to services supply. Hence, the category of ICT includes non-services-oriented cross-border movement of natural persons. GT are not in all cases considered M4. Firstly, they might not count towards M4 because they might supply services domestically, and not cross-border, when employed by a domestic supplier, rather than by an ICT. Secondly and even where they are part of an ICT cross-border services supply, part of their time is spent consuming, rather than supplying services.

Whereas the EU ICT directive includes a GT within the broader M4 category of the ICT, there are some forms of GT, which fall outside the scope of the EU ICT directive as students undergoing training as part of their studies (and not as part of their services provision qua traineeship).[34]

---

[30]Council for Trade in Services: Special Session (2007), Communication from Switzerland: Temporary Admission of Installers and Maintainers under the GATS: A Case for Mode 4 Commit-ments. World Trade Organization, TN/S/W/61, 2 April 2007.

[31]For instance: State Secretariat for Economic Affairs (SECO), Free Trade Agreement between the Swiss Confederation and the People's Republic Of China, 6 July 2013, https://www.seco.admin.ch/seco/en/home/Aussenwirtschaftspolitik_Wirtschaftliche_Zusammenarbeit/Wirtschaftsbeziehungen/Freihandelsabkommen/Partner_weltweit/china/Abkommenstexte.html, Appendix 1 of Annex VIII.

[32]For instance: European Free Trade Association (EFTA), Free Trade Agreement between EFTA States and the Republic of Korea. 15 December 2005, https://www.efta.int/free-trade/free-trade-agreements/korea.

[33]Free Trade Agreement between the European Union and the Republic of Singapore, 14. November 2014, OJ L 294/3.

[34]Directive 2014/66 OJ L 157/1; see also Peers (2013), pp. 388–389.

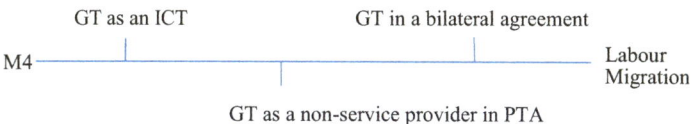

Fig. 1 Graduate trainees in bilateral migration agreements and PTAs as an example of the MMN

At first sight, the cases of GTs in the bilateral agreements of Switzerland with Morocco, Tunisia, the Philippines, etc.,[35] as well as the GT provisions in France's all-encompassing second-generation bilateral migration management agreements since 2009,[36] might mistakenly lead to conclude that GT are a category of movement, which is being simultaneously regulated in bilateral migration agreements, and M4 in PTAs. Yet, the spectrum of GTs falling under the risks associated with overlapping or multi-level regulatory frameworks, seems to dissipate when looked upon more closely: since the trainee consumes an educational service she is technically, a M2 category. Yet at the same time she is delivering cross-border services but for a foreign or domestic employer, being often the school or professional board where she is also enrolled to get an education. Hence, the element of cross-border movement with respect to a GT lies in M2 and less in M4. On the MMN continuum, the GT is more closely associated with migration, i.e. in terms of movement for getting an education, and less with a services delivery, unless that latter mobility is facilitated by a foreign ICT whose presence is e.g. in Switzerland the or EU reference to Fig. 1.

The hybrid status of the GT, uniting elements of services consumption and provision, depending on whether the employer is or not an ICT, uniting M4 movement and non-services mobility, requires an in-depth mapping study. For purposes of this cursory review of GT provisions, it can be safe to say the following: should the GT be part of the cross-border services delivery of an ICT, her movement will be considered M4-type mobility, even if she consumes domestic educational services while being trained and employed by the foreign service provider, i.e. the ICT. Should the GT be moving cross-border to consume services and work for a domestic employer as a trainee, her movement, on the MMN scale, will be considered 'migration' see Fig. 1. Oftentimes, such latter movement also falls under a bilateral labor migration/traineeship/young professionals' agreements. As the examples of Swiss GT agreements and France's agreements on young professionals

---

[35]To-date, Switzerland has traineeship agreements with the following nations: Argentina, Australia, Chile, Japan, Canada, Monaco, New Zealand, the Philippines, Russia, S-Africa, Tunisia, Ukraine, USA; out of theses, it only has a PTA with Japan, Canada, Morocco, Tunisia, The Philippines, Chile, Monaco, S-Africa; but not with Argentina, Australia, the US, Russia nor New Zealand, see https://www.sem.admin.ch/sem/de/home/themen/arbeit/berufspraktikum.html. It would be worthwhile to identify for countries with whom Switzerland has a PTA, what the bilateral traineeship agreement offers that the PTA does not, besides expedited entry conditions or a stay decoupled from employment by a foreign ICT in Switzerland.

[36]Panizzon (2010), pp. 923–956.

demonstrate,[37] GTs in bilateral agreements might enjoy a broader possibility of employment, including with domestic service providing firms, but their stay might be more heavily regulated under national immigration law and bilateral provisions against the risk of overstay. In France's agreements on migration management, the GTs will be penalized for overstaying, as strict provisions over forceful repatriation apply towards the partner country being able to send GTs to France should the person not return home voluntarily. However, there might be some administrative support for the GT to find a permanent job in France, missing from the GT provisions in PTAs.[38]

Usually, the EU writes up in horizontal M4 the different limitations which its Member States note with reference to GTs. For example, Hungary, France, Austria in the PTA with Singapore restrict the level of training to "training ... linked to the university degree...obtained", Belgium and Hungary have noted an 'economic needs test', and in terms of scope, the GT is sometimes subject to annual quotas, authorization criteria by the professional service boards, e.g. for Services provided by Nurses, Physiotherapists and Paramedical Personnel (part of CPC 93191) by BE, FR, LU. Oftentimes, the GTs face 'nationality' conditions (or residency), in the EU-Singapore PTA, GTs in lower-skilled 'other' category of services 'not included elsewhere', including washing, dying; hairdressing; cosmetic (including manicure and pedicure) and other beauty treatment, spa and non-therapeutic massage, the EU Members' unison agreement over a nationality requirement de facto functions as a barrier to all Singapore nationals desiring to access the EU market as a specialist or GT in this sector. Singapore opens up horizontally to GT from the EU, but only for the sector specified, which in this PTA are, financial services.[39]

While the EU includes GTs in its revised DDA offer, enabling PTAs,[40] it has also EU adopted 2010 the proposed Directive, to harmonize admission criteria throughout the Member States. There is however confusion among EU MS as to what sub-categories ICT divides into: GT; specialists, key personnel, business visitors? It is often seen that GT are kept separate from the ICT category and form a category of their own, while others find ICT and key personnel to be equivalent and ICT also include managers and specialist and key personnel, hence the last three being a horizontal category within any of the M4 main categories of ICT, CSS, IP.[41]

---

[37]France has bilateral agreements on young professionals with Mauritius (2009), Macedonia (2009), Montenegro (2009) Serbia (2009) and Lebanon (under ratification since 2010); https://www.immigration.interieur.gouv.fr/Europe-et-International/Les-accords-bilateraux/Presentation-generale-des-accords-bilateraux.

[38]Les Accords Relatifs a la Gestion Concertee des Flux Migratoires et au Codeveloppement, Version Actualisee Au 20 Octobre 2009, https://www.lacimade.org/wp-content/uploads/2009/01/note_cimade_accords_migration.pdf.

[39]O.J. L294/362.

[40]Tans (2017), p. 297.

[41]Tans (2017), p. 301 noting that Dutch implementing M4 legislation treats key personnel, ICT and GT as one and the same category, a fact which lead to confusion and mistakes in application.

EU Members with a long-standing tradition of exchange of youth, like France are doing a better job at aligning the GT, also called young professionals as a category of potentially highly skilled migration with its France national labor market admission categories, in this case, the of 'skills and talents'. In such cases, the GT or 'young professionals', were quite safely regulated, with the bilateral status matching the national immigration law. It is to be further researched if and when GTs liberalized in an EU PTA might also fall under the EU researcher or Blue Card directive.

Nonetheless, the bilateral opening of the French labour market to highly skilled young professionals from former colonies incurred the criticism of fuelling brain drain, graduate trainees obtaining only an add-on training by France, prior admission to the French labour market, while the elementary schooling had been paid for by the developing country.[42] To counter such criticism one could imagine an ICT-link to be requisite for any GT moving into a developed country, i.e. that France allow only GT who will be moving within an ICT scheme by Tunisian, Senegalese company operating in France.

As a WTO Member, however, France is bound by the MFN principle stated Article II of the GATS. However, because WTO scholarship is inconclusive as to whether all types of GT fall under the scope of GATS for the time being,[43] France can continue to keep the category of "young professionals" exclusively open to those countries which have signed onto a bilateral migration or a young professionals agreement with France.

In both the case of installers and maintainers and GTs, the bilateral agreements' conformity with the MFN under GATS worked as a trigger for the EU to add these two categories into its PTAs and the revised offer on M4, or otherwise risk the legal non-conformity of these bilateral MOUs and agreements under the MFN of GATS. At the same time the bilateral progress made in installers and maintainers, as well as GTs pressed the Union to draft implementing legislation in form of EU labor market directives. Finally, one observed that the interplay between bilateral and national immigration legislation worked out well, but that the risk of confusions in terms of overlapping regulation relating GTs in PTAs versus bilateral agreements occurs later on, at the transregional trade *versus* bilateral labor migration levels.

The example of how the ICT subcategory of GT is being treated by the EU in its PTAs, stands as an example in place for a two-time vertical norm diffusion process: a vertical diffusion is taking place, whereby the EU PTAs liberalize M4 in ICT, to respond to demand by EU MS to include key personnel, GTs and business sellers. At the same time, this innovation on M4 triggered the EU to harmonize the conflicting definitions, which MS immigration laws were giving to GTs, key personnel and ICT, hence the EU ICT directive was born as result of both an inverse diffusion down from PTAs to EU labor market directives and vertically from MS to the EU level. To

---

[42]Panizzon (2013); Ndiaye-Coïc (2011).

[43]Carzaniga (2009), p. 476, because the GT under an ICT contract is delivering the service to a domestic recipient and because the GT does work that is part of her education, which she consumes at home, and which is not cross-border.

complicate matters further, the EU PTAs and the EU's DDA offer over ICT take up questions from bilateral labor migration of EU MS, which for their part have also been keenly liberalizing GT, as in the France-Tunisia and France-Senegal agreements on migration management.

The Asian FTAs differ significantly from their EU counterparts. Whereas the EU and other industrialized countries have carved-out certain sectors in their M4 commitments, Asian countries have done the opposite and opened M4 not only horizontally but also sectorally, in industries or professions where they have a competitive advantage, both as an ethnic specialization (for example Thai boxing, cuisine, massage; Indian yoga, Chinese TCM) and professional advantages (such as nurses and caregivers). The M4 categories found in Asian PTAs can be broadly divided into ethnic specialization, and the professional specialization, and will be discussed separately below.

2.2 Ethnic and Professional Liberalization in the Asian Sphere

An analysis of the trade agreements in the Asian sphere shows two types of liberalisation of M4: those who have an ethnic specialisation and professionals (nurses), which are commonly observed in the Asian sphere. These are sequentially elaborated below.

2.2.1 Liberalization of M4 Workers with Ethnic Specialization

Along with the sectorisation of mode 4, a related trend appears particular perhaps for the South-South Asian geographical sphere and markets but increasingly adopted by China's, India's, Thailand's trade negotiations with counterparts in Europe, including Switzerland and the Americas: This is to identify an ethnic or cultural service[44] which has been globalized to the point that there is a labour gap on the potential market for that foreign labour in the trading partner (examples include Thai cuisine and boxing Chinese traditional medicine (TCM), martial arts and cuisine.[45])

One could thus argue that trade agreements have helped certain ethnically or culturally specific occupations to proliferate globally and to internationalize. However, this development has not been well received by national healthcare systems, or anti-immigrant political parties, as in the case of TCM.[46] An intermediate way to

---

[44]Brettell and Hollifield (2019).

[45]Gao (2017) China's evolving approach to environmental and labour provisions in regional trade agreements. ICTSD, https://www.ictsd.org/opinion/china-3.

[46]Lauder (2015) Chinese medicine's mention in free trade deal 'a tragedy for Australian science', critic warns. ABC News, https://www.abc.net.au/news/2015-06-18/chinese-medicine-free-trade-agreement-critic/6556532.

deal with on the one hand demand for ethnically-oriented occupations and resistance against these is in the compromise taken by Australia has taken in its FTA with Thailand (TAFTA 2005), which was to let in 'specialist Thai chefs' as CSS by noting down the qualifications requirements, but to subsequently flag in a side letter to the FTA that negotiations will be undertaken to overcome the challenges with the qualifications of therapists and masseurs.[47]

2.2.2   Liberalization of M4 Workers with Professional Specialization

A review of the Asian FTAs shows the liberalisation of several categories of M4 workers with professional specialisation. Unlike the EU's FTAs, where the categories of professions liberalized are quite broad (such as over 30 professions in some Franco-African agreements) the categories of professional services liberalized in Asian FTAs are quite narrow.

The category of M4 workers commonly liberalised in Asian FTAs is of 'nurses and care workers' which has been observed in several PTAs.[48,49] Other professions where M4 workers have been liberalized are professional services. Commitments have been observed for 'lawyers, accountants and taxation services' professionals,[50,51] 'engineer, specialist in humanities/international services.'[52,53] M4 commitments have also been observed for some technical and vocational education services and higher educational service providers[54] and those under a twinning or

---

[47]Department of Foreign Affairs and Trade, Side Letter on Services. Thailand-Australia Free Trade Agreement, Australian Government, 05 July 2004, https://dfat.gov.au/trade/agreements/in-force/tafta/fta-text-and-implementation/Pages/fta-text-and-implementation.aspx.

[48]Ministry of Foreign Affairs of Japan, Agreement between Japan and the Socialist Republic of Viet Nam for an Economic Partnership. 25 December 2008, https://www.mofa.go.jp/region/asia-paci/vietnam/epa0812/index.html, Annex 7.

[49]Ministry of Foreign Affairs of Japan, Agreement between Japan and the Republic of the Philippines for an Economic Partnership. 09 September 2006, https://www.mofa.go.jp/region/asia-paci/philippine/epa0609/index.html, Annex 8.

[50]Ministry of Foreign Affairs of Japan, Agreement between Japan and the Kingdom of Thailand for an Economic Partnership. 3 April 2007, https://www.mofa.go.jp/region/asia-paci/thailand/epa0704/index.html, Section 4 of Part 1 of Annex 7.

[51]Ministry of Foreign Affairs of Japan, Comprehensive Economic Partnership Agreement between Japan and the Republic of India. 15 February 2011, https://www.mofa.go.jp/region/asia-paci/india/epa201102/index.html, Part 2 of Section 4 of Annex 7.

[52]Ministry of Foreign Affairs of Japan, Agreement between Japan and the Kingdom of Thailand for an Economic Partnership. 3 April 2007, https://www.mofa.go.jp/region/asia-paci/thailand/epa0704/index.html, Section 5 of Part 1 of Annex 7.

[53]Ministry of Foreign Affairs of Japan, Comprehensive Economic Partnership Agreement between Japan and the Republic of India. 15 February 2011, https://www.mofa.go.jp/region/asia-paci/india/epa201102/index.html, Section 5 & 6 of Part 2 of Annex 7.

[54]Ministry of Foreign Affairs of Japan, Agreement between Japan and the Kingdom of Thailand for an Economic Partnership. 3 April 2007, https://www.mofa.go.jp/region/asia-paci/thailand/epa0704/index.html, Section 6 of Part 2 of Annex 7.

bridging program.[55] M4 liberalisation has also been observed in PTAs for persons with 'special skills'[56]

Similarly, the special skills category (such as hair dressing, dry cleaning services) in the CAFTA is one where the EU has made GATS-plus openings, i.e. going from unbound in GATS to fully committed. However, the liberalisation of these M4 workers will scarcely be responsible for increasing the EU-Canada trade volumes and thus has marginal relevance.

Apart from ethnic and professional specializations, a commonly observed category of M4 workers in PTAs generally is that of spouses and dependents. Some PTAs liberalise only spouses[57,58] while others liberalise both spouses and dependents.[59,60]

2.3 Side Letters

Apart from the liberalization of M4 categories in PTAs, another manner of liberalization of M4 is via side letters. The cooperation laid down in the FTA is an opportunity to formalize through a Memorandum of Understanding (MoU) other types of 'migration', including the temporary entry and stay for working holiday makers, a category outside of GATS mode 4, because it requires employment of the foreign national by a host country employer. The FTA either establishes such MNP or incorporates a pre-existing bilateral agreement on that issue. Side letters for mutual cooperation ensure that such a category of a MNP might at some point be

---

[55]Department of Foreign Affairs and Trade, Agreement Establishing the ASEAN–Australia-New Zealand Free Trade Area. Australian Government, 27 February 2009, https://dfat.gov.au/trade/agreements/in-force/aanzfta/official-documents/Pages/official-documents.aspx, Para 5 of Philippines commitments in Annex 4.

[56]Malaysia's Free Trade Agreements, Malaysia – Pakistan Closer Economic Partnership Agreement. 8 November 2007, https://fta.miti.gov.my/index.php/pages/view/malaysia-pakistan, Para E of Services Schedules of Pakistan.

[57]Department of Foreign Affairs and Trade, Australia – Chile Free Trade Agreement. Australian Government, 30 July 2008, https://dfat.gov.au/trade/agreements/in-force/aclfta/fta-text-implementation/Pages/fta-text-and-implementation.aspx, Para 1(c) and para 2 (c) of Annex 13-A.

[58]Department of Foreign Affairs and Trade, Agreement Establishing the ASEAN–Australia-New Zealand Free Trade Area. Australian Government, 27 February 2009, https://dfat.gov.au/trade/agreements/in-force/aanzfta/official-documents/Pages/official-documents.aspx, Para E of Australia's commitments in Annex 4.

[59]Foreign Trade Information System, Free Trade Agreement between the Republic of Colombia and the Republic of Korea. Organization of American States, 21 February 2013, http://www.sice.oas.org/TPD/Col_kor/Draft_Text_06.2012_e/June_2012_Index_PDF_e.asp, Section E of Annex 10-A (Both Colombia and Korea).

[60]Ministry of Foreign Affairs of Japan, Agreement between Japan and Mongolia for an Economic Partnership. 10 February 2015, https://www.mofa.go.jp/a_o/c_m2/mn/page3e_000298.html, Section 6 of Part 1 and Section 6 of Part 2, of Annex 7.

liberalized by both parties, for example service suppliers of TCM from China in Australia under the ChAFTA.[61] Side letters are also used to agree on skills assessment, recognition and licensing (ChAFTA)[62,63] or a negotiating commitment to agree in the future on such a clause (EU – CARIFORUM EPA).[64]

3 Facilitating MNP: At Which Level to Tackle M4-Tangentials?

As Sauvé and Roy (2016) have written, it is important to note that an opening in M4 of itself is not yet sufficient to enable the natural person to stay for work in the other country. As the Annex MNP defines, measures on entry, including visa, work permit and registration duties, measures on the integration, including access to social security and taxation, access to simplified linguistic and other exams, if these are contingent for the job, fall outside its scope. There is considerable literature and policy proposals on how to facilitate these M4-tangential issues, whether thru immigration legislation or in Annexes attached to a PTA.[65] The authors plea for regulation the mutual recognition of qualifications in bilateral migration management agreements and to ensure coherence between these and the GATS, while others plead for strengthening the negotiating mandate of the GATS Art. VII on mutual recognition agreement, to make it mandatory. Apart from expanding the categories of M4 workers, as seen in the section above, PTAs also facilitate the movement of natural persons by enabling regulatory co-operation regarding domestic regulations which facilitates the movement of natural persons. While some aspects are clearly GATS plus, such as mutual recognition of qualifications, faster processing times for visa applications, others have been GATS minus, such as those relating to dispute

---

[61]Department of Foreign Affairs and Trade, Side Letter on Traditional Chinese Medicine. Free Trade Agreement between the Government of Australia and the Government of the People's Republic of China, Australian Government, 17 June 2015, https://dfat.gov.au/trade/agreements/in-force/chafta/official-documents/Pages/official-documents.aspx.

[62]Department of Foreign Affairs and Trade, Side Letter on Skills Assessment and Licensing. Free Trade Agreement between the Government of Australia and the Government of the People's Republic of China, Australian Government, 17 June 2015, https://dfat.gov.au/trade/agreements/in-force/chafta/official-documents/Pages/official-documents.aspx.

[63]Department of Foreign Affairs and Trade, Side Letter on Traditional Chinese Medicine. Free Trade Agreement between the Government of Australia and the Government of the People's Republic of China, Australian Government, 17 June 2015, https://dfat.gov.au/trade/agreements/in-force/chafta/official-documents/Pages/official-documents.aspx.

[64]Official Journal of the European Union, Economic Partnership Agreement between the CARIFORUM States, of the one part, and the European Community and its Member States, of the other part. 15 October 2008, https://eur-lex.europa.eu/LexUriServ/LexUriServ.do?uri=OJ:L:2008:289:0003:1955:EN:PDF, Article 85, Article 114, and Article 121:2(b).

[65]Sauvé and Roy (2016), p. 524.

resolution and national security. This section explores both these aspects sequentially.

3.1 *GATS*-Plus *Commitments on Facilitating Mutual Recognition or Assessment of Qualifications and Licences*

GATS plus commitments are commonly observed in M4 clauses pertaining to mutual recognition and fast tracking of applications. Among these, mutual recognition is at the forefront for regional regulatory convergence, as Sauvé and Shingal have observed in a study of Asian and Southeast Asian services trade agreements (STA).[66] Several PTAs contain provisions on the mutual recognition of qualifications, as stated above regarding the recognition of TCM and other forms of traditional medicine has been incorporated in the ChAFTA via a side letter as stated in Sect. 2.3 above. The ASEAN countries on 27 June 2012 have agreed on an ASEAN Framework Agreement on Mutual Recognition Arrangements which applies to PTAs concluded with trading partners in the region.[67] The Japan – India PTA[68] and the ASEAN – India Trade in Services Agreement[69] also contain clauses on mutual recognition. As a regional regulatory approximation scheme, the ASEAN MRA might be compared to the pan-Euro-Mediterranean preferential rules of origin (PEM Convention), for trade in goods, which applies to EU Association Agreements with North African and other Euromed trading partners in the field of production of goods.

The EU PTAs with services chapters do not contain MRA schemes similar to the ASEAN framework. The mutual recognition articles in the EU-CARIFORUM FTA,[70] which promises a negotiating mandate, might be the standard so far. MRAs are not foreseen even in regional EU PTAs, such as the DCFTAs, despite the fact that DCFTAs with Eastern Partnership (EaP) countries have gone GATS-

---

[66]Sauvé and Shingal (2016).

[67]Association of Southeast Asian Nations, ASEAN Framework Agreement on Mutual Recognition Arrangements. 27 June 2012, https://asean.org/?static_post=asean-framework-agreement-on-mutual-recognition-arrangements.

[68]Ministry of Foreign Affairs of Japan, Comprehensive Economic Partnership Agreement between Japan and the Republic of India. 15 February 2011, https://www.mofa.go.jp/region/asia-paci/india/epa201102/index.html, Article 65.

[69]Malaysia's Free Trade Agreements, Agreement on Trade in Services under the Framework Agreement on Comprehensive Economic Cooperation between the Association of Southeast Asian Nations and the Republic of India (ASEAN-India Trade in Services Agreement). 13 November 2014, https://fta.miti.gov.my/index.php/pages/view/asean-india?mid=35, Article 6.

[70]Official Journal of the European Union, Economic Partnership Agreement between the CARIFORUM States, of the one part, and the European Community and its Member States, of the other part. 15 October 2008, https://eur-lex.europa.eu/LexUriServ/LexUriServ.do?uri=OJ:L:2008:289:0003:1955:EN:PDF, Article 85, Article 114, Article 121:2(b).

plus in terms of M4 by liberalising market access and national treatment for the new category of installers and maintainers and graduate trainees.

Mutual recognition of qualifications is more likely to occur between culturally close and geographically proximate trading partner is illustrated in the case of the Mainland and Hong Kong Closer Economic Partnership Arrangement (CEPA).[71] Article 15 of the CEPA, titled 'Mutual Recognition of Professional Qualifications', contains one of the most specific commitment observed for mutual recognition regime for professional qualifications in a PTA: firstly, it notes the *ratio legis* as one promoting mobility, and secondly it commits the Parties to integrate professional associations by 'competent authorities' for 'designing specific methodologies' for mutual recognition of professional qualifications. Thirdly, it disaggregates the process of mutual recognition by economic sector (accounting, printing, engineering). Similarly, the China-ASEAN (CAFTA) also contains a commitment to conclude MRA,[72] without specifying the details who will be involved in negotiating the methodologies to assess recognition.

More advanced formulas (relating to time) are observed in some FTAs as well. Under Article 65:3 of the Japan –India PTA, one party may unilaterally require the other party to "encourage its professional bodies in a specific regulated sector to negotiate and conclude within 12 months an arrangement for mutual recognition of education, experiences, requirements, certification granted".[73] Similarly, in paragraph 7 of Annex 12-A of the US-Korea FTA the Parties undertake to implement the recommendations of a working group (regarding mutual recognition of professional services) within a mutually agreed time.[74]

3.2 GATS-Plus for Fast-Tracking the Processing of Visa Applications & Facilitating Requirements

One of the proposals, during the negotiations of GATS, contained an obligation to fast-track entry for those service supplying persons falling under GATS M4.[75] Article 9 of the proposal stated that "the procedures for entry for temporary stay

---

[71]Trade and Industry Department, Mainland and Hong Kong Closer Economic Partnership Arrangement. Consolidated version, The Government of the Hong Kong Special Administrative Region, https://www.tid.gov.hk/english/cepa/legaltext/files/consolidated_main_text.pdf.

[72]China FTA Network, Agreement on Trade in Services of the Framework Agreement on Comprehensive Economic Co-operation between China and ASEAN. 14 January 2007, http://fta.mofcom.gov.cn/topic/chinaasean.shtml, Article 6.

[73]Ministry of Foreign Affairs of Japan, Comprehensive Economic Partnership Agreement between Japan and the Republic of India. 15 February 2011, https://www.mofa.go.jp/region/asia-paci/india/epa201102/index.html.

[74]Office of the United States Trade Representative, US – Korea Free Trade Agreement. 30 June 2007, https://ustr.gov/trade-agreements/free-trade-agreements/korus-fta/final-text.

[75]Group of Negotiations on Services. (1990) Communication from Argentina, Colombia, Cuba, Egypt, India, Mexico, Pakistan and Peru: Annex on Temporary Movement of Services Personnel. MTN.GNS/W/106, https://www.wto.org/gatt_docs/English/SULPDF/92100208.pdf.

shall be accomplished expeditiously so as to avoid unduly impairing or delaying the conduct of trade in services" and obliged the parties to ensure that "their embassies and immigration offices abroad, and immigration authorities at ports of entry are familiar with the visas issued pursuant to this Annex".[76] While such a provision never made its way into the final text of the Uruguay Round, many PTAs concluded thereafter have taken up some of this language by providing for simplified and expedited visa requirements (e.g. language tests, no prior application for identical visa) and application procedures (timeframe and documentation required) for M4, as also special lanes at airports, to outsourcing the process to a private company, as a way to renounce to the in-person interview at a consulate or embassy.[77]

Hence, fast-tracked processing of applications has moved from *de lege ferenda* status under GATS to a reality in PTAs and could find their way through the backdoor of a GATS-plus feature in PTAs into GATS. To some, such clauses are an aborted form of the GATS-visa, proposed by India during the Doha Round negotiations, which did not materialise.[78] These clauses often form a first step towards a harmonised regional visa policy which culminates ideally in a special visa for the categories of M4 workers, as is in force in the EU with the EU Schengen visa (SV), the EU Blue Card Directive (2009/50/EC) and the EU Single Permit Directive (2011/98/EU) for third country nationals or the ASEAN Business Travel Card (ABTC), and the ASEAN single visa to promote tourism in the region under discussion.[79]

Visa policy, in particular visa restrictiveness and facilitation, remains a key migration control and foreign policy instrument. Hence, it is unlikely that a PTA will entirely remove the visa requirement. Rather, features such as the duration of the visa validity, amount of visa renewal, visa fee, as well as the popular fast-tracking of

---

[76]Group of Negotiations on Services. (1990) Communication from Argentina, Colombia, Cuba, Egypt, India, Mexico, Pakistan and Peru: Annex on Temporary Movement of Services Personnel. MTN.GNS/W/106, https://www.wto.org/gatt_docs/English/SULPDF/92100208.pdf.

[77]Self and Zutshi (2003) and Chanda (2002).

[78]Council for Trade in Services: Special Session (2000) Communication from India: Proposed Liberalization of Movement of Professionals under General Agreement on Trade in Services. World Trade Organization, S/CSS/W/12, https://docs.wto.org/dol2fe/Pages/FE_Search/FE_S_S009-DP. aspx?language=E&CatalogueIdList=45548,89465,45733,2933,3410,31485,15703& CurrentCatalogueIdIndex=6&FullTextHash=&HasEnglishRecord=True& HasFrenchRecord=True&HasSpanishRecord=True. According to Rupa Chanda, India's proposal for a GATS visa was endorsed by other developing countries (see above), but was criticised by LDCs, who feared that the Indian proposal would target only medium-skilled service suppliers and leave out the lower-skilled services professions. Chanda R, Movement and Presence of Natural Persons and Developing Countries: Issues and Proposals for the GATS Negotiations. Trade-Related Agenda, Development and Equity Working Paper Series No 19, South Centre, May 2004, pp. 24–30.

[79]Shiny and Tewari (2019) Domestic Regulation under GATS and the Legal Regime: An Unsustainable Interaction. Center for Trade and Investment Law, Discussion Paper 1/2019, https://ctil.org.in/cms/docs/Papers/Discussion/discussion4.pdf; Mukherjee A, Goyal T (2013) Examining Mode 4 Commitments in India and the EU's Agreements: Implication for the India-EU BTIA. Indian Institute of Management, Working Paper 396; Schmitz (2015).

the application process, can be negotiated. Regional blocs, such as the ECOWAS and the EU, already contain free intra-regional travel or at least a low visa restrictiveness (less than 20%).[80] In departure, we observe that the fast tracking of visa applications can be said to be the first step in extending the free movement present within the regional blocs to trading partners with whom a PTA is concluded.

3.3   GATS-**Minus** *Commitments in PTAS:* **Lex Specialis** *on Dispute Settlement & National Security Exemptions*

This section elaborates the advancement in FTAs over GATS regarding the dispute settlement clauses and national security clauses in the chapter on temporary movement of persons. Many PTAs exempt rulings on the refusal of entry from litigation before the PTAs dispute settlement system, unless all domestic remedies have been exhausted. This, and the application of a special national security exemption specific to the Mode 4 chapter, are provisions that in many ways are more restrictive than the multilateral GATS M4 provisions. This section first elaborates the 'dispute settlement' provisions and thereafter 'national security' clauses applicable to M4 workers.

3.3.1   Dispute Settlement

The WTO Agreements and several FTAs contain dispute settlement provisions. This sub-section demonstrates that the dispute settlement clauses in FTAs are tighter than those observed in the GATS because they contain certain pre-conditions and exhaustion limits, both of which are absent in GATS for temporary movement of natural persons.

The dispute settlement provisions in the WTO Agreements, applicable to temporary movement of natural persons, do not require any pre-conditions before their invocation. As per Article XXIII of the GATS, any Member shall have recourse to WTO's dispute settlement if the Member considers that any other Member fails to carry out its obligations or specific commitments under the GATS. There are no preconditions before the invocation of the dispute settlement under the WTO Agreements apart from a consideration of a failure to carry out obligations.

At present, several FTAs contain dispute settlement provisions.[81] FTAs also contain a separate investment chapter, a majority of which have their own dispute settlement provisions.[82] Dispute settlement clauses in FTAs are either contained in a

---

[80]Czaika et al. (2018).

[81]The E15 Initiative (2018) Dispute Settlement Mechanisms in RTAs. The E15 Initiative, http://e15initiative.org/events/rta-dispute-settlement-provisions-options-for-effective-enforcement/.

[82]Crawford and Kotschwar (2018) Investment Provisions in Preferential Trade Agreements: Evolution and Current Trends. WTO Staff Working Paper ERSD-2018-14, https://www.wto.org/english/res_e/reser_e/ersd201814_e.pdf. Of the 230 PTAs analysed by this study, 111 contained

specific provision in the chapter on the temporary movement on natural persons[83] or the chapter on dispute settlement contains a provision extending the scope of dispute settlement to any dispute arising in the FTA, including on the movement of natural persons.[84]

Dispute settlement provisions in the chapter on temporary movement of natural persons often contain certain pre-conditions before the dispute settlement under the FTA can be invoked.[85] There are two types of pre-conditions which are commonly observed: firstly, a pattern of practice, and secondly, exhaustion of local remedies.[86] Furthermore, the time limit for exhaustion of domestic/administrative remedies in FTAs is often restricted to either 1 year,[87] or 2 years.[88,89]

Hence, the dispute settlement provisions for temporary movement of natural persons are more restrictive under FTAs because they contain pre-conditions and contain provisions on the exhaustion of time limits unlike the GATS which does not contain any restrictions.

substantive provisions on investment. (p. 3) Of these agreements, more than 90% contained provisions on State-to-State dispute settlement and 77% contained provisions on investor state dispute settlement (p.27).

[83] For instance, see: Government of Canada, Consolidated TPP Text – Table of Contents. Comprehensive and Progressive Agreement for Trans-Pacific Partnership (CPTPP), 08 March 2018, https://www.international.gc.ca/trade-commerce/trade-agreements-accords-commerciaux/agr-acc/tpp-ptp/text-texte/toc-tdm.aspx?lang=eng, Article 12.10.

[84] See, for instance: Comprehensive Economic and Trade Agreement (CETA) between Canada, of the one part, and the European Union and its Member States, of the other part of 30 October 2016, OJ L 11, 14.1.2017, p. 2.

[85] Sometimes, exceptions are also observed. See, for instance: China FTA Network, Free Trade Agreement between the Government of the People's Republic of China and The Government of New Zealand. 07 April 2008, http://fta.mofcom.gov.cn/topic/ennewzealand.shtml, Article 134.

[86] For instance, see: Government of Canada, Chapter 12—Temporary Entry for Business Persons. Canada-Peru Free Trade Agreement, 29 May 2008, https://www.international.gc.ca/trade-commerce/trade-agreements-accords-commerciaux/agr-acc/peru-perou/fta-ale/12.aspx?lang=eng, Article 1206:1.

[87] See, for instance, Government of Canada, Chapter 12—Temporary Entry for Business Persons. Canada-Peru Free Trade Agreement, 29 May 2008, https://www.international.gc.ca/trade-commerce/trade-agreements-accords-commerciaux/agr-acc/peru-perou/fta-ale/12.aspx?lang=eng, Article 1206:2.

[88] See, for instance: Ministry of Foreign Affairs of Japan, Agreement between Japan and Australia for an Economic Partnership. 08 July 2014, https://www.mofa.go.jp/ecm/ep/page22e_000430.html, Article 12.6:2.

[89] At times, access to dispute settlement is only allowed after the exhaustion of all local remedies. See, for instance: Centre for WTO and Economic Integration, ASEAN Agreement on Movement of Natural Persons. Vietnam Chamber of Commerce and Industry, 19 November 2012, http://aecvcci.vn/tin-tuc-n1648/asean-agreement-on-movement-of-natural-persons-mnp.htm, Article 11:2(b).

3.3.2 National Security

The national security provisions for temporary movement of natural persons appear to be more restrictive than under the GATS because they are open ended, unlike the GATS. The national security exception under the GATS restricts the application of security only to 'essential security interests' as stated in Article XIV *bis* of the GATS. The term 'essential security interests' hasn't been defined in the GATS. In *Russia — Traffic in Transit*[90] the Panel stated: *""Essential security interests", which is evidently a narrower concept than "security interests", may generally be understood to refer to those interests relating to the quintessential functions of the state...."*[91] Hence, the term 'essential security interests' stated in GATS restricts the application of national security exceptions only to functions which are 'quintessential'.

National security exceptions have been observed in the chapter on temporary labour mobility of some FTAs.[92] Furthermore, it has been observed that the term 'national security' is not defined in these FTAs, thus broadening the scope of the term relative to the GATS.

In light of the statements above, it can be stated that both dispute settlement and national security provisions in FTAs are more restrictive as compared to GATS.

4 TMNP Annex-*Plus*: Incorporating Commitments on Readmission and Return

Certain PTAs dissolve the watertight distinction, made by the GATS TMNP between the liberalization of the cross-border, temporary movement of natural persons, a theme falling into GATS jurisdiction, and the regulation of borders, territory, admission and visa, citizenship, residence and movement of persons on a permanent basis, which falls outside the scope of GATS, as laid down in Paragraph 4 of the Annex TMNP, also called the GATS *'caveat'*. However, some FTAs have removed this watertight distinction, such as the JEPA. Paragraph 7 of the JEPA states: "The Parties acknowledge that the enhanced movement of natural persons following from paragraphs 1 to 6 requires full cooperation on return and readmission

---

[90]Further details of the dispute are available at: World Trade Organization (2019) DS 512: Russia — Measures Concerning Traffic in Transit. World Trade Organization, https://www.wto.org/english/tratop_e/dispu_e/cases_e/ds512_e.htm.

[91]*Russia — Measures Concerning Traffic in Transit,* Report of the Panel. WT/DS512/R, 05 April 2019, para 7.130.

[92]For instance, see: Foreign Trade Information System, Free Trade Agreement between the Republic of Colombia and the Republic of Korea. Organization of American States, 21 February 2013, http://www.sice.oas.org/TPD/Col_kor/Draft_Text_06.2012_e/June_2012_Index_PDF_e.asp, Section E of Annex 10-A (Both Colombia and Korea), Article 10.3:1.

of natural persons staying in a Party in contravention of its rules for entry and temporary stay."[93]

It is the first time that the EU includes cooperation on readmission obligation with a trading partner in an FTA. It had already done so in DCFTAs with Eastern Partnership countries. The European Union aims to increase its leverage on return and readmission by including it as a part of the trade and visa facilitation agreements. The EU specifically aims to include the linkage of conclusion on a free trade agreement with a parallel conclusion of a readmission agreement.[94] Separately, the European Commission's 'Trade for All' strategy document explicitly states that, *"Trade policy should take into account the policy framework for the return and readmission of irregular migrants."*[95] During the TiSA negotiations, one of the discussions between the EU Commission and civil society addressed inclusion of cooperation on readmission as a conditionality to openings in mode 4.[96] The EU's proposal for the EU – Mexico FTA contains return and readmission obligations.[97]

5   Conclusion

Asian countries liberalize M4 by sectors, rather than by broadening the horizontal commitment by adding a category, which explains why they have added non-service-oriented movement of natural persons through side-letters. The EU PTAs in contrast, have been offering M4 GATS-*plus* by either adding new service provider categories in the horizontal dimension or by including persons who move cross-border without delivering services (non-services movement of natural persons, e.g. graduate trainees).

Systemic differences aside, we observe that the rationale for attaching certain types of labor migration onto a trade setting also diverges depending on the Asian or European perimeters. In the Asian arena, PTAs liberalize M4 to fill in for skill gaps and labour market needs. In contrast, M4 in EU PTAs mostly stands as bargaining

---

[93]Ministry of Foreign Affairs of Japan, Agreement between the European Union and Japan for an Economic Partnership. 17 July 2018, https://www.mofa.go.jp/ecm/ie/page4e_000875.html, Para 7 of Annex 8 – C.

[94]European Commission, Communication from the Commission to the European Parliament and to The Council: EU Action Plan on return. COM(2015) 453 Final, 9 September 2015, https://ec.europa.eu/home-affairs/sites/homeaffairs/files/what-we-do/policies/european-agenda-migration/proposal-implementation-package/docs/communication_from_the_ec_to_ep_and_council_-_eu_action_plan_on_return_en.pdf, p. 14.

[95]European Commission, Trade for All: Towards a More Responsible Trade and Investment Policy. 14 October 2015, http://trade.ec.europa.eu/doclib/docs/2015/october/tradoc_153846.pdf, p. 12.

[96]European Commission, Civil Society Dialogue: Meeting on TiSA. 3 May 2016, http://trade.ec.europa.eu/doclib/docs/2016/june/tradoc_154628.pdf.

[97]European Union, Understanding on Movement of Natural Persons for Business Purposes. Services Chapter, EU Textual Proposal, EU-Mexico Free Trade Agreement, 25 January 2018, http://trade.ec.europa.eu/doclib/docs/2018/january/tradoc_156558.pdf, Article 3.

chip in an overall trade-and migration conditionality, which require the trading partners' cooperation over combatting irregular migration, much in line with the how the EU has been previously linking trade benefits to achieve regulatory cooperation over non-trade values, including *inter alia* cooperation over combatting drug and narcotics dealing.

This chapter finds, that M4 and labor migration thus share greater areas of friction, even within trade agreements, than what the Uruguay Round trade negotiators had planned for by adopting the GATS Annex MNP. We found that foreign labor recruiting countries in the EU and Asia have elevated the recruitment of skilled labor into the trade venue to either circumvent the more cumbersome legislative process of immigration law-making (Asia) or else to pressure the law-making process at regional and national levels into drafting facilitated labor market admission for this category of workers (EU), 'inverse diffusion'. In both cases, coincidentally, it is the trade venue, via the bias of the PTAs, that has erased the watertight distinction between M4 and labor migration, which the GATS Annex MNP had sought to establish in the first place.

Asian PTAs operate some kind of parallelism between mobility and migration by introducing via side-letters non-services work in the context of a trade agreement. As the ChAFTA side-letter shows, Chinese cultural-oriented professionals (medicine, music, cuisine, martial arts) are being admitted on a quota-basis into Australia. In this case, the side-letter might be an attempt to offer labor market entry without compromising the Australian parliamentary process into drafting (yet) a modification of its immigration laws to let in the Chinese cultural professionals/laborers on a broader scale. In the Asian trading spaces, directionality is currently non-binary, in the case of cultural-oriented M4, we find a co-existence between mobility and migration, which over time will become increasingly permeable, and make place to interchangeable categories in the MMN.

In the case of the Japan-Philippines EPA and the draft EU-Mexico FTA show, migration management provisions are diffusing into trade settings—another evidence for more proximity on the MMN continuum. At the same time, migration management provisions in EU PTAs remain a 'home-affairs' issue and are regulated through soft law, including the EU Common Agendas on Migration and Mobility (e.g. EU-India/China). Hence in the EU, the MMN proximity is less accentuated, when it comes to regulating mobility, but more accentuated when it comes to liberalizing admission of foreign services/non-services/hybrid services/non-services workers, given the EU multilevel governance of labor migration.

The chapter concludes that while Asian PTAs add sectoral commitments in M4 which do not yet figure in national immigration laws and whose immigration formalities are hence included in side letters attached to a PTAs, the EU's GATS plus in M4 in PTAs are sectoral additions (installers and maintainers) which are first liberalized in a trade setting with the concomitant expectation that this category will eventually be formulated in an EU labor market directive and from there, taken up by national immigration laws.

The MMN in Asian PTAs represents a mobility approach of 'coherent fragmentation', with services-related mobility liberalized by sectors in M4, and non-services-oriented mobility in side-letters. Hence, the differences in the MMN continuum in Asian PTAs are placed in separate containers (schedules of commitments, side-letters, ASEAN mutual recognition scheme). Inversely, the EU PTAs horizontal approach to M4 commitments allows for a smooth trickling down effect onto EU labor market directives and Member States' labor market law, and thus for heightened coherence within a multi-level or fragmented system of division of competences, typical for EU law. Furthermore, the division into DGs trade and home affairs deepens the 'fragmented coherence' between liberalizing categories of services work in PTAs and regulating migration (visa, border security, returns) in the EU.

References

Brettell C, Hollifield J (2019) Migration theory: talking across disciplines. In: Brettell C, Hollifield J (eds) Migration theory, talking across disciplines, 3rd edn, pp 3–12

Carzaniga A (2003) The GATS, mode 4, and pattern of commitments. In: Mattoo A, Carzaniga A (eds) Moving people to deliver services. World Bank and Oxford University Press, Washington, DC, pp 21–26

Carzaniga A (2009) A warmer welcome? Access for natural persons under PTAs. In: Marchetti J, Roy M (eds) Opening markets for trade in services: countries and sectors in bilateral and WTO negotiations. Cambridge University Press, Cambridge, pp 475–502

Rupa Chanda, (2002) Movement of Natural Persons and the GATS. The World Economy 24 (5):631-654

Chetail V (2003) Freedom of movement and transnational migrations: a human rights perspective. In: Aleinikoff A, Chetail V (eds) Migration and international legal norms. Asser Press, The Hague, pp 47–60

Chetail V (2019) International migration law. Oxford University Press, Oxford

Cottier T, Sieber-Gasser C (2015) Labour migration, trade and investment: from fragmentation to coherence. In: Panizzon M, Zürcher G, Fornalé E (eds) The Palgrave handbook of international labour migration. Palgrave Macmillan, London, pp 41–60

Czaika M, de Haas H, Villares-Varela M (2018) The global evolution of travel visa regimes. Popul Dev Rev 44(3):589–622

de Lange T (2019) Intersecting policies of innovation and entrepreneurship migration in the EU and the Netherlands. In: Carrera S, den Hertog L, Kostakopoulou D, Panizzon M (eds) The external faces of EU migration, borders and asylum policies: intersecting policy universes, Brill, pp 224–243

Hoekman B (1996) Assessing the general agreement on trade in services. In: Martin W, Winters L (eds) The Uruguay Round and developing countries. Cambridge University Press, Cambridge, pp 88–124

Horn H, Mavroidis P, Sapir A (2010) Beyond the WTO: an anatomy of EU and US trade agreements. Bruegel Blueprint Series, 09 February 2009. https://bruegel.org/2009/02/beyond-the-wto-an-anatomy-of-eu-and-us-preferential-trade-agreements/

Jacobsson J (2015) GATS mode 4 and labour mobility: the significance of employment labour market. In: Pannizon M, Zürcher G, Fornalé E (eds) The Palgrave handbook of international labour migration. Palgrave Macmillan, London

Jurje F (2019) The EU's external labour mobility and trade—a multilayered governance approach? In: Carrera S, den Hertig L, Panizzon M, Kostakopoulo D (eds) EU external migration policies in an era of global mobilities: intersecting policy universes. Martinus Nijhoff Publishers, Brill, pp 207–221

Jurje F, Lavenex S (2018) Mobility norms in free trade agreements: migration governance in Asia between regional integration and free trade. Eur J East Asian Stud 17(1):83–117

Kemekliene G, Watt A (2010) GATS and the EU: impacts on labour markets and regulatory capacity, report 116, Brussels

Lavenex S, Jurje F (2019) Opening-up labor mobility? rising powers' rulemaking in trade agreements. In: Regulation & governance. https://doi.org/10.1111/rego.12271

Nccr – on the move (2019) The migration-mobility nexus, Neuchâtel https://nccr-onthemove.ch/about-us/the-migration-mobility-nexus/, University of Neuchatel

Ndiaye-Coïc R (2011) Sénégal: le secteur privé dans les accords de gestion des flux migratoires signés avec l'Espagne et la France, nccr trade regulation. Working paper no 2011/09. World Trade Institute, Bern

Nonnenmacher S (2012) International trade law and labour mobility. In: Opeskin B, Perruchoud R, Redpath-Cross J (eds) Foundations of international migration law. Cambridge University Press, Cambridge, pp 312–335

Panizzon M (2010) Art. 100. In: Caroni/Gächter/Turnheer (Hg.), Stämpflis Handkommentar zum Bundesgesetz über die Ausländerinnen und Ausländer, Bern, pp 923–956

Panizzon M (2013) Partenariats migratoires suisses et accords de coopération migratoire: gestion ou gouvernance des migrations internationales? Jusletter 24:2013

Peers S (2013) EU Justice and Home Affairs Law: EU Justice and Home Affairs Law: Volume II. Oxford University Press, Oxford

Reyna J (1999) Services. In: Stewart T (ed) The GATT Uruguay Round, a negotiating history (1986–1994), volume IV: the end game (part I). Kluwer Law International, The Hague, pp 775–828

Sauvé P, Roy M (2016) Introduction and overview. In: Sauvé P, Roy M (eds) Research handbook on trade in services. Research handbooks on the WTO. Edward Elgar, Cheltenham, pp 1–26

Sauvé P, Shingal A (2016) Why do countries enter into preferential agreements on trade in services? Asia Dev Rev 33(1):56–73

Schmitz J (2015) The temporary movement of natural persons in the context of trade in services: EU trade policy under mode 4 (WTO/GATS). In: Panizzon M, Zürcher G, Fornalé E (eds) The Palgrave handbook of international labour migration. Palgrave Macmillan UK, Basingstoke, pp 382–383

Self R, Zutshi B (2003) Mode 4: negotiating challenges and opportunities. In: Mattoo A, Carzaniga A (eds) Moving people to deliver services. Springer, Heidelberg, pp 27–58

Shi J (2018) Services liberalization in ChAFTA: progress assessment and the way forward. In: Picker CB, Weng H, Zhou W (eds) The China-Australia free trade agreement, a 21st century model. Hart, Oxford, pp 107–126

Shivakoti R (2019) Labor migration governance in Asia. In: Regional integration and migration in the global south. Springer, Heidelberg

Tans S (2017) Service provision and migration EU and WTO service trade liberalization and their impact on Dutch and UK immigration rules. Immigration and Asylum Law and Policy in Europe, vol 41. Brill/Nijhoff, Leiden

Tullao T Jr, Cortez M (2006) Enhancing the movement of natural persons in the ASEAN region: opportunities and constraints, ARTNeT working paper series, no. 23, Asia-Pacific Research and Training Network on Trade (ARTNeT), Bangkok

von Bernstorff J (2015) International legal scholarship as a cooling medium in international law and politics. Eur J Int Law 25(4):977–990

Ward N (2011) Facilitating the temporary movement of natural persons. In: Kunz R, Lavenex S, Panizzon M (eds) Multilayered migration governance: the promise of partnerships. Routledge, pp 143–182

Marion Panizzon, Dr. iur., LL.M. (Duke) is a privat-docent of the University of Bern, fellow of the World Trade Institute and a Member of the Board of the Center for Migration, University of Göttingen.

Harjodh Singh is an Independent Legal Consultant from India specialising in international trade law and intellectual property law.

Telecommunications and Media Services in Preferential Trade Agreements: Path Dependences Still Matter

Mira Burri

Contents

I would like to thank Rhea Hoffmann and Markus Krajewski for inviting me to the International Workshop "Coherence and Divergence in Agreements on Trade in Services" at the University of Erlangen-Nürnberg in March 2019, which provided an excellent platform for the discussion of newer developments in services trade. I am particularly indebted for the insightful comments of my discussant Christophe Kiener from the European Commission. The research assistance of Ms Zaïra Zihlmann is much appreciated; all errors remain my own.

M. Burri (✉)
Faculty of Law, University of Lucerne, Lucerne, Switzerland
e-mail: mira.burri@unilu.ch

© The Editor(s) (if applicable) and The Author(s), under exclusive licence to
Springer Nature Switzerland AG 2020
R. T. Hoffmann, M. Krajewski (eds.), *Coherence and Divergence in Services Trade Law*, European Yearbook of International Economic Law,
https://doi.org/10.1007/978-3-030-46955-9_8

169

1   Introduction

The telecommunications and the media sectors offer a fascinating study of the evolution of international services regulation. The starting point for such an enquiry is that in terms of liberalisation under the umbrella of the World Trade Organization (WTO), they stand on the opposing ends of the spectrum—the telecommunications sector is the most liberalised, with far-reaching commitments made by almost all WTO Members and added beyond-the-border regulatory duties, while the media, or "audiovisual" sector, as in the language of the WTO schedules, is the least committed for. The policy space available domestically in these services sectors is therefore strikingly different. This said, both sectors have been equally influenced by technological change—by the sweeping processes of digitisation, which not only transform the dynamics of the markets and blur the lines between the sectors but also may demand changes in the trade law framework—potentially reflecting the convergence of the sectors and involving some degree of legal innovation as the data-driven economy advances and matures. Yet, we do not see this occurring in recent preferential trade agreements (PTAs)—the divergence between the telecom and the media sectors remains and there is a strong path dependence, which translates in further liberalisation and more detailed rules for telecommunications and no commitments or specifically delineated policy space in the media services sector. This chapter substantiates this path dependence hypothesis by looking at a few recent PTAs. It examines in particular the Comprehensive and Progressive Agreement for Transpacific Partnership (CPTPP) and the update of the North American Free Trade Agreement (NAFTA), now known as the United States-Mexico-Canada Agreement (USMCA), as two key US-led treaties, and the Comprehensive Economic and Trade Agreement (CETA) and the EU-Japan free trade agreement (FTA), as two recent treaties with the participation of the European Union. The chapter maps the differences in the commitments and potentially in the treaty language in these PTAs and the corresponding chapters for telecom and media services vis-à-vis the commitments and the language under the WTO. The analysis includes also provisions that may be highly relevant for the sectors, such as on net neutrality, which are found outside of the dedicated services chapters.

In tracing these developments, the chapter also allows us to see how power has played out in trade negotiations and whether actors have changed their positions over time, in particular as in the media sector, there have been a number of highly contentious issues with regard to the debate on trade and culture. By looking at the evolution of rules over time, we may also be able to contemplate on law's adaptation and ask whether it adequately reflects the technological and policy developments that have occurred after the end of the Uruguay Round and the coming into force of the WTO Agreements in 1995.

2 State of Affairs Under Current WTO Law: GATS Rules and Levels of Commitments

2.1 Telecommunications Services

Telecommunications services are by their nature transnational and this has demanded considerable coordination between countries over time that has been mirrored in their regulation. A piece of evidence in this sense is the fact that the first intergovernmental organisation, the International Telegraph Union, is in the area of telecommunications.[1] This intrinsic need for co-operation is also reflected in the law of the WTO with regard to telecommunications, where the WTO Members have agreed on deep commitments and even provided for some regulatory safeguards that foster competition in the sector on a global scale. This level of engagement was however neither easy nor was it quick to attain, as the telecommunications sector was in a state of profound transition in the 1990s and many countries were undergoing domestic reforms in an attempt to privatise and open for competition the previously state-owned or state-controlled Post, Telegraph and Telephone (PTT) agencies. As these reforms progressed, there was a growing interest, shared in particular amongst major globally positioned corporations, that these changes become reflected in the international regulatory frameworks too. Telecommunications were to be addressed "as a distinct economic activity, a tradable service, rather than simply as a medium or a conduit for conducting trade".[2] The issue of market access as the emerging primary concern in international communications law could not be tackled appropriately within the realm of the International Telecommunication Union (ITU) and required a change of venue. The WTO provided a more apposite negotiation and regulatory forum, and ultimately established a sophisticated regime for telecommunications services, also affirming the liberalisation trend as a sound approach to telecommunications policy.[3]

The process of negotiating the commitments for telecommunication services took a while and was complicated as the national incumbents wanted to keep some of their privileges with regard to the so-called "basic" telecommunications services, while liberalising the newer and less regulated, "value-added" services.[4] Reflecting

---

[1]The International Telegraph Union was transformed into the International Telecommunication Union (ITU) in 1932 combining the International Telegraph Convention of 1865 and the International Radiotelegraph Convention of 1906.

[2]Walden (2001), p. 347.

[3]Drake (2008).

[4]The scheme used for negotiating the commitments adopted a distinction made in the US in the so-called *Computer Inquiries*. It listed as basic telecommunications services: voice telephone; packet-switched data transmission; circuit-switched data transmission; telex; telegraph; facsimile and private leased circuit services and other (lit. (a) to (g) and (o)). The remaining telecommunications services of the W/120 classification list were framed as value-added services (lit. (h) to (n)). See WTO, Draft Model Schedule of Commitments on Basic Telecommunications, Job. No 1311 (1995).

these difficulties, the resulting WTO law is structured in two instruments—the *Annex on Telecommunications*, which was agreed upon during the Uruguay Round, and the *Fourth Protocol on Basic Telecommunications Services*, which was the result of subsequent negotiations.

The Annex on Telecommunications defines its objective as "elaborating upon the provisions of the Agreement [GATS] with respect to measures affecting access to and use of public telecommunications transport networks and services".[5] In this sense, the Annex itself does not contain or lead to any market access or national treatment obligations for telecommunications services beyond the commitments that the WTO Members had already made. It comes into effect only once a Member has offered a specific commitment in a given services sector,[6] and ensures that foreign services suppliers are accorded access to public telecommunications networks and services subject to reasonable and non-discriminatory terms and conditions.[7] With the benefit of hindsight, it is clear that in practice the Annex, despite being an act on telecommunications, concerned mostly liberalised non-telecommunications services (such as banking, insurance or other financial services), which to perform effectively required access to and the use of communications networks and services. The Annex was also of importance to the earlier mentioned "value-added" telecommunications services, for which Members had already made commitments.[8] Overall, the Annex provided legal certainty and prevented that access to telecommunications becomes a non-tariff barrier to trade.[9]

After the end of the Uruguay Round, the negotiations on telecommunications continued. The agreement that was ultimately reached became known as the *Agreement on Basic Telecommunications* and was annexed to the existing schedules through the Fourth Protocol, which forms an integral part of General Agreement on Trade in Services (GATS).[10] The Agreement on Basic Telecommunications consists of a series of schedules of specific commitments, which provide for a very liberal regime for telecom services across all subsectors and modes of supply. A major breakthrough of the Agreement was the adoption of the so-called *Reference Paper*, incorporated as an additional commitment into the Members' schedules.[11]

---

[5]Section 1 Annex on Telecommunications. Section 2(b) explicitly excludes from the scope of the Annex "measures affecting the cable or broadcast distribution of radio or television programming".

[6]Section 2(c)(i) Annex on Telecommunications; WTO Panel Report, *Mexico – Measures Affecting Telecommunications Services (Mexico – Telecommunications)*, WT/DS204/R, adopted 2 April 2004, at paras 7.290–7.294.

[7]Section 5 Annex on Telecommunications.

[8]It should not be concluded however that the scope of application of the Annex is solely directed at value-added telecommunications services. As clarified by *Mexico – Telecom* (paras 7.273–7.288), the scope of the Annex also includes basic telecommunications services, when commitments for these services had been made, as is now conventionally the case.

[9]Cameron (2004), p. 21.

[10]Article XX:3 GATS.

[11]Article XVIII GATS.

The Reference Paper is a unique document in the law and practice of the WTO, which contains a set of regulatory principles for basic telecommunications. In terms of content, although only six sections long, it represents, together with the Fourth Protocol, an immense step forward in the opening of telecommunications markets and rendered telecommunications one of the best-covered sectors under the GATS. Furthermore, it ensured that the advantages of the former monopoly operators were not used to the detriment of new entrants during the precarious process of liberalising telecommunications markets.[12] The Reference Paper is particularly noteworthy, as it includes competition law-like provisions with core concepts related to market dominance and abuse of dominant position,[13] as well as some sector-specific rules. Critical amongst the latter is the obligation on major suppliers of public telecommunications networks and services to enable interconnection with their networks and services "at any technically feasible point in the network".[14] The other provisions (Sections 3–6) of the Reference Paper address universal service, licensing, regulators' independence and scarce resources, and create a fundamental framework of non-discrimination and transparency for the sector.[15]

Summing up, one can argue that in the field of telecommunications services, we have a uniquely deep intervention of the WTO rules, which not only open key telecommunications markets to foreign services and services suppliers but also in fact regulate important aspects of competition in the sector, seeking to ensure a level playing field. Another critical feature is that interconnection and interoperability are ensured and new market entrants are offered equal competitive opportunities. All these aspects have substantially contributed to the smooth functioning of the critical infrastructure layer and facilitated the emergence of global communications networks. While global Internet traffic developed later on independently, it did make use of the network basis and benefited immensely from the liberalised telecommunications markets.[16]

2.2 Audiovisual Services

The GATS and its malleability in design allowing different levels of commitment for different services sectors are at least partially the result of a pronounced and politically charged contention between trade and cultural interests. The origins of

---

[12]Bronckers and Larouche (2008).

[13]The far-reaching effect of these rules was confirmed by *Mexico – Telecommunications*. See Fox (2006).

[14]Section 2 Reference Paper.

[15]For a detailed analysis, see Geradin and Kerf (2004) and Burri (2007).

[16]Weller and Woodcock (2013).

and the positions within this clash have been well documented elsewhere.[17] Critical for our discussion here is the fact that on matters of culture, there is a rupture between the key negotiating parties in the WTO, as well as globally—the EU and the US. As a consequence of the diverging positions of the main stakeholders, we have seen the formation of very different regimes for content (audiovisual and related) and network/application (telecom, computer and e-commerce) services.[18]

The trade versus culture contention and the failure to reconcile the EU and the US positions have meant for the international regulation of services that, in spite of the arguably considerable economic gains to be reaped from the liberalisation of audio-visual media services,[19] almost all Members have made few or no commitments. For example, the EU and its Member States made no commitments[20] and tabled a number of MFN exemptions that benefit audiovisual services and providers under diverse co-production agreements and support schemes, such as the MEDIA programme.[21] The same is true for Switzerland, Canada and a number of developing countries. The exceptions to the rule of non-commitment are the US, Japan and New Zealand, as well as some of the more recently acceded WTO Members.[22] Overall, audiovisual media is the least liberalised services sector.

What is particularly interesting when looking at the Members' commitments for audiovisual services, and most illustratively those of the EU, is that they reflect a resolute "all-or-nothing" approach. The scheduling flexibility permitting different options ranging between full liberalisation and absolute non-commitment is not made use of. This is odd because for subsectors where government regulation and trade restrictions are uncommon, such as sound recording, commitments are non-existent. In a more systemic sense, this is odd because the very goals of an international trade agreement are compromised: "Indeed, absence of commitment in a given sector, while it remains an option, means that a Member can, at any time, take whatever market-access or national treatment limitation [. . .]. This absence of any guarantee of openness stands in stark contrast to the economic and trade importance of the [audiovisual] sector (and in particular its intensive use of technology and creativity) as well as the importance of the predictability and stability given

---

[17]The debate has to do with the dual nature of cultural products and services, which while being an object of trade can also be carriers of values and identities. The EU, and especially France, have pushed for the exclusion of culture-related goods and services from the economically centred rules of the WTO and for their special treatment. The US on the other hand has favoured a trade-oriented approach that does not allow for any particular special treatment of cultural goods and services and subsumes them under the basic WTO rules. See e.g. Burri (2008, 2015b).

[18]Burri (2015a).

[19]Roy (2005), p. 941; Singh (2007).

[20]WTO, European Communities and their Member States, Schedule of Specific Commitments, Trade in Services, Supplement 3, GATS/SC/31/Suppl. 3 (1997).

[21]WTO, European Communities and their Member States, Final List of Article II (MFN) Exemptions, GATS/EL/31 (1994).

[22]Roy (2005); WTO, Audiovisual Services, Background note by the Secretariat, S/C/W/310 (2010).

by commitments – that is, the certainty that certain restrictions won't be maintained or introduced in the future".[23]

The current round of trade negotiations—the Doha Development Agenda—launched in 2001 and originally to be completed by 2005, holds no promise of changes in the status quo for audiovisual services. Although the Doha round is not stalled because of audiovisual services, and the intensity of the trade versus culture clash within the WTO seems to have somewhat subsided since the Uruguay Round, the present state of requests and offers for the sector reveals precious few new commitments and no future-oriented rules-design. Despite the recognition shared by key WTO Members that the audiovisual sector has changed dramatically,[24] in particular in the face of the convergence of information technology (IT), telecommunications and media services, companies and sectors, and of the sweeping transformations caused by the Internet, there is little agreement on the way forward. The EU is adamantly pursuing its non-committal approach,[25] despite the many requests by other WTO Members to address the status quo by either full commitments in market access and national treatment, or by more targeted actions, such as binding of the current level of market opening or commitments under specific sub-headings (commonly, film production, distribution and projection services, and sometimes sound recording).[26] The US, on the other hand, is pushing for the deepest form of liberalisation possible. Switzerland has attempted to find a middle-ground and voiced proposals on how to reconcile the existing extreme positions. It has, amongst other things, suggested that WTO Members could look for more flexible design solutions that address cultural diversity safeguards, subsidies, public service, illicit content and competition issues. Switzerland made also the cautious proposal as to the form of addressing these issues and thought that an Annex on audiovisual services may be appropriate.[27] Despite the sensible as well as pragmatic nature of the Swiss proposals, they had little chance of altering the politically charged and path-dependent debate on media matters. It is also fair to note that these proactive proposals and the related discussions stem from the early 2000s and since then the regulatory environment has profoundly changed—both with regard to more recent technological advances and the new rule-making in the area of digital trade through PTAs, as well as with regard to the trade and culture debate, which has been taken out of the WTO context with the 2005 UNESCO Convention on Cultural Diversity.[28]

---

[23]Roy (2005), pp. 940–941.

[24]Graber (2004), pp. 166–170; Roy (2005), pp. 931–936.

[25]WTO, Communication from the European Communities and its Member States, Draft consolidated GATS Schedule, S/C/W/273 (2006).

[26]WTO, Audiovisual services, Background note by the Secretariat, S/C/W/310 (2010).

[27]WTO, Communication from Switzerland, GATS 2000: Audio-visual Services, S/CSS/W/74 (2001).

[28]UNESCO Convention on the Protection and Promotion of Cultural Diversity (adopted 20 October 2005; in force 18 March 2007). For appraisal, see Craufurd Smith (2007) and Burri (2010).

2.3　Appraisal of the Status Quo in WTO Law

Overall, the above sections revealed that the openness of the telecommunications is in stark contrast to the well-preserved domain of audiovisual media services. An important and logical question then is how these rules mix and what their actual impact is in the contemporary trade environment, which has been strongly influenced by the disruptive changes of the digital revolution.[29] One could of course argue that laws need not change with each and every new technological invention.[30] Indeed, the law of the WTO may lend credence to such an argument because it possesses intrinsic flexibility and resilience, both in the substance and in the procedure. The WTO often tackles issues in a technologically neutral way—for instance, with regard to the application of the basic non-discrimination principles, with regard to standards, trade facilitation, subsidies and government procurement. Moreover, the WTO has the advantage of, at least up to now,[31] an effective dispute settlement that fosters legal evolution.[32] There is strong evidence in the WTO jurisprudence for both the capacity of the dispute settlement system and its ability to deal with technological change.[33] Unfortunately, such a positive picture of the WTO's "adaptive governance"[34] does not reflect reality. In fact, there are many causes for scepticism. Some relate to the ways WTO rules, in particular the GATS provisions, were designed, allowing WTO Members to tailor their commitments. Others relate to old (pre-Internet) classifications of goods, services and sectors, upon which these commitments were based and which are becoming increasingly disconnected from trade practices.[35]

This situation has induced legal uncertainty. For instance, as the WTO law presently stands, we are unsure whether online games should be categorised as goods or services, and thus fall under the GATT or the GATS. Provided that no physical medium is involved and we decide consequently to apply the GATS, the classification puzzle is by no means solved. Online games, as a new type of content

---

[29]Burri (2017b).

[30]See famously, Easterbrook (1996).

[31]See e.g. Johnson (2019).

[32]See e.g. Sacerdoti et al. (2006) and Bernauer et al. (2012).

[33]Many seminal GATS cases have an Internet element: see e.g. Panel Report, *United States – Measures Affecting the Cross-Border Supply of Gambling and Betting Services (US – Gambling)*, WT/DS285/R, adopted 10 November 2004; Appellate Body Report, *United States – Measures Affecting the Cross-Border Supply of Gambling and Betting Services (US – Gambling)*, WT/DS285/AB/R, adopted 7 April 2005; Panel Report, *China – Measures Affecting Trading Rights and Distribution Services for Certain Publications and Audiovisual Entertainment Products (China – Publications and Audiovisual Products)*, WT/DS363/R, adopted 12 August 2009; Appellate Body Report, *China – Measures Affecting Trading Rights and Distribution Services for Certain Publications and Audiovisual Entertainment Products (China – Publications and Audiovisual Products)*, WT/DS363/AB/R, adopted 21 December 2009.

[34]Cooney and Lang (2007) and Lang and Scott (2009).

[35]Burri and Cottier (2012).

platform, could be potentially fitted into the discrete categories of computer and related services, value-added telecommunications services, entertainment or audio-visual services. We are further unsure when there is an electronic data flow intrinsic to the service, whether to classify this flow separately, or as part of the traditional services.[36] Classification is by no means trivial,[37] as each category implies a completely different set of duties and/or flexibilities. If online platforms and the services they offer were to be classified as telecom services, for example, states would lack any wiggle-room whatsoever and would have to grant full access to foreign services and services suppliers and treat them as they treat domestic ones—because of the high level of existing commitments under the GATS of virtually all WTO Members.[38] The opposite will be true, if these online services were classified as audiovisual.

The need for adjusting the existing rules of the WTO Agreements in the face of technological change has indeed been long recognised by the WTO Members who launched as early as in 1998 the Work Programme on Electronic Commerce.[39] This initiative sought to identify all pertinent issues and the need for action in all areas including trade in services, trade in goods, intellectual property protection and economic development but did not bear any fruit over a period of two decades. It is fair to note that since the launch of the Work Programme on E-Commerce more than 20 years ago, the picture of global trade has changed in many critical aspects. The significance of digital trade, both in its contribution to the economic growth of many countries and the preoccupation of governments with digital trade-related policies, have grown exponentially.[40] On the one hand, this progress and the changing interests relate to new, previously unknown or not fully developed tech-nological applications, such as mobile telephony or cloud computing, which have become important platforms for business.[41] On the other hand and more importantly, they relate to the Internet as an elemental foundation for innovation with deep implications.[42] The importance of data as a key aspect to essentially all societal activities is critical in this transformation[43] and has been recently clearly acknowl-edged in trade policy circles.[44] The sweeping transformations brought about by the

---

[36]For a discussion of the application of technology neutrality to services classification, see Peng (2016).

[37]Weber and Burri (2012).

[38]This is true not only because of traditional media policies but also because of newly adopted ones. The promotion of local content in digitally delivered services is not limited to Europe either. The Chinese Ministry of Culture reportedly has classified online games as "cultural products" and has intensely supported the domestic industry. See USITC (2013), pp. 5–7.

[39]WTO, Work Programme on Electronic Commerce, WT/L/274 (1998).

[40]USITC (2013), p. 1; USITC (2014), p. 1.

[41]See e.g. WTO, Communication from the European Union and the United States: Contribution to the Work Programme on Electronic Commerce, S/C/W/338 (2011).

[42]Chander (2013) and Burri (2017b).

[43]Mayer-Schönberger and Cukier (2013).

[44]Henke et al. (2016), Burri (2017a) and WTO (2018).

Internet have also been associated with a palette of new measures that inhibit digital trade, such as, amongst others, the so-called "data localisation" measures, which encompass diverse requirements for either the localisation of data servers and providers, local content policies, or may involve discrimination against not locally based digital services or providers.[45]

Ultimately, the lack of progress within the WTO context coupled with these new issues, which may often call for urgent regulatory action, have driven countries to seek other venues that better reflect their interests and allow for speedier solutions—in particular through PTAs, agreed upon bilaterally, regionally or between country groups.[46] The following section presents the PTA developments relevant for telecommunications and media services, with examples from some recent treaties.

3 Developments in PTAs

3.1 PTA Rules and Commitments with Regard to Telecommunications Services

Telecommunications services are regulated explicitly in almost all PTAs agreed upon in the past two decades, whose number is now above 340,[47] regardless of whether they subscribe to a negative or a positive list of committing for services.[48] A general trend that can be discerned is for very detailed and lengthy chapters that codify the WTO Reference Paper and the Annex on Basic Telecommunications and reflect the high level of commitments under the GATS, but also often go beyond them. Another observable trend is the convergence of the EU and the US templates for telecommunications chapters. To illustrate both these trends, we look at the CPTPP and the recent EU-Japan FTA, with some references to the USMCA and CETA.

3.1.1 The CPTPP and the USMCA

The Comprehensive and Progressive Agreement for Transpacific Partnership (CPTPP) builds upon the Transpacific Partnership Agreement (TPP), which was one of the most ambitious mega-regional trade deals between the US and eleven

---

[45]USITC (2013, 2014); for a country survey, see Chander and Lê (2014, 2015).

[46]See e.g. WTO (2011).

[47]The information stems from an own dataset (TAPED: Trade Agreements Provisions on Electronic-commerce and Data) that seeks to comprehensively trace developments in PTAs in the area of digital trade governance. See Burri and Polanco (2020) and find the entire dataset available at: https://unilu.ch/taped

[48]On positive versus negative list committing, see Adlung and Mamdouh (2013), Mattoo and Sauvé (2014) and Roy (2014).

countries in the Pacific Rim.[49] Upon the withdrawal of the United States under the Trump administration, with an adjusted title but without radical substantive changes, the remaining states decided to move forward and the CPTPP entered into force on 30 December 2018. The CPTPP represents 13.4% of the global gross domestic product or $13.5 trillion, making it the third largest trade agreement after the NAFTA and the single market of the European Union.[50] Beyond the broader economic impact, the CPTPP sought to be a "21st century" trade agreement that would match contemporary global trade better than the mercantilist and brick-and-mortar WTO Agreements.[51] This naturally renders the provisions with regard to telecommunications and media services of particular interest to this chapter's discussion.[52]

The CPTPP chapter for telecommunications services is very detailed (comprising 26 Articles) and seeks to ensure a level playing field for telecommunications services and service suppliers. There is a general recognition of the liberal approach towards regulation, whereby the CPTPP Parties recognise the value of competitive markets to deliver a wide choice in the supply of telecommunications services to enhance consumer welfare. Regulation is deemed unnecessary if there is effective competition, or if a service is new to a market.[53] Parties remain free however to choose how they wish to implement their obligations under this Chapter.[54]

The provisions on access to and use of public telecommunications services are strengthened in comparison to the text of the Annex and the Reference Paper by including number portability[55] and enhanced transparency requirements.[56] There is a specific provision on transparency with regard to roaming rates, whereby each Party shall endeavour to cooperate on promoting transparent and reasonable rates for international mobile roaming services with a view to promoting the growth of trade between the Parties and enhancing consumer welfare.[57] Parties may choose to take certain steps in this regard, such as: (a) ensuring that information regarding retail rates is easily accessible to consumers and (b) minimising impediments to the use of technological alternatives to roaming, whereby consumers when visiting the territory

---

[49]Australia, Brunei, Canada, Chile, Japan, Malaysia, Mexico, New Zealand, Peru, Singapore and Vietnam.

[50]Torrey (2018).

[51]See e.g. Voon (2013).

[52]For a great overview of the CPTPP and how it consolidates previous trade deals between the CPTPP partners, see Polanco Lazo and Gómez Fiedler (2017), in particular pp. 30–39.

[53]Article 13.3(1) CPTPP.

[54]Article 13.3, paras 1–3 CPTPP.

[55]Article 13.5(4). Each Party shall ensure that suppliers of public telecommunications transport services in its territory provide number portability for mobile services and any other services designated by that Party, on a timely basis and on reasonable terms and conditions. Certain exceptions apply to Brunei, Malaysia and Viet Nam (see footnote 6).

[56]Article 13.22 CPTPP.

[57]Article 13.6(1) CPTPP.

of another Party can access telecommunications services using the device of their choice.[58]

Article 13.23 CPTPP is entirely new and seeks to ensure flexibility in the choice of technology, so that suppliers of public telecommunications services can choose "the technologies they wish to use to supply their services, subject to requirements necessary to satisfy legitimate public policy interests, provided that any measure restricting that choice is not prepared, adopted or applied in a manner that creates unnecessary obstacles to trade".[59] The same rule has been reiterated in the USMCA,[60] which follows the CPTPP template in almost all elements, including the establishing of a Committee on Telecommunications, which should review and monitor the operation of the Chapter, with a view to ensuring its effective implementation "by enabling responsiveness to technological and regulatory developments in telecommunications to ensure the continuing relevance of this Chapter to Parties, service suppliers and end users".[61]

The USMCA has however added a new provision, previously unknown from other PTA templates, with regard to the conditions for the supply of value-added services.[62] Thereby the USMCA Parties recognise the importance of value-added services to innovation, competition, and consumer welfare and pledge not to impose on a supplier of value-added services requirements applicable to a supplier of public telecommunications services without due consideration of the legitimate public policy objectives, the technical feasibility of the requirements, and the characteristics of the value-added services at issue. This is a rule that seeks to provide certain safeguards for the so-called "over-the-top" (OTT) services providers and is meant to counter tendencies for increased regulatory burden on platform and digital services providers.

Net neutrality is another important digital economy topic that has been given specific attention in the CPTPP—however not in the telecom but in the electronic commerce chapter. Article 14.10 titled "Principles on Access to and Use of the Internet for Electronic Commerce", states that "[s]ubject to applicable policies, laws and regulations, the Parties recognise the benefits of consumers in their territories having the ability to: (a) access and use services and applications of a consumer's choice available on the Internet, subject to reasonable network management; (b) connect the end-user devices of a consumer's choice to the Internet, provided that such devices do not harm the network; and (c) access information on the network management practices of a consumer's Internet access service supplier".

---

[58] Article 13.6(2) CPTPP.

[59] Article 13.23(1). Paragraph 2 clarifies that when a Party finances the development of advanced networks, it may make its financing conditional on the use of technologies that meet its specific public policy interests. It is clarified further in a footnote that "advanced networks" includes broadband networks.

[60] Article 18.15 USMCA.

[61] Article 13.26 CPTPP; Article 18.27 USMCA.

[62] Article 18.14 USMCA.

While it is commendable that net neutrality is endorsed, this comes with reservations and is not linked to legal remedies for situations, such as blocking or filtering content. Other much "harder" rules that may be of critical importance for the telecommunications services and services providers are the general ban on localisation measures and the safeguarding of the free of flow of data that the CPTPP endorses.[63]

A second set of provisions outside of the telecom chapter that needs to be mentioned comes from Chapter 8 on technical barriers to trade and relates to encryption standards. It is a reaction to a practice by several countries that impose direct bans on encrypted products or set specific technical regulations that restrict the sale of encrypted products.[64] China is a prominent, but not the only, example in this context with its attempt to enforce an indigenous standard for wireless networks—the WAPI standard, which was a proprietary standard diverging from the internationally agreed upon Wi-Fi.[65] Annex 8-B, Section A.3 addresses such concerns. Pursuant to it, with respect to a product that uses cryptography and is designed for commercial applications, "no Party shall impose or maintain a technical regulation or conformity assessment procedure that requires a manufacturer or supplier of the product, as a condition of the manufacture, sale, distribution, import or use of the product, to: (a) transfer or provide access to a particular technology, production process or other information, for example, a private key or other secret parameter, algorithm specification or other design detail, that is proprietary to the manufacturer or supplier and relates to the cryptography in the product, to the Party or a person in the Party's territory; (b) partner with a person in its territory; or (c) use or integrate a particular cryptographic algorithm or cipher, other than where the manufacture, sale, distribution, import or use of the product is by or for the government of the Party". Despite certain exceptions,[66] by banning the forced provision of encryption keys or the adoption of indigenous standards, the CPTPP addresses well this newer kind of digital trade barriers and caters for the growing concerns of large companies like IBM and Microsoft that thrive on free data flows with less governmental intervention.[67] Annex 8-B adds also provisions on regional cooperation on

---

[63] Article 14.13(2) prohibits the Parties from requiring a "covered person to use or locate computing facilities in that Party's territory as a condition for conducting business in that territory". In addition, "[e]ach Party shall allow the cross-border transfer of information by electronic means, including personal information, when this activity is for the conduct of the business of a covered person" (Article 14.11(2) CPTPP).

[64] Hazucha (2013).

[65] Gibson (2007), p. 1475. The case was settled diplomatically, as China decided to forbear from mandating the WAPI standard.

[66] The provision does not prevent law enforcement actions and does not apply to networks owned or controlled by the government, or to government measures related to supervision, investigation, or examination of financial institutions or markets (Sections A.4 and A.5).

[67] Liu (2017).

telecommunications equipment,[68] as well as on the electromagnetic compatibility of IT equipment products, which are new and may be of importance to telecom operators.[69]

3.1.2 CETA and the EU-Japan FTA

With regard to cross-border trade in services, the EU's traditional approach has been to follow the GATS model and only positively (and relatively conservatively) commit, whereby different services sectors and subsectors are listed and the commitments for national treatment and market access specified. The level of commitments has largely mirrored the offers made by the EU during the Doha Round, so unlike the US, the EU has not gone substantially GATS-plus in its PTAs.[70] This is clearly reflected in the CETA, whose telecom chapter seems to be a mere reiteration of the provisions of the Annex on Telecommunications and the Reference Paper,[71] with the add-on on number portability.[72] Despite the negative list committing, with which the EU experimented for the first time in CETA, we do not see any radical differences since the levels of commitments for telecommunications were already fairly deep under the GATS. Something that is peculiar to CETA and can be mentioned is the Annex attached to the services chapter, which sets out an understanding on new services not classified in the UN Provisional Central Product Classification (CPC) in its 1991 version as used during the Uruguay Round negotiations for committing under the GATS. The Understanding specifies that the commitments made do not apply in respect to any measure relating to a new service that cannot be classified under the CPC.[73] Parties have an obligation to notify the other party about such new services and enter into negotiations to incorporate the new service into the scope of the Agreement, at the request of one of the Parties.[74] This can potentially be the case with some new services in the telecom or media context that come to the market as a result of new technological advances.

The EU and Japan's Economic Partnership Agreement entered into force on 1 February 2019 after some 7 years of negotiation. It is an ambitious and comprehensive deal and similarly to the TPP/CPTPP was meant to reflect the new practical

---

[68]CPTPP, Annex 8-B, Section C.

[69]CPTPP, Annex 8-B, Section B.

[70]EU FTAs tend to cover more WTO-plus areas while having less liberal commitments. For a detailed analysis, see Horn et al. (2009).

[71]CETA, Chapter 15.

[72]CETA, Article 15.10.

[73]CETA, Annex 9-B: Understanding on new services not classified in the united nations provisional central product classification (CPC), 1991, at para. 1.

[74]It is clarified that this regime does not apply to an existing service that could be classified under the CPC but that could not previously be provided on a cross-border basis due to lack of technical feasibility. Id., at para. 4.

reality of digital trade; for the first time in EU trade treaties, it covers all trade done by electronic means and signals of slight repositioning of the EU on issues of data.[75] The EU-Japan FTA was also negotiated in parallel to the mega-regionals endorsed by the United States and one can in this sense naturally look for certain "borrowing" and cross-references.

The EU-Japan FTA's chapter on telecommunications goes slightly beyond the GATS, and beyond CETA. Unlike other, mostly US-led, deals and typically for the EU approach (apart from CETA), the rules on telecommunications form part of the Chapter on Trade in Services, Investment Liberalisation and Electronic Commerce (Chapter 8). The Section on Telecommunications Services encompasses Articles 8.41–8.57 and in structure and in contents largely follows the US template, including also provisions on number portability[76] and international mobile roaming[77]—the latter commitment entirely missing from CETA and earlier EU PTAs. Yet, the EU-Japan FTA also misses important provisions endorsed by the CPTPP and the USMCA, such as for instance those regarding co-location,[78] access to poles, ducts, conduits, and rights-of-way,[79] as well as those on submarine cable systems,[80] and flexibility in the choice of technology.[81] Novel to the EU-Japan FTA are the recognition of the importance of the principle of technological neutrality in electronic commerce,[82] as well as the much discussed provision on the "Free Flow of Data", which states that the "Parties shall reassess within three years of the date of entry into force of this Agreement the need for inclusion of provisions on the free flow of data into this Agreement".[83] These are however to be found in the section on electronic commerce and not the one on telecommunications services.

The EU-Japan FTA, and here again typically for the EU, goes at great length in stressing that none of the commitments made apply for audiovisual services. The Telecommunications Services Section specifies in this regard that it does not apply to measures affecting: (a) broadcasting services as defined in the laws and regulations of each Party; and (b) services providing, or exercising editorial control over, content transmitted using telecommunications transport networks and services.[84]

---

[75]See Proposal for a Council Decision on the conclusion of the Economic Partnership Agreement between the European Union and Japan, COM(2018) 192 final, 18 April 2018. For updates and the text of the Agreement, see https://ec.europa.eu/trade/policy/in-focus/eu-japan-economic-partnership-agreement/.

[76]Article 8.45 EU–Japan FTA.

[77]Article 8.57 EU–Japan FTA.

[78]Article 18.11 USMCA and Article 13.13 CPTPP.

[79]Article 18.12 USMCA and Article 13.14 CPTPP.

[80]Article 18.13 USMCA and Article 13.15 CPTPP.

[81]Article 18.15 USMCA and Article 13.23 CPTPP.

[82]Article 8.70(3) EU–Japan FTA.

[83]Article 8.81 EU–Japan FTA.

[84]Article 8.41(2) EU–Japan FTA.

There are also explicit exclusions of audiovisual services in the services chapter, in general and with specific regard to investment liberalisation,[85] cross-border trade in services,[86] electronic commerce[87] and subsidies.[88] The EU also reserves the right to adopt or maintain any future measure with respect to broadcast transmission services.[89]

3.2   PTA Rules and Commitments with Regard to Audiovisual Services

3.2.1   The Approach of the European Union

As already hinted in the above section, it has been the EU approach to seek not only the clear exclusion of the entire audiovisual sector in its PTAs but also to pursue a delineation from neighbouring sectors, such as telecommunications, computer and related, or electronic commerce services. As an example, we can again refer to the CETA, where in defining the scope of the services chapter, Article 9.2 states that despite the far-reaching liberalisation commitment of both Parties, "even in this case and as a reflection of Canada's and the EU's continuing pro-cultural stance, some sectors are a priori excluded. For the EU, these are audiovisual services; for Canada, the caveat relates to its 'cultural industries'".[90] "Cultural industries" are defined as (a) the publication, distribution or sale of books, magazines, periodicals, or news-papers in print or machine-readable form; (b) the production, distribution, sale, or exhibition of film or video recordings; the production, distribution, sale, or exhibition of audio or video music recordings; the publication, distribution, or sale of music in print or machine-readable form; or (c) radiocommunications in which the transmissions are intended for direct reception by the general public, and all radio, television, and cable broadcasting undertakings and all satellite programming and broadcast network services.[91] If we compare with the W/120 classification for audiovisual services under the GATS, which includes motion picture and video tape production and distribution services; motion picture projection service; radio and television services; radio and television transmission services and sound record-ing, the scope of "cultural industries" is somewhat broader. The domestic policy

---

[85] Article 8.6(2)(c) EU–Japan FTA.

[86] Article 8.14(2)(d) EU–Japan FTA.

[87] Article 8.70(5) EU–Japan FTA.

[88] Article 12.3(7) EU–Japan FTA.

[89] Reservation 11, Annex II: Reservations for Future Measures, Schedule of the European Union, EU–Japan FTA.

[90] CETA, Chapter 32 "Exceptions".

[91] Article 1.1 CETA; also Article 32.6(1) USMCA. Canada uses this definition consistently also in other FTAs, such as for instance in its Bilateral Investment Treaty with Costa Rica.

space is further preserved though the exclusion of subsidies and government support for audio-visual services and cultural industries.[92]

It is somewhat peculiar that despite this strong commitment to the objective of cultural diversity, which the EU and Canada share and have voiced not only in the course of the "exception culturelle" debate in the Uruguay Round negotiations but also in the UNESCO negotiations on cultural diversity instruments,[93] there are no provisions on cultural exchange and co-operation in CETA, nor some sort of mutual market access commitments, which may foster cultural flows.[94]

3.2.2 The US Approach

A noted earlier, the US approach towards the audiovisual sector has been pronouncedly different when compared to that of the EU. This should be understood within the broader context of its "Digital Agenda",[95] which the United States has endorsed and made substantial efforts to implement in all trade venues. As the multilateral forum of the WTO could not move forward, largely because of the trade versus culture dilemma, the US made good use of the preferential venues. The agreements reached by the US since 2002 with Australia, Bahrain, Chile, Morocco, Oman, Peru, Singapore, the Central American countries,[96] and more recently with Panama, Colombia and South Korea, all contain critical WTO-plus and WTO-extra provisions in the broader field of digital trade. In the area of services trade, the US Digital Agenda focuses on Entertainment, Telecom and IT and seeks to ensure, when possible, that the most liberal form to schedule trade commitments (negative list) is used, so that new services are automatically covered by old commitments, as well as seeks to ensure the absence of discrimination against electronic service delivery. Furthermore, it has been specified that for audiovisual services, trade partners are not asked to dismantle existing financial support schemes for culture and content production. Neither are trade partners asked to eliminate existing regulations that discriminate against foreign content in traditional technologies like broadcasting or cinema. Rather trade partners are asked to schedule their existing audiovisual regulations and thus freeze them at a particular level. Yet, under the Digital Agenda, the US should be requesting commitments on new audiovisual services like video-on-demand, new forms of content distribution, etc.[97]

---

[92]Article 7.7 CETA.

[93]Burri (2010); CETA, Preamble, Recitals 6, 7.

[94]Cultural cooperation and market access commitments have been peaked for the EU with the EU−Cariforum and EU−South Korea FTAs, largely as an effect of the 2005 UNESCO Convention on Cultural Diversity implementation. See e.g. Burri and Nurse (2019).

[95]See US Congress, Bipartisan Trade Promotion Authority Act of 2001, H. R. 3005, 3 October 2001; Wunsch-Vincent (2003).

[96]The DR−CAFTA includes Costa Rica, El Salvador, Guatemala, Honduras, Nicaragua and the Dominican Republic.

[97]Wunsch-Vincent (2006), pp. 119−120.

In line of this agenda and despite its inflexible and adamant position in the WTO context, the US has shown deference to the culturally inspired measures of its PTA partners in the media and granted the policy space needed for these measures. In this sense, some PTAs specify that the parties are "not prevented from adopting or maintaining measures in the audio-visual and broadcasting sectors" and that the non-discrimination provision does not apply to measures affecting the electronic transmission of the so-called "linear", point-to-multipoint traditional broadcasting services. Very often however these measures are "frozen" at their present level,[98] and could relate only to conventional "offline" technologies. It is evident also that the leeway given to the US partners with respect to trade in cultural products "reflect [s] quite accurately the negotiating capacity of the states involved"—acting under the sizeable economic weight of the US, the rule of thumb is that the smaller the country, the more concessions it admits.[99] Australia, as the most affluent of these states, managed to preserve existing quotas for local content in commercial broadcasting.[100] It also remains free to maintain existing measures and adopt new ones in the areas of (a) multi-channelled free-to-air commercial television broadcasting services; (b) free-to-air commercial television broadcasting services; (c) subscription television broadcasting services (d) free-to-air radio broadcasting services; (e) interactive audio and/or video services (f) spectrum and licensing; and (d) subsidies or grants.[101] This ample policy space is subject to certain limitations pertaining either to not exceeding the existing ceilings or to the application of certain criteria for the assessment of future measures. Despite these limitations, the freedom granted to Australia in shaping its present and future cultural policy for the media is substantial, especially considering the typical US position on these matters. Singapore and Chile were also able to include relatively significant reservations, as did Costa Rica, the Dominican Republic and Morocco. On the other hand, Guatemala, Honduras, El Salvador and Nicaragua left their audiovisual sectors in practice open to imports and there is only little room for new domestic policy initiatives.

The case of the USMCA is also interesting to mention, since it brings together Canada and the US, as two countries on the opposing ends of the trade and culture debate and with regard to domestic protectionist measures for the cultural industries. Like the original Canada–US FTA and its successor, the NAFTA, the USMCA includes a broad cultural exemption to allow Canada to continue favouring its domestic cultural industries, including publishing, film, television and music; there is no discrimination as to the type of format nor as to offline or online distribution.[102] The cultural exemption under the USMCA and similarly to the NAFTA allows however the US or Mexico to retaliate, and if Canada goes too far in protecting its

---

[98]Wunsch-Vincent (2003), pp. 15–16; Voon (2007), pp. 25–26.

[99]Bernier (2004).

[100]US–Australia FTA, Annex I.

[101]US–Australia FTA, Annex II.

[102]Article 32.6 USMCA.

domestic industries, they "may take a measure of equivalent commercial effect".[103] Interestingly, there is a provision saying that all retaliation disputes are to be resolved under the USMCA[104] but not under the WTO—a reaction that may be linked to the unfortunate for Canada result of the *Canada – Periodicals* case decided under the WTO umbrella.[105] It needs to be noted that there are certain concessions made to the US: Annex 15-D requires Canada to (1) rescind the Canadian Radio-television and Telecommunications Commission broadcast regulatory policy that stopped the simultaneous substitution policy for broadcasts (the main problem being the Super Bowl) and (2) enable US home shopping broadcast services to be authorised for distribution in Canada (the main problem being the QVC).[106]

There are broad carve-outs for audiovisual services under the CPTPP as well, again mostly driven by Canada's stance on cultural matters. Some exceptions are interesting and noteworthy however: so, while under Annex II, Canada reserves the right to adopt or maintain a measure that affects cultural industries and that has the objective of supporting, directly or indirectly, the creation, development or accessibility of Canadian artistic expression or content, it cannot adopt (a) discriminatory requirements on service suppliers or investors to make financial contributions for Canadian content development; and (b) measures restricting the access to on-line foreign audio-visual content.

4   Final Observations on the Evolution of Telecom and Media Rules in PTAs: Path Dependences Remain

The chapter traced developments in PTAs with regard to the telecommunications and the media services sectors by looking at a few recent and particularly advanced trade deals of the United States and the European Union respectively. It was clearly discernible that there have been some changes vis-à-vis the status quo of the corresponding rules and commitments under the GATS but what became also apparent is that these transformations have been by no means radical. Rather they follow the same path and are dependent on previous solutions, negotiated modalities

---

[103] Article 32.6(4) USMCA: Notwithstanding any other provision of this Agreement, a Party may take a measure of equivalent commercial effect in response to an action by another Party that would have been inconsistent with this Agreement but for paragraph 2 or 3.

[104] Article 32.6(5) USMCA.

[105] Panel Report, *Canada – Certain Measures Concerning Periodicals* (*Canada – Periodicals*), WT/DS31/R, adopted 14 March 1997; Appellate Body Report, *Canada – Certain Measures Concerning Periodicals* (*Canada –Periodicals*), WT/DS31/AB/R, adopted 30 June 1997. The case signalled the unwillingness of the WTO adjudicative bodies to engage in balancing trade *versus* culture values, as the case was decided by the panel and the Appellate Body to the benefit of the US, and despite CUSFTA's cultural exception clause.

[106] See e.g. Jackson (2018).

and classifications, and even rely on the same language.[107] On critical issues, such as updated services classification, technological neutrality and other changes needed to reflect the deep changes of the digital environment and how services are traded in it, there is very little, even in these new "21st century" deals. The line of divergence between the telecommunications and the audiovisual media services regulation is also subject to strong path-dependent effect and has become even more pronounced, especially in the PTAs of the European Union. The practical reality of converged services and sectors appear to hardly matter.[108]

In the audiovisual media sector, we saw that the level of commitments and the willingness to engage in any sort of liberalisation remain low, despite the fact that the trade and culture debate has become only marginal to key trade negotiations. Interesting to note was the changed position of the United States towards concessions in the audiovisual sector, accepted however under the important condition that they do not affect digital media or this effect is explicitly contained. The detailed regulation of the telecom sectors and the liberal approach chosen in essentially all PTAs discussed, as well as the increasing similarities between the EU and the US templates, may prompt one to think that what we are observing is a good example of legal adaptation. This first impression may be flawed however simply because the language of the WTO rules, under the Annex on Basic Telecommunications and the Reference Paper, was already very detailed and far-reaching. Upon a closer look, many parts of the new PTA telecommunications chapters actually appear still somewhat stuck in 1990s and do not reflect the market reality.[109] One particular critique that has been voiced refers to the lack of proper addressing of Internet access and how it should be classified. While the USMCA adds that "public telecommunications" may include telephone and data transmission, it remains silent on Internet access.[110] Also, while the telecom chapters address "major suppliers of public telecommunications services" and contain a number of obligations for them, the market share of such operators has been reduced over time, especially after the Open Internet Order, which reclassified fixed and mobile broadband Internet access service as a "telecommunications service", was repelled by the Trump administration.[111] OTT providers, like Google, Facebook, Amazon Web Services and Microsoft, have now become the key players, for instance in the area of submarine cables.[112] Even on new rules, such as international mobile roaming, it appears that the mechanisms for

---

[107]On path dependence in law, see e.g. Liebowitz and Margolis (2000); Hathaway (2001); also Meunier and Morin (2015).

[108]See e.g. Neuwirth (2015).

[109]Paoletta (2019).

[110]Paoletta (2019); also Kotlowitz and Voon (2013).

[111]Federal Communications Commission (FCC), Restoring Internet Freedom, 33 FCC Rcd 311(1), 4 January 2018.

[112]One expert notes that 80% of new submarine capacity is built by the OTT providers like Google and Facebook, and while these "content" providers are the dominant force in new subsea capacity, they control more than 50% of global bandwidth, in any segment; the number is estimated to be over 80% by 2027. Paoletta (2019).

the reciprocal lowering of roaming rates could be difficult to implement and might be superseded by technological and market developments.[113] Whatever truly new rules on net neutrality, data flows and data localisation that we have seen, come from the electronic commerce/digital trade chapters, which have turned into a new source of rules for telecom and media services and services suppliers.

In this sense, while the path dependences still matter and the developments in PTAs have not brought about any major adjustments to the GATS framework for telecommunications and media services, it becomes increasingly apparent that change is needed, so that the data-driven economy can develop and flourish.[114]

References

Adlung R, Mamdouh H (2013) How to design trade agreements in services: top down or bottom up? WTO Staff working paper 8

Bernauer T, Elsig M, Pauwelyn J (2012) The World Trade Organization's dispute settlement mechanism – analysis and problems. In: Daunton M, Narlikar A, Stern RM (eds) The Oxford handbook on the World Trade Organization. Oxford University Press, Oxford, pp 487–506

Bernier I (2004) The recent free trade agreements of the United States as illustration of their new strategy regarding the audiovisual sector. April 2004. http://www.coalitionsuisse.ch/doss_sc/unesco_ccd/bernier_us_ftas_and_av_sector1.pdf

Bronckers M, Larouche P (2008) A review of the WTO regime for telecommunications services. In: Alexander K, Andenas M (eds) The World Trade Organization and trade in services. Martinus Nijhoff, Leiden, pp 319–379

Burri M (2007) The law of the World Trade Organization and the communications law of the European Community: on a path of harmony or discord? J World Trade 41:833–878

Burri M (2008) Trade versus culture in the digital environment: an old conflict in need of a new definition. J Int Econ Law 12:17–62

Burri M (2010) Trade and culture in international law: paths to (re)conciliation. J World Trade 44:49–80

Burri M (2015a) The international economic law framework for digital trade. Zeitschrift für Schweizerisches Recht 135:10–72

Burri M (2015b) The EU, the WTO and cultural diversity. In: Psychogiopoulou E (ed) Cultural governance and the European Union: protecting and promoting cultural diversity in Europe. Palgrave Macmillan, Basingstoke, pp 195–204

Burri M (2017a) The governance of data and data flows in trade agreements: the pitfalls of legal adaptation. UC Davies Law Rev 51:65–132

Burri M (2017b) Current and emerging trends in disruptive technologies: implications for the present and future of EU's trade policy. Study for the European Parliament EXPO_STU (2017)603 845

Burri M, Cottier T (2012) Trade governance in the digital age. Cambridge University Press, Cambridge

Burri M, Nurse K (2019) Culture in the CARIFORUM-European Union Economic Partnership Agreement: rebalancing trade flows between Europe and the Caribbean? UNESCO Policy and Research Series

---

[113]Kotlowitz and Voon (2016).

[114]See the chapter by Willemyns in this volume.

Burri M, Polanco R (2020) Digital trade provisions in preferential trade agreements: introducing a new dataset. J Int Econ Law 23

Cameron K (2004) Telecommunications and audio-visual services in the context of the WTO: today and tomorrow. In: Geradin D, Luff D (eds) The WTO and global convergence in telecommunications and audio-visual services. Cambridge University Press, Cambridge, pp 21–33

Chander A (2013) The Electronic Silk Road: how the web binds the world in commerce. Yale University Press, New Haven

Chander A, Lê U (2014) Breaking the web: data localization vs. the global internet. UC Davis Leg Stud Res Paper 378:1–50

Chander A, Lê U (2015) Data nationalism. Emory Law J 64:677–739

Cooney R, Lang A (2007) Taking uncertainty seriously: adaptive governance and international trade. Eur J Int Law 18:523–551

Craufurd Smith R (2007) The UNESCO Convention on the protection and promotion of cultural expressions: building a new world information and communication order? Int J Commun 1:24–55

Drake WJ (2008) Introduction: the distributed architecture of network global governance. In: Drake WJ, Wilson EJ (eds) Governing global electronic networks: international perspectives on policy and power. MIT Press, Cambridge, pp 1–79

Easterbrook FH (1996) Cyberspace and the law of the horse. Univ Chic Legal Forum 1:207–216

Fox EM (2006) The WTO's first antitrust case – Mexican Telecom: a sleeping victory for trade and competition. J Int Econ Law 9:271–292

Geradin D, Kerf M (2004) Levelling the playing field: is the WTO adequately equipped to prevent anti-competitive practices in telecommunications? In: Geradin D, Luff D (eds) The WTO and global convergence in telecommunications and audio-visual services. Cambridge University Press, Cambridge, pp 130–162

Gibson C (2007) Globalization and the technology standards game: balancing concerns of protectionism and intellectual property in international standards. Berkeley Technol Law J 22:1403–1484

Graber CB (2004) Audio-visual policy: the stumbling block of trade liberalisation. In: Geradin D, Luff D (eds) The WTO and global convergence in telecommunications and audio-visual services. Cambridge University Press, Cambridge, pp 165–214

Hathaway O (2001) Path dependence in the law: the course and pattern of legal change in a common law system. Iowa Law Rev 86:101–165

Hazucha B (2013) Technical barriers to trade in information and communication technologies. In: Epps T, Trebilcock MJ (eds) Research handbook on the WTO and technical barriers to trade. Edward Elgar, Cheltenham, pp 525–565

Henke N et al (2016) The age of analytics: competing in a data-driven world. McKinsey Global Institute, Washington, DC

Horn H, Mavroidis P, Sapir A (2009) Beyond the WTO? An anatomy of EU and US preferential trade agreements. Bruegel Print, Brussels

Jackson E (2018) No more American ads during Canada's Super Bowl broadcast: CRTC policy scrapped in USMCA. Financial Post, 1 October 2018, https://business.financialpost.com/tele com/no-more-american-ads-during-canadas-super-bowl-broadcast-crtc-policy-scrapped-in-usmca

Johnson K (2019) How Trump may finally kill the WTO. Foreign Policy, 9 December 2019

Kotlowitz D, Voon T (2013) Services in the TPP: a case study of telecommunications. In: Voon T (ed) Trade liberalisation and international cooperation: a legal analysis of the Trans-Pacific Partnership Agreement. Edward Elgar, Cheltenham, pp 131–155

Kotlowitz D, Voon T (2016) Telecommunications services in the Trans-Pacific Partnership: will the mobile roaming provisions benefit tourists and traders? Melbourne J Int Law 17:404–445

Lang A, Scott J (2009) The hidden world of WTO governance. Eur J Int Law 20:575–614

Liebowitz S, Margolis S (2000) Path dependence. In: Bouckaert B, De Geest G (eds) Encyclopedia of law and economics, vol I. Edward Elgar, Cheltenham, pp 981–998

Liu HW (2017) Inside the black box: political economy of the Trans-Pacific Partnership's encryption clause. J World Trade 51:309–334

Mattoo A, Sauvé P (2014) The preferential liberalization of services trade: economic insights. In: Sauvé P, Shingal A (eds) The preferential liberalization of trade in services. Edward Elgar, Cheltenham, pp 37–67

Mayer-Schönberger V, Cukier K (2013) Big data: a revolution that will transform how we live, work, and think. Houghton Mifflin, New York

Meunier S, Morin JF (2015) No agreement is an island: negotiating TTIP in a dense regime complex. In: Morin JF et al (eds) The politics of transatlantic trade negotiations: TTIP in a globalized world. Ashgate, Farnham, pp 173–187

Neuwirth R (2015) Global market integration and the creative economy: The paradox of industry convergence and regulatory divergence. J Int Econ Law 18:21–50

Paoletta P (2019) Update needed: NAFTA telecom trade provisions. The Federalist Society, 26 February 2019, https://fedsoc.org/commentary/blog-posts/update-needed-nafta-telecom-trade-provisions

Peng S (2016) GATS and the over-the-top services: a legal outlook. J World Trade 50:21–46

Polanco Lazo R, Gómez Fiedler S (2017) A requiem for the Trans-Pacific Partnership: something new, something old and something borrowed? Melbourne J Int Law 18:1–50

Roy M (2005) Audiovisual services in the Doha Round: dialogue de sourds, the sequel? J World Investment Trade 6:923–952

Roy M (2014) Services commitments in preferential trade agreements: surveying the empirical landscape. In: Sauvé P, Shingal A (eds) The preferential liberalization of trade in services. Edward Elgar, Cheltenham, pp 15–36

Sacerdoti G, Yanovich A, Bohanes J (eds) (2006) The WTO at ten: the contribution of the dispute settlement system. Cambridge University Press, Cambridge

Singh JP (2007) Culture or commerce? A comparative assessment of international interactions and developing countries at UNESCO, WTO, and beyond. Int Stud Perspect 8:36–53

Torrey Z (2018) TPP 2.0: the deal without the US: what's new about the CPTPP and what do the changes mean? The Diplomat, 3 February 2018. https://thediplomat.com/2018/02/tpp-2-0-the-deal-without-the-us/

United States International Trade Commission (2013) Digital trade in the US and global economies, Part 1. USITC Publication 4415. United States International Trade Commission, Washington, DC

United States International Trade Commission (2014) Digital trade in the US and global economies, Part 2. USITC Publication 4485. United States International Trade Commission, Washington, DC

Voon T (2007) A new approach to audiovisual products in the WTO: rebalancing GATT and GATS. UCLA Entertain Law Rev 14:1–32

Voon T (2013) Introduction: national regulatory autonomy and the Trans-Pacific Partnership Agreement. In: Voon T (ed) Trade liberalisation and international cooperation: a legal analysis of the Trans-Pacific Partnership Agreement. Edward Elgar, Cheltenham, pp 1–10

Walden I (2001) The international regulatory regime. In: Walden I, Angel J (eds) Telecommunications law. Blackstone, London, pp 346–381

Weber RH, Burri M (2012) Classification of services in the digital economy. Springer, Berlin

Weller D, Woodcock B (2013) Internet traffic exchange: market developments and policy challenges. OECD digital economy papers 207

WTO (2011) World Trade Report 2011: the WTO and preferential trade agreements: from co-existence to coherence. WTO, Geneva

WTO (2018) World Trade Report 2018: the future of world trade: how digital technologies are transforming global commerce. World Trade Organization, Geneva

Wunsch-Vincent S (2003) The digital trade agenda of the US: parallel tracks of bilateral, regional and multilateral liberalization. Aussenwirtschaft 1:7–46

Wunsch-Vincent S (2006) The WTO, the internet and digital products: EC and US perspectives. Hart, Oxford

Mira Burri is a senior lecturer at the Faculty of Law of the University of Lucerne, Switzerland. She teaches international intellectual property, media, Internet and trade law. Mira's current research interests are in the areas of digital trade, culture, copyright, data protection and Internet governance. Mira is the principle investigator of the project "The Governance of Big Data in Trade Agreements", sponsored by the Swiss National Science Foundation. She consults the European Parliament, UNESCO, the WEF and others on issues of digital innovation and cultural diversity.

Mira has co-edited the publications *Trade Governance in the Digital Age* (Cambridge University Press 2012) and *Big Data and Global Trade Law* (Cambridge University Press 2020). She is the author of *Public Service Broadcasting 3.0* (Routledge 2015). Mira's personal website is at: www.unilu.ch/mira-burri; her publications are available at: http://ssrn.com/author=483457.

"Parallel Convergences" in Free Trade Agreements on Financial Services: Select Issues

Carlo M. Cantore

Contents

The views expressed in this article are the author's only and should not be attributed to the WTO Secretariat or the WTO Members. I would like to thank Christophe Kiener, Gabrielle Marceau, Juan Marchetti, Petros Mavroidis, Alberto Osnago, Martin Roy, and the participants to the conference "Coherence and Divergence in Agreements on Trade in Services", held in Erlangen on 13 and 14 March 2019, for discussions and comments on earlier drafts.

C. M. Cantore (✉)
WTO Legal Affairs Division & University of Antwerp, Antwerp, Belgium
e-mail: Carlo.Cantore@uantwerpen.be

© The Editor(s) (if applicable) and The Author(s), under exclusive licence to
Springer Nature Switzerland AG 2020
R. T. Hoffmann, M. Krajewski (eds.), *Coherence and Divergence in Services Trade Law*, European Yearbook of International Economic Law,
https://doi.org/10.1007/978-3-030-46955-9_9

1 Introduction

Financial services are a typical component of international trade agreements. Anecdotal evidence reveals how offensive interests in the domain of financial services were the driving force behind the push by developed countries to open-up markets for services that eventually led to the launch of the Uruguay Round talks.[1] Although we lack detailed reports on the negotiations of each of the free trade agreements (FTAs)[2] notified to the Council for Trade in Services of the World Trade Organization (WTO),[3] further liberalization of international trade in financial services is, admittedly, an important reason also for the conclusion of bilateral or plurilateral agreements on services outside the WTO (although probably to a lesser extent than during the Uruguay Round). Negotiations on financial services, however, may prove problematic and trading nations may have diverging agendas, some of them being more likely to have offensive interests in this domain than others.[4] To further complicate the picture, financial services trade negotiations are typically conducted by treasury (or even central bank) officials, along with trade officials, often with different sensitivities with regard to the international constraints that domestic regulators or supervisors can afford.[5] Therefore, it is no surprise that controversies on how to conclude deals on financial services are frequent and that, as a result, the level of liberalization of international trade in financial services is not substantial. For example, Uruguay Round negotiators were only able to complete the negotiations on trade in financial services after the entry into force of the General Agreement on Trade in Services (GATS). More recently, diverging views among negotiators could have seriously caused the exclusion of disciplines on financial services from the EU-Canada Comprehensive Economic and Trade Agreement (CETA).[6]

---

[1]For instance, the US financial services industry played an active role in the early 1980s in sensitising its government about the need for international rules on cross-border trade in services and freedom of establishment. Partly due to the pressure from its domestic suppliers, the US government made it clear to its trading partners that services (and in particular financial services) should become the key ingredient for the Uruguay Round. See Marchetti and Mavroidis (2011), pp. 692–694, and, more in general, Yoffie (1990).

[2]Article V of the GATS refers to these agreements as Economic Integration Agreements. This paper uses the more common term FTAs, for ease of reference.

[3]See http://rtais.wto.org.

[4]Jarreau (1999), pp. 23–24.

[5]See Marchetti (2011) concerning the identity of the negotiators of the GATS Annex. See Cameron and Tomlin (2000) for a similar account concerning the NAFTA negotiations.

[6]Leblond (2016) reports how divergences on the introduction of a filter mechanism when the prudential carve-out is invoked in investor-state disputes led the negotiations of a trade pact between the European Union and Canada to a temporary stalemate.

This paper tries to answer two questions: (1) Do recent FTAs depart from the GATS template, and to what extent?; (2) Do financial services chapters in recent FTAs substantially converge or diverge among themselves?

Against the background of the GATS, this paper will focus on the discipline on banking and other financial services (excluding insurance) in five (relatively) recent FTAs.

The select five FTAs are: the Comprehensive and Progressive Trans-Pacific Partnership between Australia, Brunei, Canada, Chile, Japan, Malaysia, Mexico, New Zealand, Peru, Singapore, and Vietnam (CPTPP); the United States-Mexico-Canada Agreement (USMCA); CETA; the EU-Japan Economic Partnership Agreement (JEFTA); and the Korea-United States FTA (KORUS). The selection of those five FTAs is not casual. All the above-mentioned agreements adopt, in principle, a negative list approach and are systemically relevant in terms of the identity of the parties involved and trade flows. Should WTO Members ever decide to revive services negotiations, it is likely that these agreements will constitute the starting point for any discussion.

This paper compares key aspects of these FTAs, highlighting the commonalities and differences among them. In particular, this paper will examine the following elements to verify whether we are experiencing convergence in financial services FTAs: scope of application; certain aspects concerning standards of treatment and protection; treatment of new financial services; standards and regulatory cooperation; regulatory transparency; transfer of information; recognition of prudential measures; and prudential carve-outs.

It is important to stress that this paper only looks at a small set of FTAs. Furthermore, these agreements are all recent and there is limited practice (if any at all) to rely on, let alone case law concerning the interpretation of specific provisions. The understanding of the provisions and their scope of application may change in the future, depending on how the parties will give meaning to them and on how adjudicators will settle disputes and complete contracts that are otherwise naturally incomplete. Finally, it is also worth to mention that not all the five FTAs studied in the paper are already in full force, as the ratification process for USMCA is still underway and the EU and Japan are still negotiating discipline on investment protection at the time of the submission of this article.

The remainder of this paper is structured as follows: Sect. 2 compares key provisions of the select FTAs and assesses their convergence (or divergence) with the GATS and Sect. 3 provides a general assessment.

2 Key Obligations in Select FTAs Against the Background of the GATS Template

2.1 Approaches to Trade Liberalization: Positive Versus Negative List; Ratchet and Standstill Clauses

Under the GATS, certain provisions ("general obligations") apply to all measures affecting trade in all services[7] under one of the four modes of supply. The key general obligation in the GATS is the most-favoured-nation (MFN) clause, although Members can still deviate from it to the extent that they have inscribed a specific limitation in their list of MFN exemptions. WTO Members must expressly indicate the sectors (and the modes of supply) where they undertake specific commitments concerning national treatment (NT) and market access (MA). This approach, which is commonly referred to as "positive list", applies horizontally to all services, including financial services.

The GATS Annex on Financial Services (the GATS Annex) complements the discipline laid down in the GATS. Amongst other things, the GATS Annex provides an illustrative list of examples of what constitutes a "financial service" and stipulates that Members remain free to regulate according to micro- and macro-prudential policy objectives irrespective of any other obligation.

A third instrument completes the picture of the GATS discipline on financial services: the GATS Understanding on commitments in financial services (the GATS Understanding). The GATS Understanding is not part of the single undertaking, meaning that WTO Members are free to opt in (or not). Essentially, it contains a series of obligations connected to commitments in financial services sectors or subsectors that adhering Members decide to schedule.

For the purposes of this article, the three instruments taken together form part of the GATS template. However, since participation to the Understanding is voluntary, it should be stressed that not all the participants to the FTAs examined in this article also subscribed to the GATS Understanding.[8] This is a point to which we shall return in Sect. 3 below.

The GATS does not include a "standstill" clause *per se*.[9] However, the GATS Understanding lays down a general standstill obligation for WTO Members that

---

[7]To the extent that they are not excluded from the coverage of the GATS.

[8]Importantly, Mexico and several Member States of the European Union (namely, Croatia, Cyprus, Estonia, Latvia, Lithuania, Malta, Poland, Romania, and Slovenia) did not subscribe to the GATS Understanding.

[9]A standstill clause ensures that parties bind their restrictions to foreign services trade at the level existing at the time of the entry into force of the agreement. For example, if a government decides to further liberalize a specific subsector and then, following elections, a government with a different agenda decides to reverse the decision, the latter can at most fall back to the level of limitations and restrictions imposed by the party at the time of the entry into force of the agreement.

follow the Understanding's approach to the scheduling of financial services commitments.[10]

All the FTAs under analysis deviate from the approach followed by the GATS, in that they follow—in principle—a negative list approach. This means that core obligations apply to financial services, as defined by the relevant chapters, as long as a party has not expressly listed existing or future non-conforming measures.

Interestingly, all the FTAs include a standstill clause concerning core obligations such as MFN, NT, MA, cross-border trade, and commitments on the nationality of senior management and board of directors.[11] Moreover, all five FTAs introduce a "ratchet" clause, making sure that if a government decides to unilaterally make additional concessions on trade in financial services as compared to the level of liberalization agreed upon during the negotiations of an agreement, those new additional concessions cannot be reversed in the future.[12]

This is an area where FTAs depart from the GATS substantially. In particular, the introduction of ratchet clauses calls for the close monitoring of the developments taking place in the jurisdictions concerned. On paper, one could argue that ratchet clauses could even lead to unwarranted regulatory chill effects, since governments may approach further liberalization with additional caution, in light of the effects for the future that their initiatives may produce.

2.2 Scope

All the FTAs examined in this article, with the exclusion of JEFTA, introduce specific disciplines on the protection of foreign investors in the domain of financial services, including the possibility for private entities to file dispute against governments before arbitration tribunals.[13] This is not a feature in the GATS, which does not contain rules on investment protection.

---

[10]Paragraph A, GATS Understanding.

[11]Article 11.10.1 (a) CPTPP; Article 17.10.1 (a) USMCA; Article 13.9.1 (a) KORUS; Article 13.10.1 (a) CETA; and Article 8.12.1 (a) JEFTA. Article 17.6 USMCA includes a standstill clause prohibiting the adoption of measures restricting "any type of cross-border trade in financial services by cross-border financial service suppliers" of another party that were permitted on 1 January 1994 (i.e., the date of entry into force of the North American Free Trade Agreement (NAFTA)).

[12]Article 11.10.1 (c) CPTPP; Article 17.10.1 (a) USMCA; Article 13.9.1 (c) KORUS; Article 13.10.1 (c) CETA; and Article 8.12.1 (c) JEFTA.

[13]Negotiations on investment protection between the European Union and Japan are still underway.

2.2.1 Exclusions from the Scope of Application

Services Supplied in the Exercise of Governmental Authority and Government Procurement

The GATS and its Annex exclude three types of "services supplied in the exercise of governmental authority" from the scope of application of its rules: (1) activities conducted by a central bank or monetary authority (or any other public entity) in pursuit of monetary or exchange rate policies; (2) activities forming part of a statutory system of social security or public retirement plans; and (3) other activities conducted by a public entity for the account or with the guarantee or using the financial resources of the Government.[14] The second and third exclusions in the GATS only apply unless the Member concerned allows its financial service suppliers to conduct the same services in competition with its public entities.[15]

All five FTAs have similar exclusions drafted along the lines of points (2) and (3) above, including the caveat concerning domestic suppliers being allowed to trade the same services in competition with public entities.[16] JEFTA has a standalone exclusion for "activities conducted by a central bank or a monetary authority or by any other public entity in pursuit of monetary or exchange rate policies", thus similar to the GATS.[17] CPTPP, USMCA, KORUS, and CETA clarify in the "Exceptions" provision that the agreements do not apply to measures taken by any public entity in pursuit of monetary and related credit policies or exchange rate policies.[18] Ultimately the formulation does not deviate substantially from the GATS model, save for the caveat that the exclusion does not affect the parties' obligations concerning e.g. performance requirements or transfers.

Recall that Article XIII of the GATS excludes the application of Articles II (MFN), XVI (MA), and XVII (NT) to measures governing the procurement by governmental agencies of services purchased for governmental purposes and not with a view to commercial resale or with a view to use in the supply of services for commercial sale. CPTPP, USMCA and KORUS include a more straightforward exclusion of "government procurement of financial services" from the scope of application of the discipline on trade in financial services.[19] CETA follows the GATS model by excluding government procurement from the application of the provisions governing MFN, MA, NT, cross-border supply of financial services, senior management and board of directors, and performance requirements.[20]

---

[14]See para. 1(b) (i)–(iii) of the GATS Annex and Article 1.3(b) of the GATS.

[15]See para. 1(c) of the GATS Annex.

[16]Article 11.2.3 CPTPP; Article 17.2.3 USMCA; Article 13.2.5 CETA; Article 8.58.2 JEFTA; Article 13.1.3 KORUS.

[17]Article 8.58.2(a) JEFTA.

[18]Article 11.11.2 CPTPP; Article 17.11.2 USMCA; Article 13.10.2 KORUS; Article 13.17.1 CETA.

[19]Article 11.2.4 CPTPP; Article 17.2.4 USMCA; Article 13.1.4 KORUS.

[20]Article 13.10.7(a) CETA.

CETA also follows the GATS template in clarifying that the exclusions concern services purchased for governmental purposes and not with a view to commercial resale.[21] JEFTA includes a provision in the general chapter on trade in services (i.e., not in the specific section dealing with financial services) excluding government procurement from its scope of application.[22] So far, thus, the FTAs examined in this study largely converge with the GATS template as regards exclusions from the scope of application.

Subsidies

The discipline on subsidies deserves a separate section.

Article XV of the GATS acknowledges that Members could not agree on meaningful disciplines on services subsidies during the Uruguay Round and, as a result, would continue the negotiations.[23] Discussions took place in the context of the Working Party on GATS Rules (WPGR), but Members did not agree on a definition of "subsidies" or on the types of subsidies that should be notified to the Council for Trade in Services (CTS).

However, despite the language in Article XV:1 of the GATS seems to suggest that there are no hard rules disciplining subsidies, the situation is more complex. The 1993 Scheduling Guidelines prepared by the GATT Secretariat to assist Members in the preparation of their initial schedules of specific commitments report that the NT obligation applies "to subsidies in the same ways that it applies to all other measures".[24] Accordingly, a subsidy that discriminates between domestic and foreign recipients would have to be scheduled as a limitation on NT or brought into conformity with the GATS. Furthermore, the 1993 Scheduling Guidelines also warn that subsidies are not excluded from the scope of the MFN clause.[25]

The mainstream reading of the discipline on subsidies under the GATS does not challenge the language included in the 1993 Scheduling Guidelines.[26] However, it is inevitable to note a tension between the wordings of, respectively, Article XV and the 1993 Scheduling Guidelines.[27]

---

[21] Article 13.10.7(a) CETA.

[22] Article 8.12.5 JEFTA.

[23] Article XV:1 of the GATS reads, in relevant part: "Members recognize that, in certain circumstances, subsidies may have distortive effects on trade in services. Members shall enter into negotiations with a view to developing the necessary multilateral disciplines to avoid such trade-distortive effects."

[24] GATT Doc. MTN/GNS/164 of 3 September 1993, para. 9.

[25] Ibid.

[26] See e.g. Natens (2016), pp. 67–68 and the literature cited therein.

[27] Mavroidis (2020, forthcoming) highlights a number of problems. Put briefly, he argues that the language of Article XV:1 is unambiguous and that the Scheduling Guidelines, being a Secretariat document, can never override the language of the Agreement, but can at most serve as supplementary means of interpretation under Article 32 of the Vienna Convention on the Law of Treaties (VCLT).

Perhaps to avoid confusion, or to signal a departure from the GATS template, all five FTAs unequivocally exclude subsidies or government support from their scope of application.[28]

While the exclusion in CETA applies to subsidies or government support relating to "trade in services", the corresponding provision in CPTPP and USMCA is more narrowly tailored as it refers to "a subsidy or a grant provided by a party, including a government supported loan, guarantee, and insurance, with respect to the *cross-border supply of financial services* by a cross-border supplier of another party". In absence of practice, one is left to wonder whether limiting the exclusion to subsidies relating to the cross-border supply of financial services implies, for instance, that government support schemes for domestic banks in distress could be seen as discriminating against branches or subsidiaries of banks of the other party established in the territory of another party.[29]

The clear exclusion of subsidies from the scope of application of the discipline on financial services in the five FTAs marks a departure from the GATS template.

2.2.2 Definitions

All the agreements have provisions specifically dedicated to relevant definitions. It would be unduly pedantic to examine all the definitions one by one, and it would not serve any specific purpose. One specific aspect, however, deserves attention, as definitions might be key to classify the scope of application on international trade agreements.

While the GATS is silent on the notion of "financial institutions", all five FTAs except for JEFTA define financial institutions in terms of how they are regulated under the law of the party to the agreement in whose territory they are located.[30] This development is relevant to clarify the scope of application of certain rules, particularly those concerning the establishment of banks and other undertakings of a party into the territory of another party. Moreover, considering the concerns relating to the supply of financial services by non-banks, and the difficulties encountered by regulators and supervisors when dealing with the matter, this evolution in treaty drafting may prove relevant in practice. The express reference to regulation, in particular, might warrant consideration of different regulatory settings when determining the likeness of financial institutions (service suppliers). In other words, institutions obeying to different regulations may not be considered to be like financial service suppliers. This is an important development, considering the

---

[28]Article 11.2.5 CPTPP; Article 17.2.5 USMCA; Article 13.10.7(b) CETA; Article 8.12.6 JEFTA; Articles 12.1.4(d), 11.5.7 and 11.12.5(b) KORUS.

[29]Only in principle, though. Several trading nations have listed reservations on the participation of foreign banks to domestic deposit insurance schemes. Furthermore, all FTAs clarify that they do not confer foreign entities access to lender of last resort facilities.

[30]Article 11.1 CPTPP; Article 17.1 USMCA; Article 13.1 CETA; Article 13.20 KORUS.

uncertainty under the GATS as to whether regulation should play a role in likeness determinations.[31]

2.3   Developments Concerning Standards of Treatment and Protection

All five FTAs contain certain nuances or elements that depart from the GATS template. This subsection will only focus on certain issues.

CPTPP has a peculiar feature that does not appear in the GATS or other FTAs examined in this paper. Article 11.3.3 CPTPP clarifies that the NT obligation with respect to a regional level of government, consists in "treatment no less favourable than the most favourable treatment accorded, in like circumstances, by that regional level of government to investors, financial institutions and investments of investors in financial institutions, of the Party of which it forms a part".[32] Assuming a hypothetical scenario where financial investors and investments from other CPTPP parties are subject to certain requirements to be lawfully established in Ontario (a regional level of government in Canada, a CPTPP party), such requirements cannot be less favourable than those imposed to investors and investments from Quebec (another regional level of government in Canada). In other words, this clarification transforms the NT obligation into a most-favoured *region* obligation about requirements imposed at the subnational level. This is a relevant development and will require careful attention about its concrete application.

While the five FTAs generally converge as regards the discipline on MA and reproduce, in essence, the language of Article XVI of the GATS,[33] only three of them introduce a slight modification to the original template. Unlike Article XVI.2 (f) of the GATS, CPTPP, USMCA, and KORUS do not prohibit caps on foreign shareholding or on the total value of individual or aggregate foreign investment. Wang (2019) puts strong emphasis on the market-opening consequences of this deviation.

Importantly, and differently from the GATS, all five FTAs have practically identical provisions prohibiting nationality requirements for senior management and other essential personnel of financial institutions.[34] CPTPP, USMCA, and KORUS go one step further and provide that parties shall not require that more

---

[31] See the interesting discussion in Delimatsis and Hoekman (2017).

[32] Article 11.3.3 CPTPP.

[33] Article 11.5 CPTPP; Article 17.5 USMCA; Article 13.4 KORUS; Article 13.6 CETA; Article 8.7 JEFTA.

[34] Article 11.9.1 CPTPP; Article 17.9.1 USMCA; Article 13.8.1 KORUS; Article 13.8 CETA; Article 8.10 JEFTA. It should be noted, however, that most parties have made reservations on nationality requirements in their annexes to relevant agreements.

than a minority of the board of directors of a financial institution of another party be composed of nationals or residents of the party.[35]

Similarly to paragraph C.1 of the GATS Understanding, all five FTAs have a provision dealing with access to clearing and payment systems. Under NT terms, parties to these FTAs shall grant financial institutions of other parties established in their territories access to payment and clearing systems operated by public entities, and to official funding and refinancing facilities available in the ordinary course of business. All five FTAs conclude the provisions with the caveat that they are not intended to confer access to lender of last resort facilities.[36] The five FTAs also follow the GATS Understanding (paragraph C.2) in establishing that when parties require financial institutions or cross-border suppliers of another party to join the membership or have access to a "self-regulatory organization" to be allowed to supply financial service in their territories, those parties must ensure that the said self-regulatory organizations comply with both NT and MFN,[37] NT only[38] or all the obligations of the financial services chapter.[39]

Finally, CPTPP is the only FTA containing a provision dealing specifically with back-office functions. CPTPP parties recognise that back-office functions performed by the headquarters of a financial institution of one party can be essential to smoothen the operations of the branch or subsidiary established in the territory of another party. The provision allows foreign branches or subsidiaries established in the territory of a party to rely on their headquarters for the performance of certain functions (e.g., human resources; IT). CPTPP parties may impose domestic requirements, "recognising the importance" of avoiding the imposition of arbitrary requirements. Finally, the provision clarifies that parties may still require financial institutions in their territories to retain certain functions.[40] The hortatory language of the provision warrants against over-emphasising its importance.

2.4 New Financial Services

Paragraph B.7 of the GATS Understanding requires Members to permit financial service suppliers of any other Member established in its territory to offer in their territory any new financial service.

---

[35] Article 11.9.2 CPTPP; Article 17.9.2 USMCA; Article 13.8.2 KORUS.

[36] Article 11.15 CPTPP; Article 17.15 USMCA; Article 13.13 KORUS; Article 13.13 CETA; Article 8.61 JEFTA.

[37] Article 11.14 CPTPP; Article 13.12 KORUS.

[38] Article 8.62 JEFTA.

[39] Article 17.14 USMCA; Article 13.12 CETA.

[40] Article 11.17 CPTPP.

Similarly, all five FTAs have a dedicated provision dealing with the treatment of new financial services (i.e., financial services not yet traded at the time of the conclusion of the agreement). The provisions across the five agreements are very similar to each other, although it is still possible to note certain deviations. Three features are shared by all five FTAs: (1) parties shall permit a financial institution of another party to supply a new financial service that they would permit their own financial institutions to supply without amending existing legislation; (2) parties might still require a certain juridical or institutional form through which a new service be supplied, or otherwise introduce authorization requirements; and (3) when authorization is required, a decision should be made within a reasonable period of time and a negative decision might be taken only for prudential reasons.[41]

CPTPP and USMCA clarify that parties might still issue new legislation to permit the supply of a new service. KORUS and CETA reserve the right for parties to impose authorization requirements for services not yet traded in either party's territory (and CETA clarifies that the application to be authorised to supply a new service is subject to the law of the Party receiving the application and not to the obligations of CETA's new financial services provision[42]).

Examining CETA's "new financial services" provision, Delimatsis (2017) argues that it represents "an unequivocal trust vote to financial innovation in a post-crisis environment".[43] This scepticism is justified in a sense, and is at least shared by regulators and supervisors around the world.[44] However, the "new financial services" provisions in the FTAs are more narrowly drafted as compared to the corresponding provision in the GATS Understanding. If read against this background, the deviation from the standard template signals the awareness of regulators of the necessity to keep margin to intervene and address the distortions generated by the supply of new services.

2.5 Standards and Regulatory Cooperation

Since at least the 1970s, a plethora of fora and standard setting bodies have discussed ways and tools to address problems in international markets for financial services.

---

[41] Article 11.7 CPTPP; Article 17.7 USMCA; Article 13.6 KORUS; Article 13.14 CETA; Article 8.60 JEFTA. Article 8.60.2 JEFTA specifies that a negative decision may not be rendered not solely because the service is not supplied by any financial service supplier in its territory. JEFTA is also the only FTA that does not make reference to a reasonable period of time to issue a decision.

[42] Article 13.14.3 CETA.

[43] Delimatsis (2017), p. 612.

[44] In the aftermath of the 2007–2008 financial crisis, Paul Volcker, former Chairman of the Federal Reserve, is reported to have stated: "The most important financial innovation that I have seen the past 20 years is the automatic teller machine, that really helps people and prevents visits to the bank and it is a real convenience" (https://nypost.com/2009/12/13/the-only-thing-useful-banks-have-invented-in-20-years-is-the-atm/).

These discussions have further intensified after the 2007/2008 financial crisis. A comprehensive discussion of the work of these bodies would fall outside the scope of the present work. Three main points are nevertheless important in the economy of this article. First, these standards are typically not binding in nature, and do not provide for strong enforcement procedures.[45] Second, their membership is often selective, but non-members tend to comply (at least to a certain extent) with regulatory standards, or otherwise would not be able to access certain markets. Third, the GATS and its Annex are silent on the matter, and they do not refer to standard setting bodies in the domain on financial services. This has to do with various reasons, key among which is the conventional wisdom among central bankers that financial regulation is not a trade issue and is instead their *domaine réservé*.

This is another area of convergence between those FTAs and the GATS. The five FTAs, in fact, tend to not incorporate standards and recommendations adopted by relevant organisations, with notable exceptions.

JEFTA, in its Annex on regulatory cooperation on financial services, is the only FTA that requires parties to make their "best endeavours" to ensure that internationally agreed standards for the regulation and supervision of financial services be implemented in their territory. The Annex also provides a non-exhaustive list of standard-setting organizations: the Basel Committee on Banking Supervision (BCBS); the International Association of Insurance Supervisors (IAIS), the International Organization of Securities Commissions (IOSCO), and the Financial Stability Board (FSB).[46]

CETA, instead, establishes a presumption that measures are adopted for prudential reasons—and are thus sheltered by the prudential carve-out from any other type of violation—if, *inter alia*, they are in line with international prudential commitments that are common to the parties.[47]

The FTAs examined in this paper do not signal a major departure from the GATS and its provisions governing financial services trade. This is not surprising, given that standards on financial regulation are typically instruments of soft international law. While they are transposed into domestic law by legislators and then may become hard *domestic* law, it would be odd to include rigid and binding requirements of that sort in FTAs, so as to transform international standards into hard *international* law. Moreover, international standards often allow a certain degree of flexibility in terms of how domestic regulator can implement them. It is therefore understandable why the parties to these FTAs, that are also parties to the relevant standard-setting bodies, decide to not make these standards binding.

---

[45]Verdier (2013) discussed the political economy of international cooperation on financial regulation.

[46]Paragraph 5 (Principles of regulatory cooperation), Annex 8-A JEFTA.

[47]Paragraph 8(e), Annex 13-B CETA. One example might be the BCBS recommendations, although they are not explicitly mentioned in the Annex.

More in general, regulatory cooperation on financial services is not the highlight of financial services FTAs. Like the GATS, the FTAs under analysis are negative integration contracts, meaning that they do not require the harmonization of national legislations. The FTAs under analysis in this paper therefore do not differ substantially from the general FTAs landscape.

Moving to regulatory cooperation, CPTPP, USMCA and KORUS are completely silent on the issue. CETA, for its part, has a very short "Understanding on the dialogue on the regulation of the financial services sector", whereby the parties reaffirm their commitment to strengthen financial stability and to base their regulatory dialogue on internationally agreed prudential standards. Further, parties express their intention to discuss issues likely to have cross-border impact, such as cross-border trade in securities and the operation of branches.[48]

JEFTA is an outlier, in that it has a detailed Annex laying down "principles" of regulatory cooperation.[49] The language of the Annex is hortatory. Among other things, the Annex specifies the parties' commitment to cooperate on the entire area of financial regulation. Interestingly the JEFTA Annex stipulates that domestic authorities and regulators should focus on regulatory outcomes to decide whether they can rely on the regulatory framework of the other party. Furthermore, the parties committed to consider the impact that new rules may have on trade in financial services with the other party. Finally, the Annex clarifies that the principles laid down therein do not constitute binding obligations and are not subject to dispute settlement.

2.6 Regulatory Transparency

Article III of the GATS stipulates certain transparency obligations that WTO Members must comply with as regards measures affecting trade in all services, including financial services, irrespective of whether they have entered specific commitments in their schedules. Specifically, WTO Members must publish promptly (and at the latest by the time of their entry into force) all measures of general application that affect the operations of the GATS. If publication is not practicable, relevant information must otherwise be made publicly available. Members further commit to inform the Council for Trade in Services of the introduction of new laws and regulations or amendments thereto which affect trade in services. Members should also establish enquiry points to provide specific information to other Members and have the right to notify the Council for Trade in services of any measure adopted by another Member which they consider affect the operations of the GATS.

---

[48]Annex 13-C CETA.

[49]Annex 8-A JEFTA.

All five FTAs have a provision dedicated to regulatory transparency in financial services.[50] The provisions are typically very detailed,[51] and introduce certain requirements that go further than the discipline laid down in the GATS, including the following:

- Measures affecting trade in financial services should be published in advance and interested persons should be given an opportunity to comment;
- To the extent practicable, domestic authorities should address comments in writing;
- Parties must ensure a reasonable delay between the publication of the measures and their entry into force;
- Competent authorities should publish the necessary requirements for the completion of an application;
- Authorities have a deadline (120 days or an otherwise reasonable period of time) to issue a decision on the application filed by a person of the other party.

The transparency obligations laid down in the reviewed FTAs combine features of Article III of the GATS (and Article VI of the GATS, concerning the reasonable, objective and impartial administration of measures of general application) with other features that are more prominent in domestic legal systems. For instance, the possibility for interested persons to comment on legislative projects resembles domestic informal rulemaking processes where the parties affected by changes in the legislation can submit their views for them to be taken into account in the final version of the measure.[52]

These innovations from the GATS template are very important in theory, as they unequivocally amount to a signal of attention for the business community. It is too early to verify their real impact on the legislative procedures, and whether the failure to comply with these obligations would lead to.

2.7 Transfer of Information and Location of Computing Facilities

International trade in financial services is information-intensive. Reducing barriers to information sharing is essential for business. However, regulators must be careful when striking a balance between transfer of information and the protection of personal data and privacy.

Paragraph B.8 of the GATS Understanding stipulates that WTO Members cannot impose restrictions on transfers and processing of information when it is necessary

---

[50]Article 11.13 CPTPP; Article 17.13 USMCA; Article 13.11 KORUS; Article 13.11 CETA; Article 8.64.1 JEFTA.

[51]Marchetti (2020, forthcoming) has an extensive discussion on Article 11.13 CPTPP.

[52]For example, this process is known in US administrative law as "notice and comment".

for the conduct of the ordinary business of a financial service supplier. The provision further clarifies that Members retain the right to protect privacy and the confidentiality of individual records and accounts, unless that right is used to circumvent the provisions of the Agreement.

All the agreements studied in this paper contain similar language dealing with the transfer of information.[53] Whilst KORUS is the only agreement that does not further qualify the obligation to allow for free transfer of information, all other four agreements do.[54] Typically, the provisions clarify that parties retain the right to limit the transfer of information to protect privacy and personal data.[55] CPTPP also clarifies that parties retain the right to adopt or maintain measures to "require a financial institution to obtain prior authorisation from the relevant regulator to designate a particular enterprise as a recipient of such information, based on prudential considerations".[56] Finally, CPTPP, USMCA and JEFTA contain anti-circumvention language, which is drafted slightly differently from the corresponding language in the Understanding and is imported *mutatis mutandis* from the ambiguous final clause of the GATS prudential carve-out.[57]

USMCA stands out from the other examined FTAs because it has a provision specifically dealing with the location of computing facilities.[58] The provision is opened by the recognition of the critical importance for regulators and supervisors to have immediate and direct access to information concerning persons and transactions. The provision lays down the obligation that parties do not require persons to use or locate computing facilities in a given territory as a condition to conduct business therein, so long as the home country regulators or supervisors have direct access to the relevant information.[59] Before a party requires the location of

---

[53] Annex 11-B, Section B (Transfer of information) CPTPP; Article 17.17 USMCA; Annex 13-B, Section B (Transfer of information) KORUS; Article 13.15.1 CETA; Article 8.63.1 JEFTA.

[54] Admittedly, it could be argued that other exceptions can compensate for this lack of specification.

[55] Annex 11-B, Section B (Transfer of information) CPTPP; Article 17.17 USMCA; Article 13.15.2 CETA; Article 8.63.2 JEFTA. Gelpern (2016) argues, with regard to the relevant discipline in the CPTPP, that banks may still be required to keep data and servers in a particular territory and that this would entail an unnecessary duplication of data that is inconsistent with the business model of global financial firms (p. 99).

[56] Annex 11-B, Section B (Transfer of information) CPTPP.

[57] Paragraph 2(a) of the GATS Annex, final sentence, reads: "Where such measures do not conform with the provisions of the Agreement, they shall not be used as a means of avoiding the Member's commitments or obligations under the Agreement". See also Annex 11-B, Section B (Transfer of information) CPTPP; Article 17.17 USMCA; Article 8.63.2 JEFTA.

[58] Article 17.18 USMCA. Pursuant to Annex 17-D USMCA, the provision does not apply to existing measures of Canada for one year after the entry into force of this agreement. The CPTPP contains a similar provision in its e-commerce chapter (Article 14.13), but it does not apply to financial services.

[59] Footnote 9 clarifies: "For greater certainty, access to information includes access to information of a covered person that is processed or stored on computing facilities of the covered person or on computing facilities of a third-party service supplier. For greater certainty, a Party may adopt or maintain a measure that is not inconsistent with this Agreement, including any measure consistent

computing facilities in its territory, it should give the interested person adequate opportunity to provide access to relevant information. Finally, the provision is concluded with the caveat that the obligations just described do not restrict the parties' right to adopt measures to protect personal data and privacy, unless such measures are used to circumvent the obligations just described.

2.8   Recognition of Prudential Measures

Like Paragraph 3 of the GATS Annex, all the examined FTAs but for JEFTA[60] have a provision allowing for the recognition by one party of the prudential measures of another party or a non-party.[61] The possibility to recognise prudential measures adopted by another jurisdiction as equivalent to the ones applicable in the territory of the regulating party is a derogation from the MFN obligation (unless it is extended to all other countries). While CPTPP and USMCA recognise as much explicitly,[62] KORUS and CETA do not contain specific wording in this regard, but it is only logical that the same applies in those two agreements as well.

The above four FTAs stipulate that a party that accords recognition of prudential measures to a non-party (or another party) must provide "adequate opportunity" to another party to demonstrate that regulation or procedures concerning the sharing of information between the relevant parties are (or would be) equivalent.[63]

Finally, all four FTAs require those parties that recognise prudential measures of a non-party (or another party) to provide the other party(ies) with the opportunity to negotiate their accession to the existing mutual recognition agreement (MRA) or to negotiate a comparable agreement.

It is interesting to note that none of the FTAs studied in this paper includes already concluded MRAs on prudential measures as an annex to the relevant agreement. This is in line with the multilateral level, where no MRA on prudential

---

with Article 17.11.1 (Exceptions), such as a measure requiring a covered person to obtain prior authorization from a financial regulatory authority to designate a particular enterprise as a recipient of that information, or a measure adopted or maintained by a financial regulatory authority in the exercise of its authority over a covered person's business continuity planning practices with respect to maintenance of the operation of computing facilities".

[60]JEFTA does not have specific discipline on MRAs on prudential regulation, but it only has a general provision on MRAs in services akin to Article VII GATS (See Article 8.35 JEFTA).

[61]Logically, bilateral agreements only regulate the consequences of the conclusion of recognition agreements with non-parties (See Article 13.14.1 KORUS; and Article 13.5.1 CETA), whilst FTAs signed by more than two parties regulate the consequences of recognition agreements with another party or a non-party.

[62]Fn. 12 CPTPP; Article 17.12.4 USMCA.

[63]Article 11.12.2 CPTPP; Article 17.12.2 USMCA; Article 13.14.3 KORUS; Article 13.5.2 CETA.

measures in the banking sector was ever notified to the WTO Council for Trade in Services.[64]

2.9 Prudential Carve-Outs

Prudential Carve-outs (PCOs) are a typical feature of financial services chapters in trade agreements. As financial markets are frequently subject to booms and busts, governments and supervisors tend to preserve substantial space to be able to intervene *ex ante*, seeking to prevent disruptions in the financial systems, and *ex post*, trying to contain the consequences of financial turmoil and the spreading of negative externalities and contagion to other financial institutions or other sectors of the economy. The PCO plays a pivotal role in ensuring that the regulatory prerogatives of the parties are not unduly constrained by obligations concerning the liberalization of international trade.

The relevant provision in the GATS Annex, Paragraph 2(a) (Domestic Regulation) reads:

> Notwithstanding any other provisions of the Agreement, a Member shall not be prevented from taking measures for prudential reasons, including for the protection of investors, depositors, policyholders or persons to whom a fiduciary duty is owed by a financial service supplier, or to ensure the integrity and stability of the financial system. Where such measures do not conform with the provisions of the Agreement, they shall not be used as a means of avoiding the Member's commitments or obligations under the Agreement.

In the only WTO dispute so far where the provision was invoked, the Panel clarified that the provision is an exception.[65] Accordingly, the burden to show that the relevant conditions for the invocation of the defence lies with the respondent. In addition, the Panel placed emphasis on the circumstance that the list of prudential reasons in pursuance of which measures can be adopted is non-exhaustive and evolutionary in nature.[66] This means that the wording of the PCO permits to capture regulatory objectives that perhaps were not considered to be "prudential" when the GATS was negotiated, but became "prudential" in light of more recent economic thinking.[67] Importantly, the Panel clarified that the provision is broad in scope, and can justify the *prima facie* inconsistency of a measure with any GATS obligation or commitment.

Against this background, we now turn to the selected FTAs considered in this paper. As a preliminary remark, it is worth to mention that only a handful of FTAs

---

[64]For a comprehensive discussion on MRAs under the GATS, see Marchetti and Mavroidis (2012).

[65]Panel Report, *Argentina – Financial Services*, para. 7.814.

[66]Panel Report, *Argentina – Financial Services*, para. 7.873.

[67]Consider, for instance, the rules introduced on central counterparties or the FSB's guidelines on systemically important financial institutions (SIFIs). These instruments and the regulatory objective pursued were not extensively debated at the time of the GATS negotiations.

signed by sovereign states around the world does not contain a PCO.[68] The five FTAs under analysis here are no exception, as they all have a PCO, either as a first paragraph of a provision entitled "Exceptions" (CPTPP, USMCA, KORUS) or in a stand-alone provision (CETA, JEFTA).

All PCOs in the five FTAs clarify that parties can adopt or maintain measures for prudential reasons. While CETA and JEFTA clarify that this right to regulate applies notwithstanding any other provision of the whole agreement,[69] KORUS stipulates that the PCO applies notwithstanding the discipline laid down in a select number of Chapters.[70] These drafting techniques are not new, the former being in line with the model laid down in the GATS Annex, whereas the latter follows the approach adopted *inter alia* by the United States in all its FTAs signed since 2004.[71] CPTPP and USMCA, however, mark a departure from the traditional drafting techniques for preferential PCOs. In fact, the PCOs of those two FTAs apply notwithstanding the whole agreements except for the obligations in goods-related chapters.[72]

Two considerations can be made in this respect. On the one hand, this distinction may be of limited practical relevance, since obligations and commitments on financial services apply to measures affecting trade in financial services. Therefore, the clarification that violations of provisions in goods-related chapters may not be justified under the PCO may sound pleonastic. On the other hand, however, this drafting technique reveals the desire to avoid that PCOs be abusively invoked to justify, for instance, the adoption of measures taken to remedy balance of payment complications or other situations related to trade in goods.[73]

All five FTAs follow the drafting technique already used in the GATS and earlier preferential PCOs, recognising a non-exhaustive list of prudential reasons, ranging from the protection of investors to the stability of the entire financial system.[74]

---

[68]In Cantore (2018), p. 114, we reported that only four FTAs containing discipline on financial services do not have a PCO: the European Economic Area (EEA); China-Hong Kong, China; China-Macao; and Iceland-Faroe Islands.

[69]Article 13.16.1 CETA; Article 8.65.1 JEFTA.

[70]Article 13.10.1 KORUS: "Notwithstanding any other provision of this Chapter or Chapter Eleven (Investment), Fourteen (Telecommunications), including specifically Article 14.23 (Relation to Other Chapters), or Fifteen (Electronic Commerce), and, in addition, Article 12.1.3 (Scope and Coverage) with respect to the supply of financial services in the territory of a Party by a covered investment . . ."

[71]Cantore (2018), pp. 130–131.

[72]Article 11.11.1 CPTPP; Article 17.11.1 USMCA.

[73]Gari (2014), p. 434 discusses the limited scope of application of the GATS PCO to measures affecting trade in non-financial services, including capital controls.

[74]Article 11.11.1 CPTPP; Article 17.11.1 USMCA; Article 13.10.1 KORUS; Article 13.16.1 CETA; Article 8.65.1 JEFTA. CPTPP and USMCA have a footnote that reads: "The Parties understand that the term 'prudential reasons' includes the maintenance of the safety, soundness, integrity, or financial responsibility of individual financial institutions or cross-border financial service suppliers as well as the safety, and financial and operational integrity of payment and clearing systems". See Fn. 10 CPTPP; and Fn. 6 USMCA.

There is a general tendency across the five examined FTAs, shared with the majority of preferential PCOs in general, to not impose rigid conditions or requirements for the useful invocation of the PCO by the regulating party. CETA, however, establishes that only "reasonable" measures are covered by the PCO. This clarification is not likely to add much. Does it imply that only "unreasonable" measures are not covered? Or is it akin to a requirement that measures must have a rational means-ends link with their stated objective to be justified?[75] In the absence of practice, we do not know. It is important to recall that the word "reasonable" first appeared in the NAFTA PCO.[76] In the only investor-state dispute brought under NAFTA where the PCO was invoked, the arbitration tribunal clarified that a measure can be at the same time discriminatory and reasonable.[77] The tribunal further clarified that the PCO thus permits substantial regulatory autonomy for regulators, except for backhanded avoidance of significant obligations in the financial services chapter.[78]

Finally, except for CETA, the other four FTAs reproduce the convoluted (and self-cancelling) final clause of the PCO in the GATS Annex.[79] The latter has been interpreted by scholars as an "anti-abuse clause", akin to the chapeau of Article XIV GATS.[80] Case-law has not yet shed light on this score. The Panel and the Appellate Body in *Argentina – Financial Services* found it unnecessary to interpret the second sentence of the GATS PCO, since they were satisfied that the respondent in the dispute had not met the conditions laid down in the first sentence.[81]

2.9.1 Filter Mechanisms in Investor-State Disputes

As already mentioned earlier, different from the GATS, all FTAs except JEFTA include discipline on investor-state disputes. It is therefore interesting to verify how the four FTAs strike a balance between the right for governments to regulate according to prudential principles and the right for foreign investors to have their

---

[75]In line with the interpretation of the GATS PCO (which does not include the word "reasonable") provided by the Panel in *Argentina – Financial Services* (para. 7.889).

[76]Article 1410 NAFTA.

[77]*Fireman's Fund Insurance Company v Mexico*, ICSID Case No. ARB(AF)/02/01, Award (17 July 2006), para. 162.

[78]*Fireman's Fund Insurance*, para. 164.

[79]See fn. 75 above.

[80]*Ex multis*, Leroux (2002), p. 431. For a critique of the parallelism between the final clause of the GATS PCO and the chapeau of Article XIV of the GATS, see Cantore (2018), p. 182.

[81]As a final remark, we note that Japan included language in its reservations annex to JEFTA reaffirming its right to adopt or maintain prudential measures. Although it may sound pleonastic, as Japan holds this right "in any event", it is a rather recurrent feature in financial services schedules. In Cantore (2018), p. 77, we reported that the word "prudential" appears in the horizontal entries of twenty-one GATS schedules and reference to the GATS PCO is made in twenty-five GATS schedules. Adlung et al. (2013), p. 15, correctly minimize the importance of similar entries, as they refer to provisions that would apply in any event.

case heard when they lament discrimination, unfair or unequitable treatment, or expropriation.

The inclusion of filter mechanisms in investor-state disputes is an important development, as it directly responds to the concerns that, allowing private investors to sue regulating states might lead to regulatory freeze. By introducing a procedural step allowing for regulators' review in the event of disputes, the parties to these four FTAs have secured additional space to their regulatory prerogatives in a delicate domain such as prudential regulation and supervision.[82] This is even more important considering the increasing number of financial services cases brought by private parties before investor-state arbitration tribunals.[83]

Interestingly, all four FTAs containing discipline on investor-state disputes[84] introduce a "filter mechanism" coming to play when investors bring claims against a measure adopted by one of the parties and the respondent rebuts that the challenged measure is in fact consistent with the requirements of the PCO.

It is useful to recall that this feature originally appeared in NAFTA[85] and has recently found its way in other FTAs covering investment protection.[86] The main divergence among the four FTAs is that while CPTPP,[87] USMCA[88] and KORUS[89] establish that the filter mechanism can apply when any provision under the heading "Exceptions" is invoked, CETA's filter mechanism[90] may only apply in disputes where the PCO is invoked.

All four FTAs have filter mechanisms designed around the following pillars, with limited differences: (1) the respondent in the dispute may request in writing the other party (or a committee where financial regulators and supervisors from both parties are represented) to make a joint determination as to whether the PCO was lawfully invoked;[91] (2) the parties (or committee) have a deadline to issue their decision,

---

[82]It is interesting to note how, in other trade domains, similar solutions (perhaps in a less proceduralized fashion) were advocated in the past. Of particular importance is Roessler's critique to the Appellate Body Report in *India – Quantitative Restrictions*, with specific regard to the distribution of competences between adjudicators and the WTO Balance of Payments Committee. See Roessler (2000), pp. 325 and ff.

[83]See Lupo-Pasini (2018), p. 9.

[84]All the examined FTAs except for JEFTA.

[85]See Article 1415 (*Investment Disputes in Financial Services*) NAFTA.

[86]Mitchell et al. (2016), p. 795 report that Singapore and Australia amended their FTA in 2016 to include a similar filter mechanism in investor-state disputes.

[87]Article 11.22 CPTPP.

[88]Annex 17-C (*Mexico-United States investment disputes in financial services*) USMCA. Canada opted out from ISDS disciplines in USMCA.

[89]Article 13.19 KORUS.

[90]Article 13.21 CETA.

[91]Article 11.22.2(a) CPTPP; Annex 17-C.5 USMCA; Article 13.19.1 KORUS; Article 13.21.3 CETA.

which is binding for the outcome of the dispute;[92] and (3) if a determination is not reached by the statutory deadline, the arbitration panel should not draw adverse inferences.[93]

CPTPP adds an additional possible step. If the committee does not make a joint determination, parties will have the possibility to recur to state-to-state dispute settlement and ask adjudicators to decide whether the measures adopted by the regulator are covered by the PCO.[94]

2.9.2   Unique Features in CETA

CETA presents certain unique features regarding the way in which prudential concerns are addressed. Already the text of the PCO is peculiar, as in addition to the standard language it contains two additional clarifications. First, without prejudice to other prudential measures, it allows a party to require the registration of cross-border financial service suppliers or financial instruments of the other party.[95] Second, it clarifies that, subject to MFN and NT, prudential reasons may lead a party to prohibit a particular financial service or activity. This possibility is not unlimited, as the provision itself specifies that parties cannot prohibit all financial services or a complete subsector, such as banking.[96]

The unique features of CETA's approach to prudential measures are not exhausted by the foregoing. In fact, Annex 13-B to the CETA lists "high-level" principles that parties and tribunals should follow in the application of the PCO in state-to-state and investor-state disputes.

The Annex recognizes the right for parties to set their own appropriate level of prudential regulation,[97] even if that is higher than that set out in international prudential commitments that are common to the parties.[98] When reviewing the applicability of the PCO to a given measure, adjudicators should consider the urgency of the situation and the information available when the measure was adopted.[99] Importantly, the Annex recognises the specialised nature of prudential regulation, and urges adjudicators to exercise maximum deference when reviewing

---

[92]Article 11.22.2(b) CPTPP; Annex 17-C.5 USMCA; Article 13.19.1 KORUS; Article 13.21.4 CETA.

[93]Article 11.22.4 CPTPP; Annex 17-C.5 USMCA; Article 13.21.6 CETA. KORUS does not have this clarification. CPTPP and USMCA add that the party to which the complaining investor belongs is presumed to support the invocation of the exception by the respondent unless it makes a submission to argue the contrary.

[94]Article 11.22.2(c) CPTPP.

[95]Article 13.16.2 CETA.

[96]Article 13.16.3 CETA.

[97]Echoing language from the WTO Agreement on Sanitary and Phytosanitary Measures (SPS Agreement).

[98]Paragraph 8(a), Annex 13-B CETA.

[99]Paragraph 8(b), Annex 13-B CETA.

regulators' choices as well as the risk assessments conducted by financial regulatory authorities.[100]

The Annex further states that a measure meets the requirements of the PCO if it has a prudential objective and it is not "manifestly disproportionate" to achieve it. However, the same does not apply to measures that amount to a disguised restriction on foreign investment or to arbitrary or unjustifiable discrimination between investors in like situations.[101] The proviso imports language from the so-called chapeau of Article XIV of the GATS and Article XX of the GATT 1994. While CETA judges will not be bound by the WTO case law on the chapeau of Article XIV of the GATS or Article XX of the GATT 1994, they may have an incentive to do that.[102] It is therefore important to monitor developments in this area, as decisions by CETA judges could contribute to foster convergence between multilateral and preferential rules.

Annex 13-B to CETA further clarifies that, provided that it is not applied in a manner that would constitute arbitrary or unjustifiable discrimination between investors in like situations or a disguised restriction on foreign investment, a measure is presumed to be prudential if it is: (1) in line with international prudential commitments that are common to the parties; (2) adopted for the resolution of a financial institution in distress or no longer viable; or (3) adopted to preserve or restore financial stability in response to a systemic crisis.[103]

Interestingly, the Annex is subject to periodical review (every 2 years) and the Financial Services Committee may develop a common understanding on the PCO based on discussions and practice in specific disputes, mindful of developments concerning international prudential commitments.[104]

3 Assessment

The FTAs examined in this paper do not depart substantially from the GATS template, including the specific rules designed in the GATS Annex and in the GATS Understanding. Despite the different approaches to liberalization followed (negative list versus positive list), the FTAs examined in this study largely import the majority of the discipline from the GATS templates.

---

[100]Paragraph 8(c), Annex 13-B CETA.

[101]Paragraph 8(d), Annex 13-B CETA.

[102]Recent studies reveal that an increasing number of ISDS arbitration panels relies on WTO case-law in the interpretation of treaty provisions. Chevry (2020, forthcoming) provides a detailed account of this phenomenon.

[103]Paragraph 8(e), Annex 13-B CETA.

[104]Paragraph 9, Annex 13-B CETA. This paragraph also clarifies that the Annex may be amended. That is not innovative in and of itself, since any international agreement can be amended, in principle, with the consent of its parties.

Importantly, several provisions originally featuring in the GATS Understanding—which, we recall, is a voluntary instrument—are replicated in FTAs, including those where one or more parties are not signatories of the GATS Understanding at the multilateral level. Anecdotal evidence reveals that the voluntary adherence to the GATS Understanding was a compromise solution between developed Members that were ready to liberalize further their markets for financial services and developing Members that were more lukewarm in that regard.[105] This article shows how certain provisions from the GATS Understanding (e.g., on access to payment systems or transfer of information) have graduated to compulsory discipline in FTAs. This finding is important, if only because the FTAs under review here, in light of the composition of their membership, are likely to constitute the necessary starting point for any future discussion on multilateral rules on trade in financial services. This may mean, in the event of GATS reforms, that additional rules could usefully complement already existing provisions, without necessarily redrafting the entire GATS Agreement. This finding is also important because it signals the continued relevance of an early instrument allowing for "variable geometry", allowing Members willing to make deeper trade concession to do so, without imposing an unnecessary burden on other Members with different agendas or at different stages of economic development.

A general tendency towards convergence can also be noted when comparing the five FTAs among themselves. This finding, however, should probably not be overestimated for two main reasons.

First, all the FTAs concerned allow parties to make extensive reservations for existing and future measures. Second, it is certainly positive that parties introduced clarity in certain agreements with regard to specific disciplines (e.g., defining "financial institutions" by means of the legislation in force in the territory where they operate; rules ensuring the transmission of information). However, the FTAs under analysis also converge to the extent that they import verbatim language from the GATS discipline that could have benefitted from additional clarification (e.g., the vague final clause of the GATS PCO).

More interestingly, the agreements examined in this paper permit to appreciate the state of play of the dialogue between the financial services industry (with its offensive interests) and regulators (with their prerogatives). With the caveats already expressed in the previous sections, it is interesting to note that the financial services industry obtained remarkable successes, such as the possibility for private entities to sue regulators before investment tribunals or the introduction of discipline on the free transfer of information. At the same time, instruments from the past like the NAFTA "filter mechanism" in investment dispute concerning prudential measures have been revived and found their way in almost all the agreements, adding "extra-time" in investor-state disputes and safeguarding regulatory space for governments. Concerning the "filter mechanism" in CPTPP, Gelpern argues that financial firms are "more limited" than their counterparts in other sectors in the relief they can obtain

---

[105] See Mavroidis (2020, forthcoming).

from suing regulators before an investor-state tribunal.[106] *Mutatis mutandis*, the same holds true also for USMCA, CETA, and KORUS.

Commenting on the slow pace of liberalization of trade in services at the regional and multilateral level, scholars have made the case that the only way forward would be to harmonize domestic regulations.[107] In this respect, we note that the FTAs examined in this paper do not mark a substantial departure from the negative integration model of the GATS. References to regulatory cooperation were made in a minority of agreements, and even in those cases the language used is rather hortatory. In the aftermath of the 2007/2008 financial crisis, substantial work has been made in other fora (e.g., BCBS, FSB) to develop new guidelines and standards on financial regulation, to strengthen the banking sector and prevent future disruptions. However, this work has not been translated into binding requirements in FTAs. Take the example of JEFTA, whose parties are also members of BCBS. JEFTA has a lengthy annex on regulatory cooperation on financial regulation. The annex simply requires Japan and the EU to make "their best endeavours" to implement standards agreed upon in other fora. This is consistent with the idea that sovereign states prefer to keep margin of manoeuvre in the domain of financial regulation and to discuss the matter in informal institutional settings, whose outcomes take the form of non-binding instruments.[108] Most likely, financial regulation will continue to be discussed in fora other than trade agreements, consistent with what has happened since the 1970s.

Mattoo (2015) argues that regulatory cooperation is necessary to keep financial markets open, and that trust among regulators in different countries is crucial in that regard. It should be also noted, however, that international standards on financial regulation are typically drafted in such a way to permit discrepancies as to how they are effectively implemented at the national level. Therefore, irrespective of whether governments "trust" each other, a translation of standards into binding requirements would have probably not added much to the discipline of the FTAs under analysis. Against this background, the approach adopted by the EU and Japan in JEFTA, where they cautiously agreed to discuss regulatory harmonization on a case-by-case basis, is perhaps the only deliverable solution at this stage.

As a final remark, it should be stressed that important innovations have found their way in recent FTAs.[109] To name one important development, the "high level" principles concerning the interpretation of the PCO laid down in Annex 13-B to CETA are the most advanced attempt so far to meaningfully guide the adjudicators'

---

[106]Gelpern (2016), p. 96.

[107]See, *ex multis*, Mattoo (2015) and Ortino (2016).

[108]Verdier (2013). Note, however, that internationally agreed standards on banking supervision and regulation typically show high records of compliance, including in jurisdictions that are not Members of the relevant standard-setting bodies. Hohl et al. (2018) surveyed 100 jurisdictions (therefore including non-BCBS Members) and found evidence that all of them have adopted some iteration of the Basel risk-based capital regime.

[109]See also Delimatsis (2017), p. 614 on this aspect.

assessment in disputes where the PCO is invoked. Only practice will reveal how effective these innovations will be.

References

Adlung R, Morrison P, Roy M, Zhang W (2013) FOG in GATS commitments – why WTO Members should care. World Trade Rev 12(1):1–27

Cameron MA, Tomlin BW (2000) The making of NAFTA – how the deal was done. Cornell University Press, Ithaca

Cantore CM (2018) The prudential carve-out for financial services – rationale and practice in the GATS and preferential trade agreements. Cambridge University Press, Cambridge

Chevry J (2020) The impact of international trade law in international investment arbitration. Oxford University Press, Oxford (forthcoming)

Delimatsis P (2017) The evolution of the EU external trade policy in services – CETA, TTIP, and TiSA after Brexit. J Int Econ Law 20(3):583–625

Delimatsis P, Hoekman B (2017) National tax regulation, voluntary international standards, and the GATS: Argentina–financial services. World Trade Rev 17(2):265–290

Gari G (2014) GATS disciplines on capital transfers and short term capital inflows: time for a change? J Int Econ Law 17(2):399–435

Gelpern A (2016) Financial services. In: VV AA (ed) Assessing the Trans-Pacific Partnership. PIIE Briefing 16-01, pp 91–100

Hohl S, Sison MC, Stastny T, Zamil R (2018) The Basel framework in 100 jurisdictions: implementation status and proportionality practices. BCBS FSI Insights on policy implementation, No 11, pp 1–33

Jarreau JR (1999) Interpreting the general agreement on trade in services and the WTO instruments relevant to the international trade of financial services: the lawyer's perspective. N C J Int Law Commercial Regul 25(1):1–74

Leblond P (2016) CETA and financial services: what to expect? CIGI papers no. 91, pp 1–8

Leroux EH (2002) Trade in financial services under the World Trade Organization. J World Trade 36(3):413–442

Lupo-Pasini F (2018) Financial disputes in international courts. J Int Econ Law 21(1):1–30

Marchetti JA (2011) The GATS prudential carve-out. In: Delimatsis P, Herger N (eds) Financial regulation at the crossroads: implications for supervision, institutional design and trade. Kluwer, Alphen aan den Rijn, pp 279–295

Marchetti JA (2020) Financial services in the TPP. In: Gantz D, Huerta-Goldman J (eds) The Trans Pacific Partnership Agreement: its substance and impact on international trade, NAFTA, and other FTAs. Cambridge University Press, Cambridge (forthcoming)

Marchetti JA, Mavroidis PC (2011) The genesis of the GATS (General Agreement on Trade in Services). Eur J Int Law 22(3):689–721

Marchetti JA, Mavroidis PC (2012) I now recognize you (and only you) as equal: an anatomy of (mutual) recognition agreements in the GATS. In: Lianos I, Okeoghene O (eds) Regulating trade in services in the EU and the WTO. Cambridge University Press, Cambridge, pp 415–443

Mattoo A (2015) Services trade and regulatory cooperation. E15 Expert Group on Services – Think Piece, pp 1–14

Mavroidis PC (2020) The regulation of international trade (Volume III – The GATS). MIT Press, Cambridge (forthcoming)

Mitchell AD, Hawkins JK, Mishra N (2016) Dear prudence: allowances under international trade and investment law for prudential regulation in the financial services sector. J Int Econ Law 19 (4):787–820

Natens B (2016) Regulatory autonomy and international trade in services. Elgar, Cheltenham

Ortino F (2016) Regional trade agreements and trade in services. In: Lester S, Mercurio B, Bartels L (eds) Bilateral and regional trade agreements: commentary and analysis, vol 1, 2nd edn. Cambridge University Press, Cambridge, pp 213–244

Roessler F (2000) The institutional balance between the judicial and the political organs of the WTO. In: Bronckers M, Quick R (eds) New directions in international economic law: essays in honour of John H Jackson. Kluwer, The Hague, pp 325–342

Verdier PH (2013) The political economy of international financial regulation. Indiana Law J 88 (4):1405–1474

Wang H (2019) The future of deep free trade agreements; the convergence of TPP (and CPTPP) and CETA? J World Trade 53(2):317–342

Yoffie DB (1990) Trade in services and American Express. In: Yoffie DB (ed) International trade and competition: cases and notes in strategy and management. McGraw Hill, New York City, pp 367–386

Carlo M. Cantore is a dispute settlement lawyer in the Legal Affairs Division of the WTO. He is also a visiting lecturer in WTO Law at the University of Antwerp. Carlo holds a PhD in law from the European University Institute of Florence, and a law degree from the Sant'Anna School of Advanced Studies of Pisa.

Maritime Transport, the WTO, and Regional Trade Agreements: Too Many Cooks?

Lijun Zhao

Contents

Thanks to Richard Scott and reviewers who provided assistance/support. All errors remain mine. In this chapter, 'shipping' and 'maritime transport' are used interchangeably.

L. Zhao (✉)
School of Law, Middlesex University, London, UK
e-mail: L.Zhao@mdx.ac.uk

© The Editor(s) (if applicable) and The Author(s), under exclusive licence to   219
Springer Nature Switzerland AG 2020
R. T. Hoffmann, M. Krajewski (eds.), *Coherence and Divergence in Services Trade
Law*, European Yearbook of International Economic Law,
https://doi.org/10.1007/978-3-030-46955-9_10

1   Introduction

As average consumers today, we have been accustomed to driving cars assembled thousands of miles away from our home and purchasing cheap cloth and groceries, as well as inexpensive household appliances and smartphones which are indispensable by many of us. However, few of us pause to think about the significant logistical effort involved in maritime transport which bestows us this level of comfort and prosperity in our lives. The truth is that many of these goods in our everyday lives are shipped long distances via sea routes.

Maritime transport is a significant facilitator of international trade. UNCTAD estimates that roughly four-fifths of goods (by volume) are carried by sea nowadays.[1] In the breakdown of the purchase price at which consumers pay for, the freight rates only account for a very small percentage compared with the production costs of goods.[2] Maritime transport is also an essential service sector which makes gigantic contributions to the value of services trade for some countries, such as the UK, Norway, Korea and Japan.[3]

This chapter aims to assess whether services agreements on maritime transport tend to be coherent or divergent, especially in light of the today's proliferation of preferential trade agreements (PTAs) and regional trade agreements (RTAs). Because these two terms—PTA and RTA—are used interchangeably in many

---

[1]UNCTAD (2018), Review of Maritime Transport, pp. 1–15. WTO (2001), Doc. S/CSS/W/59.

[2]UNCTAD (2018), Review of Maritime Transport, pp. 1–15.

[3]WTO (2001), Doc. S/CSS/W/59.

literature and official documents,[4] so RTAs in this chapter refer both bilateral and regional agreements; however, it should be noted by readers that these two terms are different in other contexts. Furthermore, readers should bear in mind that PTA in goods trade relates to 'unilateral treatment', but PTA in services trade usually observe the 'doctrine of reciprocity'.[5]

Through examining maritime transport services and the related commitments in bilateral, plurilateral and regional frameworks under the WTO (the World Trade Organization) framework and in RTAs, as well as applied measures in services and services statistics, this chapter probes into whether and how RTAs may facilitate international trade and enhance the liberalisation of the shipping sector—maritime transport services—in the context of preferential liberalisation. In this chapter, 'shipping' and 'maritime transport' are used interchangeably. Some relevant questions have been considered as follows:

- Has the WTO's multilateral approach under the GATS properly addressed the uniqueness of the shipping sector?
- If not, to what extent, the further liberalisation of maritime transport services calls for different instruments and approaches?
- Which approach is better in liberalising the maritime transport services, through multilateral or bilateral/regional agreements? What roles will the WTO and RTAs play in the future liberalisation of the shipping sector?

2   Methodology

This study bears a multi-disciplinary nature. The analysis in this chapter is conducted from three perspectives—legal, economic and historical. History usually repeats itself, thus lessons can be learnt from history.[6] Many of the arguments made today go back three decades or more. In light of progress and regress in the existing negotiations which the WTO facilitated, experience in this part sheds light on the harmonising of all transport modes, owing to the rise of containerisation and door-to-door transport.

Moreover, law and economics interact with each other—good laws facilitate trade, but bad ones are impediments to economy.[7] Services trade liberalisation aims to improve market conditions and promote competitions, thus this chapter adopts economic analysis to examine the shipping industry in order to evaluate relevant law and trade agreements. As for the scope of the negotiating documents and achieves being covered in this research, the current author has employed the

---

[4]E.g. WTO I-TIP databases.

[5]See details in Sect. 6.1.

[6]Sturley (1991), p. 3.

[7]Sturley (1991), pp. 3–15.

WTO, UNCTAD and the World Bank public datasets and databases; some documents dated in 2013 are still confidential, so the analysis in the chapter only considered the documents which have been published by 1 January 2020.

This author employs the WTO documents databases[8] and searched all documents regarding maritime transport dated after 1 January 2010 which have not been sufficiently studied by existing literature.[9] There are totally relevant 35 documents achieved in the database, among which two documents dated in 2013 are of particular relevant but still restricts public access.

In short, this chapter employs two main methods:

- Doctrinal approach through focusing on the legal authorities, such as the WTO legal texts and those of RTAs trade agreements; and
- Empirical approach. This author uses 'The Integrated Trade Intelligence Portal' (I-TIP),[10] supported by the WTO and the World Bank, which is the only database providing a comprehensive scope of information on trade in services.

I-TIP Databases cover several useful databases providing first-hand information on Members' commitments which they made under the WTO framework and are associated to the General Agreement on Trade in Services (GATS), and services commitments made under preferential, bilateral and regional trade agreements (all of which are collectively referred as 'RTAs' in I-TIP, so this chapter also follows the database to use the term RTAs in a broad, comprehensive sense). In addition, two databases of I-TIP are particularly useful for this research:

- TIP GATS Database: this covers all GATS specific commitments and exemptions to the obligation of most-favoured-nation treatment (MFN) undertaken by WTO Members under the GATS, and
- TIP RTAs Database: this allows researchers and the public to access and search information on Members' commitments under RTAs which the WTO is notified under Article V of the GATS.

3   Selection Criteria of RTAs To Be Studied in This Research

This chapter studies maritime transport and its relevant commitments under multilateral, bilateral, plurilateral and regional frameworks (namely, commitments under the WTO's GATS and in RTAs), as well as applied measures in services and services statistics available from the WTO, the World Bank and UNCTAD.

---

[8]WTO (no date), https://docsonline.wto.org/.

[9]Parameswaran (2010) and Zhao (2014, 2015).

[10]WTO and World Bank, Services Databases "I-TIP-Services Portal" http://i-tip.wto.org/services/default.aspx. See "Users Guide" at https://www.wto.org/english/tratop_e/serv_e/itip_user_guide_e.htm.

Under the GATS, apart from Members' horizontal commitments, the current author has identified 62 sectoral commitments specifically made to the maritime transport sector, which are achieved in the I-TIP database. Furthermore, the I-TIP database has covered the majority of RTAs related to services trade, and this chapter is based on researching of a number of existing RTAs.[11]

Based on the current author's calculation, there are roughly 86 relevant RTAs[12] addressing shipping as of 1 January 2020. It should be noted that, due to the existence of a large number of identified commitments (under the GATS and RTAs) and the time restraint, it is not feasible to scrutinise all commitments. There are too many PTAs and RTAs including maritime transport commitments, so this chapter selected some important RTAs to conduct cases studies.

The standard of selection is the involvement of any of the top 5 merchant fleet owing countries (namely, Greece, Japan, China, Germany and Singapore, as shown in Fig. 1),[13] and some world-leading open registry countries. Thus, the current author decided to narrow up the scope of research through selecting some commitments (under both the GATS and RTAs) which involve these aforementioned representative countries.

---

[11]ASEAN – China; Australia – Chile; Canada – Chile; Canada – Colombia; Canada – Honduras; Canada – Panama; Canada – Peru; Chile – China; Chile – Colombia; Chile – Costa Rica (Chile – Central America); Chile – El Salvador (Chile – Central America); Chile – Guatemala (Chile – Central America); Chile – Honduras (Chile – Central America); Chile – Japan; Chile – Mexico; Chile – Nicaragua (Chile – Central America); China – Costa Rica; China – New Zealand; China – Rep. of Korea; China – Singapore; Colombia – Mexico; Colombia – Northern Triangle (El Salvador, Guatemala, Honduras); Costa Rica – Peru; Costa Rica – Singapore; Dominican Republic – Central America – United States Free Trade Agreement (CAFTA-DR); East African Community (EAC); EFTA – Chile; EFTA – Colombia; EFTA – Hong Kong, China; EFTA – Korea, Republic of; EFTA – Singapore; EFTA – Ukraine; El Salvador- Honduras – Chinese Taipei; Guatemala – the Separate Customs Territory of Taiwan, Penghu, Kinmen and Matsu; Hong Kong, China – Chile; Hong Kong, China – New Zealand; Iceland – China; India – Japan; India – Malaysia; India – Singapore; Japan – Australia; Japan – Mexico; Japan – Mongolia; Japan – Peru; Japan – Philippines; Japan – Switzerland; Jordan – Singapore; Korea, Republic of – Australia; Korea, Republic of – Chile; Korea, Republic of – Singapore; Korea, Republic of – US; Korea, Republic of – Viet Nam; Mexico – Central America; New Zealand – Chinese Taipei; New Zealand – Malaysia; Nicaragua and the Separate Customs Territory of Taiwan, Penghu, Kinmen and Matsu; North American Free Trade Agreement (NAFTA); Pakistan – China; Panama – Chile; Panama – Costa Rica (Panama – Central America); Panama – El Salvador (Panama – Central America); Panama – Guatemala (Panama – Central America); Panama – Honduras (Panama – Central America); Panama – Peru; Panama – Singapore; Panama and the Separate Customs Territory of Taiwan, Penghu, Kinmen and Matsu; Peru – Chile; Peru – China; Peru – Korea, Republic of; Peru – Mexico; Peru – Singapore; Singapore – Australia; Singapore – Chinese Taipei; Switzerland – China; Trans-Pacific Strategic Economic Partnership; Ukraine – Montenegro; US – Australia; US – Bahrain; US – Chile; US – Colombia; US – Jordan; US – Morocco; US – Oman; US – Panama; US – Peru; US – Singapore.

[12]A full list of covered RTAs under I-TIP database (up to September 2016) can be found at http://i-tip.wto.org/services/Services_RTAs_covered.pdf.

[13]UNCTAD (2018). http://stats.unctad.org/merchantfleet, http://stats.unctad.org/fleetownership.

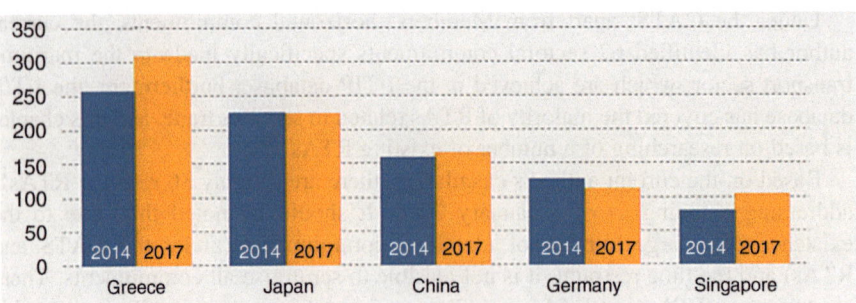

Fig. 1 Top 5 merchant fleet owning countries—2014 and 2017. Unit in the figure: millions of deadweight tons [Source: UNCTAD (2018)]

This chapter reviews the relevant RTAs governing maritime transport services. Again, not all RTAs are studied, and this chapter focuses on those involving countries meeting either of the three criteria as mentioned above. Through searching 'services databases I-TIP' created jointly by the WTO and the World Bank, this author identified all relevant PTAs which govern maritime transport services.

In summary, the selection criteria for this research are:

- Influential trading countries, such as the USA, though it is not a shipping power which provides maritime transport services in today's international shipping market
- Countries with Open registries,[14] such as Panama and Norway.
- Shipping powers. According to UNCTAD, the world top five ship owner countries, as shown in Fig. 1, are Greece, Japan, China, Germany and Singapore, which collectively account for one half of the shipping market.[15]

After calculation, the author found that the shipping sector (i.e. maritime transport services) has been covered by 86 of RTAs. Thus, an enormous amount of information on maritime transport under these the RTAs has been identified; however, they are not of equal importance, taking into account of the scale of services trade. Hence, this author selected some out of the identified RTAs to conduct further analysis; the selection criteria is that a RTA involves at least one influential country in the shipping industry.

---

[14]See details on flagging out and open registry in Sect. 6.2.3.

[15]UNCTAD (2018). http://stats.unctad.org/merchantfleet, http://stats.unctad.org/fleetownership.

4 Uniqueness and Liberalisation of Shipping: Multilateralism or Reciprocity?

4.1 Dual Nature Shared by Both Shipping and the WTO

Both the shipping sector and the WTO bear a dual nature connecting goods and services. Shipping is a globalised business with a dual nature[16] that joins trade in goods and trade in maritime transport services into one transaction. This dual nature is mirrored by the structure of WTO. Likewise, the WTO also represents a dual nature connecting goods and service. Maritime transport has gained a prominent role in the WTO negotiating agenda under the GATS,[17] along with trade in goods under the GATT (General Agreement on Tariffs and Trade). Maritime related service is an area on which WTO negotiations were scheduled under the GATS.[18] Since the Uruguay Round negotiations in the 1980s, trade in services was part of international trade negotiations, along with trade in goods.[19] The connectivity between shipping and the WTO can be traced back to the Uruguay Round, as well as the recent Doha Round, negotiations.[20]

The connectivity between maritime transport service and the global trading system—the WTO—originated from GATS related negotiations. Several annexes were negotiated along with the GATS, each representing "an integral part" of this Agreement.[21] Paralleling with all listed annexes to the GATS, it is the "Annex on Negotiations on Maritime Transport" that is of particular relevance to be discussed here in this chapter.

4.2 Liberalisation of Maritime Transport: A Broadly, Internationalised, Liberalised and Competitive Sector

Maritime transport services are largely internationalised and highly liberalised in reality. Through the World Bank's Database on 'Service Trade Restrictiveness Index (STRI)'[22] the author checked the STRI for many countries by several service sectors, and found that the restrictiveness index for transportation is lower than the majority

---

[16]UNCTADSTAT (no date). https://unctadstat.unctad.org/wds/ReportFolders/reportFolders.aspx.

[17]See Sect. 4.3.

[18]WTO (1996a). Doc.S/NGMTS/13, para 2.

[19]WTO (1994). *Marrakesh Agreement Establishing the World Trade Organization.*

[20]E.g. Zhao (2015); WTO (1996b), p. 1, para 1.

[21]GATS Article XXIX.

[22]World Bank (2019), Service Trade Restrictiveness Index Database http://iresearch.worldbank.org/servicetrade/default.htm#.

of other services sectors, such as banking, insurance, professional, telecommunications, and retail.

It should be noted that, even though the World Bank's Database does not provide the breakdown restrictiveness index figures as for air, road and maritime transports, the restrictiveness index of the maritime transport services is lower than those of other modes of transport. This is because maritime transport has been one of the most internationally integrated services and functioned beyond national boundaries (Paulsen 1983).

> [A]ny one ship may involve members of different nations – in its ownership, registration, builder, supply of engines, officers and crew, financing, insurance and chartering.[23]

Therefore, the shipping sector and its maritime services are largely internationalised and liberalised crossing countries' boundaries, and the liberalisation of maritime transport services relates to all the four modes[24] of services. This *status quo* is probably because of its importance to international trade in goods (Schoenbaum 2001). Hence, the liberalisation of maritime transport has historically been a focus of the international community.

4.3   The WTO, the GATS and Shipping

Even though the shipping sector has been largely internationalised and liberalised, compared with many other service sectors, the international community was and is still attempting to liberalise this sector through the multilateral trading system. The existing effort was part of the GATS negotiations during the 1980s–1990s and finalised as the GATS 'Annex on Negotiations on Maritime Transport'.[25] The GATS consists of 29 articles and eight annexes which represent integral parts of the GATS and address special rules for separately identified matters or service sectors. Moreover, each member country may undertake specific commitments listed in its 'Schedules of Specific Commitments' and also list MFN exemptions in its List of Article II exemptions.[26]

This GATS Annex on maritime transport is very brief, including mere 155 words and representing three sections. Section 1 of this Annex regarding negotiations delays the applications of the MFN obligations to the maritime transport sector and stipulates requirements to list MFN exemptions, to "international shipping, auxiliary services and access to and use of port facilities" beyond the effective date of the GATS, namely 1 January 1995. As seen, there have been no concrete substantive provisions under the GATS and its Annex so far.

---

[23]Degenhardt and Day (1985), p. 41. Mukherjee et al. (2013).

[24]See GATS Article II.

[25]Zhao (2015), pp. 60–118.

[26]Consolidated GATS Schedules of Commitments and MFN exemptions (by country and sector) can be viewed and downloaded at Services Database http://i-tip.wto.org/services/Search.aspx.

With regard to the *status quo* of GATS Schedules on maritime transport, through searching the GATS Commitments Database, the current author has found that apart from members' horizontal commitments, 62 WTO members included maritime transport services (Code11.A)[27] into their Schedules of Commitment and made specific commitments, and 60 WTO members included services auxiliary to all modes of transport (Code11.H)[28] in their Schedules of Commitment and made specific commitments.[29] That is to say, though the Uruguay round negotiations during the 1980s and 1990s did not progress much on this sector, many countries have voluntarily made commitments on maritime transport under the GATS.

Even so, the WTO-related negotiations on maritime transport have been stalled. To some extent, the multilateral framework and the WTO failed in further liberalising the shipping sector.[30] However, the existing negotiations and informal discussions of the maritime transport sector were not nought since some headway was made and became the basis serving the following negotiations in this sector under RTAs.[31]

The multilateral negotiations specifically laid down two cornerstones for future negotiations regardless of their approach: Firstly, the four modes of services supply[32] were followed and adapted to the maritime transport sector. Secondly, the Uruguay Round negotiations agreed that the scope of national specific commitment on maritime transport services would address 'four pillars'[33] of the maritime sector.

4.4 Four Modes of Services: Created by the WTO, Followed by RTAs

There is a wide range of maritime services. Here is a non-exhaustive list:[34]

- Commercial shipping services, including transporting bulk cargoes, manufactured goods and passengers on regular services, or as individually negotiated shipments—ship-owning, and commercial or operational management;
- Ports Loading and unloading cargoes at the intersection of land (rail, road) and maritime transport, distribution and multimodal role (logistics);

---

[27]WTO (no date), GATT (1001), Classification List, https://www.wto.org/english/tratop_e/serv_e/serv_sectors_e.htm.

[28]GATT (1001), Classification List.

[29]I-Tip database (2019).

[30]See details in Sect. 5.

[31]Zhao (2014), pp. 172–227.

[32]See details in Sect. 4.4.

[33]See details in Sects. 5.3–5.6. This categorising has been used by the WTO/GATT negotiations since the 1980s, see WTO (2013) doc. JOB/SERV/137.

[34]List created by the current author. Source: Stopford (2009), p. 49.

- Shipbuilding, repairing and scrapping (also known as recycling), including constructing new ships (hull, engines and equipment), servicing or repairing existing ships, and demolishing (recycling) old ships
- Shipping ancillary services, such as shipbroking, ship's agency, marine insurance, P&I clubs, shipping consultancy and market analysis;
- Offshore oil and gas exploration and exploitation;
- Other categories, including cruise shipping (leisure market), maritime tourism (leisure), fishing and aquaculture.

The GATS applies to services trade when the activities fall within one of the four modes of supply referred to Article I:2 of the GATS. When applying the four modes of supply[35] to shipping, maritime services can be divided into four modes:

- Mode 1: e.g. international freights (cargo shipping), passengers shipping, etc.; cabotage shipping is usually revered for national carriers instead of foreign counterparts, e.g. the USA and India;[36]
- Mode 2: e.g. vessel repair, etc.;
- Mode 3: e.g. Flagging out a vessel to a country adopts open registry,[37] etc. and
- Mode 4: e.g. Seafarers; Maritime cargo handling, Storage and warehouse in ports; Customs clearances; Container station and depot; etc.[38]

These four modes have a significant impact on maritime transport, regardless of their association with the WTO (the GATS) or with RTAs. Under the WTO framework, National Treatment regarding maritime transport sector is listed in a Member country's Schedule of Specific Commitments by stating restrictions and applied measures on the above four modes. Likewise, it is worth noting that, the negotiations and outcomes of commitments on maritime transport services in RTAs followed the four modes which were created under the GATS.

4.5 Defects of WTO Multilateral Approach in Handling Maritime Transport Services: MFN, National Treatment Obligations and Free-Rider Problem Under the GATS

Even though shipping is one of the most internationalised and liberalised industries in the world,[39] negotiations in the maritime sector turned out extremely frustrating.[40]

---

[35]Zhao (2014), pp. 172–227.

[36]See details in Sect. 5.3.

[37]See details in Sect. 6.2.3.

[38]See also Parameswaran (2010), p. 306, footnotes 1437–1440. See the four modes in GATS Article I.2.

[39]See Sect. 4.2.

[40]Zhao (2015), pp. 60–118.

Arguably, the difficulties in enhancing existing liberalisation in this sector largely are created by the existing multilateral liberalisation efforts themselves. Thus, this section examines the relevant negotiations and identifies lessons which can be learned from progression and also regression during the negotiating process.

The GATS-related maritime transport negotiations can be divided mainly into three phases; details of the negotiating history and documents can be found in existing literature,[41] this chapter does not repeat these works. The focus here is lessons extracted from these existing negotiations and possible interactions with other RTAs on maritime transport.

The Most-favoured-Nation (MFN) and National Treatment (NT) principles work as cornerstones of the WTO which employs a multilateral approach, instead of reciprocity. Albeit in slightly different ways, MFN and NT apply to trade in goods under the General GATT,[42] as well as to trade in services under the GATS. Under the GATT, both principles create general obligations.

MFN and national treatment also apply to the GATS. Unlike their counterpart provisions governing trade in goods under the GATT, two specialities are worth noting that:

Firstly, MFN is a general obligation applicable to all services sectors with some exceptions; many of the exceptions shadow their corresponding articles under the GATT, but one of them is unique.[43] The MFN principle, under Article II of the GATS, requires a country accords unconditional and most favoured treatment among the service suppliers of all Member state of the WTO. However, the MFN obligation can be exempted provided conditions listed in the GATS 'Annex on Article II Exemptions' are met. In addition, the 'Annex on Maritime Transport Negotiations' includes a proviso to MFN and prevents MFN from applying to the maritime transport sector due to two reasons. The first reason was in the negotiating practice regarding maritime transport negotiations under the GATS framework, too many Members expressed the willingness to use MFN exemptions, so a special arrangement was created under this Annex and save the efforts from the Members to include maritime transport sector into their individual Schedules. Another reason is that the multilateral approach would lead to a 'free-rider problem'[44] in the liberalisation process of maritime transport and no consensus was achieved on this service sector.[45]

Secondly, the national treatment obligations of the GATS are unique and different from its counterpart article under the GATT. It is not a general principle under the GATS.[46] Instead, it works as a *specific*[47] obligation only if a Member country

---

[41]Zhao (2015), pp. 60–118. Parameswaran (2010).

[42]GATT Articles I and III.

[43]GATS Article II.

[44]See Sect. 6.1.

[45]See Sect. 4.5.

[46]GATS Article XVII.

[47]Emphases by this author.

includes a sector into its GATS Schedule of Commitment. Moreover, Members can unilaterally restrict the market access and national treatment of a service sector, through listing any limitations in its GATS schedule of commitment (including horizontal and sectoral commitments).

4.6 The Impact of Positive/Negative List on Maritime Transport Services

The two important issues whether and how the maritime transport sector is covered by the GATS and an RTA relies on whether a 'positive list' or 'negative list' method is utilised. The National Treatment principle, under Article XVII of GATS, utilises a 'positive list' approach[48] which means that a member assumes the national treatment obligation provided a sector is being listed in its Schedule of Commitments. Namely, it is a member country's choice to make the national treatment be applicable to a sector through including the sector in its Schedule of Commitments.

It should be noted that the 'negative list' approach is being used by some RTAs, for instance, NAFTA addresses maritime transport and relevant investment (such as port infrastructures). This distinction between the MFN and National treatment principles leads to no consensus in the GATS multilateral negotiations on maritime transport sector. This explains why maritime transport services are liberalised through RTAs after the multilateral negotiations did not progress much after the WTO's Uruguay Round negotiations.

5 Recent Liberalisation of Maritime Transport Services Under the GATS and RTAs: Coherence or Divergence?

In this section, this author examines the *status quo* of liberalisation of maritime transport services, with special reference to both the GATS and RTAs (especially some important RTAs involving influential trade and shipping countries as mentioned in Sect. 3). It starts with overviews of maritime transport services under the WTO (namely under the GATS) and under RTAs. Next, because the GATS negotiations used to categorise maritime transport services into four kinds (i.e. 'pillars'),[49] this chapter follows this tradition and examines the status of the liberalisation in each of the four pillars of maritime transport under the GATS and RTAs.

As stated in Sect. 2, this author used 'I-TIP Services portal' Databases and searched 'Maritime Transport' commitments made in relation to GATS and RTAs.

---

[48]See Sect. 4.6; Mattoo et al. (2018).

[49]WTO (2013), doc. JOB/SERV/137.

Apart from Members' horizontal commitments which are applicable to the maritime transport services, it is found that there have been 62 sectoral commitments to GATS specifically made to the maritime transport sector. In addition, there are approximately 86 RTAs[50] being covered in the I-TIP Database. A large number of RTAs are identified in the database in which all of the Commitments/Reservations regarding maritime transport services and relevant investment are studied here.[51] Due to the reasons stated in Sect. 2 on methodology, the author chose some sample GATS and RTA commitments for further analysis in depth.

On the whole, based on researching the 62 GATS commitments related to maritime transport, it is worth mentioning some recent updates. Firstly, the recent liberalisation through the GATS multilateral forum is mainly fulfilled by new members' accession to the WTO, for instance, Afghanistan, Cambodia, China, Kazakhstan, Liberia, and Viet Nam. Secondly, the USA has not made any special commitment on this sector, thus unless stated in its horizontal commitment, maritime services are not bound.[52] In fact, the US submitted MFN Exemptions on maritime services to the WTO and stated the intended duration is to be indefinite. Thirdly, unlike the attitude of the USA, some shipping powers—the EU (representing Greece, Germany and others) and Japan, who decided not to submit any commitments between 1986 to 1996 because of the absence of a commitment from the USA,[53] have changed their points of view and submitted their GATS Commitment on maritime services.

More importantly, in terms of MFN Exemptions, this current author found that the EU, China and Singapore have chosen to utilise this exemption to allow themselves certain flexibility in RTAs and bilateral agreements. Surprisingly, Japan has not sought to use this exemption which means that the Japanese commitments on maritime transport services are consistent with MFN obligations and largely open its domestic market to foreign services and providers without requesting a Member country's also do the same under reciprocity principle—an approach used usually for trade in services.[54] This is possible because Japanese shipping service is highly competitive in the global market, at least in Pillar One.

5.1 The WTO and GATS: Service Schedules on Maritime Transport

In detail, maritime transport services have been further liberalised under the GATS, because of a significant expansion of WTO membership and globalisation. Many

---

[50]WTO and World Bank (2016), http://i-tip.wto.org/services/Services_RTAs_covered.pdf.

[51]Zhao (2019), http://i-tip.wto.org/services/SearchResultRTA.aspx.

[52]I-Tip database on GATS (2019).

[53]Zhao (2015).

[54]See Sect. 6.1.

restrictive maritime policies have disappeared or ceased to work. Up to date, many countries have made GATS Specific Commitment, and there have been 62 such GATS Schedules dealing with maritime transport.[55]

It is worth noting that, after 2000, further liberalisation of maritime transport mainly benefited from the WTO accession process. When new WTO members joined the WTO, many of them made GATS commitments covering maritime transport services. Since 2000, many important trading countries and blocks have joined the WTO as new members, such as China and many south-east Asian countries. For instance, all ASEAN member countries joined the WTO and made GATS commitments on maritime transport. Active participation of these new WTO members has further brought about liberalisation to maritime sectors. It is noted by the current author that these 'new' members have included sectoral commitments regarding maritime transport along with their accessions to the WTO.

5.2 WTO-Plus Liberalisation of Maritime Transport Through RTAs

The plurilateral approach is not new and should not be ruled out as a legitimate and effective approach to deepening commitments within a group of countries instead of all WTO members. The plurilateral trade agreements through RTAs can soften the rigidness of the WTO's multilateral approach and can help to overcome the defects of the GATS.[56]

Furthermore, the WTO itself commenced plurilateral negotiations in 2006.[57] Annex C of the Doha Work Programme states: "In addition to bilateral negotiations, [WTO members] agree that the request-offer negotiations should also be pursued on a plurilateral basis".[58] The wording of the plurilateral approach shifts the negotiations from a legally binding, mandatory mandate of the bilateral negotiations to act in favour of greater flexibility.[59] Similar with RTAs, some of the plurilateral negotiations under the WTO framework were sector-focused, with members acting in so-called 'friends' groups',[60] which are informal, sectoral or modal groups of like-minded members. Friends' groups allow members to benefit from an intense and close working relationship in relation to a particular sector or a mode of service. In 2006, there were approximately 14 friends' groups.[61]

---

[55]I-Tip database on GATS (2019).

[56]See Sect. 4.5.

[57]WTO (2005), Doc.WT/MIN(05)/DEC, page C-3, paragraph 9. Türk (2008), pp. 150–162.

[58]WTO (2005), Doc.WT/MIN(05)/DEC, Annex C, page C-3, paras. 7, 11.

[59]Türk (2008), pp. 151–153, 155.

[60]"Friends' groups" focus on specific sectors, such as air transport, maritime transport, but are not strictly plurilateral negotiating groups. Türk (2008), pp. 148, 159–161, 163.

[61]Türk (2008), pp. 148, 159–160.

It has been found that RTAs and the plurilateral approach considerably reduce the need to negotiate at the member-to-member level, and also help to avoid the free-rider problem associated with the WTO and GATS.[62] In addition, the plurilateral approach has already been used for negotiations in relation to the maritime transport sector, as well as in relation to air transport and logistics.[63] Thus, future maritime-related negotiations may continue using the plurilateral approach, including friends' groups.

Moreover, maritime transport is a global business, and its shipping routes include global, international, regional and local networks. Not all networks need to be addressed internationally or globally. Namely, regional and local networks of the shipping sector are effectively governed by RTAs rather than by the WTO framework. The RTAs could function as 'WTO-plus' agreements that complement the WTO and provide rules in areas in which the WTO could not reach.

5.3 First Pillar of Maritime Transport: International Shipping and Cabotage (Coastal Shipping) Under GATS and RTAs

Since the time of GATS negotiations, international shipping has been regarded as the first pillar of maritime transport services. This subsector of international maritime transport has been highly liberalised in commitments under both the GATS and RTAs. This section examines the current commitments on this subsector of shipping being made under the GATS and RTAs. Compared to international shipping, coastal shipping (i.e. cabotage transport) has been usually reversed for a country's own nationals since the 1890s, so this section also explains updates on this area of maritime transport.

5.3.1 Freight Transport and Passenger Transport

International maritime transport consists of freight and passenger shipping, but they are treated differently with regard to liberalisation. Freight transport (cargo shipping) is highly liberalised and bound. In contrast, the attitudes on the liberalisation of passengers' transport vary among countries. Still, international maritime transport of passengers is frequently excluded from a country's commitments. For instance, China includes both cargo and passenger shipping in its GATS schedule; which means that China liberalised both cargo and passenger shipping; in contrast, Japan

---

[62]Türk (2008), pp. 158–159.
[63]Türk (2008), p. 163.

chose to exclude passenger transport from its GATS schedule, which means the Japanese passenger maritime transport services are not liberalised.[64]

With regard to freight and passenger transport, salvage (which means to save goods or passengers from a ship that has sunk or been damaged or a building that has been damaged) is sometimes mentioned in commitments under the GATS and/or any RTAs. Because ship accidents are associated with freight transport and passenger shipping, a country usually stipulates whether salvage is included in its commitments under the GATS or RTAs. Currently, the author found that salvage is usually excluded from the liberalisation commitments under the GATS and RTAs by a country.

Furthermore, it is time to take a close look at some influential RTAs. One of the RTAs which deserves attention is the North American Free Trade Agreement (NAFTA).[65] It includes commitments on transport, and in its sector-specific reservations, but 'fisheries, maritime matters (including salvage)' are excluded from being bound by the MFN and NT obligations. It is noted that NAFTA does not use the terminologies or classifications of transport services which are widely used.

Turning to another important trading bloc the EU. This current author found that the EU has not entered any RTAs on maritime transport, at least not in the RTAs covered by I-TIP Databases.[66] In addition, this author checked the EU's GATS Schedule, in which the EU only states that the 'rental services with operators and with crew (CPC 7213, 7223)' are unbound and chartering of all ships is subject to notification.

5.3.2 Cabotage Transport Service and the Impact of US Harter Act of 1893 on Today's Shipping

Open registry (flagging out) has been a widely adopted practice in the shipping industry which cut the management cost.[67] One case in which flagging out can lead to market restrictions is in the area of cabotage.

Cabotage, or coastal trade, refers to the trade or navigation in coastal waters between two points within a country. Cabotage also refers to the right to engage in trade and navigation in coastal waters and to the restriction of that right to domestic carriers. The term in essence denotes the discriminatory practice of keeping foreign flags out of coastal waters and thus often constitutes an element of a government's maritime policy as a category of flag preference. The idea behind cabotage restrictions is to promote the development of national merchant fleets.[68]

---

[64]WTO and World Bank (no date), I-Tip database.

[65]USTR (no date), NAFTA, https://ustr.gov/trade-agreements/free-trade-agreements/north-ameri can-free-trade-agreement-nafta.

[66]I-Tip database on RTAs (2019).

[67]Mukherjee et al. (2013).

[68]Petrovena (1998), pp. 1039–1040.

Cabotage restrictive service dates back to the US Harter Act of 1893[69] which is still effective today. It should be noted that this Act is an example of restrictive legislation on shipping liberalisation and still being used by the USA even today. The US Harter Act was enacted in 1893 governing all sea carriage to and from the US.[70] It should be noted that by the late nineteenth century, the rise of the USA as a power equal to Europe increased the influence of US domestic law in international shipping, and this Act was introduced to protect its national shipping interests, requiring that coastal shipping must be carried out by vessels flying the US flag with US crews.

The US Harter Act had a long-lasting impact on shipping and is well known for its restrictive arrangement on cabotage.[71] Although this Act was partially superseded by the US Carriage of Goods by Sea Act of 1936, it is still effective. This aggressive[72] legislation has been followed by several countries through unilaterally enacting domestic Harter-style legislation, such as India. The Harter-style legislation generally excludes cabotage from sea transport negotiations under both the GATS and RTAs.[73] Even today, many countries are very conservative on transportation within their territories, reserving cabotage for their own national vessels and crew.

Moreover, cabotage is usually excluded from a country's commitments under many RTAs. For example, cabotage is excluded from being liberalised under Japan's GATS schedule, Japan-Austria RTA, and ASEAN-China RTA.[74]

However, an eye-catching change is that cabotage service has been gradually further liberalised than it was in the past. Under an important recent RTA between the EU and Canada, the Comprehensive Economic and Trade Agreement (CETA), European firms will have more opportunities to provide services, including specialised maritime services, for instance, dredging, moving empty containers, and shipping certain cargo within Canada.[75] This RTA arrangement between the EU and Canada on cabotage is unprecedented for cabotage service which foreigners have been excluded from running this service since the US Harter Act of 1893 until nowadays.

---

[69]United States, the Harter Act 1893, 27 Stat. 445 (1983). The Harter Act is currently codified at 46 U.S.C. app. §§ 190–196 (1998).

[70]See also Sturley (1991), pp. 11–14.

[71]Sweeney (1993), p. 1.

[72]See Sturley (1991), p. 4.

[73]E.g. WTO (1995), Doc.S/NGMTS/W/2/Add.8, p. 3. WTO (1995), Doc.S/NGMTS/W/2/Add.4, p. 8. WTO (1995), Doc.S/NGMTS/W/2/Add.21, p. 3. WTO (1995), Doc. S/NGMTS/W/2/Add.12, pp. 37–43. WTO (1995), Doc.S/NGMTS/W/2/Add.15, p. 4. WTO (1995), Doc.S/NGMTS/W/2/Add.22, p. 2. WTO (1995), Doc.S/NGMTS/W/2/Add.24, p. 6. WTO (1995), Doc.S/NGMTS/W/2/Add.23, p. 5. WTO & NGMTS (1995), Doc.S/NGMTS/W/2/Add.11, pp. 3–4. WTO & NGMTS (1995), Doc.S/NGMTS/W/2/Add.19, p. 4.

[74]I-Tip database on GATS and RTAs (2019).

[75]European Commission (no date), https://ec.europa.eu/trade/policy/in-focus/ceta/index_en.htm.

5.4 Second Pillar of Maritime Transport: Maritime Auxiliary Services Under GATS and RTAs

There are no clear definitions on this subsector of maritime transport services. However, there seems to be a coherent understanding among countries, because a list of maritime services, such as the exemplary list provided below, is commonly used by many countries in their service commitments. This current author found that commitments in maritime auxiliary services which have been stated in a large number of countries in their GATS and RTAs commitments look more or less the same.

There are usually nine kinds of maritime transport services are regarded as the Second Pillar—'maritime auxiliary services', comprising:

- Pilotage
- Towing and tug assistance
- Provisioning, fuelling and watering
- Garbage collecting and ballast waste disposal
- Port Captain's services
- Navigation aids
- Shore-based operational services essential to ship operations, including communications, water and electrical supplies
- Emergency repair facilities
- Anchorage, berth and berthing services.

These nine kinds of maritime auxiliary services listed above are largely liberalised nowadays. The commitments on their liberalisation can be found in the GATS Commitments made by many influential trade and shipping countries, for instance, China, Japan and Singapore.[76]

Attitudes towards the liberalisation of pilotage services vary among countries under the RATs and the GATS. In shipping practice, pilotage is usually an optional service for vessels calling at a port, but sometimes this service is compulsory for foreign-flagged vessels. Therefore, the extent of liberalisation pilotage service varies among countries. This statement is still true, reaffirmed by searching GATS and RATS databases on pilotage services.

5.5 Third Pillar of Maritime Transport Under GATS and RTAs: Access to and Use of Port Facilities

Regarding 'maritime auxiliary services' (Pillar 2) and 'access to and use of port facilities' (Pillar 3), the recent GATS and RTAs Commitments usually address these

---

[76]I-Tip database on GATS (2019).

two pillars together, just as the means in the previous GATS negotiation documents. This is probably because the two categories of sub-sectors are interchangeable and mingled together in the commercial and shipping reality. Unlike other subsectors, the commitments concerning the third pillar stress 'the services at port are made available to international maritime transport suppliers on reasonable and non-discriminatory terms and conditions".[77] For instance, China, Japan and Singapore have committed themselves in maritime transport services, covering Pillar 3, but the EU chose not to bound.[78]

5.6   Fourth Pillar of Maritime Transport Under GATS and RTAs: Multimodal Transport Services and Land-Based Facility and Services Sectors

Since the Uruguay Round negotiations on the GATS date back to the 1980s–1990s, multimodal transport has been addressed during the negotiations of maritime transport and was regarded as its 'fourth pillar'.[79] Progress has been achieved on two domains on the basic points. Firstly, a majority of participants recognised the need to increase transparency on various domestic shipping regulations and the value of legal certainty.[80] Secondly, the importance of multimodal transport turned out to be further highlighted at the WTO.[81] In late October 1995, the US delegation stressed the inclusion of the door-to-door supply of transport services within the GATS framework in its informal statement on multimodal transport.[82]

It is necessary to address the four pillar of maritime transport services, but the joint negotiations, together with the other three pillars of maritime transport, would make the negotiations more perplexing. Take one key element in multimodal transport—inland transport by truck and its liberalisation—as an example to illustration the complexity which would trigger; members impose various domestic instruments of the inland part of transport, which make the harmonisation of multimodal transport very difficult.[83] Owing to the absence of joint negotiations on air, sea and inland transports in the negotiations at Uruguay Round and later

---

[77]China's GATS Commitment; Japan's GATS Commitment.

[78]I-Tip database on GATS and RTAs (2019).

[79]Parameswaran (2010).

[80]These issues were initiated by a circulated EC Model Schedule, which was informally circulated among delegations shortly before the conclusion of the Uruguay Round among the participants. See WTO (1995), doc.S/NGMTS/W/2, p. 7. WTO (1996c), doc.S/L/27, p. 1, para 5.

[81]Cf. the Rotterdam Rules.

[82]OECD & WTO (1996), Doc.DSTI/SI/MTC(96)8, pp. 3–4. See also Parameswaran (2010), pp. 343–346.

[83]E.g. WTO (1995), Doc.S/NGMTS/W/2/.

NGMTS (Negotiating Group on Maritime Transport Services),[84] international multimodal transport arrangements should not be negotiated until agreements have been achieved regarding sea leg of multimodal transport, as well as cabotage[85] and inland waterways.

Since the huge economic interest and a large number of players involved in multimodal and door-to-door transport, shore-based services are ardently guarded by various interest groups and countries. Hence, land-related services are more contentious areas than the other three pillars, in the GATS and RTAs negotiations. That is to say, the fourth pillar is important but also the most difficult area as for future negotiations and further liberalisation.

6 Potential Roles for Both the GATS and RTAs in the Future Liberalisation of Maritime Transport: Legal and Economic Analyses

6.1 Multilateralism vs Reciprocity: Both Approaches Are Needed for Shipping

Traditionally, countries adopt the reciprocity approach to liberalising this sector instead of the multilateral approach that is employed under the GATS. Though the shipping sector has been highly liberalised,[86] when a country seeks to gain access to another country's services markets, they both open up the domestic markets to each other in a reciprocal way. Simply speaking, reciprocity means that when your 'backyard' is open to aliens, their home country's backyard is open to you; and this approach is adopted by RTAs.

As seen from the existing services trade agreements which govern the maritime transport sector, the reciprocity can be achieved through RTAs (or equivalents). More specifically, there are three means:

- Bilateral agreements, such as Pakistan-China RTA, China-Singapore RTA, US-Australia RTA, Chile-Japan RTA, India-Japan RTA, India-Singapore RTA
- Regional trade agreements. This is probably because the commonality shared among the countries in the same geographical region, e.g. ASEAN Service Trade Agreement, and NAFTA
- A group of countries which bears commonality, for instance, geographical proximity (e.g. ASEAN-China), or similar level of economic development between two countries with some distance (e.g. EFTA-Hong Kong RTA).

---

[84]Uruguay Round (1991), Doc.MTN.GNS/W/60.

[85]WTO (1995). Doc.S/NGMTS/W/2/.

[86]See Sect. 4.2.

However, the reciprocity is difficult to be achieved through multilateral approaches due to the 'free-rider problem'.[87] Because the GATS uses positive approach and national treatment is a specific obligation, not all countries choose to make commitments on maritime transport. Suppose if a country includes the sector in its schedule, MFN as a general obligation will require the country to open up its maritime transport sector to some members which have also opened up this sector, and to other members which have not committed to open their domestic markets. Namely, for the latter group of countries, they are 'free riders' of the liberalisation process, but their backyard is still closed to others. Thus, reciprocity is frustrated under these circumstances, and the free-rider effect discouraged many members to include the shipping sector and maritime transport services into their GATS schedules. Until today, out of 164 WTO members, there have only been 62 sectoral commitments in maritime transport; that is to say, the majority of countries, including the USA, have not made commitments on maritime transport services yet.[88] For instance, China, the EU (Greece and Germany included), Malta, Norway, Panama and Japan have made GATS commitments on maritime transport.[89] However, the USA while always taking part in relevant negotiations, has not made any commitments which are legally binding on the shipping sector.[90]

6.2 The Necessity of the WTO Regarding Shipping

6.2.1 Polycentric Governance: Multi-Forums of Shipping Related Negotiations and the Necessity of Coordination Among the Forums by the WTO

There have been approximately 30 inter-governmental organisations governing shipping, many of which are the UN agencies. There are a number of UN specialised agencies handling shipping issues.[91] The United Nations Conference on Trade and Development (UNCTAD),[92] the Organization for Economic Co-operation and Development (OECD),[93] and the United Nations Economic and Social Council (ECOSOC)[94] have published statistical data on the shipping industry for years. Moreover, the International Labour Organization (ILO), the United Nations

---

[87]See Sect. 4.5.

[88]See Sect. 5 for details.

[89]I-Tip database.

[90]Zhao (2015).

[91]These entities have different legal basis, governance structures, funding, mandates and scopes.

[92]UNCTAD, http://unctad.org/en/Pages/Home.aspx.

[93]OECD, http://www.oecd.org/home/0,2987,en_2649_201185_1_1_1_1_1,00.html. China is not an OECD country.

[94]United States Economic and Social Council (ECOSOC), http://www.un.org/en/ecosoc/.

Commission on International Trade Law (UNCITRAL),[95] and the International Maritime Organization (IMO)[96] deal with various aspects of shipping, *e.g.* seamen, the international sea cargo regime, and international sale of goods. Considering the multi-forum maritime transport, it is worthwhile to boost further cooperation.

The current author argues that the WTO possesses advantages over other forums on reinforcing the liberalisation for the shipping sector in the global scale,[97] because: firstly, the WTO is an international organization with 164 members and shipping is the most internationalised industry; secondly, as explained in Sect. 4.1, both the WTO and shipping demonstrate a dual nature that connects both trade in goods and trade in services.

6.2.2 Open Registry: A Popular Shipping Practice Contradicted with Cabotage Transport

The WTO needs to strike a balance between cabotage restrictiveness and flagging out through open registry. This is a problem unique to the shipping industry, but not for other service sectors. To fly a flag the same as the shipowner or to flag out in an open registry country is a key question.

This is because the nationality of vessels affects their rights to access port services and facilities and inland logistics network. Under maritime law and in practice, the expressions "nationality", "flag" and "registration" are usually used interchangeably.[98] The nationality of a vessel depends on its registration which is a key element of a particular ship operation because there are certain fiscal and other advantages or disadvantages attached to the registration regime and corresponding legal standards on safety and security on the operation of a ship. That is to say, nationality and registration of ships affect the provision of maritime transport service and the standards on the service quality.

Furthermore, open registry (illustrated in the Table in Appendix 2) is a kind of regulatory competition between flag states, eroding safety standards and creating harmful deregulations which allow shipowners to avoid high-safety standard in one country through flagging out in an open registry. The US shipowners pioneered the open-registry system in the 1930s and after the Second World War, so the harsh commercial climate led many shipowners from many traditional maritime states (usually high-cost countries for the ship operators/owners) and others to seek to operate under foreign flags which give them possibilities of operating at lower costs.[99]

---

[95]UNCITRAL, http://www.uncitral.org/uncitral/en/index.html.

[96]International Maritime Organization (IMO), http://www.imo.org/Pages/home.aspx.

[97]Zhao (2015).

[98]Mukherjee et al. (2013), p. 199.

[99]Mukherjee et al. (2013).

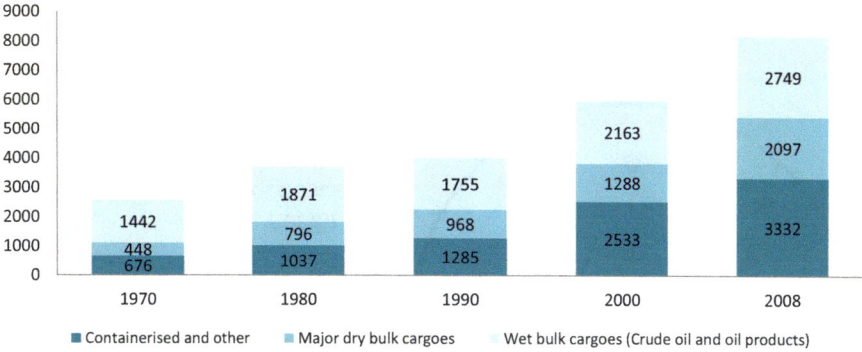

Fig. 2 International seaborne trade for selected decades (tonnes and percentage of tonnage) [see data and chart of 2008 in Hoffmann and Kumar (2010), p. 39. Source: Hoffmann and Kumar, based on data from the UNCTAD (2009). See data and charts of 2008 in Hoffmann and Kumar (2010)]. Figure is drawn up by the author [Source: UNCTAD (2018)]

Open registry sometimes undermines the quality of maritime transport services. In practice, open registry has created the phenomenon of 'bigger ships and smaller crews' which led to many shipping grounding accidents and disasters. The GATS allows regulation and international standards and this problem unique to shipping services influence the whole world need to address by the WTO multilateral framework, and particularly by the GATS.

6.2.3   Containerisation and Increasing Multimodal Transport and Door-to-Door Transport

Nowadays, multimodal transport has become increasingly significant due to the wide use of door-to-door transport and e-commerce (see Fig. 2). Containerisation significantly boosted the further development of liner carriers.[100] According to UNCTAD (see Fig. 2), goods have been increasingly carried within containers since the 1970s.[101] The increasing tendency in maritime trade boosts the multimodal transport. Accordingly, the fourth pillar of maritime transport—multimodal transport—becomes more important for the liberalisation of the entire shipping industry.

However, when searching the concluded negotiating outcomes on the liberalisation of multimodal transport, this author has not found any commitments concerning multimodal and door-to-door transport under the GATS and RTAs. As mentioned in Sect. 5.6, the multimodal transport is a tough issue, because of its connectivity with inland transport legs which occurs purely within a country's territory—which the country has exclusive authority to regulate its domestic waterways, cabotage transport and coastal territory seas. That is to say, multimodal

---

[100]Levinson (2010), pp. 1, 15, 58.

[101]Harlaftis and Theotokas (2015), pp. 8–12.

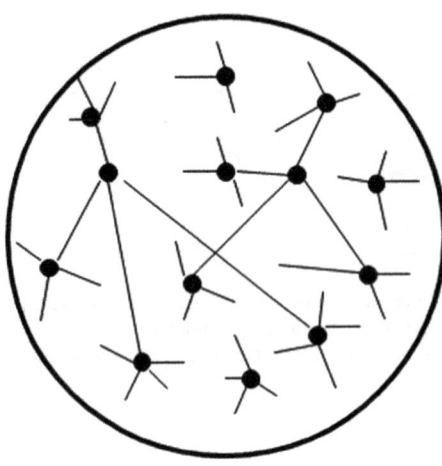

Globalised Liner Market (1970 -)

• Containerisation in the liner sector: contained cargoes (%) increased; break bulk cargoes (%) decreased

• Liner conferences lost anti-trust immunities

• Liner consortia evolved through two methods of cooperation: alliances and transnational megamergers

• Two levels of markets: international networks and regional networks

Fig. 3 Shipping—a network industry involving global, regional and local networks. Figure drawn up by the current author [Source: Zhao (2016)]

transport (with a sea leg), as a subsector of maritime transport services, is the most difficult area in the current and future liberalisation of maritime transport, even compared with cabotage transport—a less restrictive area.

The future maritime transport sector needs to address the connectivity with other modes of transport on land beyond ports areas. This is a common task facing all countries and regions around the world. As a result, the WTO which has a wide membership is justified to work on this area and coordinates with other co-existing international bodies governing shipping.

6.3   Shipping: A Network Industry Needs Both the WTO and RTAs

Shipping is a network industry, connecting two ports around the globe. The networks which shipping creates could be international, regional, or just local. As shown in Fig. 3, in practice, some shipping service connects two ports internationally, and some shipping just serves local or regional feeder ports.

At the loading and unloading ports, as well as *en route* ports, ships require extensive shore-based support for cargo storage and handling. As stated by Gilmore and Black:[102]

> Ships require a vast and bewilderingly various amount of supply and repair. An outgoing ship will normally have taken on some stores and fuel for her voyage at the port of lading. She will have run up a wharfage bill, and incurred various port fees. She will have been loaded by stevedores. She will probably be taken out by a pilot, and assisted at the start of her voyage by tugs. From time to time she will have to be repainted and repaired. A host of special callings and industries has arisen to furnish these and a hundred other supplies and services.

The WTO and RTAs meet the need of the liberalisation of maritime transport under different circumstances. On the one hand, when the shipping network is globalised and international, the WTO which bears a wide global memberships can facilitate the negotiations of this kind of maritime and logistical services. On the other hand, when the shipping network is bilateral among two regions/countries or just local, it is appropriate that RTAs which are negotiated among relevant countries and/or regions to handle the negotiations and further liberalisation of relevant maritime and even multimodal transport services.

7   Concluding Remarks and Proposals for Future Liberalisation of Maritime Transport Services

Maritime transport is a globalised business with a dual nature that joins trade in goods and trade in maritime transport services into one transaction. This dual nature is mirrored by the structure of WTO. Compared with other organisations that handle maritime transport matters, the WTO multilateral trading system is broader in its scope and membership,[103] more precise in its application, and more binding in its effect. These are the features that the global shipping routes and corresponding maritime transport requires. The WTO would, therefore, excel as a negotiation and implementation forum for promoting the future liberalisation of maritime transport services.

Nevertheless, the future liberalisation in the maritime transport sector relies on both the WTO and RTAs (including PTAs). Shipping is one of the most internationalised and liberalised industries in the world, but negotiations on the maritime transport services turned out to be extremely frustrating. Arguably, the difficulties in enhancing existing liberalisation in this sector largely are created by the existing multilateral liberalisation efforts themselves. Many lessons are extracted from the input of the effects to the multilateral negotiations from 1986 till today. From the legal and historical perspectives, the relationship between the WTO and

---

[102]Gilmore and Black (1975), p. 16.

[103]E.g. GATT, TRIPS Agreement, GATS, and the DSU.

maritime transport can be traced back to GATS and related maritime transport service negotiations. From an economic point of view, today's trade relies on shipping to carry the goods around the world, since the trade is globalised, shipping also needs such a global multilateral framework.

At the same time, shipping also needs regional and bilateral fora in which members share a high degree of commonality. For instance, ASEAN countries form a regional bloc for their culture, economies and transport networks. Since transport is a network industry, relaying port and some logistical infrastructure (e.g. road, railway, and inland waterway connected with seaports), regional transport services only need to be liberalised among the involved countries within this region (e.g. NAFTA, ASEAN, and the EU, China-Korea RTA, EU-Canada RTA). As shown in the economic analysis,[104] the shipping industry consists of both global and regional networks. A feeder port works as a connector between hub ports and local regions. RTAs among the countries sharing commonality can better facilitate the negotiations and liberalisation of maritime transport, and remove legal obstacles in the future liberalisation of multimodal transport.[105]

Moreover, because of the polycentric governance of today's maritime services, there are over 30 international bodies and agencies governing the shipping industry. That is why the current author claims that there are "too many cooks". However, the WTO and RTAs play different roles in the future liberalisation of maritime transport services. It is necessary to involve the WTO to coordinate the existing bodies governing shipping, especially matters which have global and international impact, such as open registry and cabotage,[106] and containerisation and door-to-door transport, etc. Meanwhile, regarding regional and bilateral transport logistical networks, RTAs among relevant countries and regions can deal with maritime transport and relevant service sectors. Therefore, both the WTO and RTAs are two indispensable 'cooks' who can complement their others' tasks in the field of shipping.

As the Bible says "Render to Caesar the things that are Caesar's; and to God the things that are God's", the shipping industry is a network industry, so it needs both the WTO and RTAs which involve global and regional/bilateral/local members. Therefore, it is justified that the WTO handles maritime transport services which involve countries around the world, and the RTAs deal with these maritime transport with regional or bilateral characterises and share a high degree of commonality (in culture, geographical features and other aspects).

---

[104]See Sects. 6.2–6.3.

[105]See Sect. 5.6.

[106]See Sects. 4 and 5.

Appendix 1: Services Sectoral Classification List Regarding Transport Services (Which Include Maritime Transport Services)

Sectors: Reports – Commitments – Member × Sector (GATS)

11. TRANSPORT SERVICES

    11.A Maritime Transport Services
    11.B Internal Waterways Transport
    11.C Air Transport Services
    11.D Space Transport
    11.E Rail Transport Services
    11.F Road Transport Services
    11.G Pipeline Transport
    11.H Services auxiliary to all modes of transport
    11.I Other Transport Services

HC   Horizontal Commitments

Source: the WTO

The above classifications was first used in 1991 during the preparatory negotiations for GATS. The existing Member countries' services Schedule of Commitment have utilised the above classifications, and up to date there have been 63 GATS Schedules of Commitments addressing maritime transport sector. Moreover, this classification has also been utilised by critical majority of RTAs and PTAs.

Appendix 2: Table on Open Registry (also Known as 'Flag of Convenience')

Open registry	The shipping company	The host country
Exemplars	• Shipowners who choose to flag out in open registry countries • Ship operators who runs bareboat chartered vessels and choose to flag out in open registry countries	• The first states to open their registers were those over which the US had considerable influence. Initially, they were few, the best known being Liberia, Panama and Honduras. • Today, world top 10 open registries are: Panama, Liberia, Marshall Islands, Hong Kong (China), the Bahamas, Singapore, Malta and Cyprus. Roughly 70 % of the world fleet are flagged with open registries.

(continued)

Open registry	The shipping company	The host country
Proponents	• Reduce tax liability • Lower registration fee • Lower crewing costs, because manning of ships by non-nationals is freely permitted and, thus a ship owner/operators can employ lower-cost (probably foreign) crews • Flexibility in certain aspects of the corporate structure (e.g. anonymity, through permitting greater use of bearer shares whereby the identity of the ultimate owner of the ship may be hidden)	• A new area of business activity for its national economy • A new, relatively modest, revenue source (e.g. registration fee and tax)
Opponents	• Decline in the need for crews from the states whose flags the ships had previously flown. • Lowered the shipping safety standards for the international community and the port state, because the shipowner/operator try to reduce the operation cost	• Bigger ships, smaller crew: a formula for disasters

Table complied by the current author. Source: Mukherjee et al. (2013), pp. 205–206

References

Degenhardt HW, Day AJ (1985) Maritime affairs – a world handbook: a reference guide to maritime organization, conventions and disputes and to the international politics of the sea. Gale Research Co., Detroit

Gilmore G, Black C (1975) The law of admiralty, 2nd edn. Foundation Press, New York

Harlaftis G, Theotokas J (2015) Chapter 1: Maritime business during the twentieth century: continuity and change. In: Grammenos C (ed) The handbook of maritime economics and business. Lloyds, London, pp 3–34

Hoffmann J, Kumar S (2010) Chapter 2: Globalisation – the maritime nexus. In: Grammenos C (ed) The handbook of maritime economics and business. Lloyds, London, pp 35–64

Levinson M (2010) The box: how the shipping container made the world smaller and the world economy bigger. Princeton University Press, Princeton

Mattoo A, Stern RM, Zanini G (2018) A handbook on international trade in service. Oxford University Press, Oxford

Mukherjee PK, Brownrigg M, Farthing B (2013) Farthing on international shipping. Springer, Heidelberg

Parameswaran B (2010) The liberalization of maritime transport services: with special reference to the WTO/GATS Framework. Springer, Heidelberg

Paulsen GW (1983) An historical overview of the development of uniformity in International Maritime Law. Tulane Law Rev 57(5):1065–1091

Petrovena R (1998) Cabotage and the European Community Common Maritime Policy – towards free provision of services in maritime transport. Fordham Int Law J 21(3):1019–1040

Schoenbaum T (2001) Admiralty and maritime law. West Publishing Company, College & School Division, Minnesota

Stopford M (2009) Maritime economics. London, p 49

Sturley MF (1991) The history of COGSA and the Hague Rules. J Maritime Law Commerce 22 (1):1–58

Sweeney J (1993) Happy birthday, Harter: a reappraisal of the Harter Act on its 100th anniversary. J Maritime Law Commerce 24(1):1–42

Türk E (2008) Services post-Hong Kong – initial experience with plurilaterals. In: Panizzon M, Pohl N, Sauvé P (eds) GATS and the regulation of international trade in services: World Trade Forum. Cambridge University Press, Cambridge, pp 145–171

UNCTAD (2009) Maritime Transport Review. Geneva

UNCTAD (2018) Merchant Fleet Ownership. http://stats.unctad.org/merchantfleet, http://stats.unctad.org/fleetownership

Zhao L (2014) Soft or hard law: effective implementation of uniform sea transport rules through the World Trade Organization framework. Int Organ Law Rev 11(1):172–227

Zhao L (2015) Transportation, cooperation, and harmonization: GATS as a gateway to integrating the UN's Seaborne Cargo Regimes into the WTO. Pace Int Law Rev 27(1):60–118

Zhao L (2016) The limited scope of seaborne cargo liability regime: new political–economic environments in the 21st century. Maritime Policy Manag 43(6):748–762

Zhao L (2019) Regional trade agreements covered commitment/reservation regarding services trade in maritime transport, Mendeley Data, v2. Original data collected from I-TIP Services Databases on RTAs. http://i-tip.wto.org/services/SearchResultRTA.aspx

Lijun Zhao is Senior Lecturer in Law at Middlesex University and Co-founding Director for the China-Europe Commercial Collaboration Association (cecca.org.uk). Before joining academia, Lijun worked as a Judge in P.R. China and later a consultant for several governmental law reform projects. Dr Zhao has expertise in International Business Law and International Law, and her research has been published widely in these areas of law, including International Trade, Commercial Law, Maritime and Transport Law, Comparative and Chinese Law. Many articles of hers have been published in international peer-reviewed journals. Some articles are archived by the UN Library and indexed in the UNCITRAL Bibliography on international trade and maritime law. Dr Zhao has held visiting posts at various institutions including Harvard Law School, the Max Planck Institute for Comparative and Private Law, Swansea University and Shanghai Maritime University. Currently, Lijun is conducting a research project in the support of Comité Maritime International (CMI).

Embracing Global Tax Reform in the General Agreement on Trade in Services?

Weiwei Zhang

Contents

1   Introduction

Panama launched a dispute at the World Trade Organization (WTO) in 2012 against Argentina concerning various measures that Argentina imposed on services and service suppliers from jurisdictions allegedly not cooperating with Argentina for tax

---

The views expressed in this paper are personal, and represent neither the views of Sidley Austin LLP nor its clients.

W. Zhang (✉)
Sidley Austin LLP, Geneva, Switzerland
e-mail: wzhang@sidley.com

© The Editor(s) (if applicable) and The Author(s), under exclusive licence to   249
Springer Nature Switzerland AG 2020
R. T. Hoffmann, M. Krajewski (eds.), *Coherence and Divergence in Services Trade
Law*, European Yearbook of International Economic Law,
https://doi.org/10.1007/978-3-030-46955-9_11

transparency purposes. An essential question of the dispute is whether Argentina can defend the distinct treatment based on the need to combat tax frauds.

The legal basis of that dispute is the WTO's General Agreement on Trade in Services (GATS). The GATS, concluded in 1994, is a multilateral framework of principles and rules governing all measures affecting trade in services. In fact, the negotiators of the GATS had envisaged some potential conflicts between the principle of non-discrimination underlying the GATS and taxation policies. For example, the GATS permits WTO Members to take certain discriminatory measures to ensure the effective imposition of direct taxes.[1] WTO Members are also free to conclude agreements amongst themselves to avoid double taxation.[2] However, the depth and breadth of the current global tax reform under the auspices of the Organization for Economic Co-operation and Development (OECD) and the Group of 20 (G20) to address base erosion and profit shifting (BEPS) goes beyond what could have been envisaged by the negotiators back in the early 1990s. The dispute between Panama and Argentina only touches upon one aspect of the reform to tackle BEPS in its early stage. As the BEPS Package develops, the intersections between international rules governing trade in services on the one hand, and the global tax reform on the other hand become more present and complicated.

This article identifies in a systematic manner the intersections of the two regimes. Section 2 inquires the genesis of the BEPS (Sect. 2.1) and the origin of its intersections with the GATS (Sect. 2.2). Section 3 examines whether the implementation of the BEPS Package by participating countries may cause trade concerns under the GATS—and if so, whether the policy space provided by the GATS is sufficient to accommodate the efforts to address the BEPS concerns. In doing so, it distinguishes three categories of measures relevant in implementing the BEPS Package—measures specifically recommended by the BEPS Package (Sect. 3.1); measures designed domestically, but under the guidance of the BEPS Package (Sect. 3.2); and measures countries may unilaterally adopt to counteract non-compliance or to induce compliance of BEPS Package recommendations by other countries (Sect. 3.3).

Finally, considering the overlap of the membership of the WTO and the OECD/G20 Inclusive Framework on BEPS, this article recommends that WTO Members take appropriate actions to avoid confusion when concurrently applying the rules under both regimes.

2 The BEPS and the GATS: An Introduction

2.1 The Genesis of the Current Global Tax Reform

A tax is a financial charge imposed upon a taxpayer (an individual or legal entity) by a state to fund various public expenditures. If we were living in a global village with

---

[1]Paragraph (d) Article XIV General Agreement on Trade in Services (GATS).
[2]Paragraph (e) Article XIV GATS.

one central government implementing homogenous taxation measures on everyone, there would be no need to have professionals specializing in tax planning. Nor would there be any need to conclude tax treaties. Yet we live in a heterogeneous world. Heterogeneity exists at two levels. First, at national level, all jurisdictions have different taxation policies to pursue different needs for revenue to fund government expenditures. Such needs vary depending on the terms of reference that the government has agreed with their respective constituents. For example, a government pursuing higher level of social welfare may reasonably be expected to require higher contributions from tax payers. At the same time, governments with the capacity to generate other revenues (e.g. from oil production) may need less tax contribution. Second, within each jurisdiction the distribution of the tax burden on individuals or classes of populations may not be equal. Some sectors may carry heavier tax burdens than the others, depending on how the government uses fiscal measures to encourage or discourage the development of certain economic sectors or certain groups of individuals. Since these heterogeneities arise from the fundamental differences in each government's financial needs and their terms of reference, countries often do not wish their taxation autonomy be lightly interfered at international level. For this reason, tax treaties or tax-related initiatives at inter-governmental level take these heterogeneities as a given parameter and do not interfere lightly. For example, the OECD states that their work on taxation "is not primarily about collecting taxes and is not intended to promote the harmonization of income taxes or tax structures generally within or outside the OECD, nor is it about dictating to any country what should be the appropriate level of tax rates".[3] Meanwhile, as private enterprises increasingly operate globally, countries do seek cooperation from the other jurisdictions on matters relating to taxation.

Multinational enterprises (MNEs) comprise companies or other entities established in more than one country.[4] Taxation of MNEs in different jurisdictions can have two problems. One is double taxation, generally defined as the imposition of comparable taxes in two (or more) States on the same taxpayer in respect of the same subject matter and for identical periods.[5] Double taxation became a concern, as it can impede cross-border flow of trade and investment. Since the 1920s, countries started signing bilateral tax agreements to mitigate the effect of double taxation and more importantly, to allocate tax revenue between the source and the residence country.[6] So far there are over 3000 tax treaties worldwide. Companies are profit-driven in nature and it is only natural that they plan their businesses with the international taxation regime in mind. This consideration leads to the second concern arising from MNEs exploiting the heterogeneities in taxation system in different jurisdictions or utilizing tax treaties to minimize tax base or shift their profits to low

---

[3]OECD (2000), *Towards Global Tax Co-operation: Report to the 2000 Ministerial Council Meeting and Recommendations by the Committee on Fiscal Affairs*, OECD Publishing.

[4]OECD (2011), *OECD Guidelines for Multinational Enterprises*, p. 17.

[5]OECD. (2015), Model Tax Convention on Income and on Capital 2014, OECD Publishing, p I-1.

[6]OECD. (2015), Model Tax Convention on Income and on Capital 2014, OECD Publishing, p I-1.

tax jurisdictions in which they have little or no economic activity at all. Tax planning by private economic operators is nothing new or *per se* unlawful. For a long time the debate on tax planning was mostly conducted by policy and academic experts in the field of international tax law. It became a hot topic when the recent financial crisis hit and governments struggled in dealing with decreasing revenue. Additionally, globalization and digitalization provided more opportunities for multinationals to engage in tax planning. According to the OECD, the annual revenue loss due to BEPS is conservatively estimated at US$100–240 billion.[7] For these reasons, in September 2013 G20 leaders endorsed the OECD-originated Action Plan on BEPS[8] and established the G20/OECD BEPS project.[9] In 2016, an OECD/G20 Inclusive Framework on BEPS was established to involve developing countries. As of August 2019 the Inclusive Framework has over 130 members and 14 observer organizations.[10]

BEPS refers to tax planning strategies that exploit the gaps and mismatches in tax rules to artificially shift profits to low or no-tax locations where they conduct little or no economic activities, resulting in little or no overall corporate tax being paid.[11] The BEPS Project aims to tackle the BEPS structures by "comprehensively addressing their root causes".[12] In particular, the 2013 OECD report found the following "root causes" of BEPS: domestic laws and regulations were not coordinated across the borders; international tax standards had not always kept pace with the changing global business environment; and there was a pervasive lack of relevant information at the level of tax administrations and policy makers.[13] In 2015 participating countries agreed a comprehensive BEPS Package consisting of reports on 15 actions to tackle the root causes of BEPS. As illustrated in Fig. 1, Actions 2–5 aim to address the first cause—the lack of coherence of domestic laws and regulations; Actions 6–10 focus on the second cause to make international tax standards up to date; and Actions 11–14 try to enhance transparency. Action 1 and 15 are horizontal issues. Action 1 addresses tax challenges raised by digitalisation, which the G20 agreed to develop a consensus-based solution by the end of 2020. Action 15 develops a multilateral legal instrument to facilitate the implementation of the tax treaty measures developed during the BEPS Project.

---

[7]OECD (2015), *Explanatory Statement*, OECD/G20 Base Erosion and Profit Shifting Project, OECD Publishing, para 2.

[8]OECD (2013), Action Plan on Base Erosion and Profit Shifting, OECD Publishing.

[9]G20 Leader's Declaration, September 2013, paras 50–52.

[10]OECD, Members of the OECD/G20 Inclusive Framework on BEPS (updated: August 2019), available at: https://www.oecd.org/tax/beps/inclusive-framework-on-beps-composition.pdf.

[11]OECD, "About Base Erosion and Profit Shifting (BEPS)". See http://www.oecd.org/ctp/beps-about.htm.

[12]OECD (2015), Explanatory Statement, OECD/G20 Base Erosion and Profit Shifting Project, OECD Publishing, para 6.

[13]OECD (2015), Explanatory Statement, OECD/G20 Base Erosion and Profit Shifting Project, OECD Publishing, para 5.

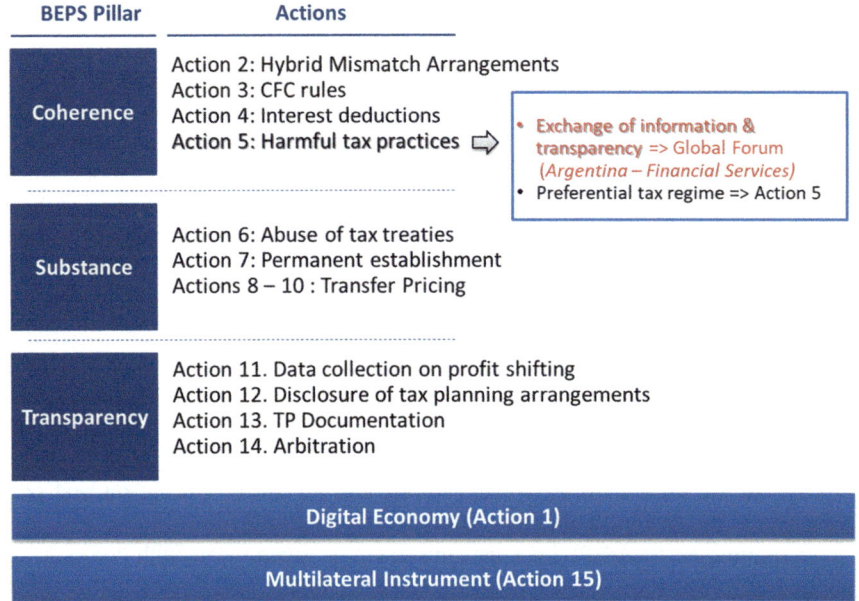

BEPS Pillar	Actions

Fig. 1 Overview of the BEPS Package

The issue touched upon by the WTO dispute *Argentina – Financial Services* relates to the need to exchange information and enhance transparency to fight against tax havens. This work, originally under Action 5, is now handled by the Global Forum on Transparency and Exchange of Information for Tax Purposes. The report on Action 5 now focuses on preferential tax regimes.[14] For this reason, *Argentina – Financial Services* only touched upon an issue in the global tax reform at its early stage. It only reveals a tip of the iceberg of the potential intersection of the two regimes.

Regarding specific recommendations, the BEPS Package provides solutions depending on the nature of the cause to BEPS.[15] First, minimum standards are developed to tackle issues in case where no action by some countries would create negative spill overs on other countries. Specifically, minimum standards are set for model provisions to prevent treaty abuse (Action 6), standardized country-by-

---

[14]OECD (2015), *Countering Harmful Tax Practices More Effectively, Taking into Account Transparency and Substance, Action 5 – 2015 Final Report*, OECD/G20 Base Erosion and Profit Shifting Project, OECD Publishing, p. 11. See also OECD (2017), *Harmful Tax Practices – 2017 Progress Report on Preferential Regimes: Inclusive Framework on BEPS: Action 5*, OECD/G20 Base Erosion and Profit Shifting Project, OECD Publishing, Paris; OECD (2019), *Harmful Tax Practices – 2018 Progress Report on Preferential Regimes: Inclusive Framework on BEPS: Action 5*, OECD/G20 Base Erosion and Profit Shifting Project, OECD Publishing, Paris.

[15]OECD (2015), *Explanatory Statement*, OECD/G20 Base Erosion and Profit Shifting Project, OECD Publishing.

country reporting to improve transparency (Action 13), a peer review process to address harmful tax practices (Action 5) and an agreement to secure effective dispute resolution (Action 14).[16] The implementation of the minimum standards is monitored by a peer review process, which evaluates the implementation by each member of each minimum standard and provides clear recommendations for improvement.[17]

Second, common approaches for domestic law measures are developed with a view to converging countries' different approaches over time and thus enabling consideration if such measures should become minimum standards. Common approaches are proposed for neutralising hybrid mismatches (Action 2) and limiting excessive interest deductions (Action 4). Although common approaches are not minimum standards, they have been adopted by many countries.[18]

Third, the BEPS Package revisits the existing international tax standards to eliminate double taxation, in order to stop abuses and close BEPS opportunities. This exercise relates to transfer pricing guidelines under Actions 8–10 and the changes recommended under Action 7 relating to permanent establishment status.[19]

Last but not least, the BEPS Package provides guidance drawing on best practices, *e.g.* in the design of effective controlled foreign company (CFC) rules.

To summarize, the BEPS Package aims to equip governments with domestic and international instruments to address tax avoidance and ensure that profits are taxed where economic activities generating the profits are performed and where value is created.

2.2 The Expanding Concept of Trade: The Origin of Intersections

In the context of trade in goods, WTO rules do not interfere lightly with domestic direct taxation, *i.e.*, a tax imposed on a person or company rather than on goods or services. The General Agreement on Tariffs and Trade (GATT) is concerned with domestic measures applied to products entering across borders.[20] In the market where domestic and foreign products compete, fiscal policies, including those

---

[16]For the implementation of the minimum standards, see OECD, *OECD/G20 Inclusive Framework on BEPS: Progress report July 2018 – May 2019*, pp. 8–19.

[17]OECD, Background Brief: Inclusive Framework on BEPS, January 2017, Section 3.2.

[18]OECD, *OECD/G20 Inclusive Framework on BEPS: Progress report July 2018 – May 2019*, Section 3.1.1.

[19]OECD, *OECD/G20 Inclusive Framework on BEPS: Progress report July 2018 – May 2019*, Sections 3.1.2 and 3.1.3.

[20]For example, Article III:8(b) carves out subsidies to domestic producers from the national treatment obligation. The concept of "border tax adjustment" is relevant in discussing the relation between the GATT and direct taxation, which has been addressed by existing literature. Since the focus of this paper is on the relation between the GATS and direct taxation, border tax adjustment will only be mentioned in passing.

relating to direct taxation, are only relevant if they were used to provide subsidies, thus falling under the ambit of the Agreement on Subsidies and Countervailing Measures (SCM).[21]

The concept of trade was expanded in the Uruguay Round of the multilateral trade negotiations to embrace trade in services. Since then the intersection of domestic direct taxation measures and trade disciplines became inevitable. Unlike trade in goods, the delivery of services often requires the presence of service suppliers. Thus, in addition to cross-border trade (mode 1), the GATS also covers three other modes of supply, namely consumption abroad (mode 2), commercial presence (mode 3) and the presence of natural persons (mode 4).[22] Under mode 3 and mode 4 service suppliers move across border. As countries mostly impose taxes on income from sources inside the country, service suppliers under mode 3 and mode 4 are often taxed in the services importing country, *i.e.* the country where they provide services. Thus, a direct tax imposed on service suppliers under mode 3 and 4 constitutes a measure "affecting trade in services" within the meaning of Article I:1 of the GATS.[23]

An underlying principle of the GATS is non-discrimination, as enshrined in Article II and XVII of the GATS. Specifically, Article II, titled "Most-Favoured-Nation (MFN) Treatment", prevents WTO Members from discriminating amongst foreign services and service suppliers. In other words, if a WTO Member accords favorable treatment to a service or service supplier from one country, it must accord "immediately and unconditionally" to services and service suppliers from all the other WTO Members "no less favorable" treatment. In a similar manner, Article XVII, titled "National Treatment", prevents WTO Members from discriminating between foreign and domestic services and service suppliers. While the MFN obligation under Article II applies to "any measures" affecting trade in services,[24] the national treatment obligation under Article XVII only applies to sectors in which the WTO Member has made specific commitments and subject to the conditions that the Member inscribed in its Schedule of Specific Commitments.

The negotiators of the GATS indeed considered the applicability of the GATS to tax measures.[25] As noted by a Secretariat note in 1993, Article II and Article XVII

---

[21]The concept of "subsidies" is narrowly defined under the SCM Agreement compared with the definition generally used by economists. Horizontally applied taxation policy could fall under the SCM Agreement under limited circumstances. For further discussion, see Daly (2005).

[22]Article I:2 GATS.

[23]As noted by a WTO Dispute Settlement panel, a direct income tax measure would generally be covered by the GATS. Otherwise, the Uruguay Round negotiators would not have deemed it necessary to create an explicit exception for such measures under Article XIV(d) of the GATS. See Panel Report, *US – FSC*, para 8.143; Appellate Body Report, *Argentina – Financial Services*, para 6.113.

[24]There are a few exceptions, including those singled out by the WTO Members in their lists of MFN exceptions upon entering into the WTO.

[25]See GATT document MTN.GNS/W/178, MTN.GNS/W/210, MTN.GNS/49.

are the most relevant provisions.[26] The note concluded at that time that "relatively few tax measures affecting service suppliers" would violate Article II and Article XVII, because "[m]ost tax measures providing distinct treatment to different categories of service supplier appear to deal with unlike service suppliers, to be based on objective considerations, or not in fact to provide less favourable conditions of competition."[27]

Nevertheless, to be on the safe side, the GATS negotiators crafted two tax-specific exceptions. Paragraph (d) of Article XIV permits WTO Members to adopt measures inconsistent with the national treatment obligation under Article XVII, provided that the difference in treatment is aimed at ensuring the equitable or effective imposition or collection of direct taxes in respect of services or service suppliers of other Members. A footnote to Article XVII provides for an illustrative list of measures that are "aimed at ensuring the equitable or effective imposition or collection of direct taxes".[28] However, this exception does not apply to the MFN obligations under Article II of the GATS.

The other exception is contained in paragraph (e) of Article XIV of the GATS. It exempts measures that accord different treatment as a result of an agreement on the avoidance of double taxation. However, this exception only applies to WTO Members' MFN obligation under Article II of the GATS.

Additionally, according to Article XXII:3 of the GATS, Members cannot resort to the dispute settlement mechanism provided by the Dispute Settlement Understanding (DSU) to make a claim under Article XVII (national treatment) of the GATS concerning measures within the scope of an international agreement "relating to the avoidance of double taxation".

These exceptions and carve-outs were considered sufficient in view of the domestic and international tax regime existing at that time. However, the current

---

[26]GATT document MTN.GNS/W/210, Note by the Secretariat, 'The Applicability of the GATS to Tax Measures', 1 December 1993. See, also, MTN.GNS/49.

[27]GATT document MTN.GNS/W/210, Note by the Secretariat, 'The Applicability of the GATS to Tax Measures', 1 December 1993, last paragraph.

[28]The GATS, footnote 6. "Measures that are aimed at ensuring the equitable or effective imposition or collection of direct taxes include measures taken by a Member under its taxation system which: (i) apply to non-resident service suppliers in recognition of the fact that the tax obligation of non-residents is determined with respect to taxable items sourced or located in the Member's territory; or (ii) apply to non-residents in order to ensure the imposition or collection of taxes in the Member's territory; or (iii) apply to non-residents or residents in order to prevent the avoidance or evasion of taxes, including compliance measures; or (iv) apply to consumers of services supplied in or from the territory of another Member in order to ensure the imposition or collection of taxes on such consumers derived from sources in the Member's territory; or (v) distinguish service suppliers subject to tax on worldwide taxable items from other service suppliers, in recognition of the difference in the nature of the tax base between them; or (vi) determine, allocate or apportion income, profit, gain, loss, deduction or credit of resident persons or branches, or between related persons or branches of the same person, in order to safeguard the Member's tax base. Tax terms or concepts in paragraph (d) of Article XIV and in this footnote are determined according to tax definitions and concepts, or equivalent or similar definitions and concepts, under the domestic law of the Member taking the measure."

BEPS Package represents the first substantial renovation of the international tax standards in almost a century. As further explained below, it calls for extensive amendments in domestic legislation and in international tax treaties to address BEPS concerns. New measures taken to implement the BEPS Package may go beyond the configuration of the "tax measures" considered in 1993. The premise upon which the conclusion was made that "relatively few tax measures affecting service suppliers would violate Article II and Article XVII" may no longer hold. For this reason, it is imperative to assess if the implementation of the BEPS Package would lead to new intersections of the GATS and the international tax regime.

3 Exploring the Intersections Between the GATS and the BEPS Package

3.1 Argentina – Financial Services: A Teaser

In *Argentina – Financial Services,* Argentina, in its various financial, taxation, foreign exchange, and registration measures, made distinction between "countries cooperating for tax transparency purposes" (cooperative countries) and "countries not cooperating for tax transparency purposes" (non-cooperative countries).[29] Panama's principle claim is that these measures are inconsistent with Article II:1 of the GATS because these measures accord less favourable treatment to services and service suppliers of non-cooperative countries than that accorded to like services and service suppliers of cooperative countries.[30]

The panel hearing that dispute found that for purposes of Panama's claims under Article II:1 of the GATS, services and service suppliers of cooperative countries are "like" the services and service suppliers of non-cooperative countries,[31] and Argentina failed to accord immediately and unconditionally, to services and service suppliers of non-cooperative countries treatment no less favourable than that which they accord to like services and service suppliers of cooperative countries.[32] For this reason, the panel decided that Argentina's measures are inconsistent with Article II:1 of the GATS.[33] The Panel also dismissed Argentina's defences under Article XIV: (c) and the Annex on Financial services.[34]

The Panel's decision was appealed. The starting point of the appeal is the panel's findings on "likeness", *i.e.* the services and service suppliers from cooperative

---

[29] Appellate Body Report, *Argentina – Financial Services,* para 1.1.

[30] Appellate Body Report, *Argentina – Financial Services,* para 1.2. Panama also challenged a few measures under Articles XVII and XVI of the GATS.

[31] Appellate Body Report, *Argentina – Financial Services,* Section 6.1.1.

[32] Appellate Body Report, *Argentina – Financial Services,* para 1.5.

[33] Appellate Body Report, *Argentina – Financial Services,* para 1.5.

[34] Appellate Body Report, *Argentina – Financial Services,* para 1.5.

countries and non-cooperative countries are like because the difference in treatment is due to origin.[35] The Appellate Body found the panel's presumption of "likeness" is problematic, because the panel failed to make a finding on whether the difference in treatment between cooperative and non-cooperative countries was based "exclusively" on origin.[36] According to the Appellate Body, "likeness" cannot be presumed if the measure providing for a distinction is not based "exclusively" on origin.[37] The Appellate Body opined that the concept of "likeness" of services and service suppliers is concerned with the competitive relationship of services and service suppliers.[38] However, the panel did not undertake an analysis of "likeness", considering various criteria relevant for an assessment of the competitive relationship of the services and service suppliers of cooperative and non-cooperative countries.[39] Thus, the Appellate Body reversed the panel's finding on "likeness".[40] Because the panel's finding on Article II of the GATS was based on the finding of "likeness", the Appellate Body also reversed the panel's finding of inconsistency under Article II of the GATS.[41]

It is interesting to note that the GATT Secretariat, back in 1993, considered a similar situation in which a list would be maintained either of "qualifying" or "excluded" countries. The Secretariat noted that "the maintenance of such a list would not in itself be inconsistent with Article II of the GATS as long as it is drawn up on the basis of objective criteria designed to safeguard the Member's tax base or counter tax evasion or avoidance and not on the basis of nationality distinctions".[42] To recall, the general exceptions under Article XIV(d) of the GATS only permits WTO Members to adopt Article XVII-inconsistent measures to safeguard the tax base. It does not apply to measures inconsistent with Article II of the GATS. The Secretariat note in 1993 indicates that this type of measures were not considered inconsistent with Article II. It proposed an objectiveness test. However, it did not specify whether the objectiveness of the measure should be considered in the assessment of "likeness" or under "treatment less favourable". Nor did it consider the competitive relationship between service and service suppliers. In light of the much more elaborated legal standard of the MFN and national treatment obligations under the GATT and the GATS since 1995,[43] the explanation offered in the 1993

---

[35] Appellate Body Report, *Argentina – Financial Services,* paras 6.2–6.8.

[36] Appellate Body Report, *Argentina – Financial Services,* para 6.60.

[37] Appellate Body Report, *Argentina – Financial Services,* para 6.61.

[38] Appellate Body Report, *Argentina – Financial Services,* para 6.25.

[39] Appellate Body Report, *Argentina – Financial Services,* para 6.61.

[40] Appellate Body Report, *Argentina – Financial Services,* para 6.70.

[41] Appellate Body Report, *Argentina – Financial Services,* para 6.71.

[42] GATT document MTN.GNS/49, p. 2.

[43] See, for example, the summary of "likeness" test in Appellate Body Report, *Argentina – Financial Services,* Section 6.1.4; the summary of "treatment no less favourable" in Appellate Body Report, *Argentina – Financial Services,* Section 6.2.4.

Secretariat note seems insufficient in providing guidance in applying Article II of the GATS to this type of measures.

The panel in this dispute was aware of the lack of an MFN-exception for measures to safeguard the tax base under Article XIV of the GATS. It tried to incorporate the consideration of the regulatory framework in which service suppliers operate in its assessment of the "treatment les favourable".[44] The Appellate Body dismissed this approach and insisted that the legal standard for "treatment less favourable" should remain as "whether the measure modifies the conditions of competition to the detriment of like services or service suppliers of any other Member".[45] This is because the GATS has provided many flexibilities for WTO Members to pursue policy objectives.[46] The Appellate Body pointed out that where a measure is inconsistent with the non-discrimination provisions, "regulatory aspects or concerns that could potentially justify a measure are more appropriately addressed in the context of the relevant exceptions".[47]

Since the Appellate body reversed the panel's finding under Article II of the GATS, it did not deal with the issue of the lack of an MFN exception for tax measures aimed at ensuring the equitable or effective imposition or collection of direct taxes. As explained below, many of the BEPS-related measures provide different treatment to services and service suppliers from different countries, just as the Argentine measures did. The next section will explore the implication of this case on the BEPS-related country-specific and other tax measures.

3.2   Applying GATS to the Measures Implementing the BEPS

As mentioned in Sect. 2.1, the BEPS Package consists of a basket of recommendations and guidelines. The WTO disciplines are only relevant if the rights and obligations of a Member are infringed by a measure of another Member. Thus, it is not the BEPS Package itself that can cause the intersection. Rather, it is the measures that the participating countries adopt to implement the recommendations and guidelines of the BEPS Package that may cause trade concerns. For the purpose of analysis, this paper categorizes measures that countries may take to implement the BEPS Package into three groups as follows:

- First, in areas such as harmful taxes and hybrid mismatches, the BEPS Package makes specific recommendations on measures or standards to be adopted by participating countries in their domestic legislation;

---

[44]Appellate Body Report, *Argentina – Financial Services,* para 6.110.

[45]Appellate Body Report, *Argentina – Financial Services,* para 6.111.

[46]Appellate Body Report, *Argentina – Financial Services,* paras 6.111–6.113.

[47]Appellate Body Report, *Argentina – Financial Services,* paras 6.115–6.118.

- Second, in areas such as treaty abuse, the BEPS Package only provides for guidance, leaving participating countries with discretion to design their own rules; and
- Third, participating countries may adopt unilateral measures to counteract non-compliance or to induce compliance, especially in areas where minimum standards have been agreed in the BEPS Package.

This section applies the GATS to these three groups of measures in turn to explore the potential intersections of the two regimes.

3.3 When Specific Recommendations Are Made by the BEPS Package

With regard to some BEPS concerns, such as harmful taxes and hybrid mismatches, the BEPS Package recommends specific instruments to be included in the participating countries' domestic law. Some are in the form of minimum standards, which participating countries have committed to implement in a consistent and prompt manner; others are in the form of common approaches or best practices. This part will go through some of these substantive recommendations to identify the potential overlap between the required amendment in domestic legislations and the GATS.

3.3.1 Measures to Tackle Harmful Taxes

A regime is considered potentially harmful if, among other things, it imposes no or low effective tax rates on income from geographically mobile financial and other service activities and is not transparent.[48] Since these regimes may unfairly erode the tax bases of other countries and may distort the location of capital and services, Action 5 of the BEPS Package aims to reduce the discretionary influence of taxation on the location of mobile financial and services activities.[49] The fact that a jurisdiction has a tax regime that offers preferential treatment for certain types of incomes is not considered problematic *per se* under the BEPS Package. What the BEPS Package requires is that such preferences not be granted to certain enterprises, *e.g.*

---

[48]See OECD (2015), *Countering Harmful Tax Practices More Effectively, Taking into Account Transparency and Substance, Action 5 – 2015 Final Report*, OECD/G20 Base Erosion and Profit Shifting Project, OECD Publishing, p. 20.

[49]OECD (2015), *Countering Harmful Tax Practices More Effectively, Taking into Account Transparency and Substance, Action 5 – 2015 Final Report*, OECD/G20 Base Erosion and Profit Shifting Project, OECD Publishing, p. 9.

enterprises that have not undertaken the qualifying income generating activities in its jurisdiction.[50]

Participating countries have agreed on standards to assess the harmfulness of the preferential regimes. For example, if a country has a preferential Intellectual Property (IP) regime, it must amend its existing legislation according to the agreed "nexus approach", which allows a taxpayer to benefit from the IP regime only if the taxpayer itself has incurred qualifying research and development (R&D) expenditures.[51] This can only happen if the taxpayer conduct R&D internally and source R&D-related services locally.[52] Indeed, as explained in the Report, such recommendation was made in line with the purpose of the IP regime, which is "to encourage R&D activities and to foster growth and employment".[53] Thus, the essence of the suggested amendment is to condition the availability of a tax advantage to the use of locally sourced R&D activities.

From the trade perspective, the requirement to use locally sourced services may cause concerns under Article XVII of the GATS. To assess claims under Article XVII of the GATS, one must establish that: (1) the relevant WTO Member has scheduled national treatment commitments under the services sector concerned; (2) that the measure in question affects the supply of services in the relevant sectors or modes of supply; and (3) that the measure does not accord to the services and

---

[50]For details, see OECD (2015), *Countering Harmful Tax Practices More Effectively, Taking into Account Transparency and Substance, Action 5 – 2015 Final Report*, OECD/G20 Base Erosion and Profit Shifting Project, OECD Publishing.

[51]OECD (2019), *Harmful Tax Practices – 2018 Progress Report on Preferential Regimes: Inclusive Framework on BEPS: Action 5*, OECD/G20 Base Erosion and Profit Shifting Project, OECD Publishing, Paris, p. 14. See also, OECD (2015), *Countering Harmful Tax Practices More Effectively, Taking into Account Transparency and Substance, Action 5 – 2015 Final Report*, OECD/G20 Base Erosion and Profit Shifting Project, OECD Publishing, p. 11. See also OECD (2017), *Harmful Tax Practices – 2017 Progress Report on Preferential Regimes: Inclusive Framework on BEPS: Action 5*, OECD/G20 Base Erosion and Profit Shifting Project, OECD Publishing, Paris.

[52]OECD (2019), *Harmful Tax Practices – 2018 Progress Report on Preferential Regimes: Inclusive Framework on BEPS: Action 5*, OECD/G20 Base Erosion and Profit Shifting Project, OECD Publishing, Paris, p. 14. "This ensures that the core income generating activities are undertaken, including with an adequate number of fulltime qualified employees and an adequate amount of operating expenditure, supported by a transparent mechanism to ensure compliance."

[53]See OECD, above OECD (2015), *Countering Harmful Tax Practices More Effectively, Taking into Account Transparency and Substance, Action 5 – 2015 Final Report*, OECD/G20 Base Erosion and Profit Shifting Project, OECD Publishing, p. 9. See also OECD (2019), *Harmful Tax Practices – 2018 Progress Report on Preferential Regimes: Inclusive Framework on BEPS: Action 5*, OECD/G20 Base Erosion and Profit Shifting Project, OECD Publishing, Paris, p. 14. "This ensures that the core income generating activities are undertaken, including with an adequate number of fulltime qualified employees and an adequate amount of operating expenditure, supported by a transparent mechanism to ensure compliance."

service suppliers of any other Member treatment no less favourable than that accorded to its own like services and service suppliers.[54]

Most WTO Members have made its specific commitments under the GATS following a GATT Secretariat document MTN.GNS/W/120 (also referred to as "W120" document). W120 lists R&D services as part of business services.[55] So far, 60 Members have made specific commitments under the R&D services.[56] Since the BEPS recommendation targets "geographically mobile activities",[57] it affects R&D services supplied through mode 1, *i.e.* cross-border supply of R&D services.

The next question is whether the measure may accord to the services and service suppliers of any other Member treatment no less favourable than that accorded to its own like services and service suppliers. In *Argentina – Financial Services*, the Appellate Body confirmed that in the context of trade in services "likeness" may be presumed if the measure at issue makes a distinction between services and service suppliers based exclusively on origin.[58] By applying the "nexus approach", countries may condition the availability of tax preferences to conducting the R&D services locally.[59] This requirement may be considered as making a distinction exclusively on origin. Accordingly, services and service suppliers locally recruited may be presumed "like" services and service suppliers provided through mode 1.[60]

As mentioned above, the Appellate Body reversed the Panel's approach to take into account "regulatory aspects" in the "less favourable treatment" analysis.[61] To condition the availability of low or zero tax upon the use of local R&D services and service suppliers may disadvantage foreign services and service suppliers because the companies which uses these R&D services may be incentivized to use local

---

[54]Panel Reports, *China – Electronic Payment Services*, para. 7.641; *China – Publications and Audiovisual Products*, para. 7.944; and *EC – Bananas III*, para. 7.314; *Argentina – Financial Services*, para. 7.448.

[55]WTO document, MTN.GNS/W/120, Section 1.C.

[56]See database on services schedules at: http://i-tip.wto.org/services/default.aspx.

[57]OECD (2019), *Harmful Tax Practices – 2018 Progress Report on Preferential Regimes: Inclusive Framework on BEPS: Action 5*, OECD/G20 Base Erosion and Profit Shifting Project, OECD Publishing, Paris, p. 14.

[58]Appellate Body Report, *Argentina – Financial Services*, para 6.52.

[59]OECD (2019), *Harmful Tax Practices – 2018 Progress Report on Preferential Regimes: Inclusive Framework on BEPS: Action 5*, OECD/G20 Base Erosion and Profit Shifting Project, OECD Publishing, Paris, p. 14. "This ensures that the core income generating activities are undertaken, including with an adequate number of fulltime qualified employees and an adequate amount of operating expenditure, supported by a transparent mechanism to ensure compliance."

[60]The company that conduct R&D services by themselves can still be characterized as a service supplier of "R&D services", even if the company involves in other businesses. In *EC – Bananas,* the Appellate Body clarified that even if a company is vertically integrated, and even if it performs other functions, to the extent that it is also engaged in providing the services at issue and is therefore affected in that capacity by a particular measure of a Member in its supply of those services, that company is a service supplier within the scope of the GATS. Appellate Body Report, *EC – Bananas*, para 227.

[61]Appellate Body Report, *Argentina – Financial Services*, para 6.111.

supply to obtain the benefit of the regime. This is a measure equivalent to a local content requirement in the context of trade in goods, which has been repeatedly found inconsistent with the national treatment obligations under the GATT 1994 or the Agreement on Trade-Related Investment Measures (TRIMS).[62]

If the measure is inconsistent with Article XVII of the GATS, the next question is if it can be justified under one of the exceptions under Article XIV of the GATS. Paragraph (d) of Article XIV GATS exempts measures "inconsistent with Article XVII, provided that the difference in treatment is aimed at ensuring the equitable or effective imposition or collection of direct taxes in respect of services or service suppliers of other Members". The term "difference in treatment" is not further defined. One might argue that such difference may only relate to the treatment of services and service suppliers directly subject to the taxation measure at issue and cannot be extended to different treatment to services and service suppliers, or goods suppliers not in direct competitive relationship with the services and service suppliers at issue. In the context of trade in goods, the Appellate Body opined that to qualify for the exemption from the national treatment obligation under Article III:8 (a) GATT 1994, the product of foreign origin allegedly being discriminated against must be in a competitive relationship with the product purchased.[63] In the context of the "nexus approach", the service suppliers of foreign origin being discriminated are R&D services and service suppliers in foreign countries. They may not be in a competitive relationship with the companies which uses the R&D services and benefit from the preference regime. Therefore, countries implementing the "nexus approach" may find it difficult to justify the measure under Article XIV (d) of the GATS.[64]

In the area of non-IP regimes, ongoing discussions concern the determination of what constitutes the core activities necessary to earn the income. These regimes relates to distribution and service center regimes, financing or leasing regimes, fund management regimes, banking and insurance regimes, shipping regimes, etc.[65] Given the intersection with the GATS identified for the IP regime, trade negotiators may want to engage more actively when new standards are being discussed in these areas under the BEPS project.

---

[62] See, for example, Appellate Body Report, *Canada – Renewable Energy* and Panel Report, *India – Solar Cells*.

[63] Appellate Body Report, *Canada – Renewable Energy*, para 5.79.

[64] Nevertheless, countries may comply with Article XVII of the GATS by not granting any tax preferences, or eliminating all the preferential IP regimes.

[65] See OECD (2015), *Countering Harmful Tax Practices More Effectively, Taking into Account Transparency and Substance, Action 5 – 2015 Final Report*, OECD/G20 Base Erosion and Profit Shifting Project, OECD Publishing, p. 38.

3.3.2   Measures to Neutralize the Effects of Hybrid Mismatch Arrangements

Hybrid mismatch arrangements exploit differences in the tax treatment of an entity or instrument under the laws of two or more tax jurisdictions to achieve double non-taxation, including long-term deferral.[66] The recommendations in Action 2 take the form of "linking rules", which align the tax treatment of an instrument or entity with the tax treatment in the counterparty jurisdiction. More specifically, countries are recommended to deny a deduction of a payment from the tax base if it is not includible in income by the recipient counterparty jurisdiction or it is also deductible in that counterparty jurisdiction. The essence of this recommendation is to apply different tax treatment if the counterparty jurisdiction has a specific taxation principle in place.

However, as acknowledged by the BEPS report, there are difficulties in identifying the hybrid element in the context of hybrid financial instruments. In other words, it is difficult to differentiate the purpose of the payment, *i.e.* whether it is for BEPS purposes or it constitutes a service supplied from the payee country. The GATS applies to this type of measures, even though the measure applies to all economic activities. In *Argentina – Financial Services,* two measures at issue are of similar nature as the one recommended by the BEPS Package.[67] The panel opined that the GATS applied to all measures affecting trade in services, "irrespective of whether service suppliers of the complaining party are engaged in trade or seeking to engage in trade with the Member applying the measure."[68] The services sectors concerned in this context should be all services sectors which have foreign service suppliers supplying their services through mode 3 (commercial establishment).[69]

Similar to the case in *Argentina – Financial Services,* the legal question under the GATS would be whether the different tax treatment based on the difference in tax regimes in the counterpart jurisdiction constitutes a violation of the MFN obligation under Article II of the GATS. The panel in that dispute considered that regulatory aspect in the jurisdictions of the service suppliers' home countries may be taken into account, provided that it was reflected in the competitive relationship between

---

[66]For details, see OECD (2015), *Neutralising the Effects of Hybrid Mismatch Arrangements,* Action 2 – 2015 Final Report, OECD/G20 Base Erosion and Profit Shifting Project, OECD Publishing, Paris.

[67]In *Argentina – Financial Services,* two measures at issue are of similar nature as the one recommended by the BEPS Package. Measure 1 of the impugned measures applies different gain withholding taxes on interest or remuneration to service suppliers in non-cooperating countries; Measure 4 applies different rules on the allocation of expenditure for transactions between Argentine taxpayers and persons of non-cooperative countries. See Appellate Body Report, *Argentina – Financial Services,* Sections 5.2, 5.5.

[68]Panel Report, *Argentina – Financial Services,* para 7.89.

[69]See the services sectors identified in *Argentina – Financial services.* Panel Report, *Argentina – Financial Services,* paras 7.97–7.98.

services and service suppliers from different jurisdictions.[70] However, the panel considered that the factual situation in the present case made it extremely difficult to undertake the required analysis of "likeness".[71] For this reason, the Appellate Body did not clarify if there would be possible to taken into consideration in the "likeness" assessment of some regulatory aspects in the jurisdictions of the service suppliers' home countries.[72]

As mentioned above, the Appellate Body reversed the Panel's approach to take into account "regulatory aspects" in the "less favourable treatment" analysis.[73]

If regulatory concerns cannot be taken into consideration in examining Article II of the GATS, the last resort of defense is Article XIV of the GATS. To recall, paragraph (d) of Article XIV provide exception for Article XVII-inconsistent measures that "aimed at ensuring the equitable or effective imposition or collection of direct taxes in respect of services or service suppliers of other Members", but is not available to justify an MFN violation. For this reason, it is not possible to justify this type of measures under Article XIV of the GATS.

This consideration might explain the Appellate Body's ambiguous statement relating to the "likeness" test under Article II of the GATS in *Argentina – Financial Services*. While acknowledging the relevance of the likeness criteria developed under the GATT, it also shows flexibility to take into account other characteristics of trade in services, *e.g.* the presence of service suppliers and the four modes of supply.[74] However, this ambiguity may render the "likeness" test under the GATS unpredictable.[75]

3.3.3 CFC Rules

CFC rules respond to the risk that taxpayers with a controlling interest in a foreign subsidiary can strip the base of their country of residence (and other countries in some instances) by shifting income into a CFC.[76] The recommended measures are designed to ensure that the jurisdictions that choose to implement them will have rules that effectively prevent taxpayers from shifting income into foreign subsidiaries. One of the building blocks that the BEPS Package recommends is that CFC rules only apply to controlled foreign companies that are subject to effective tax rates

---

[70]Panel Report, *Argentina – Financial Services*, para 7.179.

[71]Panel Report, *Argentina – Financial Services,* para 7.184.

[72]Appellate Body Report, *Argentina – Financial Services*, Section 6.1.6.1.

[73]Appellate Body Report, *Argentina – Financial Services,* para 6.111.

[74]Appellate Body Report, *Argentina – Financial Services*, paras 6.31–6.33.

[75]For this reason, the conventional debate and controversy on the process and production method (PPM) in the context of trade in goods may also find its way under the GATS.

[76]For details, see OECD (2015), *Designing Effective Controlled Foreign Company Rules*, Action 3 – 2015 Final Report, OECD/G20 Base Erosion and Profit Shifting Project, OECD Publishing, Paris.

that are meaningfully lower than those applied in the parent jurisdiction. This means if the service supplier established under mode 3 is from a jurisdiction where the effective tax rates are meaningfully higher than those of the services importing country, a higher tax rate would apply. This practice equals a border tax adjustment often debated in the context of trade in goods.

Indeed, the BEPS report highlighted that this initiative is to "level the playing field". The question is—the playing field among whom? Three situations may be envisaged. First, the "disadvantaged" service suppliers are from the same (or other) high tax jurisdictions, but they are not multinational enterprises (MNEs) which can use such tax planning techniques. In this case, the recommended measure aims to compensate these non-MNEs for not being able to employ tax planning. Second, the "disadvantaged" service suppliers, such as subsidiaries of MNEs, are from jurisdictions with lower tax rates. In this case, there may be an element of discrimination between service suppliers from high tax jurisdictions and low tax jurisdictions. In this scenario, as explained above, the measure may be inconsistent with Article II of the GATS. Also, as discussed before, Article XIV(d) does not exempt measures inconsistent with Article II. Third, if the foreign subsidiaries at issue are competing with domestic service suppliers, any measure aiming at levelling the playing field might cause national treatment concerns under Article XVII of the GATS. This is because the domestic service suppliers would not be better off but for such measure. However, as elaborated above, Article XVII-inconsistent measures can be justified by virtue of paragraph (d) of Article XIV.

3.4   When Countries Are Left with Discretion to Implement the BEPS Package

The work on preventing treaty abuse under Action 6 develops model treaty provisions and recommendations regarding the design of domestic rules to prevent the granting of bilateral tax treaty benefits in inappropriate circumstances.[77] With regard to domestic law, it recommends that countries should institute anti-abuse rules in their domestic legislations to refuse granting treaty benefits in terms of double taxation to certain foreign service suppliers. Nevertheless, it is in each country's hands to design its own domestic regulations. As envisaged by Action 14 of the BEPS Package, the application of a treaty anti-abuse provision or a domestic law anti-abuse provision may trigger disputes between the taxpayer and the tax

---

[77]For details, see OECD (2015), *Preventing the Granting of Treaty Benefits in Inappropriate Circumstances*, Action 6 – 2015 Final Report, OECD/G20 Base Erosion and Profit Shifting Project, OECD Publishing, Paris. See also recent updates in OECD, OECD/G20 Inclusive Framework on BEPS, Progress report, July 2018–May 2019.

authorities.[78] In this regard, it is requested by Action 14 that countries should provide Mutual Agreement Procedure (MAP) to ensure the timely, effective and efficient resolution of treaty-related disputes.[79] The question arises if the application of anti-abuse provision in domestic law leads to less favourable treatment (e.g. double taxation) to foreign service suppliers and consequently gives rise to national treatment concern under Article XVII GATS; and if the counterpart country can bring a case under WTO's dispute settlement to halt such anti-abuse practice.

Article XXII:3 GATS provides that Members may not invoke Article XVII under the Agreement's consultation (Article XXII) and dispute settlement (Article XXIII) provisions with respect to a measure that "falls within the scope of an international agreement between them relating to the avoidance of double taxation." Article XXII further provides that in case of disagreement on the scope of the tax treaty, "it shall be open to either Member to bring this matter before the Council for Trade in Services". The Council "shall refer the matter to arbitration" and the decision of the arbitrator shall be final and binding on the Members. It additionally provides, in a footnote, that "[w]ith respect to agreements on the avoidance of double taxation which exist on the date of entry into force of the WTO Agreement, such a matter may be brought before the Council for Trade in Services only with the consent of both parties to such an agreement." That means for disputes relating to tax agreements already existed by the time when the WTO was established, the submission of such disputes to arbitration requires positive consensus. Otherwise it requires negative consensus.

WTO Members should consider if an agreement on the avoidance of double taxation, modified according to the 2015 BEPS Package and the Multilateral Convention to Implement Tax Treaty Related Measures to Prevent BEPS can be qualified as an agreement existing on the date of entry of the WTO Agreement. If the newly amended agreement cannot "benefit" from the grandfathering, the "scope" of the newly amended tax agreement may be subject to the decision of a WTO arbitration tribunal, according to Article XXII of the GATS.

If the matter falls outside the scope of the tax treaty, for the same elaborated above, the measure may be inconsistent with Article XVII of the GATS. As already mentioned, with regard to tax agreements, paragraph (e) of Article XIV can only justify measures inconsistent with the MFN obligation.[80] Therefore, unless Article XXII can cover all the tax treaties modified by the BEPS Package, the anti-abuse

---

[78]For details, see OECD (2015), *Making Dispute Resolution Mechanisms More Effective*, Action 14 – 2015 Final Report, OECD/G20 Base Erosion and Profit Shifting Project, OECD Publishing, Paris.

[79]See recent updates in OECD, OECD/G20 Inclusive Framework on BEPS, Progress report, July 2018–May 2019.

[80]While Article XIV(d) can justify Article XVII-inconsistent measures if the different treatment is "aimed at ensuring the equitable or effective imposition or collection of direct taxes in respect of services or service suppliers of other Members", the proviso of "equitable" and the chapeau of Article XIV may operate together to ensure that the anti-abuse domestic legislation is not used as a disguised restriction on trade in services.

rules recommended by the BEPS Package in domestic law may risk being inconsistent with Article XVII of the GATS.

3.5   Unilateral Measures to Counteract Non-compliance or to Induce Compliance

To recall, minimum standards are developed under the BEPS Package to tackle issues in cases where no action by some countries would create negative spill overs (including adverse impacts of competitiveness) on other countries. Nevertheless, the recommendations in the BEPS Package are soft law legal instruments. It means that these recommendations are not legally binding, although there is an expectation that they will be implemented accordingly by countries that are part of the consensus.[81] In this scenario, can individual participating countries adopt unilateral measures to induce compliance, especially in view that the success of the BEPS Package, especially in the areas where minimum standards are developed, depends on the consistent and prompt implementation by all participating countries?

For example, Action 13 of the BEPS Package aims to improve the rules regarding transfer pricing documentation to enhance transparency for tax administration.[82] A minimum standard on Country-by-Country (CbC) Reporting was adopted. It requires that large MNEs file a Country-by-Country Report to provide, on an annual basis, information including the amount of revenue, profit before income tax and income tax paid and accrued and other indicators of economic activities. CbC reports should be filed in the ultimate parent entity's jurisdiction and shared automatically through government-to-government exchange of information. This initiative will give tax administrations a global picture of where MNEs' profits, tax and economic activities are reported, enabling them to use this information to assess transfer pricing and other BEPS risks. More specifically, BEPS participating countries are requested to adjust domestic legislation to require, in a timely manner, ultimate parent entities of MNE groups to file the CbC Report in their jurisdiction of residence; and exchange this information on an automatic basis with the jurisdiction in which the MNE group operates and which fulfills certain conditions.

As a minimum standard, the BEPS Package requests that the CbC Reporting be implemented effectively and consistently. However, the BEPS Package does not specify how implementation can be assured. Can countries take countermeasures to induce compliance when (a) a jurisdiction has not required CbC Reporting; (b) a

---

[81]OECD, "BEPS – Frequently Asked Questions", Question 4 "What is the nature of the BEPS outputs? Are they legally binding?" available at: http://www.oecd.org/ctp/beps-frequentlyaskedquestions.htm.

[82]For details, see OECD (2015), *Transfer Pricing Documentation and Country-by-Country Reporting*, Action 13 – 2015 Final Report, OECD/G20 Base Erosion and Profit Shifting Project, OECD Publishing, Paris.

jurisdiction with which no agreement has been reached for the exchange of the CbC reporting; and (c) a jurisdiction that fails to exchange information in practice?

As has been witnessed in *Argentina – Financial Services*, this type of countermeasures could inevitably give rise to either MFN or national treatment concerns under the GATS when different treatment is applied to service suppliers from complying and non-complying jurisdictions.[83] Also, as has been discussed, the exceptions under the GATS may not have been adequately equipped to except certain BEPS-related measures which are inconsistent with Article II or Article XVII of the GATS. In *Argentina – Financial Services*, the panel tried to weave regulatory considerations into its assessment of Article II and Article XVII of the GATS, but did not succeed. The Appellate Body also seemed to be hesitant to embrace regulatory considerations beyond those explicitly endorsed by the exception provisions.[84] As has been argued, the current case law has left uncertainties in applying Articles II and XVII GATS to some BEPS-related measures. Especially, it remains uncertain whether differences in regulatory framework in services exporting country may be considered relevant in assessing the "characteristics" of the service suppliers so as to make them unlike; if so, what kind of regulatory aspect be taken into the consideration; and finally, how to evaluate the appropriateness of the countermeasure at issue, *i.e.* what is the proportionality standard to be applied. Instead of leaving these uncertainties to the judicial prong of the WTO, it would be more preferable if WTO Members can take initiatives to clarify the scope of the exceptions under Article XIV of the GATS or to develop certain guidelines in view of the current global tax reform.[85]

4   Conclusion: To Keep or Level the Playing Field?

As illustrated above, the ongoing global tax reform under the BEPS Package is extensive and profound. Its intersection with the trade rules is inevitable from both conceptual and practical point of views. Conceptually, the BEPS Package aims to "level the playing field" among businesses. More specifically, it aims to modify the competitive condition between the MNEs which can engage in tax planning on the one hand, and the other types of enterprises on the other hand; and between the MNEs with their parent company or related entities located in jurisdictions with particular types of taxation principles or tax rates on the one hand, and the other MNEs on the other hand. To level the playing field, the BEPS Package makes recommendations, featuring differential treatment for different types of enterprises. Such distinctions in treatment may give rise to concerns under the MFN and national

---

[83]Panel Report, *Argentina – Financial Services*, para 7.89.

[84]Appellate Body Report, *Argentina – Financial Services*, paras 6.31, 6.34.

[85]Noting, however, not all WTO Members are participating in the BEPS Project. The Inclusive Framework on BEPS has included 125 jurisdictions, while the WTO has 164 Members.

treatment principle in trade disciplines. Under the GATS, the MFN obligation is a universal obligation applied to all services sectors unless the measure was listed by the Member concerned as an MFN exemption.[86] However, countries could not have been aware of the current BEPS concerns when they made their MFN exemption lists before 1995. Similarly, with regard to the national treatment obligation, which applies only to sectors where specific commitments are undertaken, it is unreasonable to expect that Members could have crafted their specific commitments with such BEPS concerns in mind. As argued in this paper, the two tax-specific exceptions under Article XIV, which were considered sufficient by the negotiators in the 1990s, may no longer be adequate in addressing both the MFN and national treatment-related concerns arising from the implementation of the 2015 BEPS Package. WTO Members should revisit these provisions in parallel to the reform initiatives in the international taxation field. As a temporary solution, Members may seek to reach a gentleman's agreement that certain tax measures, although potentially inconsistent with Article II and Article XVII of the GATS, should not give rise to any action under the WTO dispute settlement.[87]

Furthermore, there are areas in which the rules to tackle BEPS concerns are in making and may have an impact on the ongoing trade liberalization initiative under the GATS. Given the intersections identified in this paper, trade negotiators may need to keep a close eye on the development of rules in these areas. One of such areas is digitalization. Countries participating in the Inclusive Framework of the BEPS Package are working on rules to address the tax challenges of the digitalization of the economy, while WTO Members are exploring possibilities to upgrade the trade rules to accommodate the same challenge by digitalization.

To sum up, WTO Members should carefully consider the implication of the intersection of the GATS and the rules developed or being developed under the BEPS Package. This is an exercise to balance the goal of protecting market access and non-discrimination under the GATS on the one hand, and embrace the principle of the BEPS Package to "level the playing field" for taxation purposes on the other hand.

References

Adlung R, Carzaniga A (2009) MFN exemptions under the general agreement on trade in services: grandfathers striving for immortality? J Int Econ Law 12(2):357–392

Daly M (2005) The WTO and direct taxation. WTO discussion paper no 9, June 2005

---

[86] Article II:2 of the GATS: "A Member may maintain a measure inconsistent with paragraph 1 provided that such a measure is listed in, and meets the conditions of, the Annex on Article II Exemptions".

[87] Such approach was used by WTO Members during the extended Uruguay Round negotiations on basic telecommunications with regard to the use of differential accounting rates for the termination of international traffic. See Adlung and Carzaniga (2009), p. 389.

Weiwei Zhang is International Trade Advisor at Sidley Austin LLP's Geneva office. Dr. Weiwei Zhang is also Adjunct Professor of International Economic Law at the University of International Business and Economics in Beijing and Visiting Fellow at the Centre for Trade and Economic Integration in the Graduate Institute of International and Development Studies in Geneva.

Printed by Printforce, United Kingdom